D-DAYS IN THE PACIFIC

ALSO BY DONALD L. MILLER

The Story of World War II

City of the Century: The Epic of Chicago and the Making of America

Lewis Mumford, A Life

The Lewis Mumford Reader

The Kingdom of Coal: Work, Enterprise, and Ethnic Communities in the Mine Fields (with Richard Sharpless)

The New American Radicalism

D-DAYS IN THE PACIFIC

Donald L. Miller

A LOU REDA BOOK

Simon & Schuster Paperbacks

New York   London   Toronto   Sydney

SIMON & SCHUSTER Paperbacks
Rockefeller Center
1230 Avenue of the Americas
New York, NY 10020

First Simon & Schuster paperback edition 2005

SIMON & SCHUSTER and colophon are registered trademarks of Simon &
Schuster, Inc.

Designed by Richard Oriolo

Manufactured in the United States of America

10 9 8 7 6 5 4

LIBRARY OF CONGRESS CATALOGING-IN-PUBLICATION DATA

Miller, Donald L., 1944–
    D-days in the Pacific / Donald L. Miller.
        p.   cm.
    "Comprised of selected, greatly revised and expanded chapters from The
story of World War II, as well as additional new material"—Verso t.p.
    "A Lou Reda book."
    Includes bibliographical references and index.
    1. World War, 1939–1945—Campaigns—Pacific Area. I. Miller, Donald
L., 1944– Story of World War II. II. Title.
D767.M465   2005
940.54'26—dc22   2004065391

ISBN-13: 978-0-7432-6929-2
ISBN-10:   0-7432-6929-2

For information regarding special discounts for bulk purchases, please
contact Simon & Schuster Special Sales at 1-800-456-6798 or business@
simonandschuster.com

This book is comprised of selected, greatly revised and expanded chapters
from *The Story of World War II,* as well as additional new material.

For Gregory and Nicole

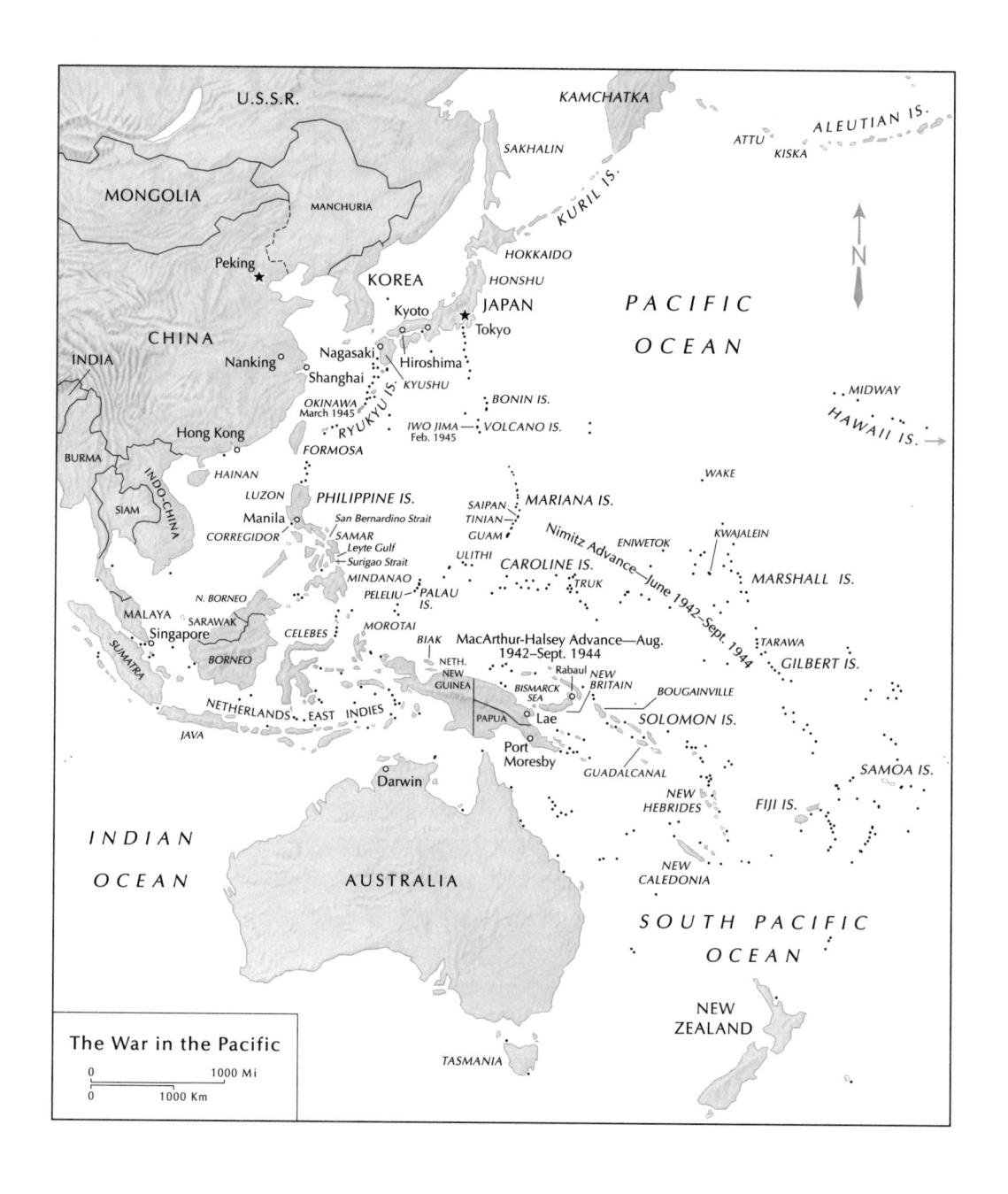

The War in the Pacific

0   1000 Mi

0   1000 Km

CONTENTS

ACKNOWLEDGMENTS

MY GREATEST DEBT IS TO MY dear, deceased friend Stephen E. Ambrose. He encouraged me to write this book and made available to me his vast archive of interviews with veterans of the Pacific theater. Over a three-year period, we engaged in an ongoing conversation about the war that he considered one of history's most vicious racial conflicts. Had he not been struck down in his prime, his next project would have been a major book on America's Pacific campaign.

Douglas Brinkley, who succeeded Stephen Ambrose as Director of the Eisenhower Center for American Studies at the University of New Orleans, gave me unrestricted access to the collections of that unique research repository and introduced me to the center's reigning expert on World War II, Michael Edwards, and its associate director, Kevin Willey, both of whom helped in a dozen significant ways. Gordon "Nick" Mueller, head of the National D-Day Museum, America's outstanding World War II museum, put at my disposal that institution's entire holdings on the Pacific war, including its large photographic collection. Martin Morgan, the museum's Research Historian, was endlessly helpful.

Whenever I was in doubt about something I called my colleague Allan R. Millett and he straightened me out.

My conversations with Hugh Ambrose, a young historian who has done fresh research on the Pacific conflict, gave me new perspectives on wartime Japan and turned a professional association into a valued friendship.

I would probably not be writing about World War II had it not been for a nudge from the documentary film producer, Lou Reda. He suggested that I write the wider book about the war, *The Story of World War II*, which turned out to be the wellspring for this new, more specialized account. Not long after I began conducting my own interviews with surviving veterans, he made available to me the transcripts and videotapes of the 700 and more interviews with participants in the war that his production teams have been conducting over the past fifty years.

Joseph H. Alexander, a world authority on the Pacific conflict and amphibious warfare, read this book in manuscript form and offered helpful suggestions. Donald Meyerson, Rod Paschall, and Mort Zimmerman also read the manuscript. My Friday nights at a local watering hole with Don Meyerson, a Marine combat veteran, gave me fresh insight into the experience of warfare.

I am pleased to thank others who helped with the book, chief among them Mark Natola, John McCullouch, and Austin Hoyt. A film producer for public television, Hoyt sent me transcripts of interviews he conducted for his film on Douglas MacArthur and his forthcoming documentary on the Battle of Okinawa and the Japanese surrender. Serving as Historical Consultant for *Victory in the Pacific*—talking with men who fought on Okinawa, with scholars who studied the battle, and with Hoyt himself—put me in a far better position to write about the last and most horrific stages of the Pacific war.

Benis M. Frank, former Director of the U.S. Marine Corps Oral History Project, put at my disposal voluminous source material on the Marines in the Pacific. He and Eugene Sledge, author of the finest combat memoir to come out of the Pacific War, *With the Old Breed at Peleliu and Okinawa*, shared with me their experiences as young warriors in the assaults on Peleliu and Okinawa.

At every juncture in my research I received enthusiastic assistance from the staffs of a number of research institutions, chief among them the National Archives, College Park, Maryland; the Library of Congress's Manuscript Division; Van Pelt Library of the University of Pennsylvania; the U.S. Naval Institute; the Imperial War Museum, London; the Naval Academy Library, Annapolis; the Naval Historical Research Center, Washington, D.C.; the Marine Corps Historical Center, Washington, D.C.; the United States Army Military History Institute, Carlisle Barracks, Pennsylvania; the United States Air Force Historical Research Agency, Maxwell Air Force Base, Alabama; the New York Public Library; the film archives of WGBH-TV, Boston; the Holocaust Museum, Washington, D.C. I owe a long-standing debt to the librarians at my home institution, Lafayette College, particularly Terry Schwartz and the library's superb director, Neil McElroy.

Grants from Lafayette College and the Mellon Foundation allowed me to assemble a research team of students that helped prepare the manuscript for publication. I am especially indebted to Emily Goldberg, my chief student researcher, who trained her able co-workers, Jessica Cygler and Alix Kenney. My secretary of many years, Kathy Anckaitis, has worked mightily to keep my chaotic working life in order. And Fred Chase, my copy editor, brought greater order and clarity to this book.

I have the good fortune of having a literary agent, Gina Maccoby, who is also a discerning critic and a dear friend. And in Bob Bender I have one of the best editors in the business. Bob and his brilliant assistant, Johanna Li, make up the entire staff of the little shop in the big plant out of which this book emerged in far better shape than when it went in.

I am immensely grateful to Bob, and to Michael Korda, Editor-in-Chief of Simon & Schuster, for reaching out to me at a time of personal need. They give the lie to the notion that a big publishing house is a relentlessly impersonal place.

This book would not have been possible without the generosity of the over 100 World War II veterans I interviewed in my research. They spoke with vigor and candor about their wartime experiences, without ever calling attention to their own heroism and self-sacrifice. As they leave us, thousands by the day, we can only hope we will see their like again.

While at work, most writers are not pleasant to have in the house. The usual author's bow to the long-suffering wife and family is more than an obligatory courtesy. My wife, Rose, has the patience of a saint, and we are together this far along in life—after seven books—because of it. I dedicated an earlier book to her, so this one is for my two devoted children, parents themselves now, but young enough to remember the moody man in the little room not far from their rooms who could only be a proper father when he turned off his writing machine.

It is the man on two feet with hand grenades, rifle, and bayonet—backed by all that modern science can devise—the man with fear in his stomach but a fighting heart, who must secure beachheads. He it is who wins the glory and pays the price, who changes the course of history. Man is still supreme in a mechanistic war.

HANSON W. BALDWIN

A POPULAR MISCONCEPTION IS THAT THERE is only one D-Day in all of history: June 6, 1944, the day the Allies landed on the beaches of Normandy and began the liberation of Northern Europe. But the term D-Day—first used in World War I by the U.S. Army—is the military code word for the starting day of any offensive. In World War II the term came to be used most commonly in amphibious operations, attacks launched from the sea by naval and landing forces against a hostile shore.

In the vast Pacific, with its hundreds of enemy-occupied islands, geography virtually dictated that all major D-Day invasions be seaborne offenses. Amphibious assaults are the most desperate and dangerous of military operations; failure means to be thrown back into the sea or slaughtered at the waterline. Many of the Allied landings in the Pacific were fiercely opposed at the point of attack; but in others, resistance was light or nonexistent on the beaches and the major fighting took place inland.

There were over a hundred D-Day invasions in the war in the Pacific. Some of them were joint operations, with American units joined by forces from one or more of the twelve other Allied nations at war with Japan. But all of them were planned and directed by American leaders and most of them, like Iwo Jima, were exclusively American affairs, with Americans doing all the fighting and dying. The last major Pacific offensive, Operation Iceberg, the invasion of Okinawa on April 1, 1945, brought to the enemy's shores the largest invasion fleet ever assembled, more soldiers, sailors, and ships than took part in the landings on that memorable June morning when most of the world heard the term D-Day for the first time.

A NOTE ON JAPANESE NAMES

IN THE INTEREST OF CLARITY, I have not followed the Japanese convention in which the family name or surname precedes the given or personal name.

PHOTO CREDITS

LRP – Lou Reda Productions
NA – National Archive
SC – U.S. Army Signal Corps
USAAF – U.S. Army Air Force
USMC – U.S. Marine Corps
USN – U.S. Navy

The Rising Sun

OIL AND EMPIRE

Foreign oil was Imperial Japan's lifeblood and fatal undoing. Japan went to war with the United States to gain access to oil in Southeast Asia it could no longer obtain from American companies, its chief supplier of the fuel that sustained its military machine. In July 1941, President Franklin Delano Roosevelt blocked the sale of American oil to Japan in retaliation for that country's occupation of French Indochina, which Japan planned to use as a launching point for an audacious move south into the Netherlands East Indies (now Indonesia), one of the world's great oil-producing regions. "Riding the Equator east for three thousand miles, a distance as great as the whole span of the United States itself, the Netherlands Indies," the *New York Times* pointed up their strategic importance, "support a population of sixty million and produce commodities—oil, tin, and rubber—which the modern world cannot do without. They are an empire in themselves, and no Pacific Power can be indifferent to their future." [1]

In the summer of 1941, Japan determined to seize these resource-rich islands, even if it meant war with the United States. It was her boldest move yet in what had been a ten-year-long campaign of conquest in Asia.

When Japan unleashed a surprise attack on Pearl Harbor on the morning of December 7, 1941, its primary strategic target was not the American fleet berthed there, but the oil fields of Sumatra and Borneo in the East Indies. Hawaii was hit to cover the flank of this great resource grab, knocking out the only naval force in the Pacific capable of stopping it.

With terrifying speed, Japan seized the territory it had long coveted in its quest for energy self-sufficiency, not just the Netherlands East Indies but also Burma, the Malay Peninsula, and the main islands in the Southwest Pacific that lay north of Australia, including the Philippines, an American protectorate. In a matter of months, it had acquired the most far-reaching oceanic empire in all of history, one blessed with every economic resource it needed to fight a major war. But the shipping lanes to these mineral-rich possessions were too far-flung to be effectively protected by the formidable, but overextended, Imperial Navy. By the late spring of 1945, a strangulating American naval blockade had cut off the Japanese home islands from the oil fields and mineral deposits of the recently conquered Asian possessions of England, France, the Netherlands, and the United States. Japan would stubbornly fight on, but the war was lost. The Pacific war was not exclusively a war over oil, but oil played a decisive role in both its origins and end.

THE ROAD TO WAR

In July 1941, the month that militants in Tokyo decided that war with mighty America was inevitable, Japan was fighting another country it could not hope to defeat. For nearly a decade, it had been at war with the Chinese, first in Manchuria, then in China itself. In these years, Japan—an ally of the United States in World War I and a nation that had been undergoing a robust Westernizing movement for almost a century—fell increasingly under the control of jingoistic military and political leaders. With Emperor Hirohito's compliance, they ruthlessly suppressed political opposition—often by public assassination—and began advancing a mystical doctrine of racialism, the superiority of the Yamato race and Japan's sacred mission to free Asia of white, Western imperialists. These ultranationalists were convinced that the world's major powers, all of them ruled by Caucasians, were conspiring to reduce Japan—"A Yellow Peril"—to second-rank status in the community of nations. Young

Japanese military officers, along with nationalistic poets and intellectuals, were also a urging a cultural renaissance, the eradication of a soft, decadent Western materialism, with its elevation of individualism and hedonism, and a return to the "divine" land's purer warrior-state greatness. They dreamed of a new age when millions of spirit warriors abandoned the pursuit of pleasure and sacrificed their lives for the spread of *Dai Nippon Teikoku*, the "Great Empire of Japan."

Economic privation fueled anti-Western xenophobia, political despotism, and an urgent drive for autarky.[2] The Great Depression, with its contraction of international trade, had a devastating impact on Japan's fragile island economy, which was heavily dependent on foreign resources. Britain, another island economy, was also hurt badly by the economic crisis, but it had an empire to help sustain its military prowess. Japan did not. It must have one, and soon, its imperialists insisted, if it was to weather the Depression and emerge as the preponderant power in a new Asia-for-Asians.

The Imperial Army was the leading agent in this drive for markets and resources. Profoundly influenced by Germany's defeat in World War I, its strategists concluded that Germany, with its tremendous continental army, had lost the war because of its vulnerability to the Allied naval blockade, which virtually sealed off the country from the outside world. The lesson was there. The world powers of the future would need more than strong armies and navies. They would have to become self-sufficient, capable of waging total war without reliance on food, fuel, or other war-sustaining materials from other nations. For Japan, this meant expanding industrial production at home and extending its imperial reach.[3]

Japan had already acquired Korea, Formosa (Taiwan), and a stake in Manchuria in earlier wars against China and Russia. Now it moved to enlarge and consolidate its holdings in that vital area of Asia that lay directly across the narrow Sea of Japan. In September 1931, soldiers of the rabidly nationalistic Kwantung Army, garrisoned in the semi-autonomous Chinese territory of Manchuria to protect a railroad system over which it had acquired rights, provoked a fight with the local warlord, overran the whole of Manchuria, and set up a new puppet state, Manchukuo. It would be a buffer against the Soviet Union and become "Japan's lifeline," proclaimed one Japanese leader, supplying iron and coal for the home country's new state-run military economy and "living space" for its exploding population, expanding at a rate of a million a year.[4] The United States refused to recognize Japan's new client state and the League of Nations issued a flaccid condemnation, but Japan ignored the American protest, withdrew from the League, and prepared to extend its Asian conquests.

In July 1937, when Chiang Kai-shek's Chinese Nationalists refused to give in to additional Japanese demands for territory and influence, the Kwantung Army stormed into China itself, overran the fertile valleys of the Yellow and Yangtze rivers, and seized all the important seaports, including Shanghai, which it bombed with vehemence, killing thousands of innocent civilians. After taking the walled capital of Nanking in December 1937, Japanese soldiers—indoctrinated to look on the Chinese as a kingdom of "chinks," of roving bandits and cowlike peasants—killed over 200,000 military prisoners of war and unarmed civilians, raping, castrating, and beheading tens of thousands of them, in what has been called a Hidden Holocaust.[5] The systematic slaughter continued for three months in Nanking and surrounding villages and got so out of control that a member of the Nazi Party who was stranded in Nanking sent Adolf Hitler a telegram pleading with him to intervene to restrain the Japanese army.[6]

Japan invaded China to exploit it economically, but this backfired. The Japanese military expected a quick victory over the politically divided Chinese—one army led by the corrupt, pro-American Chiang Kai-shek, the other by the cagey Communist Mao Tse-tung. But both leaders used China's rural vastness to great advantage. Chiang's Nationalists, who did most of the fighting, suffered defeat after defeat and by 1939 both his forces and Mao's had been virtually cut off from access to the outside world. Yet they would not be conquered, and the Japanese almost exhausted themselves killing them. "China is like a gallon jug which Japan is trying to fill with a half-pint of liquid," Mao told an American officer who visited his headquarters.[7] The long war drained Japan's human and material resources, reducing alarmingly its slender supplies of oil.

Japan was a coal-driven economy. Petroleum accounted for only about 7 percent of total energy consumption. But the navy, the air force, and the merchant fleet relied on it for their existence. And that meant an embarrassingly heavy reliance on the United States, a liberal, democratic nation whose values the military held in cold contempt.

In the late 1930s, Japan imported 93 percent of its oil, 80 percent of it from the United States and another 10 percent from the Netherlands East Indies.[8] This put Japan in a precarious position, for its major supplier of oil strongly opposed the war it was now fighting. The Roosevelt administration was committed to an autonomous China and to the Open Door policy first proposed in 1899 by Secretary of State John Hay, under which all nations would have equal trading rights in China. Although few countries, including the United States, adhered to this policy, Japan's savagely prosecuted war in China provoked the Roosevelt administration to issue more strongly worded protests to the Japanese government. Tokyo responded stridently, denouncing the Open Door as a policy inappropriate to present and future world conditions. At this point, Japan began to look elsewhere for the oil and iron ore it needed to prevail in China and become the supreme power in Asia. In 1940, it cast a covetous eye on Indochina, Burma, Malaya, and the Dutch East Indies, where these resources—along with greatly needed rubber, tungsten, and rice—were plentiful and now, suddenly, there for the picking.

Hitler's sweeping European conquests of May and June 1940, from Rotterdam to Paris, created an irresistible opportunity for Japan to snatch the Asian colonies of defeated France and the Netherlands, and of beleaguered England, which Germany was preparing to invade that summer. Three months after Hitler's legions crossed the Marne and goose-stepped through the Arc de Triomphe, Imperial Japan made a sordid agreement with the new Vichy, or collaborationist, government of France, permitting it to send troops into the northern part of French Indochina. Possession of northern Indochina would complete Japan's blockade and encirclement of China. But the Japanese government wanted more, urged on by the powerful War Minister in the new, more aggressive cabinet of Prince Fumimaro Konoe—fifty-five-year-old Hideki Tojo, a hard-line expansionist who had been chief of staff of the Kwantung Army in Manchuria. Tojo and the new extremist Foreign Minister, Yosuke Matsuoka, hoped to use Indochina as a base for an ambitious "Southern Advance" into British Malaya and the Dutch East Indies.[9] That September, Matsuoka, who preached Fascism as the force of the future, was instrumental in shaping the Tripartite Pact with Hitler and Italy's Benito Mussolini, creating what became known as the Axis alliance. The three members of the totalitarian front agreed to aid one another if "attacked by a power at present not involved in the European War or in the Sino-Japanese" conflict. This was a direct warning to the United States to stay out of the war, a war that Matsuoka assured Konoe the Germans would easily win.[10]

This put Japan on a collision course with America. President Roosevelt and Secretary of State Cordell Hull were determined to protect the Asian interests of America's future wartime allies and, more importantly, keep Southeast Asia a leading trading partner of the United States. That meant preventing Japan from gaining overwhelming influence there. The trick was how to do this without provoking a war neither statesman wanted.

America imported more goods from the Far East than any other place on earth. Three colonies alone—British Malaya, the Netherlands East Indies, and the Philippines—accounted for approximately one fifth of all American foreign purchases.[11] The United States—an automobile society with the largest rubber goods industry in the world—bought 98 percent of its rubber and 90 percent of its tin from Southeast Asia. In all, the area provided more than half of America's needs for at least fifteen vital commodities, including chromium and manganese, metals essential in the steelmaking process.[12] By 1940, key policymakers in the State Department were prepared to defend America's freedom to trade for these resources, by war if necessary, should they come in danger of falling under the control of the Japanese. A pro-Fascist Japan in possession of South Asia could cut off trade with the United States and Britain or dictate extortionate concessions to continue it. Secretary of the Navy Frank Knox put America's interest in the region in the sternest possible language in his congressional confirmation hearings of 1940: "We should not allow Japan to take the Dutch East Indies, a vital source of oil and rubber and tin. . . . We must face frankly the fact that to deny the Dutch Indies to Japan may mean war."[13]

When Japan moved into northern Indochina, Roosevelt cut off its supplies of high-quality scrap iron and aviation gas, a limited response dictated by his desire to avoid war. Roosevelt had backing for even stronger sanctions, not only from his State Department but also from an American public aroused by the suffering of the Chinese peasants they had read about in Pearl Buck's immensely popular novel, *The Good Earth*, and by news coverage of the terror bombings of Canton, Chungking, and other Chinese cities. As one protest group put it: "Japan furnishes the pilot. America furnishes the airplane, gasoline, oil, and bombs for the ravaging of undefended Chinese cities." A Gallup Poll of June 1939 found nearly three quarters of the American public in favor of a total embargo on the export of war-making materials to Japan.[14]

With war a possibility, Roosevelt had already begun to take precautionary measures. In January 1940 he had moved the base of the U.S. Pacific Fleet from San Diego to still unfinished Pearl Harbor, Hawaii. He then sent additional loans, arms, equipment, and military advisors to prop up Chiang Kai-shek's Nationalist army and allowed the creation of a volunteer air force in China—the Flying Tigers—to be commanded by a retired U.S. fighter pilot, Colonel Claire Chennault. China had to be saved, not just for humanitarian reasons, but to pin down the Japanese army, stalling its relentless southward march.

Roosevelt also began beefing up American defenses in the Philippines. Orders were issued to send to the islands over 250 B-17 Flying Fortresses, America's most formidable long-range bombers. The planes, fresh from the factory, were to be put under the overall command of General Douglas C. MacArthur, a World War I hero who had been serving as a military advisor to the Philippine government. MacArthur was recalled to active service as head of a new organization, U.S. Army Forces, Far East, made up of the Philippine army and American units in the islands.

In early 1941, the Japanese sent Admiral Kichisaburo Nomura, a sincere advocate of peace, to Washington to try to reach an agreement with the United States to reestablish trade relations and recognize Japanese interests in China and northern Indochina. The fire-eaters had not yet gained complete control of the Japanese government, and a group of navy leaders, led by Vice Admiral Isoroku Yamamoto, hoped to avoid a war that would pit its forces against the combined navies of America and Britain, an unpopular position that made Yamamoto the target of right-wing assassins.[15] Roosevelt and Hull welcomed the initiative, and Hull met regularly with the congenial Nomura, often in the secretary's private home. Seeing Hitler as the major menace, Hull and Roosevelt hoped to use diplomacy to buy time for America to rearm, making itself so formidable that the Japanese would not dare attack it. As Roosevelt told his Secretary of the Interior, Harold Ickes, an insistent advocate of tougher sanctions against Japan, "As you know, it is terribly important for the control of the Atlantic for us to help to keep peace in the Pacific. I simply have not got enough Navy to go around and—every little episode in the Pacific means fewer ships in the Atlantic."[16]

The breaking point came on July 2, 1941, when the Japanese government and the military ended their internal bickering and came together behind a plan to occupy all of Indochina "in order to consolidate the base of our national existence and self-defense."[17] American cryptologists had recently broken the Japanese diplomatic code (through an operation known as MAGIC, the equivalent to Britain's code-breaking system, ULTRA) and Roosevelt knew, therefore, that this latest move was but the first step toward the invasion of British Malaya and the Netherlands East Indies—and that the Japanese had decided to take that step even if it meant war with Great Britain and the United States. An intercepted Japanese dispatch could not have been clearer about this: "After the occupation of French Indochina, next on our schedule is the sending of an ultimatum to the Netherlands Indies. . . . In the seizing of Singapore the navy will play the principal part . . . [W]e will once and for all crush Anglo-American military power and their ability to assist in any schemes against us."[18]

A shaken Roosevelt ordered a freeze on Japanese assets in the United States. The President had not intended to cut off oil entirely, seeing this as excessively provocative, but the freeze became a de facto embargo when State Department officials, led by the young Dean Acheson, persuaded the Treasury Department to refuse to release any of the frozen funds to Japan to purchase oil.[19] This was done while the President was away from the capital at a secret meeting with British Prime Minister Winston S. Churchill. By the time Roosevelt got word of what had been done it was too late to reverse the policy. Two Japanese oil tankers that had been waiting to be filled in San Pedro Harbor, near Los Angeles, were forced to return home with their tanks empty. In the meantime, the State Department persuaded Britain and Dutch authorities in the East Indies to impose their own embargoes. Both were eager to comply; the occupation of Indochina put Japanese bombers within range of Singapore, and gave Japan two excellent harbors, Camranh Bay and Saigon, from which to strike south toward Borneo, a crown jewel of the Royal Dutch/Shell Group, one of the most powerful fuel consortiums in the world.

This virtual severing of trade with the empire damaged Japanese-American relations irrevocably, for Japan saw it as a threat to its very survival. The embargo strengthened the hand of the military leaders in the Japanese cabinet, and they, along with their civilian allies, were set on a war that even the vacillating Emperor was now willing to risk. Without American supplies, and with the nation's yearly oil production able to supply its ships for only one month, the Japanese navy's reserve of oil would last only two years unless fuel could be found elsewhere.[20] That gave war an insane logic of its own. To continue to make war against indomitable China, Japan would have to go to war against an even tougher opponent. This was kamikaze politics—state policy fueled by a desperate ideology of resource scarcity. Koichi Kido, an intimate of the Emperor and an advocate of moderation, later told the Japanese Premier in confidence, "The whole problem facing Japan had been reduced to a very simple factor, and that was oil."[21]

If Japan's reserves "[are] dribbled away," said a Japanese naval official in charge of resources mobilization, "Japan . . . [will] grow weaker and weaker like a TB patient gasping along till he drop[s] dead on the road. A grim and humiliating end. However, if we could strike boldly and get the oil in the south . . ."[22]

Roosevelt's fresh resolve removed all ambiguity from Japanese-American negotiations. Japan now faced a stark choice: continue on its present course or capitulate in response to American pressure. War was not inevitable—Konoe began backpedaling, proposing a secret summit meeting with Roosevelt (which Hull did not think appropriate, given Konoe's unmovable positions on China and the "Southern Advance"), and the Emperor wanted to give the talks in Washington more time. But after Japanese troops marched into southern Indochina on July 28 only a miracle would have prevented war. "There is no choice left but to fight and break the iron chains strangling Japan," Admiral Osami Nagano, chief of the Naval Staff, told colleagues.[23]

Hull and Roosevelt also realized that they had crossed a divide. As Hull told Undersecretary of State Sumner Welles five days later, "Nothing will stop them except force."[24]

On September 6, the Japanese made a fateful decision. At a cabinet meeting in the presence of Emperor Hirohito, Tokyo's leaders agreed to continue the talks in Washington, sending over Saburo Kurusu as a special envoy to help Nomura restore harmony to Japanese-American relations. But Japan's demands remained extreme. It refused to give up its new economic colony or disengage from China. If no agreement satisfactory to the Imperial interests was reached by the beginning of October, Japan was to prepare to go to war with the United States, the cabinet solemnly agreed.[25] When the Emperor formally ratified the decision to go to war should diplomacy fail—"the most important decision of his entire life," according to his biographer, Herbert P. Bix—the movement toward war—now tied to a rigid timetable—would continue to accelerate and all subsequent diplomatic discussion between Japan and the United States would become mere shadow boxing.[26] That the talks continued is an indication that both sides needed time to build up for the showdown, and that some leaders, including Hull and Nomura, hoped that the war they saw on the horizon could somehow be postponed.

The ascendancy of Hideki Tojo ended all hope for a compromise. In late October, with the Emperor's support, he replaced Konoe as Prime Minister. Two weeks later, on November 5, at an Imperial Conference before the Emperor, Tojo outlined the majority opinion of the cabinet he now firmly controlled. Admitting to "some uneasiness about a protracted war" with prodigiously powerful America, he went on to emphasize that, with oil reserves what they were, "I fear that we would become a third-class nation after two or three years if we just sat tight."[27] Even if the Americans softened their position in the current negotiations, Japan would be forever dependent for war-making resources on the whims of Washington bureaucrats and politicians.[28]

At this point, the government sanctioned a bold war plan put forward by Admiral Yamamoto. He proposed a secret, preemptive strike—one of staggering suddenness—on the U.S. fleet at its anchorage in Pearl Harbor. This, combined with a simultaneous attack on the Philippines, would eliminate the American threat on the northern and eastern flanks of Japan's "Southern Advance." Perhaps there was even hope for victory in this. "The coming war will be protracted and dirty," Yamamoto had told Konoe in an earlier conversation. But after Pearl Harbor he would try to bring on an early and decisive naval engagement, involving the entire fleet. If he prevailed and the Americans came to the peace table, a long and brutal war of attrition might be avoided.[29] In any event, such a strategy was, Yamamoto thought, Japan's only hope for success in a war he loyally supported, but believed his country should have avoided.

Yamamoto's respect for America's enormous material might have convinced him that a more conventional strategy would fail. The Admiral knew the enemy well. He had attended Harvard in the 1920s and traveled extensively in America before being appointed Japan's naval attaché in Washington. And though he had a low opinion of the U.S. Navy, considering it a country club for golfers and bridge players, he had the highest respect for the purposeful determination of the American people. They were not the weak-willed sybarites portrayed by Tokyo hard-liners, he reminded his naval colleagues.

What gave Yamamoto hope for his plan was that Japan had carrier planes and aviators beyond compare, along with specially designed torpedoes to sink ships in the shallow—forty-foot-deep—waters of Pearl Harbor. It was a dangerous gamble. He would be risking Japan's entire front-line carrier strength on a single, unproven operation. But against such an enemy, risks had to be taken.[30]

On November 26, while Yamamoto was making final preparations for his Hawaiian offensive, Cordell Hull handed Ambassador Nomura and special envoy Saburo Kurusu a ten-point document calling for their country to withdraw its military forces from both Indochina and China as a precondition for the resumption of trade with the United States. Interestingly, the draft document did not mention Manchuria and was headed "strictly confidential, tentative and without commitment," leaving things open, in other words, to future discussion, including, perhaps, the timetable for troop withdrawals. Nor did the document have a deadline for acceptance or rejection.[31] As Hull said later, he was not asking the Japanese to surrender their right to be a major power in Asia.[32] But Tojo chose to interpret it as a humiliating ultimatum, tantamount to a declaration of war. And he got his government to agree, thereby throwing the blame for the war on the intransigent Americans, and absolving Japan of moral responsibility for what it was about to do.[33] Japan chose war, the Imperial Conference declared, because it would not bow to American demands that "ignored our national sacrifices during more than four years of the China incident."[34]

To those who doubted that Japan could prevail against the American colossus, Tojo replied that "a reasonable prospect of victory is enough. Even if there is apprehension that we may be defeated, the nation should trust the military and move ahead."[35]

On November 27, the Pearl Harbor strike force sailed from its secret anchorages in the southern Kurile Islands. It left with the Emperor's blessing; and he himself worked closely on the war rescript, which stated, "Our empire has been brought to cross swords with America and Britain" in a war that he, the Emperor, said he had resisted but now considered "unavoidable."[36] And so His Royal Majesty sent his country into a war that would come close to destroying it, claiming, incredibly, that it was peace he really wanted.

Unaware of the location of the Japanese navy, but expecting an attack somewhere, most likely in Southeast Asia, Washington sent out a war warning to all American commanders in the Pacific. One of them was Admiral Husband E. Kimmel, commander of the Pacific Fleet at Pearl Harbor.

PEARL HARBOR

On Sunday, December 7, the two Japanese emissaries appeared at Hull's office with their government's final reply to his "ultimatum." Minutes before the meeting, Roosevelt had telephoned Hull with the news that the Japanese were at that very moment bombing Pearl Harbor. The secretary was told to receive the diplomats' reply and curtly dismiss them. After pretending to examine the document, Hull glared at the two men with undisguised disdain and declared: "In all my fifty years of public service I have never seen a document that was more crowded with infamous falsehoods and distortions—infamous falsehoods and distortions on a scale so huge that I never imagined until today that any Government on this planet was capable of uttering them." He then waved the two diplomats to the door.

Later that day, Nomura, who had not been informed of his government's plans to attack Pearl Harbor, wrote in his diary: "The report of our surprise attack against Hawaii reached my ears when I returned home from the state department; *this might have reached Hull's ears during our conversation*."[37]

The Hawaii attack was carried out with almost flawless resolve by Air Admiral Chuichi Nagumo. It was a daring move. A major base had never been assaulted in daylight by a carrier force, and many high-ranking American planners considered Pearl Harbor—the greatest concentration of American military might in the world—impregnable. But Japan had greater carrier strength than any other nation in the world, and the world's best trained carrier fliers. And its assault planes, armed with the most lethal torpedoes ever developed, were vastly superior to anything America could put in the air at the time. Even so, success depended on the strictest secrecy.

Yamamoto put to sea a massive task force composed of the Imperial Navy's six newest and largest carriers, accompanied by battleships, light cruisers, destroyers, fleet submarines, supply ships, and tankers. At sunrise, December 7, 230 miles north of the Hawaiian island of Oahu, the air was alive with the roar of enemy planes. At 7:02 two Army privates manning an experimental radar system reported a large flight of incoming planes, but their superior officer assured them that these were B-17 bombers due in from California on their way to the Philippines.

Just minutes earlier, the destroyer *Ward* had attacked a tiny two-man Japanese submarine trying to slip into Pearl Harbor. These were the opening shots of World War II for the United States.

The *Ward's* skipper, Lieutenant William W. Outerbridge, reported the attack but senior commanders were skeptical. There had been false submarine sightings in that same area—even whales had been depth-charged—so they would wait for verification. While they waited, 183 Japanese attack planes homed in on the radio beam of station KGMB in Honolulu, which guided them straight to their target.

The attack was a total surprise. American cryptanalysts, who had broken Japan's diplomatic code, but not all its military codes, had warned Washington of an imminent attack, but most indications were that the strike would occur in Southeast Asia, not at Pearl Harbor. The Japanese carrier force had moved from the remote Kurile Islands, north of Japan, across the nearly empty North Pacific, under absolute radio silence, confounding American naval intercept units. As historian David Kahn has written, "code-breaking intelligence did not prevent and could not have prevented Pearl Harbor, because Japan never sent any message to anybody saying anything like 'We shall attack Pearl Harbor.'" Japan's ambassadors in Washington had not even been told of the plan. "The real reason for the success of the Pearl Harbor attack lies in the island empire's hermetic security. Despite the American code-breakers, Japan kept her secret." [38]

Lieutenant Commander Mitsuo Fuchida led the attack from the flagship carrier *Akagi.* He was thirty-nine years old and a devoted admirer of Adolf Hitler, even to the point—with his trim black mustache—of trying to look like him. When he received orders to launch the strike at dawn, he thought to himself, "Who could be luckier than I?"

At 5:30 A.M. the flying crews of the first wave of fighters, bombers, and torpedo planes took off from six carriers that were pitching and rolling in the wind-whipped sea. The strike force climbed into heavy clouds but "the sky cleared as we moved in on the target, and Pearl Harbor was plainly visible from the northwest valley of the island," Fuchida later described the attack. "I studied our objective through binoculars. They were there all right, all eight [battleships]."

JAPANESE BOMBERS OVER PEARL HARBOR (NA).

To the disappointment of the attackers, the three aircraft carriers of the Pacific Fleet were at sea, one on the West Coast, the other two delivering squadrons of planes to Wake and Midway islands. But the seven war wagons lined up along Battleship Row, all but one of the battleships in port, presented Fuchida with a satisfying target. "Notify all planes to launch attacks," he ordered his radioman. The time was 7:49 A.M.

"Knowing the Admirals Nagumo and Yamamoto and the General Staff were anxious about the attack, I decided that they should be informed," Fuchida recalled. "I ordered that the following message be sent to the fleet: 'We have succeeded in making a surprise attack. Request you relay this report to Tokyo. . . .'

"The code for a successful surprise attack was 'Tora, tora, tora.' . . . There is a Japanese saying, 'A tiger (tora) goes out 1,000 ri (2,000 miles) and returns without fail.'"

Within minutes Fuchida saw towering waterspouts rising alongside the battleships, each of them a small city with upward of 1,500 crew. "Suddenly a colossal explosion occurred in Battleship Row. A huge column of dark red smoke rose to 1,000 feet and a stiff shock wave reached our plane. . . . Studying Battleship Row through binoculars, I saw that the big explosion had been on the *Arizona*."[39]

The USS *Solace* was the only hospital ship at anchor at Pearl Harbor that morning. On board was corpsman James F. Anderson of Fort Worth, Texas:

I REMEMBER VERY CLEARLY WHAT LOOKED like a dive-bomber coming in over the *Arizona* and dropping a bomb. I saw that bomb go down through what looked like a stack, and almost instantly it cracked the bottom of the *Arizona*, blowing the whole bow loose. It rose out of the water and settled. I could see flames, fire, and smoke coming out of that ship, and I saw two men flying through the air and the fire, screaming as they went. Where they ended up I'll never know. . . .

Almost immediately we started getting casualties, and from that point on I was very busy in our surgical ward. I remember only one of the men we got was able to tell us his name. The others were all in such critical condition they couldn't talk at all. They were all very badly burned from the oil and flash burns. The one who gave us his name did not have a single stitch of clothing on. The only thing left was a web belt with his chief's buckle, his chief-master-at-arms' badge, and the letters USS *Nevada*. He survived but he had a very long cut down the top of his head and every time he breathed his scalp would open up and I could see his skull.

We were using tannic acid for the burns. Every sheet we had in the ward was immediately brown. Many of the men who came in had their ears burned completely off, their noses badly burned, and their fingers bent like candles from the intense heat they had been in. Their bodies were just like hot dogs that had fallen in the fire and burned. All we could do for those poor fellows was give them morphine and pour the tannic acid over them.

For forty-eight hours after the assault, launches from the *Solace* combed the harbor picking up the remains of the bodies that had floated to the surface. "Our corpsmen tried very hard to salvage any part of a human body that could be identified," Anderson recalls. "We brought these parts back and tried to identify fingerprints or teeth or anything of this kind. . . . The parts were brought to the morgue, where we would clean them of oil and try to identify them." [40]

While Anderson and his fellow corpsmen went about their gruesome business, rescue crews worked frantically to reach sailors trapped in the battleship *Oklahoma*, which was hit by five aerial torpedoes and overturned.

One of the thirty-two surviving seamen caught in the doomed ship, which rested upside down at the bottom of the shallow harbor, a part of its massive hull exposed above the water, was nineteen-year-old Stephen Bower Young, a native of Massachusetts. At 9:00 A.M., Monday, December 8, Young and his fellow survivors were pulled from the overturned battlewagon by a Navy yard rescue team. They had been entombed for twenty-four hours. Oil-soaked and almost naked, they were picked by a motor launch from the *Solace*. "As our launch moved across the harbor, past the sunken *West Virginia* and the still smoking wreckage of the *Arizona*, we were too shocked to speak," Young said later. "It would take time to realize the enormity of that attack on Pearl Harbor. But we all knew that nothing would ever be the same for us. The world had changed. We knew that at the time, we really did."[41]

The *Oklahoma* lost 415 men at Pearl Harbor, more men than any other ship except the *Arizona*. That great battlewagon was hit by eight bombs. One of them penetrated the deck and exploded in the black powder magazine, setting off a tremendous explosion and fires that burned for two days. Together the crews of the two stricken battleships accounted for over two thirds of the dead at Pearl Harbor, including, on the *Arizona*, thirty sets of brothers. These were the only battleships that were not repaired and returned to duty. Today, the *Arizona* remains where it sank, with 1,177 sailors and Marines entombed in the wreckage, men who died before they knew who or why they were fighting. The volcanic explosion that sank the *Arizona* killed more human beings than any single explosion in recorded history, a record broken less than four years later by the atomic bombing of Hiroshima.

Using heavy electric winches, Navy workers righted *Oklahoma* and divers removed the remains of over 400 men who had gone down with her. The old battlewagon, however, was too badly damaged to be repaired. After the war, she was sold for scrap. While being towed to the West Coast she took on a list—the same heavy port list she'd taken on December 7, 1941—and sank. Better an honorable ocean grave, her former crew rejoiced, than to be cut up to make razor blades.

Eight battleships, three light cruisers, three destroyers, and four auxiliary ships were either sunk or damaged in the shattering attack that lasted less than two hours. *Arizona* and *Oklahoma* were wrecked beyond repair, and three battleships, *West Virginia*, *California*, and *Nevada*, were put out of action temporarily. The Army and Navy lost 165 aircraft, most of them on the ground. The Navy lost 2,008 men killed and 710 wounded, over twice as many casualties as it sustained in the Spanish-American War and World War I combined. The Army and Marine Corps together lost 327 killed and 433 wounded. Sixty-eight civilians were killed. By comparison, Japan lost five midget submarines and only twenty-nine of the 354 planes launched from its carrier task force, although many others were badly shot up. Pearl Harbor was one of warfare's most one-sided victories.

It was also America's greatest military disaster, but not as the Japanese had hoped, an irretrievable one. The three carriers in the Pacific Fleet, *Enterprise*, *Saratoga*, and *Lexington*—the fleet's main striking force in the new age of naval aer-

A NAVY RESCUE CREW STANDS ON THE UPTURNED HULL
OF THE *OKLAHOMA*, PEARL HARBOR (NA).

ial warfare that Pearl Harbor helped to inaugurate—were intact and battle-ready. And the Japanese failed to launch an additional attack on Pearl Harbor's enormous fuel dump, its submarine base, and its naval repair shops. After returning to the *Akagi* with the first wave of assault planes, while the second wave was still over Pearl Harbor, Mitsuo Fuchida had urged a third strike. But Admiral Nagumo feared that another attack might expose his fleet to the American carriers, whose whereabouts were unknown. It was a major mistake. All the oil supplies for the fleet were in tanks "that were vulnerable to .50 caliber bullets," said Admiral Chester Nimitz, who took command of the Pacific Fleet after the attack. "Had the Japanese destroyed the oil, it would have prolonged the war another two years."[42] And without fueling or repair facilities, the entire American Pacific Fleet would have had to return to San Diego. Except *Arizona* and *Oklahoma*, all of the warships that were sunk or damaged were back in active service within a year. The waters of Pearl Harbor were so shallow that ships were salvaged that would have been lost forever had they been sunk in open seas.

It was the first attack by a foreign power on American territory since the War of 1812 and the nation reacted with a deep desire for revenge. The attack on Pearl Harbor "shook the United States as nothing had since the firing on Fort Sumter," wrote Admiral Samuel Eliot Morison, the Navy's semiofficial historian.[43] Republicans and Democrats, interventionists and isolationists, labor and capital, closed ranks in a solid phalanx, and a nation of nearly 140 million people moved from peace to war with a unity it had never known before in time of crisis. Shortly after noon on December 8, President Roosevelt appeared before a joint session of the Congress to ask for a declaration of war against Japan. Congress responded with only a single dissenting vote.

Yamamoto's surprise attack had backfired. It committed an aroused America to a fight to the finish with Japan, ending in the war's opening hour all hope that Japan's leaders might have had for a short, sharp conflict and a negotiated peace. On hearing of the sinking of the American battle fleet at Pearl Harbor, the former president of Tokyo Imperial University whispered to a colleague in the dining hall, "This means that Japan is sunk too."[44]

But that was not the mood at the Imperial Palace. When told that the Hawaii attack was a complete success, the Emperor put on his military uniform and all that day was "in a splendid mood," one of his aides noted in his diary.[45]

At the White House, the atmosphere was not as somber as one would have expected. The President, said his chief aide, Harry Hopkins, was both shocked and relieved by the attack on Pearl Harbor. For well over a year, Roosevelt's secret fear was that the Japanese would avoid a war with America, that they would not attack Hawaii or the Philippines—American possessions—but would "move on Thailand, French Indo-China, make further inroads on China itself and possibly attack the Malay Straits. . . . This," said Hopkins, "would have left the President with the very difficult problem of protecting our national interests." To stop the Japanese he would have had to ask Congress for a declaration of war. But the members would have been unlikely to give him this, short of an attack on American soil. "Hence his great relief," Hopkins recalled, that Japan had struck directly at the United States. "In spite of the disaster of Pearl Harbor . . . it completely solidified the American people and made the war upon Japan inevitable." [46]

On December 11, Nazi Germany declared war on the United States, a decision that might have been more calamitous for its cause than its invasion of Russia the previous June. "Now it is impossible for us to lose the war!" Adolf Hitler told his skeptical generals. "We now have an ally who has never been vanquished in three thousand years." [47]

Hitler had long considered war with the United States inevitable and had been pressing Japan to come into the fight on the Axis side. He even proposed a surprise U-boat attack on the American Navy in port, a plan his admirals considered preposterous. One reason Hitler had not taken on the Americans earlier was because he lacked the large surface navy he thought essential to achieve total victory. But with Japan in the fight, he would have its aircraft carriers and battleships, along with his own U-boats, to deal with the United States—a combatant forced to rely on the seas to get both its ground and air forces into the fight. [48]

Fascist Italy declared war on the United States hours after Hitler's announcement. The wars in Europe and Asia became one gigantic world war, an unprecedented global conflagration.

The French correspondent Robert Guillain was under internment in Tokyo when the newspapers hit the streets announcing the attack on Pearl Harbor. He watched people's reactions as they read the papers they hurriedly bought from bell-ringing vendors:

THEY TOOK A FEW STEPS, THEN suddenly stopped to read more carefully; the heads lowered, then recoiled. When they looked up their faces were again inscrutable, transformed into masks of seeming indifference. Not a word to the vendor, nor to each other. . . .

I knew them well enough to understand their reaction. . . . They had instigated the war and yet they did not want it. Out of bravado, and to imitate their leaders, they had talked constantly about it, but they had not believed it would happen. What? A new war? For it was now added, superimposed, on the China war that had dragged on for three and a half years. And this time what an enemy: America! . . . The America which the Japanese for a quarter of a century had thought of as the champion of modern civilization, the ever-admired, ever-imitated model. . . .

Japan was at war with terrifying America. [49]

On the afternoon of December 7, Private James Jones, later the author of the novel *From Here to Eternity*, was being transported with his unit from Schofield Barracks to Pearl City. As the line of trucks passed Pearl Harbor, with smoke columns rising "as far as the eye could see," he recalls thinking "that none of our lives would ever be the same, that a social, even a cultural watershed had been crossed which we could never go back over, and I wondered how many of us would survive to see the end results. I wondered if I would. I had just turned twenty, the month before." [50]

BATAAN

To win the war that Pearl Harbor had begun the United States would send over two million men to the Pacific and launch over a hundred amphibious invasions—D-Days in the Pacific—against the widely scattered island garrisons of Japan's oceanic empire. But far into 1942, it was the Imperial Japanese forces that were the masters of amphibious conquest. In an ocean expanse dominated by their fast-striking navy, they reeled off a shocking succession of territorial conquests, all of them sea-to-land invasions.

To students of Japanese history, this Pacific blitzkrieg should not have been surprising. "For twenty-six hundred years, Japan had no war on its own soil," the Japanese ambassador to Berlin told Hitler after the attack on Pearl Harbor. "All wars that Japan was forced to fight were conducted outside the Japanese islands, each time in conjunction with amphibious operations." [51] Japan's victories in the Sino-Japanese War (1894–95) and the Russo-Japanese War (1904–05) were achieved by a lethal combination of land and sea assault. And in the succeeding decades, army and navy units conducted extensive amphibious training operations, developed new landing boats with ramps and exit rails for assault troops, and fashioned an impressive body of doctrine on modern amphibious warfare.

Japan first tested this new method of warfare on a massive scale in the months after Pearl Harbor. Landing at night whenever possible, and at lightly defended points, with heavy naval and air support, Japanese troops—many of them carrying bicycles on their backs—swept across scores of Pacific beaches, moved inland with dramatic suddenness, and began to fight independently before later and larger waves of troops arrived at the anchorage. By the time the United States could mount a counterattack, Japan held a string of island fortresses and economic colonies that stretched

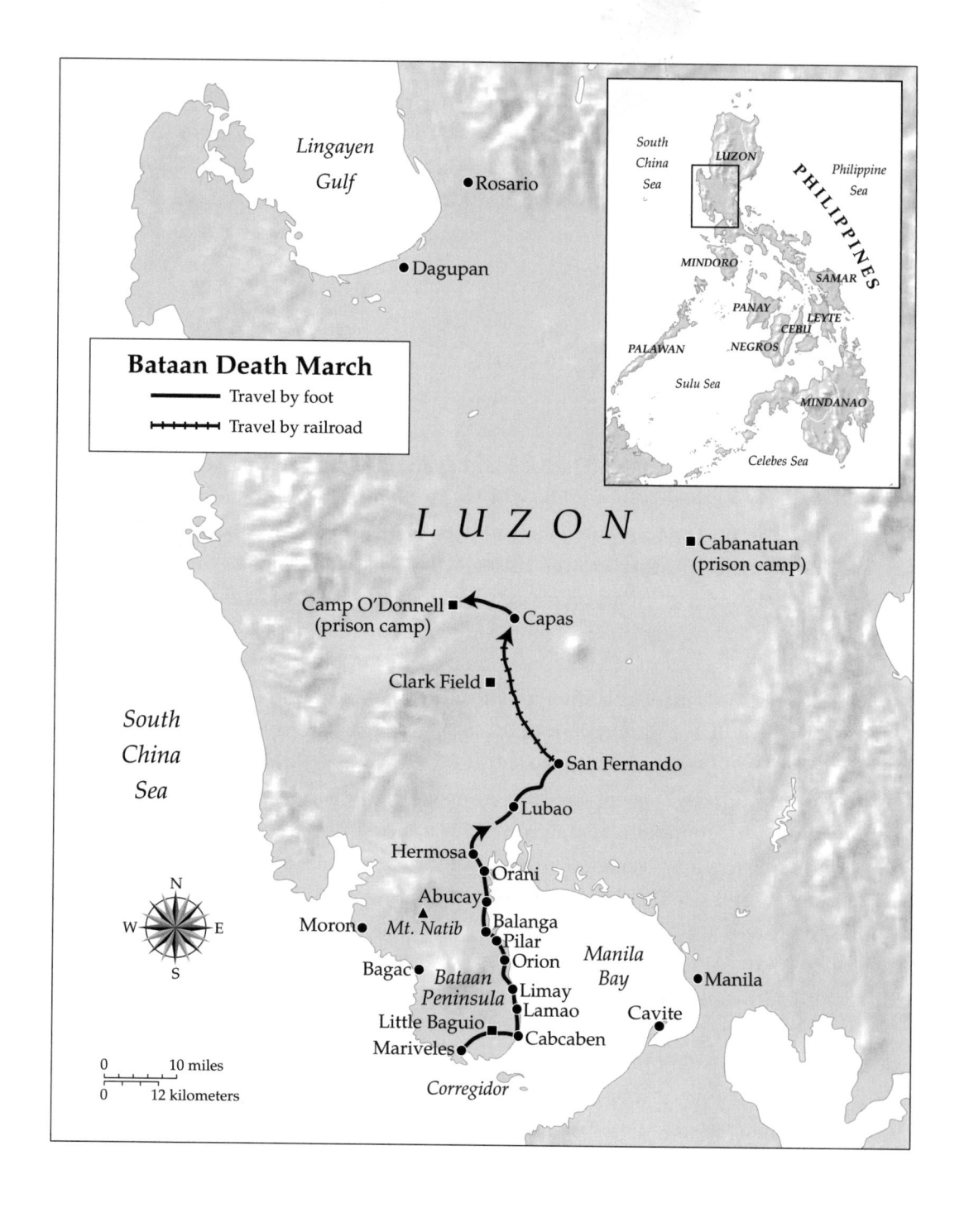

Lingayen
Gulf

●Rosario

●Dagupan

Bataan Death March

━━━ Travel by foot

┼┼┼┼ Travel by railroad

*South
China
Sea*

L U Z O N

■ Cabanatuan
(prison camp)

Camp O'Donnell ■ ◄── ●Capas
(prison camp)

Clark Field ■

●San Fernando

●Lubao

Hermosa●
●Orani

Abucay●
▲ *Mt. Natib*
Moron●

Balanga●
●Pilar
●Orion

Bagac●
*Bataan
Peninsula*

●Limay
●Lamao

Little Baguio●
Mariveles●
■ ●Cabcaben

*Manila
Bay*

●Manila

●Cavite

Corregidor

*South
China
Sea*

LUZON

*Philippine
Sea*

P H I L I P P I N E S

MINDORO

SAMAR

PANAY

LEYTE
CEBU

PALAWAN

NEGROS

Sulu Sea

MINDANAO

Celebes Sea

N
W   E
S

0   10 miles

0   12 kilometers

across the Pacific, east to west, from the Gilbert Islands to the Philippines, and north to south, from the icebound Aleutians to the mountainous jungles of New Guinea. It was a stunning assault that paralyzed the American and British fleets, overpowered the Allies' ground forces, and placed Japan's sea, air, and ground forces on Australia's doorstep—all within five months.

On the morning that Pearl Harbor was attacked the Japanese bombed Singapore and sent troops from Siam (now Thailand) toward Malaya in preparation for a full-scale assault on the fortress city. Admiral Sir Tom Phillips, commander of the British Far Eastern Fleet, put to sea with the battle cruiser *Repulse* and the battleship *Prince of Wales* to prevent an amphibious landing in northern Malaya. As the two ships steamed northward, Japanese warplanes sank them on December 10.

Even as the *Repulse* and the *Prince of Wales* went down, a Japanese task force was approaching the Philippines, determined to smash, in one sudden blow, the only enemy of consequence in its arc of aggression. Senior commander General Douglas MacArthur anticipated an attack. Work on new airfields was going forward and troop and aircraft reinforcements—mostly B-17 heavy bombers—were on the way from the United States, but all this was too late. After reading an incoming report on Pearl Harbor, Lieutenant Edwin Ramsey went to the officers club for a drink with the Army chief of intelligence for the island. " 'Lieutenant, are you religious,' he asked me. 'No sir, not particularly,' I answered. Then he said, 'I think you better give your soul to God because your ass belongs to the Japanese.' " [52]

Nine hours after the Hawaiian assault an air armada descended on Clark and Iba fields, near Manila, and destroyed most of the American planes on the ground. "At 12:35 in the afternoon . . . we heard the airplanes," recalled Lester I. Tenney, a Jewish kid from Chicago whose tank battalion was in position around Clark Airfield, expecting the landing of Japanese paratroopers. "As we looked up into the sky, we saw . . . bombers flying very high over Clark Field. Just as I was about to say, 'They're not ours,' the ground beneath us shook . . . the war we feared was upon us." [53]

MacArthur's "failure in this emergency is bewildering," writes biographer William Manchester. We will probably never know why he allowed his Air Force to be slaughtered like sitting ducks because, as Manchester notes, "we know little about his actions and nothing of his thoughts that terrible morning." [54] Arrogant, iron-willed sixty-one-year-old Douglas MacArthur, whose father had won the Congressional Medal of Honor in the Civil War and whose own Army career was a succession of stunning achievements, was never forthright about this humiliating disaster, one of the greatest in American military history. Nor was there ever an official inquiry, although Pearl Harbor was the subject of eight investigations.

After hitting Pearl Harbor, the Japanese expected MacArthur's Air Force to attack their vulnerable air base in Formosa. "We put on our gas masks," a Japanese officer recalled, "and prepared for an attack."[55] But orders for the Formosa mission were inexplicably stalled, and when the Japanese struck Clark Field the B-17 Flying Fortresses, along with the rest of the air fleet, were sitting wingtip to wingtip, with no fighter cover, while their pilots and crews were having lunch.

With the American Air Force all but destroyed and the Navy's small force of warships retreating southward, the Japanese landed 43,000 troops at Lingayen, just north of Manila, on December 22, in the largest amphibious operation of its Pacific assault. After his poorly planned strategy to stop the enemy on the beaches collapsed, MacArthur declared Manila an Open City in a futile attempt to save it and fled to the rock fortress of Corregidor, an island at the entrance of Manila Bay. From there, by radio, he commanded a fighting retreat to the wilderness peninsula of Bataan.

The mountain jungles of Bataan are ideal for defensive fighting. But MacArthur's Filipino-American army of 80,000 men was poorly armed and desperately low on food. Before long, the troops were eating horses, mules, and monkeys; 20,000 had come down with malaria; and thousands more were stricken with dysentery, scurvy, hookworm, and beriberi.

General Masaharu Homma, with his formidable Fourteenth Army, had expected to make quick work of Bataan. But in weeks of miserable jungle fighting, American and Filipino troops held him off. After pushing back the initial Japanese offensive, Major General Jonathan Wainwright, the skinny, hard-drinking leader of the jungle defense, reported to MacArthur that barely one quarter of his army was still fit to fight. Men were so sick and hungry they could barely crawl out of their foxholes. The cautious Homma, with a supply line extending back to Japan, settled in for a siege, against the advice of his superiors in Tokyo, who wanted him to launch suicidal attacks.

A gaunt and weary MacArthur, his wife and three-year-old son by his side, directed the Battle of Bataan from the 1,400-foot-long Malinta Tunnel, his huge underground command post and hospital on Corregidor, where the stench of gangrene permeated the stale, uncirculated, air. Those around him never questioned his bravery. To the alarm of his family and aides, he would stand out in the open without a helmet, coolly puffing on a Lucky Strike cigarette, as Japanese bombers pounded Corregidor. Yet the brave commander paid only one visit—in a Ford staff car—to his trapped and demoralized army on the Bataan peninsula, only three miles away by water. Perhaps he was ashamed to face his men, for the relief force that Roosevelt had promised to send never arrived.

Some troops called him "Dugout Doug," and composed poems that described their own desperate plight—abandoned by Washington because, by agreement with Churchill, priority was to be given to the defeat of Germany. Frank Hewlett, an American correspondent at the front, wrote what was to become the war's most famous piece of doggerel:

> *We're the battling bastards of Bataan;*
> *No mamma, no papa, no Uncle Sam;*
> *No aunts, no uncles, no nephews, no nieces;*
> *No rifles, no planes, or artillery pieces;*
> *And nobody gives a damn.*

After Roosevelt and Secretary of War Henry L. Stimson privately informed Churchill that they considered MacArthur's army doomed, Stimson wrote in his diary: "There are times when men have to die."[56]

But not Douglas MacArthur. He had become an American hero, commander of the only Allied army still holding out against Japan. A master of public relations, MacArthur's official dispatches gave all the credit to himself for the defense of the Philippines.

Roosevelt abhorred MacArthur—both the man and his conservative politics—but was counting on him to lead the upcoming counteroffensive in the Pacific. Others, including MacArthur's former aide, Brigadier General Dwight D. Eisenhower, admonished him severely from his staff position in Washington—mostly in private—for being caught unprepared by the enemy and losing most of the B-17 fleet in the Far East.[57] Roosevelt obviously needed MacArthur more than he did the men unjustly blamed for the Pearl Harbor attack, Admiral Husband Kimmel, commander of the Pacific Fleet, and Lieutenant General Walter Short, the Army commander at Hawaii, both of whom were relieved and subsequently retired from the service.

General George C. Marshall, the Army chief of staff, begged MacArthur to leave the Philippines. But MacArthur wired back that he and his family—the wife and son of a soldier—would share the fate of his men. Finally, on February 22, MacArthur received direct orders from Roosevelt to escape to Australia. He stalled until March 11 and then left with his family and staff in a PT boat captained by

Lieutenant John D. Bulkeley. After a harrowing 600-mile run through the Japanese blockade, MacArthur and his party arrived on the Philippine island of Mindanao and were flown to Australia. On his arrival in Melbourne he made one of the most famous statements of the war, "The President of the United States ordered me to break through the Japanese lines and proceed from Corregidor to Australia for the purpose, as I understand it, of organizing the American offensive against Japan. A primary purpose of this is the relief of the Philippines. I came through and I shall return."

The American government asked him to change this to "We shall return." MacArthur refused. Was it megalomania? Perhaps. But the original author of the phrase, the Filipino journalist Carlos Romulo, informed a MacArthur aide that this pledge was intended for Filipinos, not Americans. "America has let us down and won't be trusted. But the people still have confidence in MacArthur. If he says he is coming back it will be believed." The aide told this to MacArthur and he naturally agreed.[58]

Back on Bataan, one of his staff, Brigadier General William E. Brougher, spoke for many of those MacArthur had left behind. "A foul trick of deception has been played on a large group of Americans by a Commander in Chief and small staff who are now eating steak and eggs in Australia. God damn them!"[59]

Hunger and disease wore down the "Battling Bastards of Bataan" to the point where further resistance was suicidal. "Our stamina was gone," recalls Lester Tenney, "our food was gone, our health was deteriorating, and our ammunition and gas had just about run out. We were helpless. We troops felt let down, even betrayed. If we had been supplied with enough ammunition and guns, troops, and equipment, and food and medical supplies, we believed that we would have been able to repel the Japanese."[60]

On April 8, the Japanese launched a massive attack on the American lines. General Wainwright, who succeeded MacArthur at Corregidor, ordered a counterattack. It was the last flicker of the flame of defiance. The next day 76,000 American and Filipino troops under Major General Edward P. King, who had replaced Wainwright as commander on Bataan, surrendered to the Japanese. It was the largest surrender by the United States Army in its history.

A handful of the troops and nurses on Bataan managed to make their way to Corregidor to join the 13,000 defenders of that tunneled island rock. For almost a month the Japanese blasted it from air, sea, and land; and on May 6, they crossed the narrow channel and fought their way to the mouth of the tunnel. Concerned that the enemy would sweep through the tunnel guns blazing, killing his soldiers as well as the courageous American nurses who were caring for them, Wainwright ordered his men to lay down their arms. "In Western civilization, capture has always been viewed as being better than death," Lester Tenney wrote later. "Our bad luck was that we were being captured by a people from a civilization that believed death was preferable to surrender."[61]

The ancient Japanese code of Bushido admonished warriors not to survive the "dishonor of capture," but to "fight to the last man." It did not, however, call for the mistreatment of enemy prisoners. The warlords who took over the Japanese government in the 1930s added that to it, even though the Japanese military had treated prisoners humanely in the Russo-Japanese War of 1904–05 and in World War I. Soldiers of the new regime were fed the idea that they were members of a super race that all other people would eventually have to serve, and that prisoners of war, especially whites, were a species of cowards who deserved to be treated like animals for the dishonorable act of surrender.[62]

The prisoners at Bataan and Corregidor were not completely aware of this, but they had heard frightening reports of the atrocities committed by the Japanese in Nanking—of Chinese women raped and burned alive, and of tortured men left for dead with their penises sewed to their lips. "I was scared spitless," said Inez McDonald, one of the fifty-four Army nurses captured on Corregidor.[63]

When his Japanese captors approached him, Lester Tenney's "knees began shaking, my hands felt cold and clammy, and sweat broke out on my neck and forehead. We were all scared beyond anything imaginable."[64]

After caring for their patients in the Malinta Tunnel for two months, the nurses were sent to Santo Tomás Internment Camp in Manila, where they suffered hardships and hunger but were not physically molested. The American and Filipino troops on Corregidor were loaded onto freighters, taken to Manila, where they were marched through the streets, and then packed into ovenlike boxcars and shipped to a desolate POW camp. There 2,000 Americans died in the first two months of captivity.

The men captured on Bataan went through an unimaginable nightmare: the Bataan Death March.

When the defenders of Bataan surrendered, the Japanese expected to receive about 40,000 prisoners. They were to be marched nineteen miles to a dispatch station and then taken by truck and train sixty-six miles north to Camp O'Donnell, a former training facility for the Philippine army, in central Luzon. But General Homma found himself saddled with nearly twice that number of prisoners, almost all of them sick and starving. Some of them were taken by truck to Camp O'Donnell, but most were forced to walk much of the way under the withering April sun (April is the hottest month in the Philippines) and over sand-covered roads lined with filthy drainage ditches. "The men were in such terrible condition from malnutrition and disease, and pure physical weaknesses from long days of incessant combat, that they didn't have a chance," said nurse Hattie Brantley, who had served with them in Bataan.[65]

Before they were ordered into line, the men were stripped of canteens, food, and personal items. Japanese guards cut off the fingers of officers to get their West Point rings, and prisoners found with Japanese money were shot, on the assumption that it had been taken from a fallen soldier of the empire. Five prisoners who were too sick to make the march were bayoneted in their beds.

General Homma had instructed his officers to treat the prisoners well, but the Japanese guards were in an ugly mood. They were exhausted, sick, and hungry, and they had lost comrades on Bataan. They also came from a culture of cruelty. The officer class had the status and authority of "feudal lords," writes Japanese historian Saburo-Ienaga. The privates had no rights. They were "non-persons," and were subjected to "an unending stream of humiliation and rough treatment."[66] Japanese military training was "filled . . . with beatings," recalls Sakata Tsuyoshi, a retired World War II soldier. Senior officers would regularly inflict physical punishment on the men under them, slapping them, punching them, kicking them, and beating them with the leather straps of their swords, often while other officers stood by laughing. "This method of inflicting brutal punishment without any cause and destroying our power to think was a way of transforming us into men who would carry out our superiors' orders as a reflex action."[67]

With such training, Japanese soldiers on Bataan did not need orders to inflict violence on prisoners they already regarded with complete disdain.

The American and Filipino prisoners marched four abreast, in long columns, and were given only enough food and water to survive the march. They felt like "walking corpses." Lester Tenney was one of them:

ONE DAY OUR TONGUES WERE THICK with the dust kicked up from the constantly passing trucks, and our throats were parched. We saw water flowing from an artesian well, and . . . a marching buddy, Frank, and I ran toward the well . . . and started to swallow water as fast as we could. . . .

Within a few minutes, another ten to fifteen prisoners ran to the well. . . . At just that time a Japanese guard came over to the well and started to laugh at us. The first five of us drank our fill, and when the sixth man began drinking, the guard suddenly pushed his bayonet down into the man's neck and back. The American prisoner fell to his knees, gasped for breath, and then fell over on his face. . . .

Many of the men on the march were just too weak and had too many illnesses to continue. If they stopped on the side of the road to defecate, they would be beaten within an inch of their lives or killed.

AMERICAN POWS CAPTURED ON BATAAN (NA).

On the fourth day, as the prisoners entered the town of Balanga, Filipino civilians began throwing them food—rice cakes, small pieces of fried chicken, and chunks of sugarcane. When the guards spotted this they opened fire, killing randomly. The Japanese seemed to take malicious delight in killing Filipinos who had fought with or supported the "white devils." Lieutenant Kermit Lay saw a Japanese soldier beat to death a Filipino man with a baseball bat; and at one point in the march, Japanese guards rounded up 300 or 400 Filipino soldiers, tied them together with telephone wire, and bayoneted or beheaded them from behind. The slaughter went on for two hours.[68]

Tenney picks up the story:

WE CONTINUED MARCHING INTO THE CENTER of town, and when nighttime finally came we were herded into a large warehouse. . . . We were so tightly packed together that we sprawled on each other. When one of us had to urinate, he just did it in his pants, knowing that the following day the heat from the sun would dry them out. Those who had to defecate found their way back to one of the corners of the building and did it there. That night, the human waste covering the floor from those who had dysentery caused many others to contract this killing disease.

The stench, the sounds of dying men, and the whines and groans of those too sick to move to the back of the building had become so unbearable that I put small pieces of cloth into my ears in a feeble attempt to drown out some of the noise. Nothing could be done about the smell. . . . The Japenese guards, also unable to bear the horrible smell, closed the doors to the warehouse, put a padlock on them, and kept watch from outside.

About twenty-five men died in the warehouse that night. In the morning their bodies were tossed like garbage into a field behind the building.

Tenney:

ON THAT FIFTH DAY OF THE march, I witnessed one of the most sadistic and inhumane incidents on the entire march. . . . We had just stopped for a brief rest while waiting for another group to catch up with us. When the other group finally arrived, the guard ordered us to stand up and start walking. One of the men had a very bad case of malaria and had barely made it to the rest area. He was burning up with fever and severely disoriented. When ordered to stand up, he could not do it. Without a minute's hesitation, the guard hit him over the head with the butt of his gun, knocked him down to the ground, and then called for two nearby prisoners to start digging a hole to bury the fallen prisoner. The two men started digging, and when the hole was about a foot deep, the guard ordered the two men to place the sick man in the hole and bury him alive. The two men shook their heads; they could not do that. . . .

Without warning . . . the guard shot the bigger of the two prisoners. He then pulled two more men from the line and ordered them to dig another hole to bury the murdered man. The Japanese guard got his point across. They dug the second hole, placed the two bodies in the holes, and threw dirt over them. The first man, still alive, started screaming as the dirt was thrown on him.

As the men trudged on like zombies, twelve hours a day for several more days, they began to spot headless corpses in the roadside ditches. One American started counting heads. At twenty-seven, one head per mile, he stopped counting because what he was doing was making him crazy.

Lester Tenney witnessed one of these beheadings:

AT ONE POINT ON . . . THE MARCH, we saw an American soldier kneeling in front of a Japanese officer. The officer had his samurai sword out of the scabbard. . . . Up went the blade, then with a great artistry and a loud "Banzai," the officer brought the blade down. We heard a dull thud, and the American was decapitated. The Japanese officer then kicked his body . . . over into the field, and all of the Japanese soldiers laughed and walked away. As I witnessed this tragedy and as the sword came down, my body twitched, and I clasped my hands in front of me, as if in prayer. I could hardly breathe.

Later, Tenney said: "What made the beheading especially sickening was that the man's body shook and twitched well after he was dead."[69]

Tenney and his fellow prisoners struggled on for several more days until, barely able to stand, they were ordered to make a double-time march to the little city of San Fernando. There they were crammed into small railway boxcars used for hauling animals and taken on a five-hour ride to Capas, near their final destination, the barbed wire compound of Camp O'Donnell. In the steaming boxcars, some men couldn't breathe and died standing up. There was no room to fall down.

The exact numbers are lost to history, but about 500 Americans and as many as

2,500 Filipinos died on the march. Those that made it, said an American doctor who survived, did it "on the marrow of their bones." [70]

"If I had to do it all over again, I would commit suicide," said Kermit Lay, fifty years later.[71]

The dying did not stop at Camp O'Donnell. Over 16,000 prisoners, 1,600 of them Americans, would die in this loathsome compound in the next two months. As Tenney relates:

> THE MEN WERE DYING AT A rate of 100 and 200 a day. Malaria was a big killer and dysentery was horrible. It was so bad that men would go to sleep next to a slit trench so that if they had to defecate they would just roll over.
>
> And when they died, we had to bury these men, which meant we had to go in a field and dig a hole in marshy soil. If you dug a hole too deep, water would come up and make the dead man float. So you had to take pieces of bamboo and hold the man down with them while you threw dirt on the body.
>
> Let me tell you this. When a man said there's no use in going on any longer, he died. When he said there's no sense in waiting because the Americans are not coming, he died. The men who had positive attitudes, the men who said, "I know I'm going home," are the ones who came home.[72]

After the war, Lester Tenney began to have nightmares that never went away. They occurred with acute intensity when, as a college professor, he started writing his memoirs. He had thought he had put it behind him, but his deep hatred of the Japanese returned. In time, however, he came to consider hating "as a sickness." Today, he says he cannot blame an entire people for what happened to him during the war. The only hatred he still harbors "is for those who beat me." [73]

Kermit Lay felt differently. "I hate the Japanese. I won't talk to them, and I won't buy their products. It's just the way it is." [74]

WAKE ISLAND

Between Hawaii and the Philippines lay the three small but strategically important islands of Midway, Wake, and Guam. To control the Pacific west of Hawaii, Japan had to capture these outposts.

At 8:45 A.M. on December 8 (the calendar is one day ahead west of the International Date Line), eighteen Japanese bombers smashed the military installations on Guam. The small garrison of Navy personnel and Marines had neither antiaircraft batteries nor coastal defense guns. Their few planes were quickly put out of action. The first landing came before dawn on the 10th, and within a few hours all resistance had been overcome.

The defense of Wake is one of the heroic chapters of American history. A strategically important air base only 600 miles north of Japanese naval and air power in the Marshall Islands, Wake was lightly defended by a Marine fighter squadron equipped with a dozen new Grumman F4F Wildcats, and by a Marine Defense Battalion of about 450 men under Major James P. S. Devereux. But when the Japanese tried to land an "abominably commanded" invasion force on December 11, they were repulsed by devastating, close-range artillery fire and by the four Wildcat fighters that had not been knocked out of action in the initial bombing.[75] Wake's defenders sank or severely damaged six Japanese ships, causing the humiliated Japanese commander to call off the landing.

Back in the United States, headlines blared MARINES HOLD WAKE, and the *Washington Post* compared the desperate defense of the island to the last stand at the Alamo.

The Japanese returned on December 23, this time with six heavy cruisers and two carriers from Nagumo's Pearl Harbor strike force. Carrier-based bombers knocked out the coastal gun emplacements that had chewed up the first invasion fleet, and land-based bombers from Kwajalein, in the Marshalls, pulverized the island. A naval relief force was assembled at Pearl Harbor and sent to sea, but it was recalled when word came in that the Japanese had already landed troops on Wake. One of the last radio messages from the island defenders was a grim piece of understatement: "Urgent! Enemy on island. The issue is in doubt."

Without Navy support and with only one functional searchlight, the outnumbered Marines were helpless to stop a landing force of over 1,000 Japanese, which came in under the cover of night. After holding on for thirty hours in furious fighting, the garrison surrendered to avoid a senseless slaughter. Major Devereux walked out to meet the enemy with a white flag tied to a mop pole. Prisoners were taken to Shanghai. A hundred or so civilian construction workers were kept on Wake to rebuild it. All were later executed.

Midway was also attacked the day Pearl Harbor was hit, but its shore installations were so effective that the small task force assigned to the job turned and ran. The big fight for Midway would occur later.

SINGAPORE

The attack on the American islands in the Pacific was part of a coordinated assault that targeted British and Dutch outposts in Southeast Asia.

Hong Kong was the first to fall. This great naval base formed, with Singapore and Manila, a triangle of Anglo-American power in the Pacific. As early as 1940, however, Japanese occupation of nearby Canton had made it all but indefensible. The Japanese attacked on December 8, 1941, and for two weeks the fabled city was subjected to continuous bombardment from land and air. The British garrison might have stood up to this, but the Japanese cut off the water supply. Confronted with the responsibility for the suffering or death of thousands of civilian inhabitants, the British commander, Sir Mark Young, surrendered on Christmas Day.

Next came Penang in Malaya, then Singapore. Wearing sneakers and moving by foot and bicycle, with small bags of rice wrapped around their necks, 70,000 Japanese troops under General Tomoyuki Yamashita, one of the great commanders of the war, swept through 580 miles of rice fields, swamps, and rubber forests, crossed the Straits of Johore, and laid siege to the island city, which was packed with fleeing refugees. Running dangerously low on supplies and water, and with panic spreading through the city, British commander Sir Arthur Percival surrendered over 130,000 soldiers and internees to an army about half the size of his force.

Legend has it that Singapore's defenses "faced the wrong way," toward the sea. But that is not true. The guns faced the mainland, but were armed with the wrong ammunition, shells unsuited for battle against ground troops.

The capture of Singapore opened the way to the Dutch East Indies and was as important a victory for the Japanese army as Pearl Harbor was for the Imperial Navy.

THE DUTCH EAST INDIES

The Dutch East Indies was a vast archipelago that stretched over 3,000 miles from Malaya to the Solomons and included Sumatra, Java, Dutch Borneo, Celebes,

Dutch New Guinea, and thousands of smaller islands. Here was the storehouse of oil, rubber, timber, rice, and metal production that had driven Japan towards war; and from here it could threaten Australia, only 300 miles to the south.

From bases in Indochina, the Japanese swept down into the East Indies in December 1941. The outgunned Allies could put up almost no resistance to this inexorable land and sea blitz, speedier and on a scale vaster than anything Hitler had imagined. Two awesome Japanese attack forces "slithered into the Netherlands East Indies like the arms of two giant octopi," writes Admiral Samuel Eliot Morison, who served on eleven different ships during the war and wrote a fifteen-volume history of American naval operators in World War II. "The Western octopus worked down the South China Sea to North Borneo and Sumatra; the Eastern to East Borneo, the Celebes, Ambon, Timor and Bali. Aircraft would pound down a beachhead, amphibious forces would then move in and activate another airfield and soften up the next objective for invasion." [76]

Here off the coast of Borneo, the U.S. Navy fought its first surface engagement of the Pacific war, a battle for control of that island's tremendous petroleum wells and refineries. It took place on the night of January 23–24, 1942, in magnificent Balikpapan Bay, one of the busiest oil ports of Asia. The Americans drew first blood. When the Japanese landed an amphibious force on the south side of the bay, four blacked-out World War I destroyers, known as "cans" to their crews, slipped through the darkness and surprised a dozen enemy troop transports that were in the midst of unloading, sinking four of them, along with a patrol craft. Had they not had defective torpedoes, they would have sunk more. Shaking off their losses, the Japanese landed marines and took the island, chasing into the jungle the workers of the Royal Dutch/Shell Group who had remained behind to set fire to the wells. Of the seventy-five workers, only thirty-five survived the malarial jungle, Japanese firing squads, and prison camps. [77]

The Battle of the Java Sea was the last desperate effort to save the sprawling archipelago. Admiral K. W. F. Doorman of the Dutch navy was in command of an Allied force of five cruisers and about a dozen destroyers when, on February 27, it ran into two enemy flotillas, far superior both in numbers and firepower to his fleet. In this, the biggest surface naval battle since the Battle of Jutland in 1916, the Japanese annihilated their opponent and established their supremacy in the South Pacific.

Now there was nothing to stop the Japanese conquest of Java. From Sumatra and Borneo, 100,000 troops invaded the all but defenseless island. On March 9, the Dutch East Indies surrendered. A day earlier, the Japanese had landed troops on the north and east coast of New Guinea, at the desolate but strategically valuable jungle outposts of Lae and Salamaua.

Moving southward from bases in the Mariana and Caroline islands, Imperial forces occupied the Admiralty Islands, the Northern Solomons, and the Bismarck Archipelago, where they smashed a small but fiercely courageous Australian garrison and built their most formidable military base in the South Pacific at Rabaul, at the northern end of the island of New Britain. Blessed with a magnificent natural harbor, Rabaul is within easy reach by sea or air of New Guinea and the entire Solomon chain, stretching southward to a godforsaken disease pit called Guadalcanal. From fortress Rabaul, all major Japanese operations in the area would be launched and supported.

These easy conquests confirmed Japan's view of the capitalist West as decadent and hopelessly weakened by materialism, and spawned a dangerous spirit of overconfidence. For a time, it looked like Australia would be the next target, and it was vulnerable, for some its best combat forces were fighting with the British in North Africa. Unknown to the Allies, however, the Japanese had no intention of invading Australia. Their aim was to establish bases off Australia's northern coast in order to cut the American supply line to the island continent. The Japanese correctly saw Australia for what it became, a Pacific England, the staging area and initiating point for an immense Allied counteroffensive. Accordingly, aside from bombing the northern port of Darwin, their major military effort against the island continent was to build air bases in the South Pacific to sever its supply lines to Hawaii and the West Coast of the United States.

Allied leaders feared that the victory-drunk Japanese would drive westward into the Indian Ocean, conquer India at a time when anti-colonial sentiment there was running high, and link up with Axis forces fighting in the Mideast and the Mediterranean. But Hitler and Mussolini thought they could handle the British in that theater without Japanese help, and the Japanese army wanted to keep the burden of its forces in China and Manchuria to subdue the Chinese and prepare for a possible war with Russia. This would be a fight to take new territory and consolidate old land grabs on Russia's mineral-rich northeastern border. The Japanese were counting on the Germans to crush Soviet resistance in their great summer offensive of 1942, opening up Russia for an invasion from the east. But the Red Army held fast, and the

Chinese proved impossible to subdue, so a great part of the Japanese army remained in China for the duration of the war. This made the retaking of the Pacific, horrible though it was, a less bloody affair than it might have been. If Japan and Germany had cooperated as closely as the United States and Britain, the war would have been indefinitely prolonged. But the two Axis allies fervently mistrusted each other and failed to launch a single joint offensive.[78]

THE DOOLITTLE RAID

At this low point in the war, with Allied forces in the Pacific either defeated or on the defensive everywhere, American naval and air power delivered several critical counterpunches.

In January 1942, Vice Admiral William F. "Bull" Halsey, one of the first American heroes of the war, had sent his carriers against Japanese positions in the Marshall Islands, sinking seventeen ships and destroying forty or fifty planes. Three weeks later the carrier *Enterprise* led a force that bombarded Wake Island, and Halsey's carrier planes hit enemy bases on the north coast of New Guinea. Then, on April 18, 1942, Halsey's task force of *Enterprise* and *Hornet* stunned the Japanese by launching a bombing strike on Tokyo.

The attack had been planned by President Roosevelt and his top naval advisors and was intended to revive sinking home front morale. It was one of the great gambles of the war.

Since American aircraft carriers were unable to get close enough to Japan to send out their short-range bombers, Navy planners decided to load the deck of a carrier with mid-range Army bombers, even though planes this large had never flown from a carrier in warfare. In complete secrecy, volunteer pilots were trained at a Florida base to take off at precariously short distances. The flight decks of carriers were too short for retrieval; the bombers would have to fly 1,100 additional miles beyond Japan, to friendly bases in China. Command of the mission was given to Lieutenant Colonel James H. Doolittle, "King of the Sky," a racing pilot known for his daredevil aerial stunts, but also for his deep knowledge of aviation (he held a doctorate from MIT in aeronautical engineering).

In April, the carrier *Hornet* steamed toward Japan with sixteen twin-engine B-25s on its deck, each carrying three 500-pound bombs and one incendiary bomb.

None of the pilots had ever taken off from the deck of a carrier, and the men did not learn their target was Tokyo until they were far out to sea. When it was announced over the ship's bullhorn—"Now hear this. Now hear this. This force is bound for Tokyo"—the sailors and airmen cheered wildly. This would be payback for Pearl Harbor.

Halsey hoped to get within 500 miles of the target before launching Doolittle's bombers. But when *Hornet* and its powerful escort force reached a point 650 miles from the Japanese coast they ran into enemy picket boats. The task force destroyed them, but there was the possibility that the Japanese had already radioed the presence of the Americans. Doolittle doubted that his planes could fly from this point, hit Tokyo, and still make the Chinese mainland. It was abort or go. Halsey said to go. "The wind and sea were so strong that morning that green water was breaking over the carrier's ramps," Halsey wrote later. "Jimmy led his squadron. When his plane buzzed down . . . the *Hornet*'s deck . . . there wasn't a man topside who didn't sweat him into the air." [79]

Doolittle's raiders achieved total surprise. Swooping in at rooftop level, they hit Tokyo and five other Japanese cities, killing about fifty civilians, without the loss of a single plane. [80]

Although the raid did little damage, it lifted American morale. Asked from what base the planes had flown, President Roosevelt whimsically replied, "Shangri-la."

Aided by a strong tailwind, fifteen of the sixteen planes made it to China but ran out of fuel and crashed before they could reach their bases; one made it safely to Siberia. Sixty-four of the fliers, including Doolittle, escaped, spirited to safety by the Chinese underground. The Japanese forces in China captured eight airmen. Three were later executed, in violation of international law and with the Emperor's approval, and one died in prison after being tortured.

But it was the Chinese who suffered the most grievous consequences. In a four-month reign of terror, 250,000 Chinese were slaughtered by the Japanese in reprisal for a few brave peasants lending assistance to the downed Doolittle crews, "a scale of murder," historian Walter Boyne has written, "equal to that of the Rape of Nanking."[81]

The raid caused the Japanese to keep hundreds of planes in the home islands that otherwise would have gone to the South Pacific. More importantly, it was a deep psychological blow to the Japanese, one that led, in retaliation, to the grandiose expansion of Japanese military ambitions that brought on the Battle of Midway.

CORAL SEA

America's first attempt to stop Japanese expansion southward to secure bases to protect its newly won empire came in the waters of the magnificent sea that washes the shores of New Guinea, the Solomons, and New Caledonia. In early May, a Japanese invasion fleet steamed into the Coral Sea from Rabaul, headed for Port Moresby, a tiny but strategically important outpost that faces Australia on the southeastern tip of New Guinea's Papuan peninsula. American intelligence had decrypted the Japanese naval code and the Pacific command sent a task force of two carriers, *Lexington* and *Yorktown*, under Rear Admiral Frank Jack Fletcher, to surprise the enemy.

This was the first major engagement in naval history in which surface ships did not exchange a single shot. Separated by 175 miles of water, the two fleets never got close enough to see each other. Carrier-based planes did all the fighting; and there was so much confusion in this swirling aerial battle that several Japanese planes, in darkness and bad weather, tried to land on the deck of *Yorktown*. American planes sank one small Japanese carrier and heavily damaged a larger one, but *Lexington* was lost and *Yorktown* was badly mauled and had to limp back to Pearl Harbor.

This historic battle, which took place in the days following General Wainwright's surrender of Corregidor, was not a clear-cut American victory, but it prevented the enemy from landing at Port Moresby and taking all of New Guinea. Undeterred, the Japanese seized the mission outpost of Buna, on the north coast of New Guinea, and prepared to use it as base from which to begin an overland assault on Port Moresby. The fate of Port Moresby would be decided in a bitter land engagement in some of the most difficult terrain in the world. To support the coming fight for Port Moresby, the Japanese began secretly building an air base on a tiny island called Guadalcanal.

The Battle of the Coral Sea convinced the crews and commanders of the Pacific Fleet that they could fight on at least equal terms with the powerful and more experienced Japanese navy. At the end of May, *Yorktown*, repaired in the miracle time of sixty-eight hours, joined *Enterprise* and *Hornet* to fight another carrier-to-carrier battle in the waters off Midway Island.

MIDWAY

On the morning of June 3, 1942, a Catalina flying boat sighted a Japanese flotilla some 700 miles west of Midway Island. It was part of Admiral Yamamoto's armada of 165 ships heading toward Hawaii to deal a knockout blow to the U.S. Pacific Fleet.

Yamamoto was in personal command of the Midway operation on his flagship *Yamato*, the world's largest battleship, bearing the sacred name of the Japanese race. Infuriated by the Doolittle Raid, he had convinced Imperial Headquarters to bring on the decisive naval battle of the war. Before Pearl Harbor, he had predicted he could "run wild for a year or six months," but that the future would be gravely uncertain for Japan once prodigious America gathered its military strength.[82] Now he was about to test America's naval power in hope of a swift, smashing victory that would convince America that it could defeat Japan only at an intolerable cost.

Yamamoto's carrier commander was Admiral Nagumo. Sailing under strict radio silence, he expected to surprise and slaughter the American fleet, as he had at Pearl Harbor. A diversionary force was sent toward the American base at Dutch Harbor in the Aleutians, near the Arctic Circle. It was to draw the American fleet northward, opening the way for Yamamoto to take Midway, a strategically important atoll that guarded the western approaches to the main Hawaiian Islands. When the Pacific Fleet learned it had been fooled and raced back to Midway, it would be "annihilated," Yamamoto vowed, by the greatest assemblage of Japanese naval power ever sent to sea. "Every man was convinced that he was about to participate in yet another brilliant victory," said Mitsuo Fuchida, who had led the Pearl Harbor air attack.[83]

This time the Americans were not caught napping. Patrol planes had been sent out from Pearl Harbor to locate the incoming Japanese fleet thanks to the heady action of a naval intelligence team under Lieutenant Commander Joseph J. Rochefort, the unsung hero of the upcoming battle. Rochefort and other military cryptanalysts had broken part of the Japanese message code, and as the first reports of a tremendous concentration of enemy naval forces in the Central Pacific came into headquarters at Pearl Harbor, cool-headed Admiral Chester Nimitz, the new Commander in Chief, Pacific (CINCPAC), had taken immediate action to verify them.

The Japanese code designation for the main target they intended to hit was AF, but was AF Midway or the Aleutians or somewhere else in the Pacific? Rochefort and one of his assistants, Lieutenant Commander Jasper Holmes, tricked the enemy into revealing the answer. There was a secret—and completely secure—undersea telephone cable link between Pearl Harbor and Midway and CINCPAC sent a message over it to Midway, ordering the local commander to send back by radio, "in plain English," a spurious report that the garrison's water filtration plant had broken down, leaving Midway without fresh water.[84] A Japanese listening post intercepted the transmission and radioed Tokyo that "AF" was having water problems, a message that Rochefort's eavesdropping team picked up and decoded. The ruse had worked. The target was Midway. A few days later Rochefort broke the Japanese navy's date cipher and gave Nimitz the exact day of the impending attack, June 4.[85]

Nimitz then ordered Admirals Fletcher and Raymond A. Spruance (Halsey would have been in charge but was hospitalized with a skin infection) to ignore the Japanese feint north and concentrate all available warships in the waters around Midway. *Yorktown* sailed from Pearl Harbor with repairmen still on board, B-17 Flying Fortresses were flown in from the West Coast, and the defenses of Midway were reinforced. Nimitz had guessed correctly that the Japanese wanted to use captured Midway as a base to launch a final and decisive offensive against the Hawaiian Islands, only 1,100 miles east of Midway, invading and occupying them and forcing the Americans to the peace table.

Nimitz's greatest gamble of the war was putting quiet, self-effacing Raymond Ames Spruance, a commander with no carrier experience but with an amazing strategic mind—his men called him electric brain—in charge of one of the two carrier task forces sent out to stop the enemy. Spruance's Task Force 17, comprised of *Enterprise* and *Hornet*, along with six cruisers and ten destroyers, sailed out of Pearl Harbor first, followed two days later by Fletcher's *Yorktown*, the carrier the Japanese were confident they had destroyed in the Battle of the Coral Sea.

Nimitz's plan was elegantly simple: he would hide his three carriers until Nagumo's planes hit Midway. Then he would launch his planes and destroy the unprotected Japanese flattops. It was the Japanese, not the Americans, who would sail into an ambush.

As Nimitz expected, the great battle was fought entirely by planes and submarines, in what was to become a new and decisive form of naval warfare. As in the

Battle of the Coral Sea, the opposing carrier fleets never saw each other. The Americans struck first. On the afternoon of June 3, Flying Fortresses from Midway attacked, but missed, a squadron of enemy landing ships. The Japanese knew at once that surprise was lost and Nagumo reacted sharply with a heavy bombing of Midway the following day—an attack that severely damaged shore installations but failed to knock out the island's airfields.

When the flight leader of the raiding force urged a second strike, Nagumo rearmed the torpedo planes he had intended to use against the American fleet—if it showed up—with fragmentation bombs for another attack on Midway. But by this time, the carriers *Enterprise, Hornet,* and *Yorktown* had come within striking distance—150 miles—of his own carriers, and swarms of planes, led by Torpedo Squadron 8 from *Hornet* and dive-bombers from *Enterprise* commanded by Lieutenant Commander Clarence (Wade) McClusky, set out to find their prey. Gilbert Cant, the *New York Post*'s Pacific correspondent, describes the opening hours of this attack:

TORPEDO EIGHT, FLYING OBSOLETE DOUGLAS Devastators . . . was led by Lieutenant Commander John C. Waldron. It became separated from the other formations in the long search for the Japanese ships. A group of bombers and fighters which failed to find the enemy at the assigned position . . . had to be ordered to land on Midway as they were running out of gasoline. . . . But Waldron reasoned that if the Jap ships were not where they were supposed to be, it was probably because they had found the welcome too warm for their comfort and had decided to retire some distance, if not entirely. He therefore backtracked along their previously known course. McClusky arrived at the same conclusion, but not until after he had overshot the enemy's reported position by seventy-five miles or more. Then he too set out to intercept them to the northwest. The effect of these identical decisions made at different times was to bring Waldron's squadron within sight of the enemy. . . .

Waldron found the main enemy force with few fighter planes in the air, but his squadron had been out a long time and was running short of gas. It had accomplished part of its mission merely by locating the retiring Japanese and reporting their position. Waldron radioed his information and added: "Request permission to withdraw from actions to refuel." The admiral to whom the request was passed had an awful decision to make. To permit these planes to withdraw might make all the difference between sinking or crippling three carriers (Waldron had not sighted the fourth) and giving them a chance once more to slip out of sight under a squall. Three carriers could determine the balance of power in this 1942 sea war, in which the carrier was a capital ship . . . of greater importance . . . [than] the battleship. . . .

Hypothetical scores of ships and hypothetical thousands of lives were on one side of the scale; on the other side were fifteen planes and the lives of their three-man crews. The admiral ordered: "Attack at once." [86]

Before taking off, Waldron had met with his pilots: "I want each of us to do his utmost to destroy our enemies. If there is only one plane left to make a final run in, I want that man to go in and get a hit. May God be with us all." [87]

Flying directly into the enemy's gun barrels, all fifteen of Torpedo 8's low-flying Devastators were blown into the sea by whirling Zeros and murderous sheets of anti-aircraft fire, "and for about one hundred seconds the Japanese were certain they had won the Battle of Midway, and the war," writes Samuel Eliot Morison. [88]

Ensign George Gay, the only only flier in Torpedo 8 to survive this American-style kamikaze attack, was shot down and wounded, and watched the rest of the air battle from his floating seat cushion. Two other torpedo squadrons attacked the carriers. The Zeros, flying at deck level, cut them up, too; out of the eighty-two airmen who attacked the carriers in their slow, two-seater torpedo planes—little more than flying coffins—only thirteen survived. Jack Waldron was last seen diving toward an enemy carrier, standing straight up in his cockpit, which had been turned into a blazing furnace by exploding gasoline. [89]

Not a single Japanese ship was hit in this massacre. The torpedo planes, however, had been unintended sacrificial lambs. With Nagumo's protective cover of fighter planes preoccupied with them at sea level, Clarence McClusky's dive-bombers appeared suddenly overhead. They, too, had initially failed to find Nagumo's fleet, but had accidentally located an enemy destroyer, which had been pursuing the American submarine *Nautilus*. Abandoning the search, it had headed back to the fleet, creating a foaming white wake, which the fast-thinking McCluskey had followed. The Japanese destroyer had led the American squadron straight to its prey.

Ensign Gay watched as McClusky's dive-bombers came pouring out of the sun "like a beautiful silver waterfall." [90] They were about to catch Nagumo's carriers in their most vulnerable position, without their protective fighter "cap" and with their decks crowded with planes refueling and rearming, this time with torpedoes, for an expected wipe-up attack on the American carriers. *Akagi* was the first to be hit.

"At 10:20 Admiral Nagumo gave the order to launch when ready," Matsuo Fuchida recalled. "The big ship began turning in the wind. Within five minutes all her planes would be launched.

"Five minutes! Who would have dreamed that the tide of battle would shift completely in that brief interval of time." [91]

At 10:25 A.M. McClusky's dive-bomber group was about to deliver what historian John Keegan has called "the most stunning and decisive blow in the history of naval warfare." [92]

Lieutenant Clarence E. Dickinson was in McClusky's *Enterprise* group:

AS I PUT MY NOSE DOWN I picked up our carrier target in front of me. I was making the best dive I have ever made. . . . We we coming down in all directions on the port side of the carrier, beautifully spaced. . . . I recognized her as the *Kaga;* and she was enormous. . . .

The target was utterly satisfying. . . . I saw a bomb hit just behind where I was aiming. . . . I saw the deck rippling and curling back in all directions exposing a great section of the hangar below. . . . I dropped a few seconds after the previous bomb explosion . . .

I saw the 500-pound bomb hit right abreast of the [carrier's] island. The two 100-pound bombs struck in the forward area of the parked planes. . . .

Then I began thinking it was time to get myself away from there and try to get back alive. [93]

When McClusky's dive-bombers bore down on the Japanese carriers, Matsuo Fuchida learned what it was like to be on the other end of a surprise air strike. He was on the *Akagi* but was not flying that day, having come down with a case of appendicitis:

AT 10:34 THE ORDER TO START launching came from the bridge by voice-tube. The Air Officer flapped a white flag, and the first Zero fighter gathered speed and whizzed off the deck. At that instant a lookout screamed: "Hell-Divers!" I looked up to see three black enemy planes plummeting towards our ship. Some of our machine guns managed to fire a few frantic bursts at them, but it was too late. [94]

Within less than a minute the ship was turned into an inferno. Nagumo, with tears in his eyes, had to be forced by his officers to abandon the doomed *Akagi*. Fuchida stayed behind to try to hold off the inevitable, but broke both his ankles jumping from one deck to another to avoid the explosions and raging fires. He was strapped to a bamboo stretcher and lowered to a boat, which carried him to a rescue ship.

"The [Japanese] carriers . . . resembled a very large oil-field," Ensign Gay reported later. "The fire coming out of the forward and after end looked like a blowtorch, just roaring white flame and the oil burning. . . . Billowing big red flames belched out of this black smoke . . . and I was sitting in the water hollering Hooray, hooray!"[95]

That night *Akagi* and *Kaga* both sank. A third carrier, *Soryu*, received three direct hits and horribly damaged. When its commanding officer, Captain Ryusaku Yanagimoto, refused to abandon ship, Chief Petty Officer Abe, a Japanese wrestling champion, was sent aboard to bring him to safety, by force if necessary. But Abe respected the will of the greatly loved commander and left him on the bridge, his samurai sword in hand, calmly singing "Kimigayo," the Japanese national anthem. The crippled *Soryu* was scuttled by the Japanese destroyer *Isokaze*.

The attack had taken less than six minutes. After it was over, Ensign George Gay was pulled from the sea. He had participated in and witnessed one of history's greatest naval engagements.

The Japanese were battered, but still capable of fight. Dive-bombers from the carrier *Hiryu*, which had become separated from the other carriers during the American air attack, struck back, fatally damaging the *Yorktown* after flying through a hornet's nest of American fighters in an act of "Oriental desperation."[96] But then around four o'clock, American planes reached the *Hiryu*, bombing and burning it from stem to stern.

"When it was ascertained that the ship was in a sinking condition, Admiral [Tamon] Yamaguchi and Captain [Tomeo] Kaku decided that they would go down with the ship," one of their fellow officers recalled. "They all shared some naval biscuits and drank a glass of water in a last ceremony. Admiral Yamaguchi gave his hat to one of his staff officers and asked him to give it to his family; then there was some joking among them—the captain and the admiral—that their duties were finished when the ship sank."[97]

When told that there was still money in the ship's safe, Yamaguchi, one of the greatest of the Japanese naval commanders, ordered it be left alone. "We'll need money for a square meal in hell," he said.[98]

USS *YORKTOWN*, HIT AT MIDWAY (NA).

Not wanting to fight a night battle with Yamamoto's battleships and unknown numbers of carriers that might be in the area, Rear Admiral Spruance steamed east, away from the enemy he had hurt far more than he realized at the time.

After reassembling his damaged but still dangerous battle fleet—two light carriers, eleven battleships, eight cruisers, and dozens of destroyers—Yamamoto, still hoping for a last-minute victory, waited for the Americans to reengage. Only when he determined that Spruance and Fletcher wanted no part of him did he turn west and sail for home. It was the eighth of June, one of the blackest days in Japanese history.

The Japanese lost four fleet carriers in the Battle of Midway and the Americans only one, *Yorktown*. Abandoned by her crew, she was sunk two days later by a Japanese submarine as the Navy tried to tow her home. Midway was the Imperial Japanese Navy's first major defeat since 1592. When Yamamoto ordered a withdrawal, he turned to his worried officers on the *Yamato*: "I'll apologize to the Emperor myself." [99]

The Japanese people were not told of the shattering defeat at Midway. Even the Army was not informed of the extent of the losses. When Mitsuo Fuchida returned to Japan on a hospital ship, he was not taken ashore until dark "when the streets were deserted. I was taken to the hospital on a covered stretcher and carried through the rear entrance. My room was in complete isolation. No nurses or corpsmen were allowed in and I could not communicate with the outside. It was like being a prisoner of war among your own people." [100]

Military intelligence as well as military might won the Battle of Midway; two letters, AF, changed the direction of the Pacific war. "Had we lacked early information of the Japanese movements, and had we been caught with carrier forces dispersed . . . the Battle of Midway would have ended differently," said Admiral Nimitz.[101] Working a twenty-hour day in a windowless basement at Pearl Harbor, dressed in a red smoking jacket and slippers, Commander Joseph Rochefort had given Nimitz the key to victory. It was the most important intelligence coup of the Pacific war.

The Battle of Midway changed the course of the war in the Pacific. The Japanese First Air Fleet, the most modern in the world, lost not only four of its most powerful carriers but, just as critically, fully a third of its crack pilots. From this point on in the war, just six months after Pearl Harbor, the Imperial navy was thrown back on the defensive by America's newest weapon, the carrier task force. "After Midway," recalled Japanese navy minister Mitsumasa Yonai, "I was certain there was no chance of success."[102]

Later that summer, back at Honolulu, James Jones, now a corporal, watched "the victorious carrier pilots of Midway drunk and having fist fights on the lawns of the Royal Hawaiian. . . . None of them expected to come back, and they wanted everything they could get of living on the way out, and that included fist fighting."[103]

NEW GUINEA

While American carrier power was altering the direction of the Pacific war, General Douglas MacArthur was planning a major offensive against Japanese strongholds in the dense, mountainous jungles of New Guinea. Most of the forces available to him were Australian infantry; Americans had not yet arrived in this theater in any numbers. This was to be the starting point for his march of revenge to retake the Philippines and liberate the men he had left behind.

MacArthur had arrived in Melbourne on March 17, 1942, to take charge of the pathetically weak Allied force in Australia. With enthusiastic bravado, he decided to defend Australia by going on the offensive. He would begin at Port Moresby with a force that was a corporal's guard compared to the Japanese arrayed against him. But by late July his engineers had built airfields and bomber strips. Then they moved 150 miles down the coast to Milne Bay at the extreme southwestern tip of New Guinea, and in this "green hell" they cut an air base out of the jungle, a starting point for a drive on Japanese concentrations at Buna and Gona on the island's northeast coast.

MacArthur hoped to move troops there by air. He did not believe it possible to mount an offensive over the towering, jungle-clothed Owen Stanley Mountains that divide New Guinea as the breastbone divides a chicken, for only a single narrow trail leading through the village of Kokoda crossed this forbidding range. The Japanese thought otherwise. In July they ascended the Kokoda Trail from the Buna area and, on reaching the reverse slope, began to drive MacArthur's Australian outposts before them. The fighting was prolonged and vicious. On August 25, Australians, reinforced by elements of the American Army, repulsed an attempted Japanese landing at Milne Bay, in what was the first Allied land victory in the Pacific war, and the first time a major Japanese amphibious landing had been stopped ashore. But it was not until mid-September that starvation, bombing, and stiff resistance on the ground halted the Japanese advance against Port Moresby and the Australians began chasing them north, back across the forbidding Kokoda Trail.

RETREAT IN BURMA

If the outlook in the Pacific was somewhat brighter late that summer, it was positively gloomy in Burma, where the Japanese had routed the undermanned Allies.

Burma, a British colony, was one of the vital points in the Far East. From Lashio in the northeast ran the Burma Road, connecting at one end with Mandalay and Rangoon, at the other with Chungking in China. After the Japanese occupied the main Chinese seaports in 1937–38, this road was China's lifeline to the outside world. Burma was also the key to India.

By December 1941, Japan had massed some 200,000 troops in Siam (Thailand) and Indochina and had powerful air forces operating from bases in Siam. The invasion was launched in December but the main attack was made late in January by Siamese puppet troops. The British fell back on Rangoon, Burma's largest port. Pounded by air, they called upon the Flying Tigers, the volunteer American pilots commanded by Claire Chennault.

The Flying Tigers had been hired by Chiang Kai-shek in the summer of 1941 to defend the Burma Road. Flying obsolete P-40s, they had destroyed over 300 Japanese planes. When the Japanese invaded Burma, they shot down another forty-six planes, but there was no stopping the enemy onslaught. Late in February, the Japanese drove British Indian troops back toward Rangoon, which was evacuated in March, severing all supply routes for Allied troops in the interior. Chinese forces under American general "Vinegar Joe" Stilwell came down from the north to help hold the line, but the

Japanese brought another army in from Siam, cut the Burma Road north of Lashio, and forced Stilwell to retreat through an almost impenetrable jungle filled with king cobras and other vipers. "The retreat from Burma," wrote correspondent Jack Belden, who was with Stilwell, "was one of the bitterest retreats in modern times. . . . Remnants of the Allied armies, six months after the finish of the Burma campaign, were still lost in the jungles, wandering at the base of the Tibet fastness, fed by airplane drops, but slowly dying of malaria, exhaustion, starvation, still unable to escape." [104]

By the end of May the Japanese conquest of Burma was complete, and so, too, the isolation of China. With the Burma Road gone, the only supply route to China was by air "over the Hump," the Himalayas—one of the most hazardous air routes in the world.

With Great Britain's energies concentrated in Europe, North Africa, and the Atlantic, where it was fighting for both its Mediterranean empire and its very survival, it was never able to sufficiently supply its beleaguered forces on the Asian mainland or lend more than token assistance to the American naval effort in the Pacific. The Pacific war—not the war in China or Burma—became increasingly an American war, run by American commanders and fought mostly by American men, with invaluable assistance in the South Pacific from the Australians. And in the late summer of 1942 it was a war the Japanese were still winning.

The Hard Way Back

GUADALCANAL

The first phase of the battle for the Pacific ended at Midway. The second began with Guadalcanal, a remote island in the Solomons chain, ten degrees below the Equator. An epic land, air, and naval struggle, the Guadalcanal campaign stopped Japan's triumphant expansion and put America on the offensive for the first time in the war. Guadalcanal was also the only Pacific campaign that American forces came perilously close to losing.

From the sunny deck of his incoming troopship, Corporal James Jones looked out at what he thought was a piece of paradise: "the delicious sparkling tropical sea, the long beautiful beach, the minute palms of the copra plantation waving in the sea breeze, the dark band of jungle, and the dun mass and power of the mountains rising behind it to rocky peaks."

But when he landed, Jones found himself in "a pestilential hellhole."[1] It was oppressively hot and humid, with torrential downpours that soaked the men's clothing and bedding and led to appalling outbreaks of skin infection and fungal diseases.

The vine-choked rain forest blocked out the sun and was filled with slimy mud and rotting vegetation. This damp undergrowth gave off a vile, unforgettable smell and was a breeding farm for voracious insects and dozens of debilitating jungle diseases. And everywhere there were snakes and scorpions, and spiders as big as a man's fist.

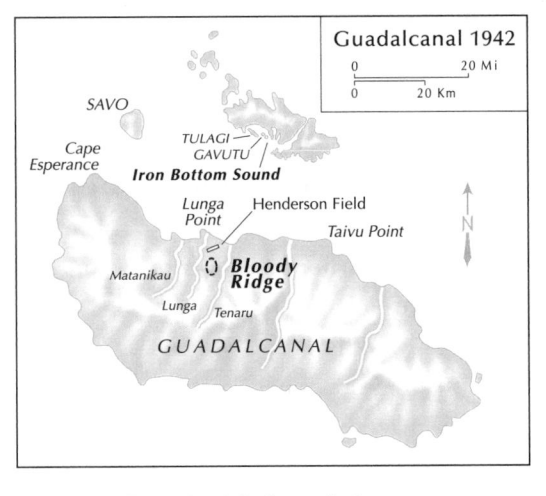

A massive wall of blue-green mountains cut the island lengthwise, and in places coral ridges reached down from them to sweeping white beaches. Kunai grass grew on these ridges and looked splendid blowing in the tropical breeze. But the blades of the grass cut like a knife and the grass grew so high it sawed at men's throats. And bordering the magnificent beaches were swamps infested with malaria-bearing mosquitoes. "If God ever created a hell-on-earth contest the island . . . would have made it to the finals," said one Marine.[2]

Guadalcanal was thinly populated by about 25,000 Melanesians and had no economic value. But recently and unexpectedly it had become the most important strategic spot in the Pacific. The Japanese had occupied the Solomons in the spring of 1942, and during that summer their army had begun constructing an airfield on Guadalcanal. Thanks to the intelligence of Commander Rochefort, the Americans learned of the airstrip even before the Japanese navy did. If the Japanese completed the airfield by August, as expected, their land-based bombers would control American shipping lanes to Australia, over which great amounts of men and supplies were moving weekly to reinforce Australian units that were being called back from North Africa. Admiral Ernest J. King, commander in chief of the United States Navy, was determined that this 6,500-mile long lifelife not be severed, and it was he who pressed for and prosecuted the first major American offensive in the Pacific theater, using every ship and Marine at his disposal.

In the gray morning light of August 7, exactly eight months after Pearl Harbor, the 1st Marine Division, commanded by Major General Alexander A. "Archie" Vandegrift, a veteran of jungle warfare in Central America, landed 19,000 troops on Guadalcanal and the tiny neighboring islands of Tulagi, Gavutu, and Tanambogo. It was the first American D-Day of World War II and America's first large-scale amphibious landing since the Spanish-American War. Opposition was unexpectedly tough on Tulagi, where, with the exception of a mere twenty-three men captured, the garrision of nearly 900 combat troops and laborers fought to the last in bunkers, caves, and tunnels, showing what General Vandegrift called an "astonishing" willingness to die defending a small seaplane base.[3] But the Guadalcanal landing was unopposed and the Marines moved inland to seize the airfield that was abandoned that morning by the badly outnumbered Japanese. The Marines named it Henderson Field in honor of a Marine pilot killed at Midway, and from this day it became the focus of the campaign.

When the Marines landed, the Japanese had only about 2,300 men on an island not much larger than the state of Delaware, most of them construction workers at the crushed coral airfield. But in the coming months, both sides poured in reinforcements—the Americans to hold the airfield, the Japanese to retake it.

MARINE CAMP, GUADALCANAL (USMC).

HENDERSON FIELD, GUADALCANAL. THIS "PAGODA" WAS HEADQUARTERS FOR U.S. MARINE AND NAVY FLIERS (USMC).

At first, things went badly for the Marines. A carrier force commanded by Vice Admiral Frank Jack Fletcher, a veteran of the Battles of the Coral Sea and Midway, covered the initial landing operations by a task force headed by Rear Admiral Richmond Kelly Turner, the tactician who would plan and direct most of the great Marine amphibious assaults in the Pacific. Fletcher feared his three carriers were sitting targets for Japanese aircraft in the area and abruptly left a day earlier than planned. This necessitated the withdrawal, as well, of Turner's transports, which at the time were bringing in supplies and almost 2,000 additional men. It was a cowardly decision, and it left the abandoned Marines short of artillery, ammunition, and food— and without air cover and those extra 2,000 fighting men. After the Navy left, "there was a lot of talk about Bataan," said one Marine.[4] It was a siege now, and not even Washington was confident the Marines could be saved.

Enemy reaction to the American landing was swift and devastating, for the American invasion was seen as a threat to Rabaul on New Britain and to Japanese plans for further expansion in the South Pacific. The next evening a naval strike force came racing through the Slot, the Americans' name for the deep channels through the central Solomons, and pounced on the unsuspecting fleet that was in Savo Sound screening the American beachhead. Marine combat photographer Thayer Soule was nearby in a troopship waiting orders to head in to the beach. Most of the men had gone to bed. "At 0200 we were awakened by general quarters. The Japanese had arrived early. The sky near Savo [Island] was ablaze with orange and white flashes. Tremendous explosions shook our ship. After only a few minutes, the firing stopped. We could hear only the rain falling on the canvas overhead. . . . Except for the glow of a burning ship, the night was black once more."

Without losing a single ship, Vice Admiral Gunichi Mikawa's expert night-fighting force, equipped with Long Lance torpedoes, the most devastating underwater weapons in the world, sank four heavy cruisers and inflicted nearly 1,800 casualties. Predatory sharks tore into the men as they hit the water. Sailors pulled out of the sea were so badly burned that corpsmen could find no place to stick hypodermic needles. It was the most devastating defeat suffered on the high seas by the U.S. Navy. Yet it could have been worse. "They could have crushed our landing, marooned our troops, destroyed our supplies, and crippled our navy for months to come. But they sailed away," Soule wrote later.[5] Mikawa had not dealt the "mortal blow" because he feared American carrier planes would hit him at first light. It was one of the great mistakes of the war, for Fletcher was fleeing south, out of range of Mikawa.

That was thin consolation for the Marines who watched the last of the transports leave the next evening. "Bastogne was considered an epic in the ETO [European Theater of Operations]," writes historian William Manchester, a Marine veteran of the Pacific Theater. "The 101st Airborne was surrounded there for eight days. But the marines on Guadalcanal were to be isolated for over four months. There have been few such stands in history."[6]

The correspondent Hanson Baldwin summed up the Marines' predicament after the Battle of Savo Sound. "It is as if the marines held Jones Beach, and the rest of the Long Island were loosely dominated by the enemy."[7]

Back in Washington, when Admiral King was awakened by a duty officer and handed a dispatch describing the disaster at Savo Sound, he couldn't believe it. "They must have decoded the dispatch wrong. Tell them to decode it again," he told the duty officer. As King said later, "That, as far as I am concerned, was the blackest day of the war. The whole future then became unpredictable."[8]

Douglas MacArthur wired Chester Nimitz recommending that the Marines be evacuated. Nimitz disagreed.[9]

Thereafter the battle for Guadalcanal was a seesaw affair, a series of ferociously fought sea and air engagements and a long, punishing land campaign. Except in the mountains and jungles of New Guinea, Americans had never waged war under harder conditions than those that the Marines—and later Army infantry reinforcements—encountered on Guadalcanal.

The Marines had to hold the airstrip until they had enough men to drive the Japanese off the island. The Navy had to resupply and reinforce Guadalcanal and stop the Tokyo Express, the swift-running destroyer convoys that brought troops and supplies down the Slot from Rabaul. The Marines helped out with their own small air arm, the Cactus Air Force, commanded by Major General Roy S. Geiger. The pilots at Henderson Field lived on meager rations, battled malaria and dysentery, and were pounded day and night from both sea and air. Led by their ace, Captain Joseph J. Foss, who downed twenty-six enemy aircraft and won the Congressional Medal of Honor, they covered the naval supply effort and did excellent work against Japanese bombers and Zeros. They were helpless, however, to prevent the Tokyo Express from building up Japanese troop strength on the island. The Tokyo Express brought in reinforcements at night; the Marine and Navy pilots could fly effectively only in daylight. They flew every day and the pace and ferocity of the action began to wear them down. "When the medics used to tell us about pilot fatigue," a haggard pilot told a war reporter, "I used to think they were old fuds. But now I know what they meant. There's a point when you just get to be no good; you're shot to the devil—and there's nothing you can do about it." [10]

Some airmen broke under the strain, but most continued to fly, and their efforts helped the Marines to hold on. As two historians of the battle write, "During the time when adjacent waters were in dispute (which was also the critical period of the fighting ashore), it was marine airmen, assisted by navy and army pilots, who were instrumental in saving Guadalcanal by making it difficult for the Japanese to land reinforcements," forcing them to rely on the Tokyo Express, which came under steady attack by American naval vessels as they gained proficiency in night fighting.[11] When American carriers were sunk or knocked out of action in the waters of the Solomons, their orphaned fighters, dive-bombers, and torpedo planes flew to Henderson Field and operated from there. As one American Army officer cynically put it, "What saved Guadalcanal was the loss of so many carriers." [12]

It became a war of attrition. In a succession of tremendous naval struggles, the tide swung back and forth, with both sides suffering alarming losses, including, for the United States, the *Hornet*, the carrier that had ferried Jimmy Doolittle's planes to the waters off Japan. The Americans won some victories. But until October, when aggressive, hard-drinking Bull Halsey took over command in the South Pacific from the super-cautious Vice Admiral Robert Lee Ghormley and began pressing his commanders to challenge the enemy in night fighting, the Japanese controlled the waters around Guadalcanal. The turning point was what became known to history as the Naval Battle of Guadalcanal.

On the night of November 13, two Japanese battlewagons, with a screen of destroyers, came barreling through the Slot, headed for Guadalcanal. Yamamoto had sent them to bomb Henderson Field into submission and provide cover for a landing force of 10,000 fresh troops arriving on fast transports and destroyers. American intelligence had once again broken the Japanese code, giving Halsey time to prepare. First to meet the Japanese fleet was a badly outnumbered destroyer-cruiser force under Rear Admiral Daniel J. Callaghan, a close personal friend of President Roosevelt's. Defying the odds, Callaghan attacked, fighting at dangerously close range, in what was the seagoing equivalent of hand-to-hand combat.

It was a moonlit night and the American correspondent Ira Wolfert was on shore with the Marines to witness what Admiral Ernest King called "one of the most furious sea battles ever fought." [13]

THE LAND FORCES HAD GIRDED THEMSELVES for a . . . [heavy] bombardment. Men huddled in foxholes, and asked each other silently with their embittered faces, "Where's our Navy?" and wondered what would be left to stop the Jap transports.

Those seven hours of darkness, with each moment as silent as held breath, were the blackest our troops have faced since Bataan, but at the end of them our Navy was there, incredibly, like a Tom Mix of old, like the hero of some antique melodrama. It turned the tide of the whole battle by throwing its steel and flesh into the breach against what may be the heaviest Jap force yet engaged by surface ships in this war. . . .

The beach had a front-row seat for the devastating action. Admiral Callaghan's force steaming in line drove headlong into a vastly more powerful Jap fleet which was swinging around tiny Savo Island with guns set for point-blank blasting of Guadalcanal. . . . Matching cruisers and destroyers against battleships is like putting a good bantamweight against a good heavyweight, but the Japs unquestionably were caught with their kimonos down around their ankles. They could have stayed out of range and knocked out our ships with impunity, and then finished us on the ground at their leisure.

We opened fire first. The Jap ships, steaming full speed, were on us, over us, and all around us in the first minute. . . . The range was so close that the Japs could not depress their guns enough to fire at the waterline, which is why so many hits landed on the bridge and two of our admirals were killed.

The action was illuminated in brief, blinding flashes by Jap searchlights which were shot out as soon as they were turned on, by muzzle flashes from big guns, by fantastic streams of tracers, and by huge orange-colored explosions as two Jap destroyers and one of our destroyers blew up within seconds of one another. . . . The sands of the beach were shuddering so much from gunfire that they made the men standing there quiver and tingle from head to foot.

From the beach it resembled a door to hell opening and closing, opening and closing.[14]

It was over in twenty-four minutes, "a barroom brawl after the lights had been shot out," an American officer described it.[15] Watching the naval gunfire from a distant foxhole, the tall, twenty-six-year-old combat correspondent Richard Tregaskis, author of the now classic *Guadalcanal Diary*, realized that the fate of the Marines hung on these tremendous naval collisions in the waters of the Solomon Islands. "One had the feeling of being at the mercy of great accumulated forces far more powerful than anything human. We were only pawns in a battle of the gods, then, and we knew it."[16]

The Japanese lost a battleship and were prevented from bombing Henderson Field and landing troops. But the American flotilla had ceased to exist as an effective fighting force. Callaghan and another admiral, Norman Scott, were killed on the bridges of their ships and a cruiser and four destroyers were lost.

The next day, the light cruiser *Juneau*, with a crew of nearly 700 men, was blown to pieces by a torpedo from a Japanese submarine. On board were the five Sullivan brothers from Waterloo, Iowa. They had enlisted together after Pearl Harbor, convincing the Navy to break its policy of splitting families in wartime. The Navy claimed that all five Sullivans went down with the ship and it launched a publicity campaign, featuring their parents, to boost war production. But one of the brothers,

George Sullivan, along with 140 other men on *Juneau*, had actually survived the spectacular blast that took the ship under, only to die later in a shark attack—a fact not revealed for forty years. The men had lived hour to hour, without food or water, under an unforgiving sun, and were assaulted by sharks as they clung to rafts and life nets. The last of the survivors—only ten men—were not found for over a week because of a botched search-and-rescue mission by the Navy.

The damaged but still lethal Japanese fleet steamed on toward Guadalcanal. Vice Admiral Willis A. Lee, with a force of four destroyers and two battleships—*Washington* and *South Dakota*—met the enemy head-on in Savo Sound. It was another night fight and one of the only full-scale battleship engagements of the entire war. Almost the instant the two fleets collided, the Japanese sank two destroyers and damaged the other two. At this critical moment, *South Dakota*, nicknamed the Big Bastard by its crew, experienced a power failure that put out its radar. Without its "night eyes," it became an easy target for Japanese night fighters. They put forty-two hits into it, smashing the ship's superstructure, knocking out its communications, and killing and mangling crewmen.

Robert L. Schwartz, a reporter for *Yank*, the GI paper, interviewed men on the *South Dakota* and pieced together what went on inside the ship after it was hit. His story is one of the most powerful accounts of naval combat in print.

HODGEN OTHELLO PATRICK . . . TALKER ON THE Big Bastard's sky patrol, highest lookout post where the ship took its first hit during the Battle of Savo Island, came as reasonably close to being killed as can be expected of any man.

Patrick remembers squaring for battle and from his high perch seeing the Jap ships come up. He saw the first salvo leave the flagship up ahead. His next recollection is of being thrown against a bulkhead and finding somebody's arm, without a body, across his face. A dead weight lay across his chest, pinning him.

"I'm dead," he thought, and the remembrance of it is still clear in his mind. "Here I am dead. This is what it's like to be dead." But the earthly touch of shrapnel in his knee and his hip convinced him that he was still alive. He looked around. The two officers lay dead. Seven enlisted men were still. Four wounded looked at Patrick, not knowing what to do next.

Patrick pressed the button on his headset. "Sick bay," he called, "send help." . . . But no help came.

Patrick ordered two wounded to go below and then put tourniquets on the other two, using their own belts. He applied the same treatment to his own leg above the bleeding knee. . . . He hunted a long time for morphine before he found it and divided it with the others. As he was about to take his share of the sedative he noticed that several of the men he had thought dead were stirring. Without a moment's hesitation he divided his share among them. . . .

Despite his injuries, Patrick found that he could get to his feet. He saw that he could report better while standing and remained that way until the end of the battle. Afterward, he fell again to the deck but never stopped his regular reports until he was relieved the next morning.

Patrick was the only enlisted man of the crew who was recommended for the Navy Cross.

When general quarters sounded on the Big Bastard, Rufus Mathewson . . . took his post as a talker in the conning tower.

"It'll be a push-over," he heard someone say. "Just a bunch of armed transports. We'll knock 'em off like sitting ducks."

Mathewson said to himself, "I wish I was home." . . .

Hours ticked by. Shortly after midnight the loudspeaker carried a cold steady voice from the plot room. "Target 20,000 yards, bearing 240° . . . target 19,800 yards, bearing 241° . . ." Slowly the target drew closer.

There was a terrific explosion up ahead. Mathewson dashed to one of the slits and felt his stomach drop as he saw a battleship ahead silhouetted by flame. "Lord, let me out and I'll change my ways," he said aloud. A direct hit had dissolved one of the [American] destroyers. . . .

Over the lookout's phone came a voice, "Destroyer sinking on our starboard bow." The captain ordered left rudder, and the helmsman swung the wheel. They skirted the destroyer, then came back on their course. From over the phone came the Admiral's voice: "Fire when ready." . . .

Thirty seconds later shells screamed out. The captain and the navigator were jarred away from their positions at the 'scopes, but voices came in over the phone.

"Right on!"

"The damned thing has dissolved!"

"Looked like a cruiser."

"That was a battleship!"

In rapid succession Mathewson heard a loud crash, a rolling explosion, and then the searing rattle of metal fragments as they crashed into cables, guns, and superstructure. The ship shrugged, leaned back into a volley of 6- and 8-inch shells that raked through the sky control tower, topmost position on the ship.

Quickly Mathewson called sky control on the battle phone. "Patrick, you there?"

"Here, but our officers are dead, and all of us are wounded."

Mathewson asked for permission to go relieve Patrick but his request was denied. Mathewson and Patrick were close friends, and now the thought of Patrick lying wounded on sky control beyond the help of anyone because of fires burning below him almost brought tears to his eyes.

Methodically Big B went on firing. . . .

Six- and 8-inch shell fire peppered the bridge with steel fragments. It was almost impossible for shrapnel to penetrate the armor of the bridge but the men inside heard one shell smack through the gun director just aft of the bridge and then explode against the chart house. Directions for course and bearing stopped coming in.

Over the amplifier from the chart house came a voice. "My God, this man's bleeding to death. Send help. Hurry. Please hurry."

Melvin McSpadden, the engine control talker, was first to answer. "Sick bay is on this circuit and they'll send a doctor. Give us some bearings."

"This poor guy's bleeding to death. Have you got any bandages? I can't leave him like this."

McSpadden tore down a blackout curtain hanging over one of the slots, stuffed it through the aperture and shouted to a seaman on the catwalk outside, "Take this to the chart house quick." . . .

Batt II, which is the auxiliary control room situated inside the superstructure below the sky control tower, was the hardest hit portion of the ship. One of the talkers in Batt II was Tom Page. . . .

Page remembers it was a beautiful night. There was a big moon and it was very warm and quiet. The smell of gardenias was strong from off Florida Island. The association of the gardenias with the action that followed caused Page to lose all desire to smell a gardenia again.

Over the amplifier came a voice, "Guadalcanal on our starboard hand." Big vivid flashes lit the sky—some of it gunfire in the distance, some of it lightning. . . .

Page sat in a corner on an overturned bucket, feeling comfortable now that the big guns were booming. He noticed that the commander, usually a very nervous man, was very calm. Then he was knocked off his bucket by a shell hit. The molten metal from the shell ran across the floor like lava and he stepped out of the way. Steam pipes were broken, electrical fires sputtered. Noise and heat from the steam were unbearable. He screamed over the phone to engine control to shut off the auxiliary steam line. . . .

During the entire action one of the lookouts standing by a slot kept repeating in a low voice: "Lord, I'm scared. Nobody has any idea how scared I am. How could anyone be this scared? My God, I'm scared." He said that over and over for about 10 minutes. Nobody thought it was strange.

Men began crawling to their feet. . . . Only the noise of the steam escaping could be heard above the gunfire below. Then the gunfire ceased and within a minute the steam went off. A new noise could be heard now—the moans of the injured and the dying. Pharmacist's mates went among them, injecting shots of morphine. . . .

[At that moment] John P. Buck [the ship's] after-battery lookout. . . . could see the big 16-inch barrels poked out over the starboard rail. He was lazily watching them when they suddenly fired a salvo with a deafening roar. Buck was picked up bodily and thrown [several feet through the air]. He heard his helmet fly off and strike a bulkhead 30 feet away, then roll around the floor. The explosion blinded him for about 15 minutes, during which time he groped on the floor and found his helmet. . . .

Over five miles away a 14-inch shell came screaming out of the muzzle of a gun on a Jap battleship. Buck first saw it when it was about two miles away from him, looming larger and larger as a red dot in the sky. He knew it was going to hit and knelt down. . . .

The shell came through at exactly deck level. . . . There was a blinding flash and roar, and shrapnel rained down like cinders. Buck mentally marked turret No. 3 off his list. But when he went out to look he found that the turret was still there but beside it was a yawning hole in the deck.

Looking over the starboard rail he saw a Jap ship racing up. He reported it but worriedly wondered how they were ever going to hit it with the after turret almost certainly out of action. Then he heard the secondaries open fire with a staccato bang-bang-bang, finally reaching the ear-splitting regularity of machine-gun firing. . . .

The after turret, meanwhile, turned slowly toward the approaching ship, now so close that the elevation on the barrels was almost nil.

Nobody was more amazed than Buck when the after turret fired. He had no idea it was still in action. Then he saw that the Jap ship had been hit almost point-blank by all three shells. There was a big flash where the ship had been and then smoking, bubbling water. . . .

The firing stopped and Buck left to help in the care of the wounded. At sick bay he found men stretched out on every available table with doctors and pharmacist's mates working over them while standing in 4 inches of blood and water on the deck.

He was sent with a doctor to the top of the superstructure to help the wounded men who had been cut off there. Only Patrick was still there. The doctor stayed with Patrick, giving Buck Syrettes of morphine to administer inside the superstructure on the way down.

Descending on the inside of the tower, Buck found a man lying on one of the upper levels with one leg shot off. He took out his knife and walked over to a dangling electrical wire, cut it loose and wrapped it around the injured man's leg. He wrenched loose the shattered rung of a ladder and used it to twist through the wire, making a tourniquet.

On the next level down he felt his feet get tangled in something in the water on the deck. An officer came along with a flashlight and they discovered that his legs were entwined by someone's insides floating on the water.

He kicked himself loose and went down to the main deck where he saw a man sitting wearily against a bulkhead.

"Hey, Mac, are you okay?" asked Buck.

No answer came so Buck asked him again. When he got no answer this time, Buck reached down to feel his pulse. The man was already cold. Buck left and went back to his post.

Up above the deck the wounded Patrick was giving out morphine. Page was trying hard to keep breathing above the escaping steam, and Buck was trying to recover his sight after being dazed by shell fire. Below decks, in the engine control room, was Chief Yeoman Cheek reading an old issue of the *Reader's Digest*.

The huge panel of gauges in front of him was functioning perfectly. The engine was at top speed, the boilers were maintaining a magnificent head of steam, and the blowers were keeping the room quite cool and comfortable. When a command came through, Cheek carried it out, then returned to his reading.

There was nothing else to do.

The noise of the battle was distant and removed. . . . So Cheek kept on reading the *Reader's Digest*. . . .

It was morning when Cheek walked up onto the deck and saw the destruction. Then he realized, for the first time, how many shells had ripped into the ship during the night.

After he saw the damage, he couldn't sleep for three days.[17]

The Japanese couldn't put the Big Bastard out of action and its powerful batteries helped the *Washington* sink the battleship *Kirishima*. When that happened the superior Japanese force withdrew. On the morning of November 15, American planes, ships, and artillery pounced on the abandoned troop carriers. In this bloodbath, the Japanese were able to land only about 2,000 men. Running in transports under Japanese guns, the Navy, meanwhile, had built up the fighting force on Guadalcanal to over 35,000 men, and many of the steadily outnumbered Japanese were beginning to starve and run short of medicine and ammunition.

After the Naval Battle of Guadalcanal, victory in the Solomons was no longer in doubt. There was plenty of hard fighting ahead—not until February were the last Japanese cleared out of Guadalcanal, and the fight for New Georgia, Choiseul, and Bougainville in the northern Solomons continued through most of 1943. But the naval losses the enemy suffered in this prolonged campaign constituted a disaster second only to that of Midway: two battleships, twenty-three other warships, 600 aircraft, and almost 2,300 irreplaceable aviators. The United States lost two carriers and about as many other combat ships as the Japanese, many of them in the waters between Guadalcanal and Savo Island, called Ironbottom Sound for the number of ships sunk there. What went unreported to the American public was the loss of almost 5,000 sailors in some of the most savage naval fighting in history. With the war beginning to go well for the Allies, not only in the South Pacific but also in French North Africa, where American troops landed in November 1942, and at Stalingrad on the Volga River, where the Red Army was beginning to win one of the most ferociously fought battles of history, the Navy thought it prudent to suppress these grim figures. While mourning the death of his friend Daniel Callaghan, Roosevelt announced that the "turning-point in this war has at last been reached."[18]

But before American seamen and airmen gained the upper hand in November, Marines and infantry on Guadalcanal fought a series of survival battles in the malarial jungle and around the grassy perimeter of Henderson Field. Most of General Vandegrift's Marines were fresh-faced, hastily trained recruits who had enlisted right after Pearl Harbor. One of them was Paul Moore, Jr., just out of Yale College. Years later, in an interview, Moore described the making of a Marine on Guadalcanal:

SOMEBODY TOLD ME ABOUT THE MARINE Corps. I knew so little about the Marine Corps that I thought it was just like the Navy except you had a prettier uniform. There was a young Marine Corps officer at Yale who drove around the campus with his blues on, in a convertible car with whitewall tires, and I thought he was the best thing I'd seen in a long time. I wanted to be just like him, so I enlisted in the Marine Corps.

Moore was sent to Quantico for basic training, where, in his words, he made "a damned fool" of himself.

I REMEMBER WRESTLING WITH A MACHINE gun, trying to take it apart. It suddenly came apart and I hit myself in the forehead and blood streamed out of my head all over the classroom. The lieutenant turned around and said, "There's an example of a man who cannot follow orders." No sympathy. In any case, the first marking period I was tenth from the bottom of the class of four hundred and way below qualification level for an officer.

I went in to the lieutenant and asked him what I could do about it. He just put his head in his hands, and then shook his head and said, "Moore, you just don't look like a Marine and you never will." . . . Luckily, we went out on the rifle range shortly after, and I did very well at rifle shooting. I'd had a little bit of experience. We used to do it in the Adirondacks. . . . So I did pass and qualify to get my commission.

After qualifying as a rifle platoon leader, Moore was sent to the Pacific with 5,000 other Marines in July 1942. They embarked on a converted ocean liner that Moore had recently sailed on, first class, on a European vacation. When they arrived in Wellington, New Zealand, the locals were happy to see them, but they had some concerns.

ALL OF THEIR YOUNG MEN WERE away fighting in the [North African] desert, and to have 20,000 Marines piling into a rather old-fashioned Victorian

English city, with all the young women there, I think made them a litt'
ous. Understandably! So we were given this very elaborate cultural l
deliver to our platoons about how conservative English society was. T
"You never speak to a young woman in New Zealand, whoever she is, without
being properly introduced. You don't go out without a chaperone." Well, we
landed in New Zealand. I had duty so I didn't get off for about an hour. By the
time I walked up the main street of Wellington, every Marine had a girl on
his arm.

After a short training stint in New Zealand, Moore's company went to the Fiji
Islands for maneuvers.

ALL WE HAD WAS ONE OR two days in the Fiji Islands. Then we got back
on board, and as we were steaming toward our next destination, they told
us . . . our battalion was to join a Raider battalion [a battalion of Marines
trained for difficult landings in the Pacific] and attack Tulagi, which was a
small island across the gulf from Guadalcanal. The rest of the division disem-
barked on Guadalcanal.

As we went on our way we were protected by a few destroyers and a couple
of cruisers, but each morning as we got up and looked across the sea, we'd see
more and more naval vessels. It was the most incredible experience, to look out
at these battleships, aircraft carriers, destroyers, cruisers—this enormous fleet of
I suppose a hundred ships. It seemed like a thousand. It felt like the Greeks
going to Troy. . . . You felt totally invincible.

There had been no attack by United States troops before this time. This was
the first.

The night before the landing . . . we were anxious and excited and tense.
Dawn broke. We got up in the darkness and got ready to go over the side. In
those days [before landing craft were equipped with metal ramps on their bows]
you went down a sort of landing net, a webbing made out of stout rope which
they would otherwise use to load cargo. They'd put these nets over the side and
we'd use them as a rope ladder to go down into the Higgins boats . . . [shallow
draft] wooden powerboats [manufactured by a New Orleans boatbuilder named
Andrew Jackson Higgins]. Even with a fairly medium-sized sea the Higgins
boat would go up and down and the ship would go up and down, and to try to

get down that swaying cargo net with about eighty pounds of equipment on your back without killing yourself or getting jammed between the Higgins boat and the ship was quite a stunt. . . .

When the signal was given the Navy ensign in command of the Higgins boat would take off and the boats would go in a preordained pattern toward the beach. All during this time, from dawn on, the cruisers and destroyers had been shelling the shore. We'd never seen a shot fired in anger before, and we didn't see how any animal, much less any human being, could live under this enormous barrage.

Although resistance was strong on Tulagi, Moore did not see any combat. After two weeks, his company was sent across Ironbottom Sound to Guadalcanal. On landing, he was told his best friend from college was one of the first Marines killed on the island.

OUR OUTFIT WAS ON THE MOVE all the time—first we were moved over to Henderson Field, and then within a few days there was a counterattack by those Japanese who were still there, on so-called Bloody Ridge, where a Raider battalion [led by Lieutenant Colonel Merritt "Red Mike" Edson] was dug in. It was the first big battle of Guadalcanal itself, and our troops resisted it, but the Japs almost broke through to Henderson Field and so our battalion was rushed up the second night to support this unit.

One thing I noticed was the relationship between being in one place and emotional stability. . . . We were always on the move. We never had a chance to really make our foxhole our home. If a Marine can dig his foxhole, and dig out a little shelf for his canteen and another little shelf to put a photograph of his girlfriend on, have a little shelter of palm trees to keep the sun off, and make a little home for himself, it makes a tremendous difference to his emotional stability. . . .

The second night the Japanese . . . attacked again and we were thrown into combat, which merely amounted to holding the line against some fairly light Japanese fire. . . . The strange thing was that after the battle was over, one of my men flipped and went into total hysterics, screaming and yelling in the middle of the night. . . . I didn't know whether a Japanese had snuck through the wire and knifed him to death or what. It turned out this guy went absolutely out of his mind. . . .

This kind of thing happened all the time. . . . I had three or four men who went crazy in my platoon, which was 15 percent . . . and this was true of the other platoons in my company. . . . And though it was not a scientific experiment, it seemed to me there was a direct relationship between this and the fact that we were moving all the time.

After Bloody Ridge we were put into another emplacement at the other end of the line. . . .

I was in one of the battles at the Matanikau River. It was a jungle river about 200 yards wide where it emptied into the bay. The Matanikau was outside of our lines, and for a long time there was sort of a seesaw between the Japanese troops and our own—sometimes the Matanikau was ours, sometimes it was theirs. So from time to time troops would be sent out to try to secure the river. I went out there on patrol, coming at it from inland with our company. I was responsible for leading 700 men single file through this impenetrable jungle, with machetes and a compass. . . . When we got within maybe a tenth of a mile of the coast, we heard this battle going on. . . . Another unit had gone up the beach, tried to cross the Matanikau, and was being thrown back by the Japanese.

Lieutenant Colonel Lewis "Chesty" Puller [perhaps the most renowned Marine combat leader of the war] was in charge of this operation, and his tactics were to send one platoon after another across a totally exposed sand spit which closed off one end of the river. . . . The order given to each of these platoons was to run across the sand spit until they were opposite the bank, wade across the river, and attack the Japanese battalion, which was dug in with automatic weapons and hand grenades and mortars in the bank. . . . Well, one platoon went over and got annihilated. Another platoon went over and got annihilated. Then another. We were lined up just behind the shore, ready to go. Ours was the fifth platoon to go over, and you know, we all realized it was insane. We heard what had happened to the other platoons. But if you're a Marine, you're ordered across the goddamn beach and you go. So we went . . . zigzagging and running as best we could so that we wouldn't be exposed, and finally we lined up along the ocean side of the sand spit, just peeking over the top, with our weapons trained on the embankment across this little river. . . . The intelligence was that we could wade across. Well, our two scouts went out and found the water over their heads. . . .

Art Beres, one of my corporals, got to the opposite bank. I remember him holding on to a root, with the bank about a foot over him, and when he turned

CROSSING THE MATANIKAU RIVER ON GUADALCANAL (USMC).

around I saw his whole face had been shot away. Two other guys had been killed at that particular moment, and I went across to get Art. . . . He was swimming. But by that time I'd called for us to attack (even though we were swimming we were told to attack, so we attacked). First of all I retrieved Art . . . and got him back so that he could get behind the sand spit and be protected until he could be taken to the aid station. Then I turned around to continue swimming across the river with the rest of my platoon, and I remember—this sounds absolutely impossible but it actually happened—looking up and seeing mortars and hand grenades going over my head and the water as if it were raining, with bullets striking all around us.

I guess we got almost to the opposite bank and at that point realized two or three people had been killed, two or three others wounded, and there was just no way we could do it, so I called for retreat. We . . . swam back, and when we got to the bank I found two men who were unconscious on the beach. I and another fellow looked to see how they were and found out both of them were dead. So we just left them there and ran back to the protection of the sand spit.

I remember when I was leaning over trying to bring one of my men to safety seeing bullet marks in the sand around my feet and thinking, you know, if I get out of this, maybe it means I should do something special. . . . I don't know . . . whether it's superstition or what, but certainly I felt that I had been extremely fortunate, and that I was, in a sense, living on borrowed time, and that this was another good reason to give my life to the Lord, and it seemed that being a priest was that way.

Four years after the war Moore was ordained a priest in the Episcopal Church. In 1972 he was installed as the thirteenth bishop of New York.

WHEN I GOT BACK, I ASKED if I could see Colonel Puller, to report to him what had happened. I wasn't particularly proud of the fact that we had retreated, but it seemed to be the necessary thing to do. Otherwise we would all have been killed and the emplacement still would not have been taken. I can still see him. He had a fat belly. He was sitting under a coconut tree. . . . I saluted and told him . . . what had happened, what I saw of the Japanese emplacement. He not only didn't answer me, he didn't even turn his head to speak to me. It's as if I hadn't been there. After a while I just left.

We did not get across the Matanikau River at that point. We fell back to our lines on the perimeter of the airfield. . . .

We took off the next morning and went up again to the Matanikau River, but this time we went across way up in the headwaters where there wasn't any resistance. . . .

Morale was very bad. But there was something about Marines—once we were ordered to attack we decided we damn well were going to do it. . . . You're very nervous before you go in, of course, like before a football game. . . . But once you get in it . . . your psyche gets sort of numbed, and therefore you can do acts of bravery, so-called, without necessarily having to be very brave. You just do them because in the excitement of combat you see this is the thing you're supposed to do, and you do it. It isn't making a decision that requires an enormous amount of courage. . . . Also, once you get into the excitement of the action you tend to forget about being vulnerable. When the machine gun nest needed to have a hand grenade, I got up and threw the hand grenade, without timidity, though obviously it made me very vulnerable. I'm fairly tall even on my knees, and I got up and threw it, and as I threw it, got shot.

I received the Navy Cross for that. . . . But it really wasn't any great act of bravery. Some of the more extraordinary heroic actions that take place in combat, I think, are understandable. You read about them and say, "Oh my God, I would never do that!" But when you get in combat you do it without thinking too much about it. You do it automatically. And the flip side of the coin is brutality, the imperviousness to killing other people, even brutally; some of the people, I think, become sort of sadistic. Also the act of being fairly impervious to the death of your colleagues—not that you don't regret it, and not that you aren't trying to prevent it and care for them, but you don't burst into tears when you see this guy you've worked with for a few months lying there dead. "So he's dead. I wonder who I'll get to replace him, to take his place on the line?"

To get back to the Matanikau. . . . Although I was shot I was not unconscious. The bullet . . . came through my chest between two ribs, slightly shattering them, went past my heart, as the doctors later told me, when it must have been on an inbeat instead of an outbeat, and then missed my backbone as it went through the other side of my body about an inch. So it was a very close shave. . . . The air was going in and out of a hole in my lungs. That didn't mean I was finished, but I thought I was dead, going to die right then. . . . I wasn't breathing through my mouth but through this hole. I felt like a balloon going in and out, going pshhhh.

I was thinking to myself: now I'm going to die. And first of all it's rather absurd for me, considering where I came from, my early expectations of a comfortable life and all the rest, for me to be dying on a jungle island in combat as a Marine. That's not me. . . .

Shortly, a wonderful corpsman crawled up and gave me a shot of morphine, and then a couple of other people got a stretcher and started evacuating me. . . . At Henderson Field they had deep dugouts for the wounded. I spent the night in a dugout, then the next day I was flown out. That night I'll never forget, because in this dugout, which I remember was about ten feet deep and about twenty feet square, the wounded were packed just like sardines, and it was terribly hot, there was bad ventilation, terrible smells, and these poor guys were yelling and screaming all night. That was a real horror story. The next morning a plane was able to get in, and they put us aboard and flew us back to Espíritu Santo, a Navy medical hospital.[19]

From there, Moore was taken on the hospital ship *Solace* to Auckland, New Zealand.

One problem that historians have in re-creating the past is that their readers know how it will turn out, so events often seem inevitable. But they are not. An Allied victory in World War II was not preordained; nor was an American victory at Guadalcanal. "If our ships and planes had been routed in . . . [the Naval Battle of Guadalcanal], if we had lost it, our troops on Guadalcanal would have been trapped as were our troops on Bataan," Admiral Bull Halsey wrote later. "We could not have reinforced them or relieved them. Archie Vandegrift would have been our 'Skinny' Wainwright and the infamous Death March would have been repeated. (We later captured a document which designated the spot where the Japanese commander had planned to accept Archie's surrender.) Unobstructed, the enemy would have driven south, cut our supply lines to New Zealand and Australia and enveloped them."[20]

Halsey and the Navy deserve much of the credit for driving the Japanese from Guadalcanal. But, in the end, it came down to the men in the mud. They fought two enemies: the jungle and the Japanese. In that unfathomable jungle, a friend of Paul Moore's was shot by one of his own men when his part of the line got lost and doubled back without realizing it. In total darkness, the men would hear "strange jungle noises for the first time," Moore recalls. "Whether these were birds squawking in the middle of the night or some strange reptiles or frogs, I don't know, but we were terrified by any noise whatsoever because we'd been told that the Japanese signaled each other in the jungle by imitating bird calls. So we knew we were being surrounded by them, and once in a while our men would fire. We lost two or three men in the company by that kind of tragic mistake."[21]

Other companies suffered losses under similar circumstances. "We were not fully prepared for the mysteries of those jungles," says Guadalcanal veteran Major Carl W. Hoffman.

The enemy was the other surprise. Before the war, "our instructors . . . used to joke about the fact that the [near-sighted] Japanese couldn't hit anything on the rifle range," Hoffman remembers. "When we got [to Guadalcanal] we realized that we'd been too quick to write off these little men." They were "courageous, bright, and tenacious . . . and [they] could fire [their] weapons pretty well."[22]

The *New York Times* reporter Hanson Baldwin, who arrived late in the campaign, wrote with grudging respect for the enemy. "The Japanese are full of tricks, deceit and cunning; the unorthodox is their rule. Hard, ruthless, brave, well-equipped, they are the best jungle-fighters in the world.

"[They] are . . . good at bird calls and animal cries, which they use at times to cover their rustling progress through the jungle or to distract the Marines' attention. When they want to be, the Japanese jungle fighters can be almost completely noiseless and invisible. Carefully camouflaged, they inch their way through the tall grass or wait motionless and supremely patient for hours, lashed to treetops or almost neck deep in swamps."

And they fought with fanatical courage, tearing out of jungle hideaways in the black of night on screaming banzai charges. "They never stop trying until they are killed or crushed," Baldwin wrote. "The Marines have stopped trying to help the Japanese wounded since the early days of the Guadalcanal fighting, when badly wounded Japanese, playing dead, suddenly flung hand grenades in the faces of hospital Corpsmen who were trying to help them.

"The war in the Pacific is, therefore, a cold, hard, brutal war. The foe is supremely tough and supremely confident." In order to beat them in jungle fighting, General Vandegrift told Baldwin, "we shall have to throw away the rule books of war and go back to the French and Indian Wars again."[23]

The suicidal bravery of the enemy was incomprehensible to American troops, and their adeptness at jungle warfare was positively terrifying.

"They take to the jungle as if they have been bred there," wrote reporter John Hersey.[24] This led some American troops to believe that "the enemy isn't truly human but a furtive jungle animal," a Marine remembered.[25] "I wish we were fighting against Germans," said another Marine. "They are human beings, like us. . . . But the Japanese are like animals."[26]

Most frightening of all was the way the Japanese treated their prisoners. Early in the fighting, a report swept through the American camp of the beheading of several Marine captives. In his novel *The Thin Red Line*, James Jones probes the reaction of raw recruits to such enemy atrocities: "A cold knifing terror in the belly was fol-

JAPANESE DEAD NEAR THE ILU RIVER, GUADALCANAL (NA).

lowed immediately by a rage of anger. . . . There was a storm of promises never to take a . . . prisoner. Many swore they would henceforth coolly and in cold blood shoot down every Japanese who came their way, and preferably in the guts."[27]

Beginning at Guadalcanal, the war in the Pacific would be a war without quarter. Prisoners were rarely taken and atrocities were answered in kind. Marine Donald Fall tells of the moral reversal that began to occur: "On the second day on Guadalcanal we captured a big Jap bivouac [and] found a lot of pictures of Marines that had been cut up and mutilated on Wake Island. The next thing you know there are

Marines walking around with Jap ears stuck on their belts with safety pins. . . . We began to get down to their level." [28]

Or as Guadalcanal veteran Ore Marion put it:

WE LEARNED ABOUT SAVAGERY FROM THE Japanese. Those bastards had years of on-the-job training. But those sixteen-to-nineteen-year-old kids we had on the Canal were fast learners. Example: on the Matanikau River bank after a day and night of vicious hand-to-hand attacks, a number of Japs and our guys were killed and wounded. At daybreak, a couple of our kids, bearded, dirty, skinny from hunger, slightly wounded by bayonets, clothes worn and torn, whack off three Jap heads and jam them on poles facing the "Jap side" of the river. . . . Shortly after, the regimental commander comes on the scene. . . . The colonel sees the Jap heads on the poles and says, "Jesus, men, what are you doing? You're acting like animals." A dirty, stinking young kid says, "That's right, Colonel, we are animals. We live like animals, we eat and are treated like animals, what the fuck do you expect." [29]

Marines were told that mutilation was a court-martial offense, but it was hard to take that order seriously when Admiral Halsey was constructing billboards all over the Solomons with this unambiguous message: *Kill Japs, Kill Japs, Kill more Japs.*

"When we first started out I held one of our men equal to three Japanese," Halsey publicly declared his contempt for the enemy. "I now increase this to twenty. They are not supermen, although they try to make us believe they are. They are just low monkeys. I say monkeys because I cannot say what I would like to call them." [30]

In his deeply personal history of World War II, novelist James Jones writes that the great question of 1942 was: "Did we have the kind of men who could stand up eyeball to eyeball and whip the Japs." America was "a peace-loving nation, had been anti soldiering and soldiers since the end of World War I. And we were taking on not only the Japs in the Far East, but the Germans in Europe as well. The Japanese with their warrior code of the bushi, had been in active combat warfare for ten years; the Germans almost as long. Could we evolve a soldier, a civilian soldier, who could meet them man to man in the field? . . . Not everyone was sure.[31] As the novelist James A. Michener recalled years later, "Many observers considered us a lost generation and feared we might collapse if summoned to some crucial battlefield." [32]

This was the significance of Guadalcanal. In its green vastness, American boys evolved into the gritty island fighters who were needed to turn back the equally tough Japanese. In two night attacks on Henderson Field, one in September, the other in October, the Japanese were thrown back in hellish fighting at bayonet range. In the first attack, Red Mike Edson and 700 Marines, including Paul Moore, held off 3,000 Japanese troops for two nights on a small ridge in front of the airport. The enemy made excellent use of the terrain and charged entrenched positions as if impervious to death. Four of the attackers reached Vandegrift's command tent and killed a Marine sergeant with a sword before they were gunned down. When pinned down by heavy mortar and machine gun fire, Japanese soldiers shouted insults to the Marines to get them to expose themselves. When dawn broke on the 14th of September, over a thousand Japanese dead and wounded lay in heaps on the blasted slopes that ran up what the Marines would call Edson's Ridge, or Bloody Ridge.

"I hope the Japs will have some respect for American fighting men after this campaign," Edson told John Hersey. "I certainly have learned respect for the Japs. What they have done is to take Indian warfare and apply it to the twentieth century. They use all the Indian tricks to demoralize their enemy. They're good, all right, but I think we're better." [33]

Bloody Ridge caused both sides to bolster reinforcements and on October 25, Chesty Puller and a force of Marines and Army infantry made an equally epic stand on the ridge, in darkness and driving rain. In this all-out attack, the Japanese lost over 3,000 seasoned troops and any chance of taking Henderson Field and Guadalcanal.

After the September raid, reporter Richard Tregaskis hurried to Red Mike Edson's headquarters to get his story of the battle. "He told us about the individual exploits of his men and their collective bravery, but did not mention the fact that he himself had spent the night on the very front line of the knoll, under the heaviest fire.

"He did not mention it, but the fact was that two bullets had actually ripped through his blouse, without touching him."

Edson and his officers "told us some good stories of valor," Tregaskis wrote. "The outstanding one was Lewis E. Johnson's." He was hit three times in the leg, and "at daybreak placed in the rear of a truck with about a dozen other wounded, for evacuation. But as the truck moved down the ridge road, a Jap machine gunner opened up and wounded the driver severely. The truck stopped." Johnson dragged himself into the cab and tried to start the engine. When it wouldn't start, he "pulled the truck a distance of about 300 yards over the crest of the ridge. Then he got the engine going and drove to the hospital."

Feeling revived, he drove back to the ridge and picked up another load of wounded Marines.

Days later, over breakfast, Major Kenneth Bailey, one of the heroes of the ridge, said something to Tregaskis about taking chances in combat. "You get to know these kids so well when you're working with 'em . . . and they're such swell kids that when it comes to a job that's pretty rugged, you'd rather go yourself than send them." [34]

Bailey was killed three days later.

At Guadalcanal, Bailey's boys "fought bravely and better than the enemy," wrote John Hersey. "They had shown themselves to be men, with the strength and weaknesses of men. That had given me, an unprofessional onlooker, a new faith in our chances of winning the war in the visible future." [35]

What turned "kids" like Paul Moore and James Jones into ruthlessly focused jungle fighters? For Jones, it was the acceptance that you were going to die, that you were "written down in the rolls of the already dead." Only when a soldier makes "a compact with himself or with Fate that he is lost" can he fully function under fire. Then he has "nothing further to worry about."

Yet strangely, the "giving up of hope" creates a compensatory kind of hope, Jones adds. "Little things become significant. The next meal, the next bottle of booze, the next kiss, the next sunrise, the next full moon. The next bath."

When you know you're going to die, "every day has a special, bright, delicious, poignant taste to it that normal days in normal times do not have. Another perversity of the human mechanism?" [36]

At Guadalcanal both sides fought with desperate determination. "Every day I was there," wrote reporter Ira Wolfert, "the Jap gave new evidence of his intense willingness to go to any lengths to win, or, if unable to win, to go on fighting until his breath stopped." Wolfert did not see a single Japanese officer taken alive on the island, "and the great majority of the few soldier prisoners we have taken have been wounded and in a condition where their minds have not been up to par." There "[is] one thing nobody in the world can be better at than the Japs," he wrote admiringly, "and that's in the guts department."

And yet the Americans, on land, at sea, and in the air, were licking them. "We've shown that we have more military brains than they have, are better at war, all kinds of war, from strangling and knife-fighting and head-trampling on up into the complicated mechanized operations of modern battle."

Guadalcanal would not be a battle won by heroes. "Heroes don't win wars," Wolfert wrote, "They help. . . . But the heroes are the exception, and it's the ordinary run-of-the mill guy who doesn't feel tempted to do more than his share who has to be relied on to win for our side. . . .

"Our fellows . . . don't look like actors being brave. They look mostly like fellows working.

"Nobody looks young in a fight. I've seen lots of twenty-year-olds out there in the middle of all that stuff flying around and some eighteen-year-olds, but I never saw anybody who looked much under forty while the fight was going on. That's one way our fellows show what they're up against. The blood in their young faces gets watered with a kind of liquid of fear and takes on that blued-over color of watery milk. Their skin looks clothlike, with the texture of a rough, wrinkled cloth.

"Then when things get really thick, like when fellows start getting hit and dropping and crying out with pain all around you . . . sometimes the flesh around their mouths starts to shake as if they were whimpering and their eyes . . . you can see their eyes coated over with a hot shine as if they were crying. But they go right on doing what they have to do . . . doing the work of war."

It was important that these young fighting men were learning to be tough because even greater battles lay ahead, Wolfert cautioned. But the people back home would have to be tough, as well "able to stand the losses, stand all the terrible sorrow and misery that the dead leave in their wake.

"Our losses have been very small thus far. That is because we have been on the defensive in the Solomons since the day we took the place. The Japs have had to come after us. Soon we'll have to start north and go in after them. Then our losses are very likely to increase. There are a lot of people better able than I am to guess how the people back home are going to stand up under that. What I can say is how our fighting fellows are going to stand up under it because I've seen them do it."[37]

In December, the 1st Marine Division was pulled out of Guadalcanal. Although the division had been reinforced earlier by Army units, it had done most of the fighting up to then and the men were tired, sick, and emotionally drained. Almost all of them had malaria and great numbers of them also had dysentery and dengue—"break-bone fever," the doctors called. But they had been told that no one would be pulled off the line unless he was a litter case.

By the time General Vandegrift turned over command at Guadalcanal to Army Major General Alexander M. Patch, the Japanese high command had decided that Guadalcanal was a lost cause. Many of its soldiers on the place they called "starvation island" were so undernourished and wracked by jungle diseases that their hair and

HASTILY DUG GRAVE OF A U.S. MARINE (USMC).

nails had ceased to grow. In the next two months, infantry soldiers and remaining Marines, using trained war dogs to seek out the enemy, began a great push westward from Henderson Field that ended when about 11,000 Japanese troops were evacuated by destroyer convoys at Cape Esperance, a Pacific Dunkirk. On February 9, 1943, General Patch sent a radio message to Admiral Halsey: "Tokyo Express no longer has terminus on Guadalcanal."

Approximately 60,000 Army and Marine Corps ground forces fought on Guadalcanal. Almost 1,600 were killed in combat. Over 4,700 were wounded and twice that number were evacuated after being struck down by jungle diseases or battle psychosis. The Japanese lost close to 21,000 ground troops, about two thirds of those who fought on the island. It was the first defeat suffered by the modern Japanese army.

Samuel Stavisky, a reporter for the *Washington Post*, was there for the "mop-up," when worn-down American troops went into jungle hellholes to hunt down the Japanese who had not been able to get off the island and refused to surrender. "Killed all the yellow slant-eyed bastards," a Marine announced to no one in particular as he emerged with his death squad from a growth-covered gorge. He said it matter-offactly, almost wearily, for he and his fellow Marines were too tired and sick to feel any elation in victory. Just then, Stavisky saw "four skinny, starved, wounded, and unconscious Japs . . . dragged out. The rest were dead: shot, bayoneted, blasted by grenades. Rooted out. Grubbed out. Rubbed out."

"It's over guys," the lieutenant told his men.[38]

It was for them, that day, in that place, on that island. But in stopping the Japanese juggernaut at Guadalcanal, these never-to-be-the-same boys had committed themselves and their country to the greatest reconquest effort in all of history.

Great battles, said Winston Churchill, are those that "won or lost, change the entire course of events, create new standards of values, new moods, new atmospheres in armies and in nations."[39] That was Guadalcanal.

ANONYMITY

Two weeks after a vicious firefight on Guadalcanal, James Jones was assigned to Graves Registration detail. His unit was ordered to go up into the hills and dig up the bodies of dead comrades:

THE DEAD WERE FROM ANOTHER REGIMENT, so men from my outfit were picked to dig them up. That was how awful the detail was. And they did not want to make it worse by having men dig up the dead of their own. Unfortunately, a man in my outfit on the detail had a brother in the other outfit, and we dug up the man's brother that day.

As they dug up the bodies, the officer in charge told them to take one dog tag off each man before putting him into a body bag. It was awful work anyway, but these men had been dead for two weeks.

WHEN WE BEGAN TO DIG, EACH time we opened a hole a little explosion of smell would burst up out of it, until finally the whole saddle where we were working was covered with it up to about knee deep. Above the knees it wasn't so bad, but when you had to bend down to search for the dogtag (we took turns doing this) it was like diving down into another element, like water, or glue. We found about four bodies without dogtags that day.

"What will happen to those, sir?" I asked the lieutenant. . . .

"They will remain anonymous," he said.

"What about the ones with dogtags?" I asked.

"Well," he said, "they will be recorded."

As Jones wrote later, "To accept anonymity, along with all the rest he has to accept, is perhaps the toughest step of all for the combat soldier. . . . It is one of the hardest things about a soldier's life." [40]

NEW GUINEA

While the battle of Guadalcanal still raged, General Douglas MacArthur's forces were fighting an equally ugly war of attrition in the tangled jungles of New Guinea, where the Army, not the Marines, ran the campaign and did most of the suffering and dying. In September 1942, after the Japanese failed to take Port Moresby in their forced march over the Owen Stanley Range, MacArthur's troops chased them back over these forbidding mountain jungles toward their bases at Buna and Gona on the north coast of New Guinea. The Australian correspondent George H. Johnston describes the road back over the treacherous Kokoda Trail at the height of the rainy season. The Australians, with American support, led the advance:

I MAY BE WRONG, FOR I am no soothsayer, but I have an idea that the name of the "Kokoda Trail" is going to live in the minds of Australians for generations, just as another name, Gallipoli, lives on as freshly today, twenty-seven years after it first gained significance in Australian minds. . . .

The weather is bad, the terrain unbelievably terrible, and the enemy is resisting with stubborn fury that is costing us many men and much time. Against the machine gun nests and mortar pits established on the ragged spurs and steep limestone ridges our advance each day now is measured in years. Our troops are fighting in the cold mists of an altitude of 6,700 feet, fighting viciously because they have only a mile or two to go before they reach the peak of the pass and will be able to attack downhill—down the north flank of the Owen Stanleys. That means a lot to troops who have climbed every inch of that agonizing track, who have buried so many of their cobbers [mates] and who have seen so many more going back, weak with sickness or mauled by the mortar bombs and the bullets

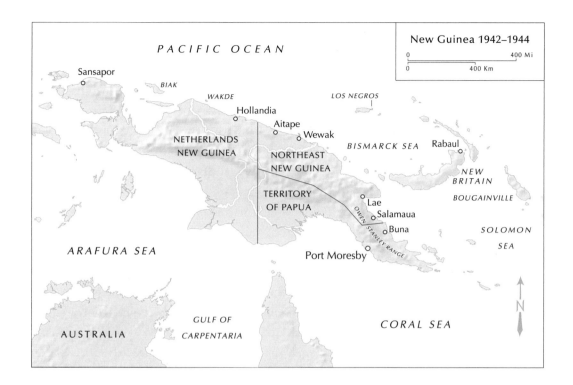

New Guinea 1942–1944

and grenades of the enemy, men gone from their ranks simply to win back a few hundred yards of this wild, unfriendly, and utterly untamed mountain. . . .

Fresh troops are going up the track. . . . The men are bearded to the eyes. Their uniforms are hotch-potches of anything that fits or is warm or affords some protection from the insects. . . .

In the green half-light, amid the stink of rotten mud and rotting corpses, with the long line of green-clad Australians climbing wearily along the tunnel of the track, you have a noisome, unforgettable picture of the awful horror of this jungle war. . . .

The Japs have made their stand in the toughest area of the pass through the Owen Stanleys—a terrible terrain of thick mountain timber, great rocks drenched in rain, terrifying precipices and chasms. Often the troops have to make painfully slow progress by clawing with hands and feet at slippery rock faces overlooking sheer drops into the jungle. The almost constant rain or mist adds to the perils of sharp limestone ridges, narrow ledges flanked by chasms, slimy rocks, and masses of slow moving mud.

In this territory the Japanese are fighting, with a stubborn tenacity that is almost unbelievable, from an elaborate system of prepared positions along every ridge and spur. Churned up by the troops of both armies, the track itself is now knee deep in thick, black mud. For the last ten days no man's clothing has been dry and they have slept—when sleep was possible—in pouring rain under sodden blankets. Each man carries all his personal equipment, firearms, ammunition supply and five days' rations. Every hour is a nightmare. . . .

The Australians have reconquered the Owen Stanley Range. Today, on November 2 [1942], they marched into Kokoda unopposed, through lines of excited natives who brought them great baskets of fruit and decked them with flowers. . . .

Kokoda, "key to the Owen Stanleys," has been abandoned by the Japanese without a fight.[41]

The Allies trapped the Japanese at the coastal villages of Buna, Gona, and Sanananda. The Americans under Major General Edwin F. Harding concentrated on Buna, while the Australians moved against Gona and Sanananda. At Buna, the Japanese dug in behind massive camouflaged bunkers, fronted by nearly impassable swamps. Under orders from MacArthur at Port Moresby, Harding's green, poorly equipped infantry regiments, lacking heavy artillery, flamethrowers, or tanks, attacked repeatedly and recklessly and were massacred. With the remaining troops of Harding's 32nd Division near collapse from hunger, fever, and energy-sapping heat, a frustrated MacArthur replaced Harding with Lieutenant General Robert L. Eichelberger. "Bob, I want you to take Buna, or not come back alive," MacArthur told him.

When Eichelberger landed near Buna on December 1 the horrible stink of the coastal swamp told him that he and his army were "prisoners of geography. . . . We would never get out unless we fought our way out." The troops were "riddled with malaria, dengue fever, tropical dysentery, and were covered with jungle ulcers." But Eichelberger quickly found out that "sick men can fight."[42]

Eichelberger was an inspirational leader, but his men could never have held on without supplies flown in over the Owen Stanley Range by MacArthur's new Air Force chief, Major General George C. Kenney, one of the greatest air commanders of the war. On December 9, the Australians broke through and took Gona; then Eichelberger, with Australian reinforcements, reopened the assault on Buna.

"It was a sly and sneaky kind of combat," Eichelberger wrote in his memoirs, "which never resembled the massive and thunderous operations in Europe, where tank battalions were pitted against tank battalions and armies the size of city popula-

tions ponderously moved and maneuvered. The Pacific was a different war. In New Guinea, when the rains came, wounded men might drown before the litter bearers found them. Many did. No war is a good war, and death ignores geography. But out here I was convinced, as were my soldiers, that death was pleasanter in the Temperate Zone."[43]

In jungle fighting, troops didn't bother to build elaborate trenches; the daily rains would have filled them up. And the fighting was "informal," reported *Yank* correspondent Sergeant Dave Richardson:

WHEN AMERICANS, AUSTRALIANS, AND JAPS CLASH, no more than a few dozen men on either side are involved. There's none of that dramatic "over the top" stuff here. Patrols go out every day to feel out the Jap pillboxes and strong points. Then stronger forces come in to knock them out, supported by mortar and light artillery.

When the pillboxes and machine-gun nests are gone, more Yanks and Aussies come in to mop up the snipers and occupy the area.

The Yanks, most of them from Wisconsin's thickly wooded country, are beating the Japs with tactics borrowed from America's original fighting men—the Indians. These tactics involve swift, silent movement, sudden thrusts out of jungles. The rifle is the basic weapon.[44]

The last fighting around Buna took place in torrential rains that prevented the Japanese from burying their dead. The stench of decomposing bodies stacked in heaps just outside the Japanese lines was overwhelming. "We wondered," said a combat reporter, "how the live Japs had borne it until we discovered they were wearing gas masks as protection against their own dead."[45]

On January 2, 1943, Buna fell, and three weeks later Sanananda was overrun. The cost of the campaign was high for both sides. The Americans suffered 3,000 casualties and almost three times as many men were treated for serious diseases. Japanese and Australian losses were horrifying: 21,000 Australians troops killed, wounded, or treated for disease; 13,000 Japanese killed.

Eichelberger attributed the victory to sheer stubbornness. "The Japanese morale cracked before ours did."[46] But it cracked only because the besieged enemy ran out of food.

The diaries of Japanese soldiers found in the enemy's bunkers and dugouts record the grinding attrition of the battle and slowly changing Japanese perceptions of the American combat soldier. These excerpts, taken from several diaries, follow chronologically the progress of the siege:

THE ENEMY HAS RECEIVED ALMOST NO training. Even though we fire a shot they present a large portion of their body and look around. Their movements are very slow.

The enemy has been repulsed by our keen-eyed snipers. In the jungle it seems they fire at any sound, due to illusion. From sundown until about 10 P.M. they fire light machine guns and throw hand grenades recklessly.

The enemy has become considerably more accurate in firing.

The nature of the enemy is superior and they excel in firing techniques.

Artillery raking the area. We cannot hold out much longer. Our nerves are strained; there is a lack of sleep due to the continuous shelling.

Mess gear is gone because of the terrific mortar fire. Everyone is depressed. Nothing we can do. It is only fate that I am alive today. This may be the place where I shall find my death. I will fight to the last.

Now we are waiting only for death. . . . Can't anything be done? Please God." [47]

In the final stages of the siege, the hemmed-in Japanese ate the flesh of dead enemy soldiers. When hope ran out, they attacked and died rather than surrender. As an Australian reporter wrote: the battle had to be fought until there was "not one Japanese left who was capable of lifting a rifle." [48]

Eichelberger had done the impossible, but MacArthur took complete credit for the victory, even though he had never left his headquarters in Port Moresby, forty minutes away by air. After Buna was taken, Eichelberger wrote with unconcealed wrath: "The great hero went home [to Australia] without seeing Buna before, during, or after the fight while permitting press articles from his GHQ to say he was leading his troops in battle." Not long after the war, MacArthur approached Eichelberger and said, "Bob, those were great days when you and I were fighting at Buna, weren't they?" Eichelberger took this as "a warning not to disclose that he never went to Buna." [49]

Coming just a month before the Japanese evacuation of Guadalcanal, Buna was the first great victory by American ground forces in the Pacific. It gave Kenney air bases from which to attack Japanese strongholds in the region in preparation for a great push toward Rabaul, the center of Japanese power in the South Pacific. Guadalcanal would be a defensive victory; this was an offensive strike, the beginning of what the troops called "The Hard Way Back."

For MacArthur, the victory had personal meaning. "The dead of Bataan will rest easier tonight," he told reporters after Buna fell. [50]

AFRICA AND THE ATLANTIC

On November 8, 1942, a week before its great naval victory at Guadalcanal, the United States launched its first great land offensive against the German army. An

Anglo-American force headed by Lieutenant General Dwight D. Eisenhower landed at Casablanca, on the Atlantic coast of French Morocco, and two other task forces made up of British and American troops landed at Oran and Algiers on the Mediterranean coast of Algeria. Altogether, 65,000 troops were put ashore in a beautifully synchronized amphibious operation. In a gigantic pincer movement, they would pressure Axis troops from the west while General Bernard Law Montgomery's British Eighth Army, which had just broken through General Erwin Rommel's Afrika Korps at El Alamein, barely sixty miles west of Alexandria, Egypt, the gateway to the Suez Canal, came at them from the east.[51]

While the converging Allied forces battled the German army in brutal desert warfare, President Roosevelt and Prime Minister Churchill, together with high-ranking officers of the Anglo-American coalition, met for ten days at Casablanca to plan future military operations. Roosevelt's chief military advisor, General George Marshall, pushed hard for a 1943 invasion of northwest Europe, the Second Front that Russian premier Joseph Stalin claimed he needed to turn back the Nazi invaders. Churchill thought an invasion of northern France was premature. With thousands of landing boats diverted to the Pacific, an adequate invasion fleet had not yet been built, German U-boats were inflicting catastrophic damage on Atlantic convoys headed from America to England and Russia, and the Luftwaffe had air mastery of the skies over Northern Europe. Marshall was persistent, but Britain was then the stronger of the two partners, and Churchill had immense persuasive powers over Roosevelt. The next offensive, it was decided, would be in the Mediterranean the following summer, probably against Sicily and then Italy. As a concession to the Americans and to Admiral King, a larger percentage of the war effort was to be allocated to the Pacific theater. Churchill and Roosevelt also agreed to continue the bombing campaign the Royal Air Force had begun against the cities and industries of the Third Reich, launching a stepped-up, around-the-clock offensive from England by the RAF and the American Eighth Air Force, the British bombing at night and the Americans in daylight.

At a press conference at the conclusion of the Casablanca Conference, Roosevelt sprang a surprise, announcing that the Allies would demand nothing less from the Axis powers than "unconditional surrender." It was apparently a spontaneous statement, but Churchill immediately endorsed it, for the two leaders had recently discussed the idea. This meant nothing at the time, as it was made from a position of military weakness, but it was to have huge consequences later in the war when a fully mobilized America had the unrivaled power in both the Pacific and European theaters to back up its bellicose language.

After the disorganized Americans barely stopped an audacious offensive by Rommel near Kasserine Pass, command of the American II Corps was given to General George S. Patton, with General Omar N. Bradley as his deputy. Patton performed a minor miracle, turning the corps into a crack desert fighting force. Now Montgomery from the south, and Patton from the north, closed in for the kill, beginning the great push that ended in the annihilation of the Axis forces in North Africa and their surrender on May 3, 1943. All Africa was now cleansed of the Axis stain and restored to Allied control.

That May, the Allies won another huge victory, the Battle of the Atlantic, the life-or-death struggle to prevent German U-boats from severing the ocean lifeline between Britain and her allies, as well her fighting forces around the world, including those in Burma, India, and the South Pacific. In 1942, it had had looked like the Allies might lose the battle for control of the sea lanes. That year the U-boats sank over 1,000 Allied ships in the Atlantic, at a cost of only eighty-six submarines. Later that year, however, a brilliant intelligence coup helped change the course of this desperate sea battle, and of the war itself.

U-boat captains used sophisticated little Enigma machines, each with a complex system of three rotors and a typewriter-like keyboard, to encode and decode messages. The Germans were confident this message system could not be compromised. But beginning in 1940, British cryptographers operating out of Bletchley Park, a top secret facility near Oxford, began using computer-like machines called "bombes" and Enigma machines and codebooks seized from captured U-boats to break the supposedly unbreakable German naval codes, allowing the British naval office to deflect convoys from prowling U-boat wolf packs. The Germans never learned their code was broken but they kept changing it to insure its security, making it necessary to continue raiding U-boats to capture Enigma machines and codebooks. All the while, the carnage continued at an alarming rate.

Then came the most sudden and dramatic turnaround of World War II. In May 1943, the Allies gained supremacy in the Atlantic, sinking forty-one U-boats, more than they had sunk in the first three years of the war. Using small escort carriers, fast destroyers, and long-range bombers and other planes equipped with sophisticated radar and homing torpedoes, Allied hunter-killer teams forced Admiral Karl Doenitz,

commander of the German submarine service, to pull his boats from the North Atlantic and put them in safer waters.[52] "We had lost the Battle of the Atlantic,"
Doenitz privately admitted in May 1943. "Black May," the German would call it.[53]

From this point on, the Allies would apply ever-growing American industrial
might with crushing impact, on land, on sea, and in the air. That May, after initial
successes unlike any in modern warfare, both Germany and Japan had been stopped.
Now the Allies, building up for the kill, would begin the great drives toward Tokyo
and Berlin. "The age of managerial, organizational war was in full flex," James Jones
recalls of that May 1943, "almost without having realized it had been born."[54]

In a dispatch he filed just after Tunisia was won in the spring of 1943, war correspondent Ernie Pyle wrote that there were days in 1942 when he sat alone in his
tent "and gloomed with the desperate belief that it was actually possible for us to lose
this war." The home front didn't seem to be contributing with full energy and the
raw GIs he loved seemed no match for the battle-toughened Germans. But then
American production went into high gear. The world's greatest automobile society
stopped making cars and transformed its auto plants into production machines for the
making of every imaginable instrument of mobile warfare—tanks, planes, ships,
landing gear, and mobile artillery that Eisenhower, Patton, MacArthur, Halsey, and
Nimitz began using with devastating effect. And after going through the hell of combat initiation, GIs and Marines became calloused, hard-cursing warriors whom their
folks back home would hardly have recognized.

"Apparently it takes a country like America about two years to become wholly at
war," Pyle wrote. "We had to go through that transition period of letting loose of life
as it was, and then live the new war life so long that it finally became the normal life
to us." America had finally become "a war nation." While Pyle was not sure how it
would happen or how long it would take, "no longer do I have any doubts at all that
we shall win."[55]

On Guadalcanal, John Hersey had come to the same conclusion months before
this. But neither reporter, embedded with the fighting men he was covering, could
give his readers the big picture. Along with Guadalcanal and Buna, El Alamein and
Stalingrad, Midway and the Battle of the Atlantic, Tunisia "clearly signified to friend
and foe alike," Eisenhower wrote later, "that the Allied nations were at last upon the
march."[56]

Amphibious Advance

The Aleutians

With Guadalcanal secured, the United States sent an Army amphibious force in May 1943 to retake two barren islands far to the north, in the Bering Sea sealing grounds off Alaska. During the Battle of Midway, a Japanese diversionary fleet had attacked and occupied Attu and Kiska in the Aleutians, the long string of islands between Asia and the American continent, on the roof of the Pacific. This occupation, by which the enemy hoped to block any American assault against the Kuriles and northern Japan, caused a surge of concern in the United States. Alaska and the Pacific Northwest now seemed vulnerable to an enemy invasion. These fears were unfounded, but America wanted to finish the business the Japanese had started, expelling them from U.S. territory.

On May 11, the Army's 7th Infantry Division, which had recently undergone amphibious training, began landing on the forbidding Arctic landscape of Attu. Seventeen days later the cornered and starving Japanese, outnumbered five to one, staged a desperate banzai charge, screaming that they would drink American blood. The few hundred who survived the slaughter pressed hand grenades to their chests and pulled the pins. The Americans buried some 2,400 Japanese and took only twenty-nine prisoners, but they suffered an appalling 1,700 casualties. Attu turned out to be one the bloodiest island battles of the Pacific war in proportion to the number of men engaged. *Time-Life* correspondent Robert Sherrod was there and saw this "primitive, man-against-man fighting" as an ominous harbinger of the approaching island warfare in the Central Pacific.[1]

Three months later, American and Canadian forces invaded Kiska, but discovered that the entire Japanese garrison had evacuated under the cover of night and heavy fog. A report said they had left only a few dogs and some hot coffee. "What does this mean?" Navy Secretary Frank Knox asked the irascible Admiral Ernest King, who was with him when this report reached Washington. "The Japanese are very clever," replied King. "Their dogs can brew coffee."[2]

RABAUL

While this campaign of fog and ice was being fought, General Douglas MacArthur was advancing across the long north coast of New Guinea, an island twice the size of France. At the same time, Bull Halsey's South Pacific Fleet, with Marine and Army amphibious troops, was moving up the long ladder of the Solomons—through New Georgia, Rendova, Munda, and Vella Lavella—toward the northernmost island, Bougainville. The objective of this coordinated offensive, code-named Cartwheel, was the Japanese air and naval bastion at Rabaul, at the northeastern tip of New Britain, just northwest of Bougainville.

In early March 1943, the Japanese had tried to stop MacArthur by landing 7,000 troops from Rabaul on New Guinea's northeastern coast. Land-based American and Australian bombers from George Kenney's Fifth Air Force swooped in at mast-high level, and in the three-day Battle of the Bismarck Sea sank four Japanese destroyers and all the transports. Three thousand troops drowned or were machine-gunned in the water by PT boats and fighter planes, a reprisal, the men said, for similar atrocities by the enemy. MacArthur would later call this the "decisive aerial engagement" in his theater of operations.[3]

Even the air war was an escalating battle of attrition, one that Japan, with its smaller economy, could not possibly win. In the first twenty-one months of the war in the South Pacific, the Japanese navy lost 26,000 warplanes, almost a third of its total

JUNGLE WARFARE, SOUTHEAST ASIA (USMC).

force, along with thousands of exquisitely trained pilots. American losses were also heavy, but the U.S. was replacing its fliers and planes at a far quicker rate, and doubling and tripling its forces in the region.[4] With the Allies enjoying air superiority, Japanese hopes of holding Papua, the southeastern part of New Guinea, ended. The following month Admiral Yamamoto launched a last-ditch air attack on American shipping and air bases in the area, but his planes did little damage. In an effort to rally his pilots, the admiral flew to inspect air bases in the Solomons. The Americans broke the Japanese code, and under orders straight from Nimitz ambushed the plane from the sky, sending it spinning and burning into the jungle. Admiral Mineichi Koga—a vastly inferior military strategist—replaced Yamamoto as commander in chief of the Combined Fleet.

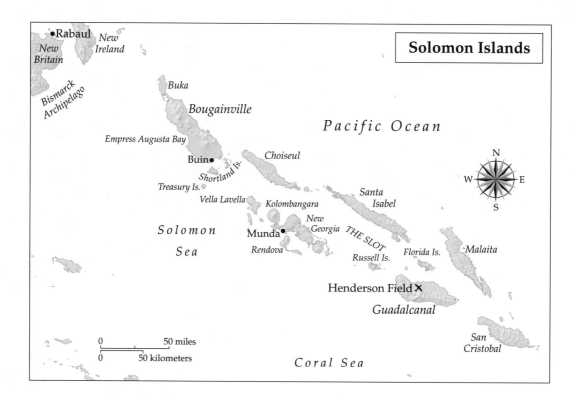

By mid-September, MacArthur's troops had retaken the small ports of Lae and Salamaua, just north of Buna, battling boiling heat, jungle leeches, tropical ulcers, and starving and desperate enemy troops. MacArthur was now nearly halfway up the long northern coast of New Guinea, with the Philippines as his supreme objective. He then swung north and west, landing the 1st Marine Division, veterans of Guadalcanal, in the rain-soaked jungles of Cape Gloucester, at the western tip of New Britain, on the day after Christmas. One month later the Marines seized the airfield there. With that and Halsey's establishment of airfields in the contested swamps of Bougainville the previous November, Rabaul was caught in the deadly American pincer. Bombers from Bougainville and Cape Gloucester pounded Rabaul relentlessly, destroying most of the planes the Japanese had sent to hold on to its South Pacific Gibraltar. With 100,000 of the Emperor's infantrymen, Rabaul prepared for an invasion, the troops vowing to die in a final fight. They waited for the Americans, but the Americans never came and this proud and embittered Imperial Guard was forced to live out the entire war in humiliation on the bypassed island fortress.

The American high command decided there was no need to try to take Rabaul in a costly offensive; it had been outflanked and neutralized. As Samuel Eliot Morison noted: "Tarawa, Iwo Jima, and Okinawa would have faded to pale pink in comparison with the blood which would have flowed if the Allies had attempted an assault on Fortress Rabaul." [5]

At first, MacArthur angrily protested the decision to avoid Rabaul, but this tactic, first employed by Halsey in the Solomons, would become his signature strategy in the South Pacific, a strategy he later claimed to have invented. Instead of hitting Japanese strongholds, he flew over them, letting them "die on the vine," saving lives and time. Beginning in the spring of 1944, his forces started that series of leaps along the New Guinea coast—Wewak, Hollandia, Biak—that eventually brought them within striking distance of the Philippines. This "leapfrogging" movement was one of

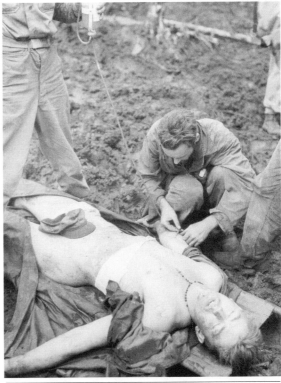

A NAVY CORPSMAN ADMINISTERS BLOOD PLASMA TO A BADLY INJURED MARINE ON CAPE GLOUCESTER, NEW BRITAIN (NA).

the most brilliantly conceived offensives of the war, conducted without a major carrier force, with a small air arm, and only a minimal number of divisions. "If you force the Japs into a corner," MacArthur explained his thinking to a reporter, "they'll fight viciously to the death. They can live a long time on a little rice and few supplies. Flank them, give them a line of retreat even though it may lead nowhere and you have them." [6]

After the war, a high Japanese military official declared that MacArthur's offensive "was the type of strategy we hated most." MacArthur, he said, "with minimum losses, attacked and seized a relatively weak area, constructed airfields and then proceeded to cut the supply lines to [our] troops in that area. . . . Our strongholds were gradually starved out. The Japanese Army preferred direct [frontal] assault, after the German fashion, but the Americans flowed into our weaker points and submerged us,

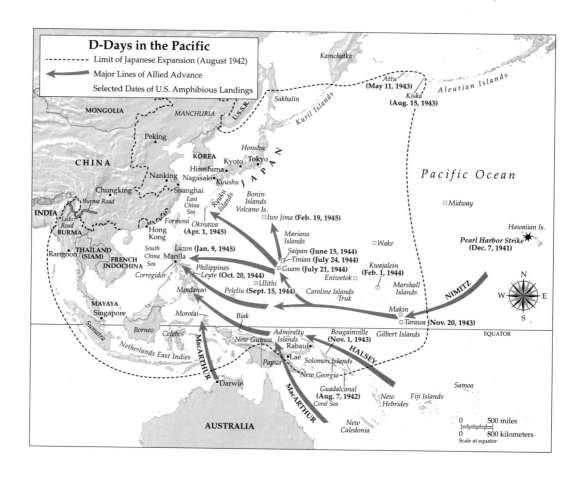

D-Days in the Pacific

- - - - - Limit of Japanese Expansion (August 1942)

⬅ Major Lines of Allied Advance

Selected Dates of U.S. Amphibious Landings

MONGOLIA

MANCHURIA

U.S.S.R.

Kamchatka

Sakhalin

Kuril Islands

Attu
(May 11, 1943)

Kiska
(Aug. 15, 1943)

Aleutian Islands

Peking

CHINA

KOREA

Honshu

Kyoto Tokyo

Hiroshima

Nanking

Nagasaki

Kyushu

Chungking

Shanghai

Burma Road

INDIA

Ledo Road

BURMA

Formosa

Okinawa
(Apr. 1, 1945)

East China Sea

Ryuku Islands

Bonin Islands
Volcano Is.

☐ Iwo Jima **(Feb. 19, 1945)**

Pacific Ocean

☐ Midway

Hawaiian Is.

Pearl Harbor Strike
(Dec. 7, 1941)

THAILAND
(SIAM)

Rangoon

FRENCH INDOCHINA

Hong Kong

South China Sea

Luzon **(Jan. 9, 1945)**

Manila

Philippines

Leyte **(Oct. 20, 1944)**

Corregidor

Mindanao

Mariana Islands

Saipan **(June 15, 1944)**

Tinian **(July 24, 1944)**

☐ Guam **(July 21, 1944)**

☐ Ulithi

Peleliu **(Sept. 15, 1944)**

☐ Wake

Kwajalein
(Feb. 1, 1944)

Eniwetok ☐

Marshall Islands

Caroline Islands
Truk

NIMITZ

N
W   E
S

MAYAYA

Singapore

Sumatra

Morotai

Biak

Borneo

Celebes

Netherlands East Indies

MacARTHUR

New Guinea

Admiralty Islands

Rabaul

Papua

Lae

New Georgia

Bougainville
(Nov. 1, 1943)

Solomon Islands

Gilbert Islands

Makin

☐

Tarawa **(Nov. 20, 1943)**

EQUATOR

HALSEY

Darwin

Coral Sea

Guadalcanal
(Aug. 7, 1942)

New Hebrides

Fiji Islands

Samoa

MacARTHUR

AUSTRALIA

New Caledonia

0   500 miles
0   800 kilometers
Scale at equator

just as water seeks the weakest entry to sink a ship. We respected this type of strategy . . . because it gained the most while losing the least."[7] For every one of his men that was killed, MacArthur killed ten Japanese.

TWO ROADS TO TOKYO

New Guinea opened one road to Tokyo. Another was through the vast Central Pacific—the Gilbert, Marshall, Caroline, and Mariana islands. Clearing this tremendous bluewater highway would be the job of the United States Navy, with Marine and Army ground forces. MacArthur pleaded for supreme command of the Pacific theater and a single offensive, led by the Army, along the line he had been pursuing. But the Navy was unwilling to risk its big carriers in the treacherous shoals of New Guinea, where they would be exposed to land-based bombers; and Admirals King and Nimitz wanted the war in the Central Pacific to be an entirely Navy affair. Roosevelt, in consultation with his Joint Chiefs of Staff,* made the final decision: the offensive against Japan would be twin-pronged and simultaneous, with two separate commanders. MacArthur would continue his drive toward the Philippines while Nimitz cut across the Central Pacific, capturing strategically important islands all the way to the innermost reaches of the enemy's defensive system. There, airstrips would be built to bomb Japan, and submarine bases would be carved out of coral to house the underwater fleets that would be sent out to decimate enemy shipping, with the aim of cutting off Japan from its resource-rich colonies in the South Pacific. It was a cumbersome command structure and strategy, a compromise between two insistent prima

---

*The Joint Chiefs of Staff, formally constituted in February 1942, was the President's foremost advisory body on the planning and conduct of the war. From mid-1942 to the end of the war, its members were General George C. Marshall, Army Chief of Staff, Admiral Ernest J. King, Commander in Chief of the U.S. Fleet and chief of American naval operations, Lieutenant General Henry H. "Hap" Arnold, the commanding general of the U.S. Army Air Forces, and Admiral William D. Leahy. Although Leahy, an old confidant of Roosevelt's, was the committee's chairman and the President's chief of staff, the committee was dominated by Marshall, who became Roosevelt's chief military advisor.

The Combined Chiefs of Staff, formed immediately after Pearl Harbor, was the supreme Anglo-American military authority. It was made up of the U.S. Joint Chiefs of Staff and its equivalent, the British Chiefs of Staff. The committee advised the President and Prime Minister on military strategy and carried out military decisions taken by them. The committee sat in Washington and was chaired by Leahy.

donnas—King and MacArthur—but it turned out to be surprisingly effective. It forced the overextended Japanese to repulse two concurrent, though independent, offensives, both of them pressed without cease by two of the most aggressive commanders of the war, MacArthur and Nimitz.

The Japanese were rendered more vulnerable to this two-pronged strategy by the very scope and magnitude of their stunning opening offensive. In 1942, the empire's defensive perimeter extended 14,200 miles, a distance equal to over one half the earth's circumference. This made it virtually impossible for the fuel-starved Imperial Navy to sufficiently reinforce or supply the nation's distant garrisons or prevent American submarines and planes from disrupting and eventually severing the empire's far-flung supply lines, along with its economic lifeline to the oil, rubber, rice, and metals of the South Pacific.[8]

Both offensives, each conducted in an area larger than the European and Mediterranean theaters combined, would employ amphibious warfare, but with a difference. Distances between neighboring islands were not nearly as great in the Southwest Pacific as they were in the Central Pacific. Employing excellent intelligence, MacArthur's Seventh Amphibious Force, commanded by Rear Admiral Daniel "Uncle Dan" Barbey, the most accomplished amphibious naval commander of the war, preferred surprise landings, usually at night, using newly developed landing craft to ferry troops and heavy armor from shore to shore, with a small fleet of PT boats and destroyers covering the sea lanes and Kenney's land-based planes providing air support. It was a march of the airfields. Once MacArthur and Halsey captured positions in the Solomons or New Guinea, their engineers would cut an airstrip out of tangled jungle and the troops would move under an umbrella of air cover to the next objective. This was triphibious warfare—ground, air, and sea—and it revolutionized the way wars were fought.

MacArthur would make headlines in the American press by invidiously comparing the "island hopping" strategy of Navy and Marine commanders in the Central Pacific—the application of "direct frontal pressure, with the consequent heavy casualties"—with his own "hit 'em where they ain't, let 'em die on the vine" strategy.[9] But the geographic and strategic situation in the Central Pacific was vastly different than in MacArthur's theater.

Nimitz and the Marines were also committed to triphibious warfare but they would conduct it in their own way in the wide-open spaces of the Central Pacific, where distances between enemy strongholds were daunting. Great carrier fleets

SOLDIERS OF THE ARMY'S 27TH INFANTRY DIVISION ATTACK A
BEACH ON MAKIN ATOLL, GILBERT ISLANDS (NA).

would make these giant leaps, landing troops at daybreak on D-Day, on small, hotly defended islands, where they expected to be met, head-on, at the water's edge. These would be high-risk Storm Landings, usually by Marines, who would apply maximum killing power on a concentrated objective, getting in and out as fast as possible. There would be none of the deliberateness of MacArthur's big-unit jungle campaigns, which were conducted either against large land areas with long coastlines, like New Guinea, and later, the Philippines, or closely grouped islands, like the Solomons, where there was room for surprise and tactical feints, opportunities to "hit 'em where they ain't." As a result, almost all of the Allied amphibious landings in the South Pacific were either unopposed or lightly contested; the bigger and unbelievably brutal battles occurred off the beaches, in the dense, miasmic jungles.[10]

The geography of the Central Pacific made amphibious assault almost inevitable.[11] Most of the islands the Americans attacked were too small and isolated for the invading forces to use deception or maneuver. And the assault armadas were so enormous and had to travel such great distances that it was relatively easy for the enemy to track them and read their intent. The only chance of prevailing was to go in straight ahead behind overwhelming naval and air firepower.

The small size of these Central Pacific islands was actually a source of enemy strength. Iwo Jima, as Admiral Nimitz pointed out, "had no extensive coast line affording to the attackers a choice of numerous landing points, where the invading troops would meet little opposition."[12] In an attack against a large landmass, such as New Guinea or Normandy, the defender, not knowing where the landing force will strike, and not being strong enough to stoutly defend all likely landing beaches, has to leave the coast relatively lightly defended and concentrate most of his forces at a strategic location from which they can be moved against the invader, once the main landing place has been located. The attacker can choose the place where he wants to land and achieve tactical surprise, or hit the enemy in a spot where he is weakest.

It was different with assaults on small, heavily defended islands, the most difficult of all amphibious operations. As Marine General Vandegrift explained to a United States senator who was concerned about the high casualties the Marines began to suffer in the Central Pacific in late 1943, "The defender can readily diagnose the point of attack, and due to the small distances involved, can . . . concentrate his forces against any landing attempt . . . [and] pour concentrated fire against the attacker at the moment when . . . comparatively helpless and exposed, the attacking troops are approaching the beach in small craft."

Small coral islands derived additional strength from their surrounding reefs. Until the Navy, in 1944, was able to develop amphibious tractors in sufficient numbers and with sufficient firepower to surmount these reefs without taking heavy losses, Marines were forced to disembark from landing craft a good distance offshore and wade in against lethal fire. Losses in such operations were always high, Vandegrift explained, because "there are no foxholes offshore."[13]

Many of these small, widely separated islands could not be avoided or "leapfrogged." They had to be taken to provide air, naval, and supply bases to support the next island campaign, hundreds, sometimes thousands of miles away. Even before the fighting ended, the Seabees, naval construction battalions, would begin building airfields, submarine pens, port facilities, roads, and hospitals—an entire island infrastructure garrisoned by support troops, including small numbers of African-American Marines. After rest and recuperation, the reassembled strike force would head out for the next Storm Landing.

In the Central Pacific—a Navy-run war—speed was everything, every island assault bringing the Americans closer to Japanese cities to slaughter from the air and shipping lanes to strangle.

These were more than amphibious invasions. They were amphibious assaults, operations in which the invasion was an assault from start to finish.[14] And the Marine Corps was superbly qualified to carry them out. Beginning in the years immediately after World War I, Marine Corps planners had begun searching for a unique mission for the Corps to guarantee its continued existence at a time when Army commanders were claiming that their own troops could easily take over the redundant responsibilities of the Marines. This provoked the Marines, led by Major General Holland "Howlin Mad" Smith, a former Alabama attorney and a combat veteran of World War I, to fashion a new doctrine of warfare: ship-to-shore assaults against heavily defended enemy islands.

As early as the 1920s, the United States Navy had expected to fight the next war in the Central Pacific, following a surprise Japanese attack on one of America's island outposts, most likely the Philippines. The Navy's War Plan Orange envisioned the American fleet steaming across the Central Pacific toward the Japanese home islands and bringing on a decisive battle with the Imperial Navy. In this, the Marines saw an opportunity. To navigate the extreme distances of the Central Pacific, the Navy would need island bases currently held by the Japanese. The Marine Corps proposed to invade and secure these farflung garrisons, using new amphibious tactics it had begun to develop in the 1930s.

"To the minds of many interwar military leaders, the marines might as well have proposed to land on the moon," writes historian Ronald H. Spector.[15] While daylight assaults from the sea against fortified beaches were as old as organized warfare, critics argued that modern land-based and air weapons made them unfeasible—almost suicidal. British and French forces had attempted such a landing in 1915 at Gallipoli, in the Dardanelles, to force Turkey out of the war. But the miserably trained, poorly led troops—most of them Australians—were defeated on the beach-head, a military fiasco that almost ended the career of the invasion's architect, Winston Churchill, First Lord of the Admiralty.

But Marine Corps visonaries, beginning with Major Earl H. "Pete" Ellis, one of the first to study the operational necessities of a war against Japan, were confident that seaborne assaults against heavily defended beachheads were possible with careful logistical planning, aircraft and submarine reconnaissance, massive air and naval bombardment, close and continuous air support, and new landing craft to put men and arms on the beaches suddenly and in overmastering force. The Marines made pioneering contributions to the technology as well as the theory of amphibious warfare, encouraging the development and mass production of shallow-draft Higgins boats (LCVPs, Landing Craft Vehicle, Personnel) as well as amphibian tractors (LVTs, Landing Vehicle, Tracked) capable of carrying assault troops over the treacherous coral reefs that rimmed the atolls of the Central Pacific.* The Army introduced its own amphibian truck, the DUKW, nicknamed "Duck." These ungainly-looking six-wheeled workhorses carried supplies, artillery, and ammunition from ship to shore, to both Marines and Army infantry, beginning with the invasion of Kwajalein in early 1944. In most Central Pacific operations, amphibian tractors and DUKWs were carried to their launching sites in the bellies of huge, shallow-draft Landing Ship Tanks (LSTs), where they entered the water through clamlike bow doors. Although the Japanese began the war far ahead of the Americans in landing craft design, these and at least a dozen other assault vehicles helped make the U.S. Marine Corps, by 1944, the world's most feared amphibian warriors. By then they were what Pete Ellis, writing in 1921, had hoped they would become—not just "skilled infantry men and jungle men" but "skilled water men" as well.[16]

---

*The LVTs was also called amphtracs or amtracs, although most Marines called them Alligators, the name their inventor, Donald Roebling, had given them.

The first LVTs were modified versions of vehicles used by Roebling for hunting trips in the Florida swamplands. They were excruciatingly slow, with a maximum speed of nine miles per hour on land and four in the water. Lightly armored, they were essentially seagoing light trucks. By 1944, improved versions were capable of speeds of seventeen to twenty mph on land and five to six in the surf, which made them still slower than the DUKWs. But unlike the DUKW, the tracked LVT could crawl over almost anything, including, most importantly, the fringing reef of a coral island.

By 1944, the greatly improved LVT (A) was virtually an amphibious light tank. It had a snub-nosed, turret-mounted 75mm howitzer, along with four machine guns. And its armor could withstand machine gun fire and exploding shell fragments, although not direct artillery hits.

When the Japanese attacked Pearl Harbor, the United States Marine Corps, hamstrung by budgetary restrictions, lacked both the manpower and the landing craft to conduct ambitious amphibious operations. Guadalcanal had been aptly named Operation Shoestring. By late 1943, however, with as many American fighting men— Army, Navy, and Marines—deployed against Japan as against Germany, the Marine Corps had the men, equipment, and experience to begin an epic island offensive against history's greatest oceanic empire. And thanks to prescient planners at its Quantico, Virginia, training and strategic planning facility, it knew how to do the job. After the war, General Alexander Vandegrift, then the Marine Corps Commandant, claimed that the Marine Corps' greatest contribution to victory was "doctri-nal . . . The basic amphibious doctrines which carried Allied troops over every beach-head of World War II had been," he said, "largely shaped—often in the face of uninterested or doubting military orthodoxy—by U.S. Marines." [17]

Storm Landings in the Central Pacific were operations of vast distances, great speed, and terrible striking power. The Navy would spearhead seven of them, begin-ning with Tarawa, and the battles would be short, violent, and decisive, battles of "a magnitude and ferocity that may never again be seen in this world," writes historian Joseph H. Alexander. [18]

For the Japanese army, these would be fights to the last; there would be nowhere to retreat to and no prospect, as at Guadalcanal, of evacuation. The American ar-madas covering the invasions would make sure of that.

The prodigious expansion of the Pacific Fleet made these lightning land-ings possible. By late 1943, the United States Navy had grown to the point where it was not only the largest and most powerful in the world, but larger than the combined navies of all other warring powers. Seven new battleships had joined the fleet, mostly to provide ship-to-shore fire. Even more significant was the astonishing growth of the Navy's air arm. The Pacific Fleet added seven enor-mous *Essex*-class carriers and eleven lighter carriers, augmented by numerous escort carriers. The new *Essex*-class carriers were fast and heavily armed, and each of them was capable of carrying from eighty to a hundred aircraft—the most for-midable of them the new F6F Hellcat, which could outfight the feared Japanese Zero. The ships formed carrier task forces made up of troop transports and am-phibious vessels protected by battleships, cruisers, destroyers, submarines, and minesweepers. And each task force had a "sea train" of fuel, cargo, repair, and hos-pital vessels that allowed it to operate out of port for as long as seventy days. Car-rier groups were refueled every four days by oilers, which also brought the mail and the latest movies.

Vice Admiral Marc A. "Pete" Mitscher's Task Force 58, controlling a large part of the fast carriers—each of them carrying 2,600 men, the size of a small town—was alone more powerful than the entire Japanese Navy. "Task Force 58 is really some-thing new under the sun," wrote two reporters who covered the war in the Pacific. "It is so big that one captured Jap pilot said he knew they'd lost the war when he got his first bird's-eye view of its hundreds of ships, from destroyers to huge carriers and 45,000-ton battlewagons, spread over 40 square miles of ocean. It is so fast that no pre—Pearl Harbor battleship could keep pace with it. And it is relentless, because it never has to go home." [19]

TARAWA

Now this remorselessly modern Navy was ready to strike a series of hard blows in the Central Pacific. The first was aimed at Tarawa in the Gilbert Islands, 2,400 miles west of Hawaii and at the far end of the defensive perimeter Japan had established to protect its island empire. The landing here was significant both strategically and tactically, strategically because it inaugurated America's great ocean-borne amphibious offensive and was the first real test of American amphibious doctrine, tactically because it taught valuable and painful lessons in island landing.

Tarawa is an atoll, a ring of tiny coral islands that nearly encloses a picture-pretty lagoon. The target on Tarawa was Betio, its largest island, but only a tiny speck in the vast Pacific, about the size of New York's Central Park. It is less than two miles long and little more than 700 yards wide at its center, and it is pancake flat, with no point rising more than a few feet above the surf line. While Marines reduced it and seized its nearly completed airfield, the 27th Army Division would storm lightly defended Makin atoll, 100 miles to the north.

Nimitz placed Raymond Spruance, a hero at Midway and the newly appointed commander of the Fifth Fleet, in charge of Operation Galvanic, the invasion of the Gilbert Islands. Thirty-five thousand troops and 6,000 vehicles were carried by fast transports protected by the Fifth Fleet's nineteen carriers, twelve battleships, and a supporting flotilla of cruisers, destroyers, and minesweepers. The entire armada covered fifty square miles of ocean. And a good part of it was committed to Betio.

Betio was garrisoned by 4,600 men, over half of them Japanese Imperial Marines, volunteers known for their fighting spirit and stoic discipline. These elite troops would be

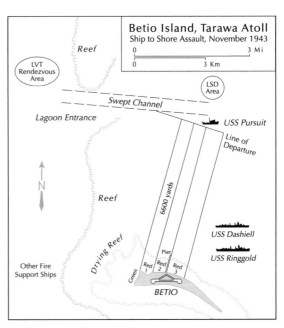

positioned behind the most formidable system of defenses Americans had yet to encounter in the Pacific. The assault force was Major General Julian C. Smith's 2nd Marine Division, half of them veterans of Guadalcanal who had been recuperating from malaria in New Zealand. They were under the overall command of salty-tongued Major General Holland "Howlin' Mad" Smith, one of the Marines' chief architects of amphibious warfare, and the commander who would direct almost every major island assault in the Central Pacific.

U.S. Marine Corps correspondents described the island garrison their comrades were sent against:

THE JAPANESE OVER A PERIOD OF fifteen months did a very sound job in perfecting their defenses for . . . Betio. They transformed its flat insignificance into one solid islet fortress which they felt, with considerable justification, would prove impregnable.

For its beaches and the reef were lined with obstacles—concrete pyramid-shaped obstructions designed to stop landing boats, tactical wire in long fences, coconut-log barricades, mines, and large piles of coral rocks.

And for its beach defense there were numerous weapons—grenades, mortars, rifles, light and heavy machine guns . . . antiboat guns, [and] . . . coast-defense guns. . . .

The emplacements for these weapons were often seven feet thick, of solid concrete, reinforced by steel, coral sand, and coconut logs.

The pillboxes for the automatic weapons, and even the riflemen's pits, were scientifically constructed to withstand heavy bombardment. Around a concrete floor in a three- to five-foot excavation was built a twelve-inch reinforced concrete wall. Over this were alternate layers of coral sand, coconut logs, and sandbags. The roof was made in the same way with coral sand covering the entire outside, then tapering off gradually to prevent the casting of shadows which would show in aerial photographs.

In places the blockhouses were of concrete with a roof thickness of five feet, on top of which were palm-tree trunks with a diameter of eighteen inches, and a final layer of angle irons made of railroad steel.

Guarded by these defenses was a landing field: the long, dusty airstrip that gave the Japanese a position of strategic importance in the Central Pacific because it was their nearest point to our travel routes from San Francisco to

Hawaii to Australia, because it was our first major obstruction on the road to Tokyo.

In addition to these Japanese-made defenses there were the barriers and hazards of nature. There was the reef. There were the tides.

The Japanese who manned this islet fortress of Betio were not of the ordinary run. They were all volunteers. They possessed a finer physique and training than any other group in the Emperor's forces. . . . Their rear admiral in command at the atoll [Keiji Shibasaki] is known to have stated that the invading Americans faced certain annihilation, for "a million men could not take Tarawa."

The Admiral's confidence was based on realism. . . .

We were not underequipped for Tarawa. Offshore stood the mightiest fleet ever assembled up to that time in the Pacific. In the two years since Guadalcanal, an amazing variety of special landing craft had been developed to meet the needs of transporting men and materiel for massive seaborne invasions.

Yet Tarawa . . . was a gamble. For the first time in martial history a seaborne assault upon a heavily defended coral atoll was to be launched. As General Julian Smith told his troops on the eve of D-Day:

"We are the first American troops to attack a defended atoll. What we do here will set a standard for all future operations in the Central Pacific area." [20]

As Major General Holland Smith said later, after inspecting Shibasaki's fortifications: "The Germans never built anything like this in France. No wonder those bastards were sitting back here laughing at us! They never dreamed the Marines could take this island, and they were laughing at what would happen to us when we tried." [21]

On the morning of November 20, three hours before the Marines climbed down the cargo nets and boarded their landing craft, the Navy unleashed a spectacular bombardment, the largest yet of the war. "We will not neutralize; we will not destroy; we will obliterate the defenses of Betio," declared Rear Admiral Harry W. Hill.[22] "We thought that most of the Japanese would be dead by the time we got on the island," reporter Robert Sherrod recalled. "There was even a debate on the troop transport I was on as to whether or not the Japanese had evacuated the island, as they did at Kiska. B-17 pilots who bombed the island the day before reported seeing no signs of life—no return fire, nothing. What we hadn't figured out, of course, was that this was the most heavily defended beach in the world, yard by yard, and that there were an awful lot of Japanese waiting for us." [23]

Unknown to the Marines, the naval bombardment failed to destroy the enemy's craftily disguised blockhouses and pillboxes, almost 500 of them. The fleet assaulted the island from its lagoon side, where the defenders least expected it, but the Navy stopped the bombardment twenty minutes before the troops landed because of visibility problems. This gave the Japanese time to switch their mobile defenses from the south, or sea beach, to the north side of narrow Betio, turning the dreamy lagoon into a murderous fire zone for their machine guns and mortars.

But the most forbidding defense the enemy possessed was the jutting coral reef that extends 300 to 900 yards into the placid blue-green lagoon formed by the atoll. On the morning of the invasion the tide was unusually low, and the defenders did not believe the invaders could get over it with their heavily loaded Higgins boats. But the Americans had a new weapon that could climb over reefs and operate as an assault vehicle on land. The Americans did not, however, have enough of them, only 125.

The first wave of Marines went in on amphibious tractors—LVTs—whose caterpillar tracks could move them through water and over land. They had been used at Guadalcanal, but only to carry supplies, not troops, for they were slow, difficult to steer, and lighly armored. Admiral Richmond Kelly Turner, head of the Amphibious Task Force, the force responsible for getting the troops to the target, was against using them, but hot-tempered "Howlin' Mad" Smith, commander of all American ground troops in the Gilberts campaign, had insisted, "No LVT's, no operation." [24]

The Alligators crawled over the wide reef and churned onto the beach, machine guns blazing. The sight of these strange metal monsters that could move across both water and land struck fear into some defenders, but the Japanese quickly recovered and hit the invaders with a crushing crossfire, forcing them to take protection behind a low seawall of coconut logs that ran along the beach. Still, the LVTs delivered 1,500 men to the beaches in the first fifteen minutes, with only minor casualties. America's first Storm Landing was off to a good start. The problem would be maintaining momentum.

Almost everyone else coming ashore on D-Day rode in Higgins boats, which were larger and had a deeper draft than the amphtracs. They needed four feet of water to get over the reef, but the tide that day was not accommodating. It was an exceptionally unusual "dodging tide" that stayed low for the next thirty hours, confounding the predictions of Marine intelligence experts that there would be at least five feet of water covering the reef. The diesel-powered Higgins boats slammed into the reef and grounded, forcing the Marines to wade in to shore in chest-deep water, under searing fire. "I couldn't even see the beach because of the tremendous smoke," said Major Michael Ryan.[25] His battalion, like others landing after the first wave, was cut to shreds.

It was now 0920. "Back home," wrote Hanson Baldwin, "the football crowds [were] gathering; chickens and turkeys, dressed and ready for Thanksgiving, crowd[ed] the markets; on Broadway 'Life With Father' [was] in its fifth year, and 'Oklahoma!' [took] the mind off war."[26]

But in the bullet-swept lagoon at Betio, young Americans were dying.

Marines in the slow-moving Alligators returned to the reef to try to ferry in stranded comrades and were blown out of the water, men leaping from them with their clothes aflame. "In the distance I could see the beach," recalled Marine Karl Albrecht. "It was lined with amphtracs, all of which appeared to be burning and smoking. . . . The attack appeared to have dissolved in confusion. I was terror stricken and amazed at the same time. We were Americans and invincible. We had a huge armada of warships and a division of Marines. How could this be happening? . . . I discovered the rows of Marines along the beach weren't lying there waiting for orders to move. They were dead. There were dead all over. They appeared to outnumber the living."[27]

The pilot of a Navy patrol plane described the scene: "The water never seemed clear of tiny men, their rifles over their heads, slowly wading beachward. I wanted to cry."[28] Only at the northwestern tip of Betio did the Marines have any success. There Major Ryan led ashore survivors of the 3rd Battalion, 2nd Marines after spotting a lone Marine landing through a gap in the Japanese defenses. Ryan took charge of these scattered Marine units and created the only organized fighting force on Betio for a day and a half. He had just 200 men and two tanks.

Later that morning Robert Sherrod started in with the fifth wave. He was part of a small band of civilian and Marine Corps correspondents and cameramen, ranging in age from seventeen to fifty-four, who would cover the battle. World War I veteran Kerr Eby, one of America's greatest combat artists, was the oldest man to land on Betio; Harry Jackson, an aspiring sculptor, was the youngest. Sherrod would write a superb book on Tarawa; Kerr Eby would capture the battle's ferocity with his brooding charcoals of anonymous Marines, their helmets hiding their faces; and Staff Sergeant Norman Hatch and a team of Marine Corps photographers, headed by Hollywood star Captain Louis Hayward, would produce a film documentary of the fighting that would win an Academy Award. On this morning, all the correspondents and cameramen put themselves in as much danger as any Marine in the assault force. Two of them would die and three would be wounded or injured.

The pilot of Sherrod's landing boat dropped him off near the reef, in neck-deep water. "No sooner had we hit the water than the Jap machine guns really opened up on us. . . . It was painfully slow, wading in such deep water. And we had seven hundred yards to walk slowly into that machine-gun fire, looming into larger targets as we rose onto higher ground. I was scared, as I had never been scared before." [29]

"The water was red," recalls Harry Jackson. "It takes a lot of blood to make water red." Jackson waded through the lagoon with his buddy Whitey Cronin, a still photographer. "A mortar hit and I looked around and said, 'Whitey, Whitey where are you?' There was a gyrene [Marine] behind me and he said, 'Is this Whitey?' And I looked and there is Whitey for sure. The whole front of his skull had been blown off, and I looked right into the cave, this incredibly red-black cave of his being. There is no way to describe what one feels in that instant. I was standing shoulder to shoulder with a Marine, and he said to me, 'You've been hit.' And I looked at him and said, 'You are, too.'" [30] When enemy fire took down the Marine next to him, Associated Press photographer Frank Filan dropped his cameras in the water to help him. Later, he would borrow a camera to take a famous shot of battered Betio.

One coxswain went out of his mind. "This is as far as I go!" he screamed after running into a hail of bullets. He then dropped the ramp of his Higgins boat and twenty Marines, loaded down with gear, jumped out and drowned in fifteen feet of water. [31]

Robert Sherrod's aiming point was a long pier that stretched from the beach to the reef. Its coconut log stanchions offered him some cover. From there he crawled 400 yards to the beach and jumped into a foxhole in the sand. "I took my first close look at . . . Betio. . . . From the water's edge to the seawall there was twenty feet of sand and brown green coral. These twenty feet were our beachhead. The Japs controlled the rest of the island." [32]

He was in a sector of the beach commanded by a big, red-mustached major named Henry "Jim" Crowe. After catching his breath, Sherrod walked over to Crowe and asked if he had seen any other war correspondents or photographers. Crowe said he hadn't but unknown to him, sitting in a foxhole not thirty yards away was Norman Hatch, the only motion picture cameraman on the beach. Hatch had gone in to Betio with Crowe and become separated from him on the reef. His film footage, along with Sherrod's reporting, would make Crowe an American hero.

MAJOR "JIM" CROWE DIRECTS ACTION FROM HIS IMPROVISED COMMAND
POST ON THE CROWDED BEACH OF TARAWA, GILBERT ISLANDS (USMC).

Years later, Staff Sergeant Norman Hatch gave his story of the first day on
Tarawa:

BACK IN NEW ZEALAND, WHEN I was put in charge of a group of motion
picture photographers for the Tarawa engagement, I selected the one man that I
wanted to go into the beach with. His name was Jim Crowe and he had been a
hero on Guadalcanal. I wanted to go in with him because he was aggressive.
Wherever he went there was bound to be plenty of action to film.

I went to see him and said, "Major, I'm a motion picture cameraman and I'm assigned to go with you in the upcoming engagement." And he barked, "I don't want any goddamn Hollywood Marines with me." I said, "I'm not a Hollywood Marine, I'm a regular, I shot expert with the rifle." I also told him that the film that I would shoot would be as useful to the Marine Corps as the physical combat would be. He looked at me for a minute and said, "You can go, but stay the hell out of my way." When it came time to go in on the Higgins boat I sat on the engine hatch with him and he took one look at me and muttered, "Jesus, you're here."

He was battalion commander and was not due in until the fifth or sixth wave; his executive officer had gone in with the first wave. As we approached the reef all the boats were hung up, and Crowe looked in toward the beach and saw that his men were packed together against the seawall, with enemy fire and shattered assault craft pinning them into a tiny square of sand and coral. And all of a sudden Crowe yells, "I've got no beachhead." So he shouts to the coxswain, "Put this goddamn boat in right now. I've got to get in there and straighten out that beach." He was afraid he was losing his beachhead and wouldn't have room for the next companies that were scheduled to come in.

There was no water on the reef and we ran up on it fast and hit it hard, sending everyone flying. Then the coxswain tried to drop the metal ramp of the plywood boat and it wouldn't go down. It was panic time, for all hell was breaking loose around us, and we were a sitting duck. Crowe told everyone to go over the side, and that's not easy to do on an LCVP, especially under the fire with all your battle gear, weighing about sixty to seventy pounds. The gunwales are almost shoulder high and we had to climb over them and drop into water that was about chest level. My assistant, Bill Kelliher, and I had to be very careful. We couldn't get our cameras and film wet. So Kelliher went over the side first, and I loaded him with his cameras and gear, which he carried on his shoulders. Then I went over the side and one of the boat handlers loaded me with my camera equipment.

It was about 400 yards to the beach and we followed the men who had gotten out of the boat ahead of us. But they were all low in the water; all that was sticking out was their helmets. They looked like a herd of turtles. Nobody was standing up and walking, except Kelliher and me. This was my first time in combat and I could see the bullets hitting in the water all around me, and there was a sniper firing at us from under the pier. And I kept saying to Kelliher, "We got to stay upright, don't get down, don't get under the water."

If you ever walked through water you know what an effort it is, and we were weighted down and were wearing heavy boots. . . . When we got to the beach I fell into a shell hole and started shooting film. But before I did I got a sense of what a mess we were in when I looked up and saw a Marine lying right in front of me with his left buttock shot off. All the flesh was exposed and bleeding. My face was about two feet away from his wound, and I thought, Jesus! That could be me!

While I was lying in that hole I got a graphic shot of Jim Crowe standing up and leaning on an LVT, while everyone around him was sucking sand. He was an inspiration to some mighty scared boys who were hugging that seawall. He was walking around cradling a shotgun in his arm and clenching a cigar in his teeth and barking, "Look, the sons of bitches can't hit me. Why do you think they can hit you? Get moving. Go over that wall and kill some goddamned Japs." This got people up and moving to establish a perimeter in front of us, some kind of toehold on that beach. But these guys soon got pushed back. There were too many of them and not enough of us. And we couldn't see the bastards. They were dug in like rodents. But Crowe had the right idea. Unless we went over that wall we were going to die.

Here we were in this big mess, and all I could think about was getting it on film. It's like your camera is your gun. You have no sense of danger; you block it out. When you're looking through the viewfinder you're divorced from what's going on around you. What you're doing is looking at a movie out there—that's right, the battle seems like a movie—and your entire intention is to get that movie. Subconsciously, you know guys are shooting at you, but you dismember yourself by looking through that viewfinder. Capturing the story of the battle becomes the most important thing in your life.

And I had a big responsibility, after all. This was the first time the Marines had made an assault on a fortified beachhead, and I was the only Marine cameraman to get onto the beach that day. The rest couldn't get in until the next day. I had a job to do. If I didn't capture this on film, no one would.[33]

A Marine killed on D-Day wrote in the last letter to his wife: "Marines have a way of making you afraid—not of dying, but of not doing your job."[34]

As the battle deteriorated, General Julian Smith, on the bridge of the flagship *Maryland*, radioed General Holland Smith, on the battleship *Pennsylvania*, near Makin. He wanted reinforcements, the 6th Marine Regiment, which was being held in reserve, and he ended with the ominous words, "ISSUE IN DOUBT."

This message had been sent after getting word of the situation on Betio from the commander of the assault forces, Colonel David M. Shoup, a bull-necked, profane man who wrote poetry in his private moments and later became Commandant of the Marine Corps. "He was awfully nervous about whether we were going to lose the battle or not," Sherrod recalled, "but his troops would never have known it. He's one of the reasons the battle was not lost. Directing the fight from an improvised command post right behind a Japanese blockhouse, with the enemy still in it, he was a rock. I can see why he got the Medal of Honor at Tarawa after being wounded and refusing to be evacuated." [35]

Five thousand Marines assaulted the beach on D-Day. By midnight, 1,500 of them were dead or badly wounded, making this the bloodiest day up to then in Marine Corps history. This was the crisis moment of the battle, when it could easily have been lost. That night, the Marines were packed so tight on the narrow beach that no one could move without stepping on somebody else, and hanging in the tropical air was the stench of their own dead, piled up behind them on the water's edge. Lots of guys thought they were trapped and doomed. It was "like being in the middle of a pool table without any pockets," said one Marine.[36] The men expected a banzai attack, but Jim Crowe told them, "I don't want a single shot fired on the beach tonight unless the Japs hit us with everything they got." He said if any Japanese came crawling in over the seawall, "get 'em with your knives." That was because there were so many troops on the beach that if they started firing at enemy infiltrators they would kill their own comrades.

"I remember drifting off to sleep," Hatch recalls, "and in the middle of the night I heard somebody yelling, 'There's a Jap in here and he's killing people, he's killing the wounded . . . ' I reached for my knife . . . [but] all of a sudden the guy yells, 'I've got him.'

"You know, we probably would have pulled out that night if we could have because I'm convinced that if the Japanese had been able to mount a force, they would have pushed us right off the beach. I don't think there's anything we could have done about it because we didn't have enough people ashore. They really missed a big chance." [37]

For fifty years after the battle, historians surmised that the Japanese did not attack because Admiral Shibasaki's wire communications had been knocked out by the naval bombardment, making it impossible for him to orchestrate a coordinated counterstrike. But recently translated Japanese war records reveal that Shibasaki was killed by the initial naval bombardment, cut down out in the open with most of his staff while they were moving from one bunker to another. This is why his Imperial Marines were in no position to mount a countercharge.

The following morning Norman Hatch and Robert Sherrod sat at separate spots against the seawall looking out into the lagoon, one taking notes, the other scanning the action with a camera, recording a slaughter even worse than the one they had just survived.

After spending the night in their boats—seasick, wet, and scared—a group of Marine reinforcements started coming in on Higgins boats, only to smash into the reef and ground. "The Japanese were zeroed in on that reef edge," says Hatch. "It was almost uncanny to watch a ramp go down and a bunch of guys make a surge to come out and a shell explode right in their faces. . . . Boats were blown completely out of the water and bodies were all over the place. If Hollywood tried to duplicate that it would not be believed."

Hundreds of Marines died in the water; it was worse than the first day.[38]

Seasick Marines caught on the reef began to be rescued by a Navy salvage boat officer named Edward Heimberger, whom some of them recognized as the movie star Eddie Albert. He was sent out to salvage broken boats, but all he did was salvage Marines. "As I looked around I saw a lot of men in the water, wounded, so I tried to pick them up," Albert recalled years later. His boat was carrying drums of high-octane gasoline and was taking fire from at least five machine gun nests. "The bullets were incendiary and armor-piercing and they came right through the boat and skittered around on the floor. Fortunately somebody was watching over us and the bullets didn't hit any of those tanks."

A group of Marines who were not wounded, but had lost their rifles, refused Albert's offer to evacuate them. "They said 'take the wounded in.'" Then they asked Albert if he was coming back. "And I said, 'Yeah.' And they said, 'Bring some rifles.' So I dropped off the wounded [on the hospital ship] and came back. By that time they had all been killed."[39]

"We were losing, until we won," General Julian Smith would say years later.[40] The Marines started winning on the afternoon of the second day. But even on that dismal morning some things began to go right. It all started when Major Michael Ryan took a ragtag unit of "orphans" from other battalions and, with the help of two tanks and naval gunfire, fought his way down the west coast of the island and captured a large beach, called Green Beach. Now General Julian Smith could land reinforcements securely, along with heavy weapons. While Smith was assembling a landing force of the 6th Marines, the men on the main invasion beaches started to move out over the seawall and take enemy bunkers. As Hatch recalled, the inspiration was Major William Chamberlin:

> HE WAS AN OLD MAID, IN training and aboard ship, a college professor who was always telling the guys to put on their T-shirts so they wouldn't get sun-

A PARTIALLY CAMOUFLAGED JAPANESE BLOCKHOUSE
ON HEAVILY FORTIFIED TARAWA (USMC).

burned. But on the beach that second day he was a goddamned wild man, a guy that anybody would follow in combat.

Early in the morning he came over to me and said, "We're going to take that command post," pointing to a monstrous bunker about forty feet high and on a slope. "Are you interested in coming along and getting some good pictures?" Staff sergeants don't argue with majors, so I told him that sounded like a good idea.

He got his junior officers around him in a foxhole and said, "All right. We're going to jump off at 0900 and we're going to go right over the top of that thing and blow them the hell out." Then he told everybody to synchronize their watches, just like they do in the movies. "When I give the signal, we're off and running."

We were in a foxhole together and at 0900 sharp the major gets up and looks at me and says, "Are you ready?" Then he charges out yelling, "Follow me." We ran right up to the top of that blockhouse. When we got there I looked around and it was only the major and me. And there were about a dozen Japanese looking up and wondering what the hell we're doing on top of their command post. I said, "Major, where's your weapon?" And he said, "I gave my carbine to somebody else and I lost my pistol." All I had in my hands were my cameras, so I said, "We'd better get the hell out of here." So we turned and ran down back off the other side and jumped into a foxhole.

Then there was a little ass-chewing and he got everybody together again and they took that blockhouse by dropping charges down the air vents, shooting in fire from flamethrowers, and firing their weapons through the gun slits. After they did that, we waited, and several squads of troops came rushing out to engage us, figuring we were surrounding them. We annihilated them, and I was able to capture this on film. This is where my forty-five seconds of fame started which lasted me sixty years. In the Pacific war one hardly ever saw the Japanese, and this was the only time we caught a shot of the enemy in some strength fighting us at point-blank range.

After this, the battle became an island-wide search-and-destroy mission.[41]

It was called "blind 'em, blast 'em, and burn 'em." That's how Tarawa would be taken, just the way Chamberlin took that big blockhouse. Withering rifle fire drove the Japanese defenders away from their firing slits so that demolition men could heave TNT satchel charges into the bunkers. Then Marines carrying napalm tanks on

U.S. MARINES STORM A JAPANESE "BOMB
PROOF" ON TARAWA (USMC).

their backs poured fire and flame through the openings, burning up the oxygen inside
and suffocating the defenders. The work was done in teams, but one Marine, Scout
Sniper William Deane Hawkins, went on a one-man rampage, attacking pillbox after
pillbox—crawling up to them in the sand, firing into the gun ports, and tossing
grenades inside—until he was ripped apart by mortar fire. He was awarded the
Medal of Honor posthumously, and the airfield at Betio was named Hawkins Field.

Some bulldozers and additional light tanks were landed on the afternoon of the second day, when the tide finally rose, and they were used to break the bunkers. The tanks went in close and blasted away. Bulldozers, manned by Seabees, were brought up to seal the entrances to blockhouses. Gasoline was poured into the vents and ignited with explosives. The charred corpses were not removed. The bulldozers finished the job, entombing the victims under tons of coral and sand.

"The improved situation is reflected in everyone's face around headquarters," Sherrod wrote in his notebook late that afternoon. "The Japs' only chance is our getting soft, as they predicated their whole war on our being too luxury-loving to fight. Of this much I am certain: the Marines are not too soft to fight. More than three thousand of them are by this time assaulting pillboxes full of the loathsome bugs, digging them out." [42] It is about this time that Shoup sent the fleet his now famous situation report: "Casualties: Many. Percentage Dead: Unknown. Combat Efficiency: We Are Winning." [43]

On the evening of the second day, the 6th Marines began landing on Green Beach, with Mike Ryan's "orphans" providing cover. They came in across the heavily mined lagoon on rubber rafts, led by Ryan's good friend Major William Jones, the "Admiral of the Condom Fleet," his men called him. Beginning at dawn the next day, Jones's men moved slowly, but with violent effect, across the south coast of Betio, in the wilting heat, reducing one enemy stronghold after another. They took heavy hits from infantry in log and sand forts and from snipers who had tied themselves to the trunks of coconut trees, but they fought "like men who were anxious to get it over with," in Sherrod's vivid description. [44] Another battalion landed on Green Beach, and these fresh troops marched through Jones's depleted forces, "walking beside medium tanks which bored into the fading Japs."

With enemy resistance collapsing, Merritt "Red Mike" Edson, who had become a Marine Corps legend at Guadalcanal, came in to relieve an exhausted David Shoup as beach commander. With him came more tanks and other heavy armor. The tanks "had a field day with the Japs," Sherrod wrote later, and "armored half-tracks, mounting 75-mm. guns, paraded up and down Betio all day . . . pouring high explosives into pillboxes." Observing the progress his Marines were making, Edson smiled and said, "It won't last as long as Guadalcanal." [45]

In every part of the island, Marines found Japanese who chose suicide over surrender. The accepted way was to lie down, remove the split-toed jungle shoe from the right foot, put the barrel of an Arisaka rifle in the mouth, or up against the forehead, and squeeze the trigger with the big toe.

With most of the island under American control, the reporters went out to a

transport ship and began writing their stories on typewriters borrowed from the Navy.
Less than an hour after they left, the Japanese staged the first of a series of all-night
assaults on William Jones's thin front lines, culminating in an early morning banzai
charge, with the troops screaming "Marine you die!" and officers swinging samurai
swords. "We're killing them as fast as they come at us, but we can't hold out much
longer. We need reinforcements," the company commander pleaded with Jones on
the field phone. "We haven't got them," Jones replied. "You've got to hold." Supported by naval guns that fired within 500 yards of the American lines, the Marines
locked up in hand-to-hand combat with knives and bayonets. "Everyone got into the
fight," said Jones. "It was a madhouse." [46] The next morning, a stunned Marine with
bloodshot eyes crawled out of his foxhole, looked at the 300 or so massacred Japanese
lying around him, and said, "They told us we had to hold . . . and, by God, we held." [47]

Marine veteran William Manchester would write later: "At the time it was impolitic to pay the slightest tribute to the enemy, and [Japanese] determination, their refusal to say die, was commonly attributed to 'fanaticism.' In retrospect it is indistinguishable from heroism. To call it anything less cheapens the victory, for American valor was necessary to defeat it." [48]

These desperate attacks hastened the end of what could have been a prolonged battle had the Japanese decided to hold out in their bombproof bunkers. "I had a chance to walk the lines in front of my front lines," Major Jones recalls. "And tears came to my eyes because of all the dead Marines mingled with dead Japanese." Marine photographers came up and took moving pictures of the bodies. Then Jones called for the big gallon cans of "torpedo juice" (straight alcohol used by the Navy as torpedo fuel) that a sailor had given him back in New Zealand. "And we opened it up and had a cocktail party in one of the tank traps." [49]

The next day, November 23, 1943, the fighting ended. Betio was declared secured at 1312 hours on the fourth day. It had been seventy-five hours and forty-two minutes since the Marines had hit the beach. Makin was taken, with light casualties, on the same day, giving the Americans control of the Gilbert Islands. (At Makin, the Navy took most of the losses when the escort carrier *Liscome Bay* was torpedoed by an enemy submarine, sending 644 crewmen to their deaths.) What they had did not seem like much. "I'm on Tarawa in the midst of the worst destruction I've ever seen," a Marine officer wrote his wife. [50] But as Admiral Nimitz said, they had kicked open the door to the Japanese heartland. Already, Hellcats were landing on Betio's airstrip; and from there, reconnaissance planes would soon be flying over the Marshall Islands, gathering intelligence for the next Storm Landing.

THE DEAD OF TARAWA

At Tarawa, the Marines and Navy suffered 3,407 casualties. That was nearly 1 percent of the entire Marine Corps of 390,000 officers and men. Losses were similar at Guadalcanal, but "this was . . . worse than Guadalcanal," said the old Marine Raider Evans Carlson as the fighting wound down. "It was the damnedest fight I've seen in thirty years of this business." [51] Tarawa was a horror because the killing was so compressed in time and space. Marines were in Guadalcanal, a much larger island, for six months. They were at Tarawa four days, and the total acreage of Betio is only one-half square mile. In this compacted space there were almost 6,000 dead soldiers, enemy and American.

MARINE DEAD ON THE BEACHES OF TARAWA (USMC).

In an awful indication of the ferocity of the fighting, burial details were able to identify only half of the 997 dead Marines. The fighting was so brutal and continuous that the men had almost no time to eat or sleep. "There was just no way to rest; there was virtually no way to eat. Mostly it was close, hand-to-hand fighting and survival for three and a half days. It seemed like the longest period of my life," Major Carl Hoffman recalled.[52]

At Guadalcanal, the Japanese evacuated their forces when the cause became hopeless. On Betio, they left crack troops to fight and die. Only seventeen Japanese soldiers were captured. It wasn't an American victory; it was a small holocaust. Even the killing ground was massacred. There was nothing left standing on Betio but the blackened stumps of palm trees and the defiant walls of empty, blown-out blockhouses. The air was still, and the stink of death was in it.

When the correspondents came back to Betio at the end of the fighting their senses were assaulted. "As I walked up the pier, from the comparatively clean-smelling sea, the overwhelming smell of the dead hit me full in the face," Sherrod recalls, "and I vomited a little. By dark I was used to it again." No picture, he said, could capture the devastation of Betio. "You can't smell pictures."[53]

On the final day, Eddie Albert was back in the lagoon picking up marble white corpses that had been in the water for two days. "In the heat, they float very quickly in the warm water. And so I picked them up and took them back for a proper burial."[54] When the tide came in, it carried the mangled and swollen bodies of men who died off the reef. Corpsmen waded in and fished them out of the water and placed them on the sand. Some of the men had been in the water so long their hair had washed off. "I always expected them to lift their heads for air but they never did," said one Marine.[55]

The bodies were placed in a long line on the sand. Nearby, a man in a bulldozer prepared a large trench. The uncovered bodies were placed in it, and a chaplain performed the last rites. "The bulldozer pushes some more dirt in the Marines' faces and that is all there is to it. Then the bulldozer starts digging a second trench."[56]

It was high tide. Watching the water splash against the seawall to a depth of three feet, carrying the dead who were on the beach to the seawall itself, where they floated grotesquely, it struck Sherrod that the death tide of Tarawa might have saved more Marines than it killed. If the tide had come in earlier the invaders would not have had a beachhead on D-Day. They would have had to go over the seawall and into killing fire, or else back into the lagoon.

When the battle was over, Sherrod walked the island's perimeter, recording what he saw in his notebook. "Betio would be more habitable," he wrote, "if the Marines could leave for a few days and send a million buzzards in." [57] Meeting up with a group of generals who had come on the island to assess the damage, he spotted something that ennobled all this human savagery. It was a dead Marine, leaning forward against the seawall, with one upraised arm on it, supporting his body. Just beyond his hand, on the top of the wall, was a blue and white flag, a beach marker to designate the spot where his assault wave was to land. Looking at it, General Holland Smith said: "How can men like that ever be defeated?" [58]

Sherrod would say later: "If we ever fought a battle in which courage was the dominant factor, it was at Tarawa." [59]

When the Marines left the island, William Jones and his men had to stay behind to bury the Japanese who had killed so many of their friends. They buried them as their fellow Marines had been originally buried, in big trenches, the bodies stacked like the coconut logs of the Betio fortifications. "Then we unburied our dead," Jones recalls, "and put them on a ship to take them back to Honolulu. After the war, the Japanese came back and removed their dead for proper burial." [60]

Robert Sherrod left Tarawa convinced of something people back home did not want to hear: that there was no way to defeat the enemy except by extermination. In late 1943, when American production began to reach its fabulous potential, a lot of Americans expected the war to end soon, brought to a sudden conclusion by fire from the sky. We would bomb Germany and Japan back to the stone age; close combat would be unnecessary. Tarawa put the lie to this. The road from Tarawa to Tokyo would be one of the bloodiest campaigns in all of history, and every fight would be to the death. There would be no more enemy evacuations as at Kiska and Guadalcanal, a chilling thing to contemplate. "When I told my mother what the war was really like, and how long it was going to take, she sat down and cried," said a bomber pilot who returned home from the Pacific in 1943. "She didn't know we were just beginning to fight the Japs." [61] But how was this to be made known to the American public?

Sherrod and a number of others who covered the war believed the American people were being lied to. There were combat correspondents who filed unvarnished reports, but government censors and cooperating news agencies rewrote them, playing up the positive and shielding the public from the bloody harvest of the war. After Tarawa, Sherrod returned to an America that was "not prepared psychologically," he wrote, "to accept the cruel facts of war." [62]

Sherrod's stories in *Time* and *Life* gave the double-barreled bad news of Tarawa's butcher's bill and the certainty of higher costs to come. But it was the visual evidence that really struck home. Since World War I, the government had prohibited the media from showing pictures of dead American soldiers, even of bodies covered with blankets. This changed two months before Tarawa, when the head of the newly

THIS PHOTO OF A SHATTERED JAPANESE PILLBOX REVEALS THE
FEROCITY OF THE FIGHTING ON TARAWA (USMC).

created Office of War Information, Elmer Davis, the "Mount Everest" of radio news commentators, asked President Roosevelt to lift the ban on the publication of photographs of dead American soldiers. The public, Davis insisted, "had a right to be truthfully informed" about the war, subject to restraints dictated by military security. Roosevelt relented, and *Life* magazine led the way, publishing a photograph by George Strock of three dead American soldiers lying on a desolate beach at Buna. This provoked tremendous controversy, and readers and other news writers assailed *Life* for giving people more of the war than they could take, or for engaging in "morbid sensationalism." [63]

This was the situation when Norman Hatch returned from Tarawa with 3,700 feet of film. The Marines had imposed no censorship restrictions on photographers and correspondents at Betio; they had been free to document the battle as they witnessed it. Still, Hatch expected to run into trouble with the military censors. He was shocked when the Navy released all of his film to the newsreels. Theaters across the country began showing the first unrestricted combat shots that the American public had ever seen, and Hatch's name was put on the marquees. Hatch's footage was also used in a color-tinted documentary film the Marine Corps produced for general distribution. But the film, *With the Marines at Tarawa*, could not be released without Roosevelt's approval.

The President was in a quandary. Photographs of the carnage at Tarawa had already appeared in the press, along with a statement from Holland Smith that Tarawa was taken only because of the willingness of the assault forces to die.[64] This caused a storm of outrage, as did the release of the casualty lists. Why, people wondered, had American boys paid such a frightful price to take an obscure stand of coral that should have been blasted into oblivion. Was this some horrible intelligence blunder by the Navy? Some congressmen called for a special investigation, and Nimitz's office was flooded by mail from mothers who accused him of killing their sons.

Roosevelt had heard that the Tarawa film was graphic and wondered if the public was ready for it. On the other hand, the war bond drive was flagging, and a film like this, showing what America was up against in the Pacific, might give it a boost. Robert Sherrod helped the President make up his mind, as he recounted years later.

I WAS TOLD ABOUT THIS TARAWA film and allowed to see the rough cuts before it was edited. And they were pretty raw, pretty bloody. People didn't know the war was that bad.

I went to one of Roosevelt's press conferences and stayed afterward and had a chat with him, as I had done before many times during the war. He had been in Teheran meeting with Stalin and Churchill at the time of the Tarawa battle and they hadn't told him a great deal about it apparently, because he said to me, "Why didn't they use the battleship shells to blow up the island?" And [I told him] they had used the battleship shells. They used everything they had. Then the President said, "What about that movie they shot? I hear it's pretty raw, pretty rugged."

"Yes sir," I said. "That's the way it is out there." And I recommended that he release it.

The movie was shown. Not the rawest part, but enough to indicate that this is going to be a hard war to finish fighting in the next two years. [After] it was released, I saw the chief of public relations at Marine Corps headquarters, and he said, "What were the consequences of releasing that film? Enlistments fell off 35 percent." [65]

But war bond sales increased dramatically, the film won an Oscar in 1944 for best documentary, and the wide-angle photograph that Frank Filan shot on the first day from the beach, *Tarawa Island,* won a Pulitzer Prize. Like Mathew Brady's Civil War exhibition, "The Dead of Antietam," the film and photographs of Tarawa showed Americans on the home front a war they had not yet seen. In doing this, they helped strengthen public resolve for even grimmer struggles ahead. "We must steel ourselves now," the *New York Times* warned, "to pay [the] price." [66]

Tarawa, the first great test of Marine amphibious assault doctrine, rewrote the book on Storm Landings, pointing up the need for greater and more accurate naval gunfire and air bombardment, for frogmen and underwater demolition teams to clear obstacles and scout beaches and tides, for more and better-armed amphibious assault vehicles. [67] But the principal weapon on Tarawa needed no improving: a Marine wading ashore with his rifle at the ready.

Tarawa was the culmination of almost two decades of Navy and Marine Corps amphibious planning. "At Tarawa," wrote General A. A. Vandegrift, "we validated the principle of the amphibious assault, a tactic proclaimed impossible by many military experts. . . . Hereafter no matter what the strength of [the enemy's] bastion he could never feel secure. This was the real lesson of Tarawa." [68]

CHAPTER 4

Saipan

ITALY

While American Marines were storming the beaches of Betio in late November 1943, Ernie Pyle's foot-slogging infantry was fighting the mud, the snow, and the Germans in the forbidding mountains of central Italy, in a campaign that was as abysmally planned and ferociously fought as Tarawa. It was a campaign that had begun in controversy the previous summer.

With North Africa cleared and control of the waters of the Mediterranean assured in the late spring of 1942, the Allies prepared the first blow against Europe. The objective was not northern France, as the Americans had hoped, but what Churchill called Europe's "soft underbelly."

Sicily was the first target. One of the principal objectives of the Italian campaign would be to bring down the weakened regime of dictator Benito Mussolini, taking one of the three main Axis partners out of the war. The airfields at Foggia, in southwest Italy, would also enable Allied air forces to reach southern Germany and the vast oil fields of Romania, Hitler's chief source of crude oil. And an Allied offensive in Italy would force Hitler to divert combat divisions from the Russian front, relieving the pressure on Stalin's Red Army, which was bearing the overwhelming burden of the land war against Germany. The Italian campaign, which began with the invasion of Sicily from bases in North Africa in July 1943, achieved every one of these objectives, but at a terrible cost in lives. Italy also siphoned off men and resources that could have been used in the Pacific to hasten the surrender of Japan.

After taking Sicily, the Allied high command was convinced that the Germans would not commit to an all-out fight in Italy because of long supply lines and British-American mastery of the air in the Mediterranean basin. But when Mussolini was ousted in a palace coup and the new government signed an armistice with the Allies, an infuriated Hitler disarmed the Italian army, shipped off 600,000 Italian troops to slave labor camps in Germany, rescued Mussolini from his Italian captors in a daring airborne raid on a mountaintop hotel, and poured in massive reinforcements. The Germans held on for over 500 days, fighting a brilliant defensive campaign, not surrendering until May 2, 1945, the day the Berlin garrison capitulated, effectively ending the war in Europe.

The Italian campaign was, in reporter Robert Capa's words, a nightmare of "mud, misery, and death."[1] It was the longest campaign fought by the Western Allies and a horrid throwback to the useless bloodletting of World War I. The Allies would suffer 312,000 casualties, 188,000 of them Americans. The Germans would lose 435,000 men. But the largest loser was Italy itself. Museums, archives, cathedrals, archaeological treasures, and ancient monasteries were blasted and burned, and hundreds of towns were pulverzied beyond recognition, their half-starved survivors turned into war-shocked refugees.

The Allied forces invaded Italy on September 3, 1943. British General Bernard Montgomery's Eighth Army crossed the Strait of Messina from northern Sicily and advanced up the toe of the Italian boot, hoping to draw German troops away from the main invasion force, which was to land six days later at Salerno, just south of Naples. Lieutenant General Mark Clark's Fifth Army, a multinational force made up of troops from nearly every Allied nation, with Americans predominating, would make that landing. Montgomery was to push up from the south and link up with him.

The plan unraveled when Field Marshal Albert Kesselring guessed exactly where the Allies would land and was waiting for them in the hills overlooking the beachhead. And Montgomery was not there to help. He had been held up by German engineers, who were blowing up mountain roads and bridges along his tortuous line of advance.

On September 12 Kesselring made a slashing counteroffensive. When his panzer divisions smashed through the American lines, Clark considered calling in the Navy and evacuating the entire invasion force. But the Germans ran into overwhelming American artillery fire, causing them to pull back temporarily. Clark then got support from Allied airpower and Navy ship-to-shore fire—and from the 82nd Airborne Division, which made a perilous night drop on the beach. By September 15, the counterattack had lost its force and the Germans began an orderly withdrawal to the north. Clark's Fifth Army joined with Montgomery's Eighth, coming up from the south, and pursued them.

It had been a close call. Of all the American amphibious landings of the war, this one and Tarawa came nearest to failing. The Allies entered Naples on October 7, but the campaign turned into a bloody stalemate when the Germans retired to strong defenses in the mountains of central Italy. "Between Naples and Rome Mr. Winston Churchill's 'soft underbelly of Europe' was pregnant with hard mountains and well-placed German machine guns," wrote Robert Capa. "The valleys between the mountains were soon filled with hospitals and cemeteries."[2] By this time, Generals Montgomery, Patton, and Eisenhower had gone to England to prepare for the cross-Channel invasion, taking with them troops and military equipment that were desperately needed in Italy's murderous mountain combat. Relegated to a secondary role in the big strategic picture, Clark's men slogged ahead, wet, tired, and miserable, fighting on ridges of solid rock where Army mules were more valuable than jeeps and tanks.

THE MARSHALLS AND THE SOUTH PACIFIC

As Mark Clark's troops were battling the Germans in the rugged mountains south of Rome, halfway across the world calm, colorless Chester Nimitz was preparing to move on the Marshall Islands, only two months after taking Tarawa. This would be the necessary prelude to the decisive event in Nimitz's sweeping Central Pacific offensive: the invasion and conquest of Saipan, as important to victory over Japan as the Normandy invasion was to victory over Germany. The invasions took place within nine days of each other, and inaugurated a year of unprecedented car-

U.S. SOLDIER GIVES A WOUNDED JAPANESE A DRINK ON
KWAJALEIN, MARSHALL ISLANDS (SC).

nage for Americans—and in the Pacific, barbaric fighting fueled by racism and revenge. The final year of the war in the Pacific would be a death embrace with an
enemy determined never to surrender.

The Marshalls lay 500 miles north of Tarawa and about 1,000 miles east of the
Japanese naval base on the island of Truk. Kwajalein Atoll, at the center of the Marshall chain, was the main invasion target. Applying lessons learned at Tarawa, the
Americans used underwater demolition teams to destroy mines and beach obstacles,
and seized two nearby islets, placing heavy artillery on them, which, along with Navy
ships and planes, pounded the world's largest coral atoll into rubble. Only then did
the 4th Marine Division, seeing its first combat duty as a unit, and the Army's 7th Infantry Division, amphibian veterans of the Aleutian campaign, land on February 1.

COFFEE ABOARD SHIP FOR THE MARINE CONQUERORS OF
ENIWETOK ATOLL, MARSHALL ISLANDS (USMC).

The Marines went after the Japanese supply complex and airfield on the twin islands of Roi and Namur, at the northern end of the atoll, and the Army stormed Kwajalein, the main islet of the atoll.

This time the first wave of troops advanced to the beaches behind armored amphibious tractors equipped with machine guns and rocket launchers, and every troop-laden tractor had machine guns as well. The Japanese fought with predictable fury, suffering a casualty rate of over 98 percent, but by the fourth day, in a masterfully executed operation, Kwajalein Atoll was secured at a cost of 800 American lives out of an assault force of 53,000. Eniwetok Atoll, 326 miles to the west, was taken several weeks later, before the Japanese had time to build a formidable defense.

Nimitz's swift victories in the Marshalls and the Gilberts were made possible by the pressure of MacArthur's advance in northern New Guinea and the Solomons, which drew the Japanese fleet away from the Central Pacific just before the invasion of Tarawa. This was an unexpected dividend of the divided American command structure in the Pacific.[3]

In the steaming jungles of the South Pacific—at New Georgia, Bougainville, Biak, and other places—American and Australian forces fought small, desperate battles of annihilation as savage as Tarawa, and in even viler terrain and weather. There were no cities, or even large towns, only small, isolated settlements; maps were primitive or nonexistent; and there was not a single decent road in all of New Guinea and the Solomons, where the combined wartime population barely reached two and a half million. And because it was so difficult to see the enemy in the dark, enclosing jungle, or to move heavy military equipment through its wretched terrain, most fighting was at close quarter. "In no theater of war during the twentieth century did infantry experience as much combat at point-blank range as they found in the South Pacific," writes historian Eric Bergerud.[4]

The jungle itself caused as much human harm as the enemy. The pitiless heat and suffocating humidity broke the spirits and stamina of strong men; fetid tidal swamps, thick with crocodiles, were breeding basins for mosquito-borne diseases; and the high, interwoven canopy of forest growth—great trees that seemed to reach to the sky—shut out the light, casting men into a perpetual darkness that drove some of them crazy. Soldiers and Marines went for weeks without seeing either the sun or the stars; and everywhere there was the smell of death and decay from rotting bodies and vegetation. "In the jungle, we were enveloped by a matted tangled tree canopy, 200 feet or so up," an Australian soldier described the upland jungle of Papua. "Thorn vines descended. Beneath us on the track was a slimy ooze of stinking death. The smell of bodies from both sides decaying just below fungus level. Buried just to the side of the track, they leaked their filth into the mash of mud and millions-of-years-old root systems that covered the ground. It drove some of our less strong soldiers to total nervous breakdown and weeping frustration."[5]

Then there were the incessant rains. "The swamp and mud were knee deep at times," Marine Charles Meacham recalls of his service on Bougainville. "On occasion when we were quote 'sleeping' at night, sometimes we'd have to hold our buddy's head up in our lap as he slept because you were floating in mud and water. When it came your time to sleep, he'd hold your head up."[6]

In this terrain, and under these conditions, opposing armies fought the most savage light-infantry war ever waged by modern industrial nations, a war without rules or restraint, one in which the Japanese suffered even more than Allied soldiers.[7] With their supply lines severed by American air and naval power, they died in staggering numbers from disease and starvation.

With death upon them, some desperate men resorted to cannibalism. "There was absolutely nothing to eat, and so we decided to draw lots," recalled a Japanese army lieutenant. "But the one who lost started to run away so we shot him. He was eaten. . . .

"All we dreamed about was food. I met some soldiers in the mountains who were carrying baked human arms and legs. It was not guerrillas but our own soldiers who we were frightened of."[8]

Moving into a position evacuated by the enemy on Noemfoor Island, off the coast of northern New Guinea, Chester Nycum of the 503rd Parachute Infantry Regiment spotted the body of his company's scout lying on the ground. "It had been carved as though he were a piece of beef. All the flesh was gone from his legs, buttocks, and chest, and his heart and kidneys were missing. We had no doubt that they were eating our dead. We vowed right then never to take another prisoner!"[9]

The greater the desperation of the enemy the more dangerous he became, in the eyes of American soldiers, who lived in terrible fear of Japanese night attacks on their positions. Private First Class David C. Krechel was at Aitape, on the northern coast of New Guinea, when a Japanese soldier crept into the headquarters for his regiment and decapitated a radio operator with a sword blow. The next night Krechel was sleeping in a hammock strung between two towering coconut trees when he was awakened by a sharp pain in his legs. "I thought I had lost my legs because I figured a Jap had come up with his sword and chopped my legs off at the knees. . . . I lay there scared to death, afraid to move. I didn't want him to swing again. . . . [Then] the numbness wore off and I was able to reach down and feel that I had legs. . . . I didn't know what happened. But you didn't dare to get out of where you slept. If you got up and moved around you got shot. So there was nothing I could do but wait till morning. [When] I got up the next morning, here's this coconut lying right across the top of my shins."[10]

THE MARIANAS

Control of the Gilberts and Marshalls, and shortly after, the Admiralty Islands to the west, just north of Rabaul, which were seized by MacArthur's forces, enabled

Task Force 58, the striking arm of Admiral Raymond Spruance's Fifth Fleet, to deliver devastating blows at Japanese air and naval bases in the area. In mid-February, Admiral Marc Mitscher's air fleet destroyed over 200 planes and sank 200,000 tons of merchant shipping in two days of nonstop raids on Truk.

With Truk neutralized, as Rabaul had been, Task Force 58 steamed with impunity into the waters of the Marianas, only 1,300 miles from Tokyo. "The Marianas are the key of the situation," Admiral King declared, "because of their location on the Japanese line of communications between the home islands and the empire.[11] King and Nimitz were convinced that Japan could be brought down by economic strangulation. American naval bases in the Marianas would quicken the inevitable, depriving Japan of the oil, rubber, rice, iron, and other commodities essential to wage modern warfare.

General Henry Harold "Hap" Arnold, commander of the Army Air Forces, had another idea. The Air Force would defeat Japan, as it expected to defeat Germany, with long-range strategic bombing, the executing instrument a fearsome weapon just off the assembly line, the B-29 Superfortress, the world's first intercontinental bomber. The air barons had originally intended to deploy these "Superforts" almost exclusively from bases in China, but Chiang Kai-shek's inability to contain Japanese incursions in the area of the airfields made the Marianas a better location. From long island airstrips, American bombers could, in the words of George Marshall, "set the paper cities of Japan on fire."[12] With the capture of the Marianas, the Navy and Air Force together could apply overwhelming power, making a costly land invasion of the home islands unnecessary, in the opinion of both Nimitz and Arnold. Three tremendous weapons of war—the aircraft carrier, the long-range submarine, and the Superfortress—would finish off the enemy by blockade and bombardment. But as journalist Robert Sherrod wrote, "No man who saw Tarawa . . . would agree that all the American steel was in the guns and bombs. There was a lot, also, in the hearts of the men who stormed the beaches."[13]

With the capture of the Marshalls, the war of the coral atolls ended. "We are through with the flat atolls . . ." declared General Holland Smith. "Now we are up against mountains and caves where the Japs can really dig in. A week from now there will be a lot of dead Marines."[14] The principal targets in the Marianas—Guam, Saipan, and Tinian—were large volcanic islands with developed infrastructures of sugar plantations and towns. Tinian was relatively flat, but Saipan and Guam, which had been an American possession since the 1880s, had a varied, luxuriant topography, much like Hawaii's, with flat sugarcane fields, precipitous cliffs, jungle-carpeted mountains, and "big rawboned valleys."[15] Unlike Tarawa, all three islands had sizable native populations—on Saipan, mostly Japanese immigrants. But like Tarawa, all were strongly defended, especially Saipan. It was Tojo's Pacific bastion, and he assured the Emperor it was invincible.

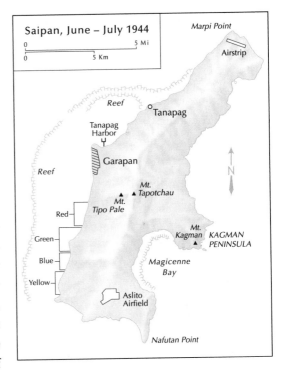

Saipan, June – July 1944

0   5 Mi
0   5 Km

Marpi Point
Airstrip
Reef
Tanapag
Tanapag Harbor
Garapan
Reef
Mt. Tapotchau
Mt. Tipo Pale
Red
Mt. Kagman   KAGMAN PENINSULA
Green
Blue
Magicienne Bay
Yellow
Aslito Airfield
Nafutan Point
N

There were nearly 40,000 Japanese troops on Saipan, about 6,000 of them Marines under the command of Vice Admiral Chuichi Nagumo, the hero of Pearl Harbor, who had been sent to the Marianas after being disgraced at Midway. The island's army commander, Lieutenant General Yoshitsugu Saito, was under orders from Tokyo to hold Saipan until the Imperial Fleet arrived from the Philippines with the intention of driving off and destroying the American carrier force.

Saito had every muzzle trained on the reef the Americans would come over. The island's defense system, however, was not nearly as formidable as it could have been. American submarines had been conducting an effective interdiction campaign against supply and troop transports headed for Saipan, sinking ships laden with men and tanks, cement and steel. After Saipan was taken, a Japanese prisoner claimed that if the American assault had come three months later the island "would have been impregnable."[16]

When Marc Mitscher's Task Force 58 sailed from Majuro in the Marshall Islands to launch the Marianas operation, it took nearly five hours to clear the lagoon. The armada of 800 ships, nearly 1,000 planes, 100,000 sailors and aviators, and 127,000 troops, two thirds of them Marines, would be almost as large as the one assembled for the Normandy D-Day landings. "I was at sea on an amphibious assault vehicle, on the 7th of June, when word reached us of the Allied landing at Normandy," recalls Marine officer Edwin Simmons. "From the deck, as far as I could see, were the gray shapes of hundreds of Navy ships plodding in convoy toward their targets in the Marianas. I had a realization then of the overwhelming strength of our country—that we could do this at the same time that we were landing in Normandy and reopening a front in Europe."

The joint expeditionary force was under the command of Admiral Richmond Kelly Turner, nicknamed Terrible Turner for his volcanic temper. This was his fifth major amphibious operation, going back to Guadalcanal. The expeditionary troops were under General Holland "Howlin' Mad" Smith, who while perhaps not as brilliant as Turner, was equally irascible. "The two men struck sparks like flint against steel," Simmons says. But their partnership, "though stormy, spelled hell in bold red letters for the Japanese." [17]

There was a thunderous preliminary bombardment, but naval guns were unable to destroy vital targets on the large mountainous island, where the enemy hid in caves and "spider holes." As Admiral Nimitz said later, "The enemy met the assault operations with pointless bravery, inhuman tenacity, cave fighting, and the will to lose hard." [18]

Here, unlike Tarawa, the reef would not be a problem. Underwater demolition teams had scouted the conditions of the reef, the currents, and the beach, and had blown up concrete and steel landing obstacles, taking sixteen casualties in this perilous operation. On the clear, windless morning of June 15, strong surf pounded over the reef, its sound blocked out by the rumbling of the big battleship guns. Over the loudspeaker of the transport that carried Robert Sherrod to yet another Pacific D-Day came the chaplain's voice: "With the help of God we will succeed. . . . Most of you will return, but some of you will meet the God who made you. . . . Repent your sins." [19] When they heard this, more than a few men winced.

After the signal went up from the flagship, over 700 Alligators [LVTs] went tearing ashore, ninety-six abreast in every wave, many of them with turret-mounted cannons. They poured out of what looked to a Japanese defender "like a large city that had suddenly appeared off shore," and by nightfall they had carried 20,000 men to the beach. [20] The Alligators were to press inland almost a mile in a coordinated, four-mile-wide blitz, securing a strong defensive position to shield the beach. But their thin skin of armor could not stand up to the heavy Japanese guns, and they were cut to pieces, big plates of steel flying everywhere as they tried to cross the beach.

From their hiding places on the shoreline cliffs the Japanese put down a deadly line of fire on the beaches. That first night and the next day Major William Jones's unit, heroes at Tarawa, helped to hurl back three enemy counterattacks, one of them a spectacular tank assault—the largest of the island war in the Pacific—which they broke apart with bazookas, naval fire, and their own "Steel Goliaths." It was the "damned artillery and mortars," veterans would say later, that made Saipan so tough to take; that and the rugged terrain—steep gorges and cliffs and a spine of volcanic mountains culminating in towering Mount Tapotchau. "Down our throats came this avalanche of artillery fire," recalls rifle platoon leader John C. Chapin, who had just graduated from Yale with honors in history.

THE SHELLS HIT AHEAD, BEHIND, ON both sides, and right in our midst. They would come rocketing down with a freight-train roar and then explode with a deafening cataclysm that is beyond description. . . . We had no place to

SAIPAN. MARINES UNDER ENEMY FIRE ON THE BEACH (U.S. NAVAL INSTITUTE).

go. We had no foxholes. It was right out of the blue. Later we realized that sitting up on Mount Tapotchau, 1,554 feet high, Japanese observers had preregistered every possible location before we landed. . . . They were zeroed in on us and were hitting us with pinpoint accuracy.

All around us was the chaotic debris of . . . combat: Jap and Marine bodies lying in mangled and grotesque positions; blasted and burnt-out pillboxes; the burning wrecks of LVTs that had been knocked out by Jap high-velocity fire; the acrid smell of high explosives; the shattered trees; and the churned-up sand littered with discarded equipment.[21]

Circling offshore in General Red Mike Edson's LVT, listening to the radio reports from the beach, Robert Sherrod penciled in his notebook, "looks like a real crisis."[22]

One of the first of over 1,500 casualties on the beach was Jim Crowe, the Tarawa iron man. He and his aide were hit coming in, and Crowe was in agony with a severe sucking wound near his heart. "I thought I was dying," he later described his final hour in combat. "And I thought maybe I'd better take a little interest in things. So I put my carbine in my hand [and] put my fist in this hole, which the doctors said saved me. . . . D'Natilly, my corporal, lying there, pulled his left arm up and looked at his wristwatch. And I said, 'Why are you looking at your wristwatch, Bill?'

"He said, 'Sir, I want to see what time I die.'"

A corpsman and a surgeon bent over them to try to help. "But then a shell hit down around my knees [and] just laid [the corpsman] wide open . . . and everything in him flew out against me." The doctor also got hit, but survived, and Crowe took some shrapnel in one leg. Then a shell hit a tree right next to his head and wounded him further in the arm and wrist. "So I got up and left. I wasn't going to stay there any longer."[23] Norman Hatch, the Marine Corps photographer, says that "Crowe had made a $20 bet with the division surgeon that if he got hit, no matter where, he would get to the aid station. Spotting his big red handlebar mustache, men on the beach offered to help him, but he insisted on walking, holding himself together with one hand while firing his carbine at snipers. When he got to the aid station, he barked at the surgeon, 'Give me my twenty bucks.'"[24]

As Sherrod and Edson passed the battalion aid station, they spotted Crowe sitting in a shell hole, heavily bandaged and "breathing hard," waiting to be evacuated. The surgeon administering morphine looked up and murmured, "not much chance,

I'm afraid." But Crowe refused to accept the verdict. "I hate like hell for this to happen, General," he told Edson in a clear voice, "but I'll be all right." Then he turned to Sherrod, "I'll see you stateside. We'll throw a whizdinger." [25] Crowe survived, but he and Sherrod never did meet again. Crowe's battalion was taken over by another hero at Tarawa, the bespectacled, soft-spoken economics professor from Northwestern University, Major William Chamberlin.

Some of the stretcher-bearers at the battalion aid station that day were the first African-American Marines to see combat in the war. The United States Marine Corps had not accepted blacks since 1798 and had hoped to fight World War II as an all-white organization. "If it were a question of having a Marine Corps of 5,000 whites or 250,000 Negroes, I would rather have the whites," said the defiant Marine Corps Commandant, Major General Thomas Holcomb. [26] But under mounting pressure from President Roosevelt, the resolutely segregationist Marines had been forced to accept black volunteers and, later, draftees. The Corps formed and trained two Defense Battalions, the 51st and 52nd, and made sure they never saw combat, assigning them to outposts far in the rear of the Central Pacific advance. Ironically, it was the African-American Marines who were not trained for combat who saw heavy action all across the Pacific, beginning, 800 strong, on the beaches of Saipan. These were laborers in military support units.

As soldiers and Marines swept ashore on D-Day, African-American depot and ammunition companies, standing knee-deep in surf, with mortar shells raining down on them, offloaded shells, food, and water from landing vehicles and hustled them to front-line troops. When they were shot at, they returned fire with rifles and machine guns they picked up on the beach. "My company landed about 2 P.M. on D-Day," Captain William C. Adams, commander of the 20th Marine Depot Company, told a combat correspondent. "We were the third wave, and all hell was breaking when we came in. It was still touch and go when we hit shore, and it took some time to establish a foothold.

"My men performed excellently. . . . Among my own company casualties, my orderly was killed." [27]

The orderly was Private Kenneth J. Tibbs of Columbus, Ohio, the first black Marine killed in combat in World War II. Later that afternoon, Private Leroy Seals of Brooklyn, New York, was mowed down. He died the following day. Coming into the beach, four men of an African-American depot company were wounded by mortar fire and had to be evacuated, but the others went in, found guns, and fought as infantry, helping to maintain a precariously held position and to kill enemy infiltrators. The next day, they evacuated hundreds of wounded men to a hospital ship offshore, and under heavy rifle fire they "rode guard on trucks carrying high octane gasoline from the beach." [28]

"The Negro Marines are no longer on trial," said the new Commandant, Alexander A. Vandegrift, leader of the Guadalcanal invasion. "They are Marines, period." [29] It would have been good if it were true, but throughout the war African-American Marines continued to be treated as separate and unequal.

That first night the Marines and Army reinforcements were pinned to the sand, but there was never any doubt that the landing would succeed. The Americans were here in greater numbers and with more firepower than at Tarawa. Still, in the words

DEAD JAPANESE SOLDIERS ON THE BEACH AT SAIPAN (USMC).

of one Marine, "There is something definitely terrifying about the first night on a hostile beach. No matter what superiority you may boast in men and matériel, on that first night you're the underdog, and the enemy is in a position to make you pay through the nose."[30]

THE BATTLE OF THE PHILIPPINE SEA

That evening Admiral Spruance got word that the Japanese fleet was steaming toward Saipan. The newly assembled First Mobile Fleet, with almost every warship in the Japanese Navy, had been sighted by American submarines in the Philippine Sea, that part of the Pacific Ocean between the Philippines and the Marianas. Its commander, Vice Admiral Jisaburo Ozawa, had sailed out to slaughter the American landing forces and destroy the United States Pacific Fleet "with one blow."[31] For the still confident Japanese high command, this would be the decisive naval battle that would bring the Americans to the peace table. "Can it be that we'll fail to win with this mighty force?" a Japanese admiral wrote in his diary. "No! It cannot be."[32]

The U.S. Fifth Fleet had more firepower—fifteen carriers and over 900 warplanes—to Ozawa's nine carriers and 430 combat aircraft. But Ozawa was counting on using Japanese airfields in Guam to refuel and rearm his planes and hit the American carriers in a devastating shuttle action. Observing radio silence, Ozawa had no idea that Marc Mitscher's carrier planes had knocked out those airfields in preparation for the invasion of Saipan.

The fast-approaching Japanese fleet presented Spruance with an agonizing decision: to steam westward after Ozawa or to wait for him near Saipan while protecting the landing force, whose transports and cargo ships were still being unloaded. Remembering Guadalcanal, where the Navy had suffered the greatest defeat in its proud history after Frank Jack Fletcher's carrier fleet pulled out and abandoned the Marines, Spruance stayed in a covering position, against advice from the aggressive Marc Mitscher. "I will . . . try to keep the Japs off your neck," Spruance told Turner.

As Spruance sent out scout planes to search for the Japanese, he learned from Nimitz, at Pearl Harbor, that he was under the same imperative as Ozawa. "We count on you to make the victory decisive."[33]

Spruance put his carriers and battlewagons in a blocking position to the west of Saipan, out of sight of the fighting men on the beaches. "Those of us on the ground of course knew nothing [of the impending naval battle]," says John Chapin. "The

NAVY GUNNERS STAVE OFF JAPANESE AERIAL ATTACK (NA).

morning when [we] turned and looked out to the sea and saw that this vast fleet was gone—the sea was empty—I want to tell you, that's a sinking feeling." [34]

Ozawa's search planes found Mitscher's fleet on the afternoon of June 18. Mitscher wanted to push out into combat range, but Spruance doubled back toward Saipan to prevent a Japanese force from passing him in the night and hammering the beachhead. The next day, Ozawa launched four massive raids against Task Force 58. With the enemy air fleet closing in from 130 miles, the old circus rallying cry of "Hey, Rube!" went up, and fighters scrambled and flew west to meet the threat. This would be the greatest carrier battle of World War II, with almost four times the forces engaged at Midway. But with the inexperienced, poorly trained Japanese pilots outnumbered and fighting superior Hellcats, it was less a battle than an eight-hour aerial massacre. Ozawa lost 373 planes to the Americans' thirty. The pilots called it "The Great Marianas Turkey Shoot." But it was more than a fighter fight. Torpedoes from submarines *Albacore* and *Cavalla* sent two Japanese carriers to the bottom of the Philippine Sea.

One of the last of the planes to return to the USS *Lexington* was Lieutenant Stanley Vraciu's F6F Hellcat. As his fighter screeched to a stop on the carrier deck, he pulled back the canopy, looked up at Mitscher standing on the deck with his long-billed lobsterman's cap pulled low over his tanned face, and held up six fingers. Six kills! "The skill, initiative and intrepid courage of the young aviators made this day one of the high points in the history of the American spirit," writes Admiral Samuel Eliot Morison.[35]

"Now," says Morison, "the hunter became the hunted."[36] The next day the thin, leather-faced Mitscher sent three carriers after the crippled but still dangerous Japanese fleet. Scout planes failed to locate the enemy's position until 5:40 in the afternoon, but Mitscher, aware of the extreme risks of a night raid, launched 216 planes from ten carriers in an astonishing ten minutes. "Give 'em hell, boys; wish I were with you," he told them before the cry went out to "Man Aircraft!"[37]

At 6:40, after flying almost 300 miles, they spotted the Japanese fleet. With the setting sun barely touching the horizon and the sky splendid with brilliant orange and red clouds, the Hellcats struck. They sank the carrier *Hiyo* and blasted from the night sky another sixty-five enemy planes, while losing only twenty of their own, in an engagement that has been called the Battle of the Philippine Sea. This left the retreating Ozawa with only thirty-five out of the 430 planes he had had in his command on the morning of June 19.

The dusk raiders who smashed Ozawa's fleet now faced a new danger. They had begun this mission knowing they had only a slim chance of returning because the Japanese carriers had been spotted at the maximum range of their planes. And after they had taken off they learned that Ozawa was sixty miles further west than first reported. Now, after a fuel-draining attack, they had to fly back over 250 to 300 miles of ocean on a moonless night to the blackened fleet. The ships' lights had been turned out to avoid detection by Japanese submarines. Many of the pilots were dizzy with fatigue and none of them had been trained to land on a carrier at night.

When the gas-starved planes came within range, the group commander of four carriers, Rear Admiral Joseph "Jocko" Clark, turned on the deck lights and pointed searchlights into the sky to act as homing beacons. Mitscher ordered all of Task Force 58 to do the same, a decision that Clark considered "one of the war's supreme moments."[38] A pilot who was sent up in a night-fighting Hellcat to help guide the planes home said the scene was like "a Hollywood premiere, Chinese New Year's and Fourth of July rolled into one."[39]

Lieutenant E. J. Lawson, returning to the *Enterprise,* saw plane after plane go plunging into the sea. Almost half the planes landed on the wrong carriers; one plane tried to land on a red-lit destroyer and had to veer off at the last second and splash into the sea. Pilots and crewmen were scattered all over the waters around the gigantic fleet, blowing the boatswain's whistles they carried for such emergencies and "blinking their little waterproof flashlights." [40] All but forty-nine pilots and crewmen were recovered by the end of the next day.

Although neither the Navy nor the Army recognized it at the time, this great sea battle was yet another vindication of America's "double-thrust" strategy in the Pacific. [41] The American victory in the Philippine Sea, part of Nimitz's Central Pacific offensive, made it impossible for the Japanese to give full attention to MacArthur's final drive up the coast of New Guinea, toward the Philippines.

TAKING SAIPAN

Back on Saipan, the ground troops had no idea that this battle had been fought and won, reducing the options of the island defenders to death by one of two ways: at the enemy's hands or by their own. As the Americans gathered up their strength and moved off the beach, the Japanese fell back into a hastily organized defense in depth, using the terrain to advantage. They burrowed into caves all over the islands, and from Mount Tapotchau they poured down fire on the advancing Marines and Army infantry.

Private Robert F. Graf describes the system for flushing Japanese soldiers out of caves:

QUITE OFTEN THERE WOULD BE MULTI-CAVE openings, each protecting another. Laying down heavy cover fire, our specialist would advance to near the mouth of the cave. A satchel charge would then be heaved into the mouth of the cave, followed by a loud blast as the dynamite exploded. Other times it might be grenades thrown inside the cave, both fragment type, which exploded sending bits of metal all throughout the cave, and other times [white] phosphorous grenades that burned the enemy.

Also the flame thrower was used, sending a sheet of flame into the cave, burning anyone that was in its path. Screams could be heard and on occasions the enemy would emerge from the caves, near the entrance. We would call upon

MARINES HURLING HAND GRENADES AT ENTRENCHED
JAPANESE SOLDIERS ON SAIPAN (USMC).

the tanks, and these monsters would get in real close and pump shells into the openings.[42]

The cave teams had to be on guard for snipers in nearby trees, or for Japanese who "played possum," as one Marine related, "by smearing blood of other Japs [we had killed] on themselves and lying still as [we] came up. However, within the battalion my instructions were, 'If they didn't stink, stick it.'"[43]

Of the approximately 29,000 civilians on the island, 22,000 were Japanese, the

A MARINE FINDS A WOMAN AND CHILDREN
HIDDEN IN A CAVE IN SAIPAN (USMC).

vast majority of them from the prefecture of Okinawa. There were also Korean slave laborers, and Kanaka and Chamorros people, the original inhabitants. The local natives surrendered willingly, but some Japanese and Koreans hid in caves. American soldiers often put their own lives on the line to try to help them. "The thing that really got to me," said one Marine officer, "was watching these boys of mine; they'd take all kinds of risks; they'd go into a cave never knowing whether there would be soldiers in there, to bring out these civilians. The minute they got them out, they began to feed them, give them part of their rations, and offer their cigarettes to the men. It made you feel proud of the boys for doing this." [44]

But as the Americans began to lose friends in these cave operations, and as water supplies grew short and polluted, forcing some men to chew on napalmed sugarcane stalks to try to kill their thirst, distinctions were often not made between armed resisters and defenseless civilians. The troops learned a Japanese phrase, which translated loosely meant: throw your rifle away and come out with your hands up. "We tried this," recalls John Chapin, "[and] I never got anybody to come out."[45] If a flamethrower was called for, the people inside the cave, who had learned the English word for it, would usually kill themselves. The cave would then be sealed by a bulldozer.

When sick and scared civilians did come out of their hideouts, there were some heart-tearing scenes. A captured Japanese woman who was crying uncontrollably approached Robert Graf and began hitting him on the arm and pointing to his pack. "I

A MARINE ESCORTS AN ELDERLY SAIPAN WOMAN AND
CHILDREN IN HER CARE TO AN INTERNMENT DEPOT (NA).

didn't know what she wanted until an interpreter came over and explained that she wanted some food and water for her dead child. She pointed to a wicker basket that contained her dead infant. I gave her what she requested, and she placed the food and water in the basket so that the child could have nourishment on the way to meet [its] ancestors.

"Every illness that we had been briefed on was observed: leprosy, dengue fever, yaws, and many cases of elephantiasis. Most of them were skeleton-thin, as they had no nourishment for many days. Many were suffering from shock caused by the shelling and bombing, and fright because they did not have the vaguest idea as to what we would do to them."

This is a part of the Pacific War few historians deal with, "civilians," in Graf's words, "caught in a war that was not of their making." [46]

Some injured women and children found their way to a small American field hospital, where they were taken care of by ten Navy nurses led by First Lieutenant Birdie B. Daigle. "We found Saipan a scorched island with many killed and wounded," Daigle wrote in her diary. "All buildings had been completely demolished and the populace had taken a horrible blow. . . . We worked, day and night, behind the lines. . . . During the day we tended civilians, at night servicemen became our patients. I wish the people at home could have seen the results of war bombardments on those civilians. . . .

"At first we had so many wounded to take care of, and so few facilities, the job seemed too tremendous. Sometimes we felt like crying. It was just that we needed so much in order to do our best work." [47]

On June 23, after capturing the main towns, airfields, and strongholds in the southern half of the island, Marine and Army troops launched a great three-division drive to clear the island of all resistance. It would be a desperate fight. The Japanese commanders on Saipan had just received a message from Tojo: "If Saipan is lost, air raids on Tokyo will take place often; therefore you will hold Saipan." [48]

Holland Smith spread his forces across the entire middle of Saipan, from east to west, and ordered them to push northward with resolve. The Marines moved on the right and left flanks and the Army's 27th Division, a New York National Guard unit, took the center, fighting slowly and in disorganized fashion through some of the toughest terrain on the island. The plodding movement of the 27th, which had not fought well at either Makin or Kwajalein, incensed Holland Smith, for it dangerously exposed his Marines on the flanks. After a sharp warning to the commander of the 27th, Major General Ralph Smith, and a consultation with Spruance, he relieved Ralph Smith, setting off an interservice feud that continued long after the war. "Ralph Smith is my friend," Holland Smith told Sherrod later that day, "but, good God, I've got a duty to my country."[49] Nimitz, a diplomat as well as a warrior, was not sympathetic. He made sure Holland Smith never again held an active combat command.

On June 25 the Marines took Mount Tapotchau, a turning point in the battle. There was no celebration; everyone realized that the island would not be taken until nearly every Japanese soldier had been killed. General Saito, wounded and cornered

A LONE MARINE WATCHES FROM HIS FOXHOLE AS A MARINE FLAMETHROWING TANK FIRES ON A JAPANESE PILLBOX (USMC).

in the cave that served as his command post, sent a final message to his troops, imploring them to follow him in a sacrificial charge against the enemy. In another island cave, Admiral Nagumo sent a similar message to his sailors and Marines. But neither the general nor the admiral went forth to lead his troops. Nagumo put a bullet in his brain. Saito fell on his ceremonial sword but failed to strike cleanly. Writhing in agony, he was finished off by a pistol shot from his adjutant.

The final fight, the most fearsome banzai charge of the Pacific war, came at 4:30 in the morning on July 7, 1944. Over 3,000 screaming Japanese soldiers and sailors broke through a gap in the lines of the 27th Division. Some had rifles, grenades, and mortars, but many carried only clubs, rocks, swords, and rusty bayonets wired to bamboo sticks. After this "human storm" overran elements of two Army battalions, a second wave came through and killed the wounded. Those Japanese soldiers who remained hit three artillery battalions of the 10th Marines and were blown to pieces at point-blank range by 105mm howitzers, but not before overrunning twelve guns, engaging in hand-to-hand combat with artillery gunners and reinforcements, and blowing up an ambulance that tried to evacuate the wounded. "It reminded me," said an American officer, "of one of those old cattle stampede scenes of the movies. The camera is in a hole in the ground and you see the herd coming and then they leap up and over you and are gone. Only the Japs kept coming and coming. I didn't think they'd ever stop." [50]

Later that day, the Marines gathered up their dead. Lying on the field when Sherrod arrived was Major William L. Crouch, commander of the Marine battalion. His helmet and carbine were close to his body and near his hand were two letters from home, which he was probably trying to read as he bled to death. In a field not far away, the shattered bodies of the enemy were being stacked three feet high. Sherrod wrote in his notebook, "They are thicker here than at Tarawa." [51]

Mitsuharu Noda, a paymaster for Admiral Nagumo, survived this grisly fight:

ABOUT TWENTY MEMBERS OF [NAGUMO'S] headquarters participated in the final battle. We drank the best Japanese whiskey—Suntory Square Bottle, we'd saved it to the last minute. We smoked our last tobacco—Hikari brand. We were even able to smile. Maybe because we were still together as a group. . . .

On July 7 at 4 A.M., shouting all together, we headed toward the enemy camp. . . . We were not going to attack enemies. We were ordered to go there to be killed. Some probably may have gone drunk, just to overcome fear, but that last taste of Suntory whiskey was wonderful. It was a kind of suicide. We didn't crawl on the ground, though bullets were coming toward us. We advanced standing up.

We had hardly any arms. Some had only shovels, others had sticks. I had a pistol. I think I was shot at the second line of defense. Hit by a machine gun, two bullets in my stomach, one passing through, one lodging in me. I didn't suffer pain. None at all. But I couldn't stand either. I was lying on my back. I could see the tracer bullets passing over. This is it, I thought.

Then I saw a group of four or five men, Japanese, crawling toward each other on their hands and knees. Their heads were now all close together. One of them held a grenade upward in his right hand and called out an invitation to me: "Hey, sailor there! Won't you come with us?" I said, "I have a grenade. Please go ahead."

I heard "Long live the emperor!" and the explosion of a hand grenade at the same instant. Several men were blown away, dismembered at once into bits of flesh. I held my breath at this appalling sight. Their heads were all cracked open and smoke was coming out. It was a horrific way to die. Those were my thoughts as I lost consciousness.[52]

After this, the fight went out of the enemy. They waited in their holes to die or committed hara-kiri with knives or grenades—or by drowning themselves in the sea. (Before this battle only about 600 Japanese had been captured by all of the Allied powers.)[53]

On July 9 the battle was over, although here, as on every other island in the Central Pacific, there was no surrender. It would take over a year to kill or capture the Japanese who remained hidden in caves.

The Battle of Saipan lasted twenty-four days and the cost was steep—16,525 American casualties, including 3,426 killed or missing, more casualties than Americans had suffered in any previous Pacific battle. Only 921 Japanese of a garrison of nearly 40,000 were taken prisoner. Approximately 14,500 civilians were put into an internment camp, where they would live when they were not working on construction projects.

The Japanese, Koreans, and native peoples were each put in separate, fenced-in sections. Each racial group appointed its own police force to keep order and patrol its perimeter.[54]

While the camp was being set up, and the dead were being buried, American wounded were being taken out to hospital and troop ships anchored offshore. One of

A U.S. STOCKADE CAMP ON SAIPAN (USMC).

the four hospital ships was the *Solace,* which had taken in the wounded in the attack on Pearl Harbor. When Robert Sherrod went on board to gather material for a story, *Solace* had just returned from Guadalcanal for a second shipload of patients. The hospital ships were painted pure white, and the doctors, nurses, and corpsmen wore "spotless white. . . . Everything about the ship was intended to make the wounded man forget about mud and foxholes . . . and the whine of artillery."

Each ship had beds for 480 men, but there were so many wounded at Saipan that patients were put on cots, sofas, and the bunks of ship's personnel. Still, there was not enough space. Only one in five of the wounded could be taken aboard hospital ships. The rest, except for a few evacuated by planes, "sweated it out on the crowded bunks of transports."

The types of wounds the men suffered described the nature of the battle. At Tarawa, 57 percent of the *Solace*'s cases had been bullet wounds. At Saipan, artillery and mortars caused 65 percent of the wounds, and there were five times as many wounds caused by bayonets and knives. Saipan had been an artillery fight, punctuated by brutal, close-in fighting and more and larger banzai charges than veterans in the Pacific had ever experienced. And because it was a far longer battle than Tarawa, there were many more cases of combat fatigue. The disorder was treated as callously here as it was in Europe. A third of the men suffering from combat fatigue in the early fighting were returned to shore with only one or two days' rest.

The *Solace* had a crew of seventeen doctors, 175 corpsmen, and seventeen nurses. "Until long after the Saipan battle, the Central Pacific campaign," Sherrod wrote, "was a womanless war except for the nurses aboard the hospital ships [and in a few field hospitals]. They were a source of curiosity for men who had not seen a woman in months or years." [55]

DEAD JAPANESE TROOPS ON TINIAN
AFTER A BANZAI CHARGE (USMC).

That was one of the major differences between the war here and in Europe, along with the climate and the incredible distances between the battlefields, often a thousand miles and more, with nothing but water in between. Fighting men felt isolated in the Pacific as they rarely did in Europe, where there were nearby civilizations like their own. "And another adjustment I'll have to make," wrote Ernie Pyle, who was transferred to the Marianas from Northern Europe after Saipan was captured, "is the attitude toward the enemy. In Europe we felt our enemies, horrible and deadly as they were, were still people. But out here I've already gathered the feeling that the Japanese are looked upon as something inhuman and squirmy—like some people feel about cockroaches or mice." [56]

Just before Sherrod left the *Solace*, about 9:00 P.M., the ship began to receive wounded fighting men. As they were loaded from amphtracs, an embarkation officer, Dr. Richmond Beck, looked at the red-bordered casualty tag that each man had pinned on him and examined the wound, which had been dressed ashore. He made a quick diagnosis and sent the man to the proper ward. There the wounded man received another tag. "When we run out of tags we know we've got a shipload," another doctor told Sherrod.[57] The clothing of each man was cut off and tossed overboard. Then they sailed away from Saipan.

For many of those ashore that evening, sleeping on the bare ground, tired and so far from home, Tinian and Guam were next. Tinian, just across the straits from Saipan, was overrun in nine days. Less important strategically but far more gratifying to the American public was the reconquest of Guam, which was completed by August 10 after weeks of fighting that was as vicious as that on Saipan. It was the first conquered United States territory to be retaken from the enemy. The fall of Guam ended the Marianas campaign. Even as the fighting raged, Seabees had been expanding the runways on Saipan, Tinian, and Guam for the arrival in a few months of the new B-29 Superfortresses. "Saipan was to Japan almost what Pearl Harbor is to the U.S.," Robert Sherrod wrote after the battle, "except that it is a thousand miles closer to Japan's coast than Pearl Harbor is to America's."[58]

MARPI POINT

Before the bombing of the Japanese home islands began, there was a profound perceptual change in both Japan and the United States that would make the last year of the war in the Pacific bloody beyond belief. The triggering incident occurred at Saipan.

As the battle wound down, a group of Marines on amphibious tractors saw seven Japanese soldiers on a coral reef and went out to capture them. As they approached the reef, one of the Japanese, undoubtedly an officer, pulled out his sword and began cutting off the heads of the men who were kneeling in front of him. Before the Marines could get to him, there were four heads floating in the lagoon. The officer, swinging his sword wildly, charged the Marines and was gunned down, along with the two remaining men. Marines had seen this kind of behavior before. No one was prepared for what happened next.

On July 11, two days after Saipan was declared "secured," two American reporters, Keith Wheeler of the *Chicago Times* and Frank Kelley of the *New York Herald Tribune,* and a photographer for *Life,* Peter Stackpole, arrived at press headquarters on the island with a story almost too horrifying to believe. During the final days of the fighting, remnants of the Japanese army and about 4,000 panic-stricken civilians had escaped to Marpi Point, on the northern tip of the island. There they began killing themselves, often in the most gruesome manner. Parents tossed their children from the high cliffs into the sea, or onto jagged piles of rocks. Mothers waded out in the water with their babies and disappeared in the surf. Fathers, mothers, and children stood in circles holding grenades given to them by the Japanese soldiers and pulled the pins.

Marine interpreters tried to stop them. They and civilians who had surrendered spoke through amplifiers, pleading with the people on the cliffs to give themselves up, assuring them they would be treated humanely. But their government had told them that the sadistic, hairy-faced Americans would rape, torture, and kill them. Tragically, even some who did choose life over death did not survive. Japanese soldiers assassinated many civilians who showed an inclination to surrender.

The next morning, Robert Sherrod drove to Marpi Point. After he returned he wrote one of the most influential pieces of journalism to come out of the Pacific war, "The Nature of the Enemy," which appeared in *Time* magazine:

MARPI POINT . . . IS A LONG PLATEAU on which the Japs had built a secondary airfield. At the edge of the plateau there is a sheer 200-foot drop to jagged coral below; then the billowing sea. The morning I crossed the airfield and got to the edge of the cliff nine marines from a burial detail were working with ropes to pick up the bodies of two of our men, killed the previous day. I asked one of them about the stories I had heard.

"You wouldn't believe it unless you saw it," he said. "Yesterday and the day before there were hundreds of Jap civilians—men, women, and children—up here on this cliff. In the most routine way, they would jump off the cliff, or climb down and wade into the sea. I saw a father throw his three children off, and then jump down himself. Those coral pockets down there under the cliff are full of Jap suicides."

He paused and pointed. "Look," he said, "there's one getting ready to drown himself now." Down below, a young Japanese, no more than 15, paced back and forth across the rocks. He swung his arms, as if getting ready to dive; then he sat down at the edge and let the water play over his feet. Finally he eased himself slowly into the water.

"There he goes," the marine shouted.

A strong wave had washed up to the shore, and the boy floated out with it. At first, he lay on the water, face down, without moving. Then, apparently, a last, desperate instinct to live gripped him and he flailed his arms, thrashing the foam. It was too late. Just as suddenly, it was all over: the air-filled seat of his knee-length black trousers bobbed on the water for ten minutes. Then he disappeared.

Looking down, I counted the bodies of seven others who had killed themselves. One, a child of about five, clad in a ragged white shirt, floated stiffly in the surf.

I turned to go. "This is nothing," the marine said. "Half a mile down, on the west side, you can see hundreds of them."

Later on I checked up with the officer of a minesweeper which had been operating on the west side. He said: "Down there, the sea is so congested with floating bodies we can't avoid running them down. There was one woman in khaki trousers and a white polka-dot blouse, with her black hair streaming in the water. I'm afraid every time I see that kind of a blouse, I'll think of that woman. There was another one, nude, who had drowned herself while giving birth to a baby. A small boy of four or five had drowned with his arm clenched around the neck of a soldier—the two bodies rocked crazily in the waves. Hundreds and hundreds of Jap bodies have floated up to our minesweeper."

Apparently the Jap soldier not only would go to any extreme to avoid surrender, but would also try to see that no civilian surrendered. At Marpi Point, the marines had tried to dislodge a Jap sniper from a cave in the cliff. He was an exceptional marksman; he had killed two marines (one at 700 yards) and wounded a third. The marines used rifles, torpedoes and finally, TNT in a 45-minute effort to force him out. Meantime the Jap had other business.

He had spotted a Japanese group—apparently father, mother, and three children—out on the rocks, preparing to drown themselves, but evidently weakening in their decision. The Jap sniper took aim. He drilled the man from behind, dropping him into the sea. The second bullet hit the woman. She dragged herself about 30 feet along the rocks. Then she floated out in a stain of blood. The sniper would have shot the children, but a Japanese woman ran across and carried them out of range. The sniper walked defiantly out of his cave, and crumpled under a hundred marine bullets.

Some of the Jap civilians went through considerable ceremony before snuffing out their own lives. The marines said that some fathers had cut their children's throats before tossing them over the cliff. Some strangled their children. In one instance marines watched in astonishment as three women sat on the rocks leisurely, deliberately combing their long black hair. Finally they joined hands and walked slowly out into the sea.

But the most ceremonious, by all odds, were 100 Japs who were on the rocks below the Marpi Point cliff. All together, they suddenly bowed to marines watching from the cliff. Then they stripped off their clothes and bathed in the sea. Thus refreshed, they put on new clothes and spread a huge Jap flag on a smooth rock. Then the leader distributed hand grenades. One by one, as the pins were pulled, the Japs blew their insides out.

Some seemed to make a little game out of their dying—perhaps out of indecision, perhaps out of ignorance, or even some kind of lightheaded disrespect of the high seriousness of Japanese suicide. One day the marines observed a circle of about 50 Japanese, including several small children, gaily tossing hand grenades to each other—like baseball players warming up before a game. Suddenly six Japanese soldiers dashed from a cave, from which they had been sniping at marines. The soldiers posed arrogantly in front of the civilians, then blew themselves to kingdom come; thus shamed, the civilians did likewise.

What did all this self-destruction mean? Did it mean that the Japanese on Saipan believed their own propaganda which told them that Americans are beasts and would murder them all? Many a Jap civilian did beg our people to put him to death immediately rather than to suffer the torture which he expected. But many who chose suicide could see other civilians who had surrendered walking unmolested in the internment camps. They could hear some of the surrendered plead with them by loudspeaker not to throw their lives away.

The marines have come to expect almost anything in the way of self-destruction from Japanese soldiers. . . . But none were prepared for this epic self-slaughter among civilians. More than one U.S. fighting man was killed trying to rescue a Jap from his wanton suicide.

Saipan is the first invaded Jap territory populated with more than a handful of civilians. Do the suicides of Saipan mean that the whole Japanese race will choose death before surrender? Perhaps that is what the Japanese and their strange propagandists would like us to believe.[59]

This is precisely what the Tokyo warlords wanted their own people as well as the Americans to believe. They wanted the Americans to believe it in order to frighten them into backing off from their insistence on unconditional surrender, which would mean the invasion of Japan and the mobilization of its people into a "Hundred Million Special Attack Force," ready to die like the victims of Marpi Point. And they wanted the Japanese people to believe it in order to prepare them for the sacrifice they would be called on to make if the enemy invaded the home islands.

"Saipan was the decisive battle of the Pacific offensive," Holland Smith wrote.[60] It brought down the government of Hideki Tojo and paved the way for the withering bombing campaign on the home islands that Tojo clearly foresaw. "When we lost Saipan," said one of the Emperor's military advisors after the war, "Hell is on us."[61] A

MARINES GATHER TO PAY RESPECTS TO THEIR COMRADES WHO FELL ON SAIPAN (USMC).

war cabinet headed by General Kuniaki Koiso replaced Tojo's government. With the Americans less than 1,400 miles away, it began making preparations for an expected invasion.

The new government correctly read American intentions. Saipan led to a major change in U.S. policy in the war against Japan. Only a few days after the fall of Saipan, at a meeting of top commanders of the American and British armed forces, General Marshall made the following motion:

"As a result of the recent operations in the Pacific it was now clear to the United States Chiefs of Staff that, in order to finish the war with the Japanese quickly, it would be necessary to invade the industrial heart of Japan."

The Combined Chiefs of Staff then redefined the aims of the war in the Pacific:

"To force the unconditional surrender of Japan by: (1) Lowering Japanese ability and will to resist by establishing sea and air blockades, conducting intensive air bombardment, and destroying Japanese air and naval strength. (2) Invading and seizing objectives in the industrial heart of Japan." [62]

That September, at a meeting in Quebec, Roosevelt and Churchill formally approved the new war policy.

With the likelihood of an American invasion, the Japanese government began a massive propaganda effort to convince the general population to prepare to embrace death, as had the martyrs of Marpi Point. Heavily censored versions of Sherrod's article began to appear on the front pages of Japanese newspapers alongside editorials celebrating the "patriotic essence" of Japanese women and children who chose "death rather than to be captured alive and shamed by the demonlike American forces." [63] Stricken from the Sherrod article were references to Japanese soldiers killing their own countrymen, and to the thousands of Japanese citizens who did surrender and were treated humanly. These official versions of Sherrod's article "became fuel for an unprecedented orgy of glorification of death," writes historian Haruko Taya Cook. [64] When the American "beasts" appeared, the government declared, the "one-hundred million" must be victorious or die together. Beginning in August, all citizens were to receive military training, with bamboo spears as their chief weapons. [65]

At the same time, Marpi Point convinced many Americans that Japanese civilians were as "fanatical" as Japanese soldiers, and that Japan could be defeated only by a war of mass extermination, a war not only against combatants but also against noncombatants, as Robert Sherrod had suggested after Tarawa. That kind of war would be fought from the air, from bases in the Marianas, culminating in the flight of the *Enola Gay* from Tinian to Hiroshima. But another kind of total war had already begun at Tarawa and Saipan, a war to the finish with an enemy who would not surrender, no matter how badly he was beaten.

This merciless island fighting was fed by inflamed racism. To the Japanese people, who prided themselves on being genetically "pure," uncontaminated by immigration, Americans were mongrelized brutes—devils and demons. After the fall of Saipan the Japanese government stepped up its organized campaign of racial vilification. Here is an article from a popular Japanese magazine:

IT HAS GRADUALLY BECOME CLEAR THAT the American enemy, driven by its ambition to conquer the world, is coming to attack us, and as the breath and body odor of the beast approach, it may be of some use if we draw the demon's features here.

Our ancestors called them Ebisu or savages long ago, and labeled the very first Westerners who came to our country the Southern Barbarians. To the hostile eyes of the Japanese of former times they were "red hairs" and "hairy foreigners," and perceived as being of about as much worth as a foreign ear of corn. We in our times should manifest comparable spirit. Since the barbaric tribe of Americans are devils in human skin who come from the West, we should call them Saibanki, or Western Barbarian Demons.[66]

Posters in classrooms and other public places exhorted students to "kill the American animal." American soldiers in the Pacific, on the other hand, did not need propaganda slogans to feed *their* hatred of the enemy. Japanese atrocities against war prisoners and their suicidal banzai charges were seen as signs of their barbarity. The Marine Corps film shot on Tarawa depicted Japanese defenders as "living, snarling rats." As one veteran of the Pacific fighting wrote: "The Japanese made a perfect enemy. They had so many characteristics that an American Marine could hate. Physically, they were small, a strange color, and, by some standards, unattractive. . . . Marines did not consider that they were killing men. They were wiping out dirty animals."[67]

After the fall of Saipan, Japanese military leaders knew the war was lost. Their weakened fleet was powerless to break the American naval blockade, which was able to pull the noose tighter from advanced bases on Saipan. And they had no air arm to protect their cities of wood from the long-range B-29s that would soon begin taking off from the Marianas. "Our war was lost," said a Japanese admiral, years later, "with the loss of Saipan."[68] Yet Emperor Hirohito and his chief ministers refused to accept defeat; and out in the Pacific, the soldiers of the empire continued to fight with undiminished bravery, confident of victory.

"Do you think Japan will win the war?" an Army interrogator in the Philippines asked a Japanese prisoner not long after the fall of Saipan.

A. "Of course Japan will win the war."

Q. "Why?"

A. "Japan can beat anybody."

Q. "What makes you think Japan will win?"

A. "Japan has never lost a war. She cannot be beaten. All of Japan is one mind."[69]

How does one defeat such an enemy? Justice M. Chambers, a Marine at Marpi Point, answered for countless American troops in the Pacific. "[General William Tecumseh] Sherman was right. To win the war and get it over with, just kill off many of the other side, make it terrible, and the war will stop."[70]

That is what America eventually did. That is how the war against Japan was won. The debate over the morality of it was left to history.

Pacific Strategy

The invasion of the Marianas had supported MacArthur's drive up the coast of New Guinea by luring the Imperial Fleet into the Battle of the Philippine Sea. This prevented it from coming to the aid of Japan's beleaguered garrison on the island of Biak, off the coast of New Guinea, the site of a strategically important airfield the enemy could not afford to surrender.

The battle for the island of Biak had been preceded by some of the most inspired campaigning of the war by a sixty-two-year-old military marvel who had lost nothing to time. On April 22, 1944—less than two months before D-Day on Saipan—Douglas MacArthur had sent General Robert L. Eichelberger on an audacious 600-mile leap over several enemy strongholds to desolate Hollandia, on the north coast of Netherlands New Guinea. After taking Hollandia and another airstrip at Aitape, just to the east, the Americans withstood a furious counterattack by the Japanese Eighteenth Army, weakened and depleted by its long jungle march to reach the enemy that had just bypassed them. In weeks of murderous fighting, the Eighteenth Army lost nearly 9,000 men to enemy fire and tropical disease, leaving no Japanese force of consequence to stop MacArthur from completing the conquest of New Guinea.

The American Army had then continued to sweep westward and northward along the coast, in search of hard ground in the rain-soaked region on which to build airstrips for the heavy bombers MacArthur needed for his reconquest of the Philippines. That May, MacArthur's forces had finally secured firm terrain for General Kenney's bombers on the coastal island of Wakde and, MacArthur thought, on the larger, heavily defended island of Biak, east of New Guinea's Vogelkop Peninsula. But Biak would not be pacified. With the enemy holed up in cave-pocked ridges and gorges, the fighting there was as rough as anywhere in the Pacific. It turned into a stalemate that could easily have been an American disaster had the enemy brought in reinforcements and naval gunpower. But just as Japan's two largest battleships were steaming southward to bombard the American beachhead, word reached Tokyo of Admiral Spruance's arrival in the Marianas. The Biak operation was abruptly abandoned and the Combined Fleet headed out to meet its fate in the deep waters of the Philippine Sea, dooming Biak's starving cave-dwellers.

And now it was nearly over—MacArthur's two-year-long campaign over a distance of 2,000 miles, through some of the most fearsome terrain and weather on earth. His plan had unfolded almost flawlessly. And his officers, William Manchester writes, "now thought of him as almost supernatural, a view he of course encouraged." [71]

That summer and early fall, after taking the island of Noemfoor, some sixty miles west of Biak, and the village of Sansapor on the extreme western tip of New Guinea, MacArthur's forces leaped ahead to the island of Morotai, bypassing a Japanese garrison of 25,000 troops on the large island of Halmahera. With the securing of Morotai, all of New Guinea was isolated and the interminable battle—the longest of the war—ended, except for the still lethal process of cleaning out the remaining enemy troops, a thankless job left to the Australians. Of the over 157,000 Japanese soldiers sent to fight in New Guinea, only 10,000 or so survived. Most of the dead succumbed to starvation and disease.

On September 15, just after his troops landed unopposed on Morotai, Douglas MacArthur arrived to inspect his new island outpost, only 300 air miles from the Philippines. "He gazed out to the northwest," an aide remembers, "almost as though he could already see through the mist the rugged lines of Bataan and Corregidor." [72] Then he said, "They are waiting for me up there. It has been a long time." [73]

As MacArthur pondered his next move, America's Pacific strategy was shifting under his feet. The issue was where to strike next. MacArthur's plan had been to climb the ladder of the Philippine archipelago from Mindanao, at the southernmost tip, to Leyte, and finally to Luzon. Admiral Ernest King, however, wanted to bypass the huge island group, which would be difficult to conquer and hold, and invade Formosa, which was closer to Japan.

For a time, the President, George Marshall, and most of the Joint Chiefs had sided with King, but in July 1944, at a stormy strategy session with MacArthur and Nimitz in Hawaii, Roosevelt had given "the nod, though no final decision, to Luzon." [74]

MacArthur had been insistently persuasive. As he told Roosevelt, he had promised both his imprisoned troops and the conquered Filipino people that he would return to liberate them. "Promises must be kept," he pleaded with Roosevelt, his voice cracking with emotion; this was as much a moral as a military issue. [75]

The general also made his case on solid strategic grounds, and this was probably more persuasive. It would be better to control the Philippines than far smaller Formosa. From the long archipelago, American forces could command the 700-mile-wide South China Sea, completely cutting off Japan from her southern conquests. And the Filipino partisans, who had been waging a ceaseless guerrilla war against 400,000 Japanese occupation troops, would greatly aid the liberation movement. What's more, Luzon could not be easily bypassed on the way to Formosa, as King proposed; it was simply too big. Any attempt to sail around its flanks would expose American ships to bomber attacks from the island's excellent airfields.

Although the wily President had not committed himself, MacArthur had left Pearl Harbor confident that the two Pacific offenses—his own and Nimitz's—would converge at Luzon, not Formosa.

Several MacArthur biographers have suggested that the general and the President, both master schemers, may have struck a covert deal in Hawaii—Roosevelt to back the Luzon invasion in return for MacArthur's agreement to issue a stream of press releases announcing great battlefield successes in the Pacific achieved with Washington's unwavering support. [76] Since there are no official transcripts of the meeting, this plausible idea is unprovable. But MacArthur had been overpowering in his own defense. "Give me an aspirin before I go to bed," the President called to his physician after three hours in the general's company. "In fact, give me another aspirin to take in the morning. In all my life nobody has ever talked to me the way MacArthur did." [77]

PLANNING THE PACIFIC OFFENSIVE IN HAWAII, JULY 1944. LEFT TO RIGHT: GENERAL DOUGLAS MACARTHUR, PRESIDENT FRANKLIN ROOSEVELT, ADMIRAL WILLIAM LEAHY, AND ADMIRAL CHESTER NIMITZ (SC).

That September, at the time of the Morotai operation, the Combined Chiefs of Staff gave MacArthur the official go-ahead to invade Mindanao in November and Leyte in December. A final decision on the next objective would be made later, but Formosa was now off the table. A recent Japanese offensive against the Chinese Nationalists deprived the Allies of the China air bases they had been counting on to subdue Formosa. This forced even King to waver, but he did not relent until he was informed by Allied planners that the conquest of Formosa would require air bases on Luzon and more troops than MacArthur and Nimitz, together, had at their disposal.[78]

To protect MacArthur's right flank, the Navy and Marines would take Japanese-held Peleliu in the Palau Islands, 550 miles east of Mindanao, knocking out its excellent air base and building a support facility for initial operations in Mindanao. But within a week almost everything changed. In conducting softening-up carrier raids on the Philippines and nearby islands, Admiral Bull Halsey downed an incredible 500 planes and met unexpectedly light resistance. Seeing an opportunity here, he immediately sent a top secret message to Nimitz recommending that the Mindanao operation be canceled and that MacArthur strike at Leyte as soon as possible. This, he argued, would make the invasion of Peleliu, which he feared would be "another Tarawa," unnecessary.[79] Nimitz sent Halsey's recommendation, with his approval only of the acceleration of the Philippines operation, to the Combined Chiefs of Staff, which were meeting in Quebec. After getting MacArthur's consent, they changed the timetable. MacArthur would bypass Mindanao and make an amphibious assault on Leyte on October 20.

Nimitz's decision not to call back the Peleliu invasion force, which was only three days from the island, was a major mistake. The rationale for the invasion had disappeared. He might have been trying to appease MacArthur, who wanted all the air support he could get, but Nimitz had also been informed by American intelligence that Peleliu would be easy to take, a two- or three-day operation.

It was one of the worst intelligence blunders of the war. When finally subdued after months of fighting, Peleliu was virtually worthless. The swiftly advancing Pacific war had passed it by, turning it into a backwater fuel depot. But the cost of taking it was unconscionable—almost 10,000 Marines and Army infantry killed or wounded in perhaps the most savage major battle of the Pacific theater. "The only difference between Iwo Jima and Peleliu," remarked General Roy Geiger, who commanded the assault troops at Peleliu, "was that at Iwo Jima, there were twice as many Japs on an island twice as large, and they had three Marine divisions to take it, while we had one Marine division to take Peleliu."[80]

The defenders of Peleliu put up a sign. "We will build a barrier across the Pacific with our bodies."[81] That foretold the ferocity of the fight.

A Marine at Peleliu

WITH THE OLD BREED

The 1st Marine Division was given the ugly assignment of taking Peleliu, the main island of the Palaus, an eighty-mile arc of islands halfway between Guam and the Philippines. D-Day was scheduled for September 15, 1944. That summer the division was in rest camp on Pavuvu in the Russell Islands, eighty miles from Guadalcanal. The 1st Marine Division had done most of the fighting in the epic battle of Guadalcanal and had just completed a tough assignment with General MacArthur, taking Cape Gloucester, on the island of New Britain, in miserable jungle fighting at the peak of the monsoon season. They were a spirited, veteran outfit, nicknamed the Old Breed, even though over three quarters of the men had not yet reached the age of twenty-one. Already legendary among their warriors was Colonel Chesty Puller, whose reckless audacity had won him a Navy Cross and a Purple Heart on Guadalcanal.

One of their newest replacements was a skinny, soft-voiced twenty-year-old from Mobile, Alabama, named Eugene B. Sledge, "Sledgehammer" as he was known

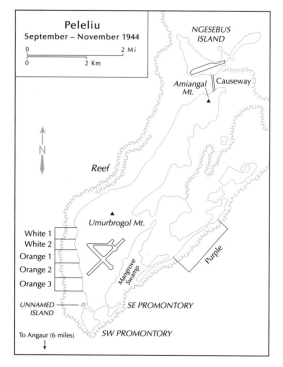

Peleliu
September – November 1944
0   2 Mi
0   2 Km

to his buddies in K Company, 3rd Battalion, 5th Marine Regiment, 1st Marine Division. Sledge was a doctor's son, a quiet, thoughtful boy who read widely and knew what the war was about and wanted to get into it. Impatient to see combat, he had deliberately flunked out of a Marine officer training program at Georgia Tech to become an enlisted man. By the time he finished officer training the war might be over, he told his protesting parents. He had joined the Marines, he said, to fight not to study. Even so, he wondered if he could face up to combat—and whether he could kill.

Sledge was patriotic and deeply religious. He neither smoked nor drank, and one of his passions was bird watching. After the war he became a professor of biology, specializing in ornithology, at a small Alabama college. There, in his free moments, he completed the war memoir he had begun immediately after returning from Peleliu, *With the Old Breed at Peleliu and Okinawa.* Published in 1981, it has become a small classic, one of the finest personal accounts of combat ever written.

The book is based on a secret diary Sledge kept during the war. "My parents taught me the value of history," he told the writer Studs Terkel after the war. "Both my grandfathers were in the Confederate Army. They didn't talk about the glory of war. They talked about how terrible it was.

"During my third day overseas, I thought I should write all this down for my family. In all my reading about the Civil War, I never read about how the troops felt and what it was like from day to day. We knew how the generals felt and what they ate.

"We were told diaries were forbidden, because if we were killed or captured, any diary might give the Japanese information. So I kept little notes, which I slipped into the pages of my Gideons' New Testament. . . .

"Some of the supervisors never knew I was keepin' notes: 'We just thought you were awfully pious.'" [1]

When Sledge joined the 1st Marine Division as a mortarman in a rifle company the men were "bone-tired and decimated from the bloody fighting on the rain-drenched jungle island of New Britain, off the eastern coast of New Guinea," recalls another new replacement, James D. Seidler. "Most of the division was dumped on Pavuvu Island, which had been a British coconut plantation before the war, so there were four years of rotting palm fronds and coconuts, along with thousands of land crabs, huge rats, snakes, and other assorted critters. And mud. It took three months' hard work to make it habitable."[2]

EUGENE B. "SLEDGEHAMMER" SLEDGE (LRP).

Years later, Sledge described the place: "Huge fruit bats came out all night and flew around and got into fights with rats in the palm trees right above our tents. Land crabs scuttled through the tents all night and each day you had to shake your shoes out to get them out. Morale should have been low, but most of us were in our teens and early twenties and were part of an elite and proud outfit.

"There was no recreation except volleyball, baseball, and B-grade movies we watched on log seats in a coconut grove. But I think this is one of the things that bonded us all so closely together. . . . We didn't have any distractions. We had to lean on each other." In a recently published sequel to *With the Old Breed*, Sledge writes that the veterans "treated us replacements like brothers—with the understanding we had to prove ourselves in combat. They were the best teachers in the world in how to kill Japs because, simply said, that is the infantryman's job, to kill the enemy. . . .

"A passionate hatred for the Japanese burned through all the Marines I knew." When Sledge asked a veteran of Guadalcanal why, he got an unbelieving stare and this emphatic reply, "Because they're the meanest sonabitches that ever lived."[3]

The high point of Sledge's stay on Pavuvu was a visit by Bob Hope. "While we were preparing for Peleliu, which incidentally we weren't told about until the day before we shipped out, Bob Hope was over in [the nearby island of] Banika entertaining the troops in the naval hospital. When he heard the 1st Marine Division was on Pavuvu he flew over with his entertainment group in a Piper Cub and put on a wonderful show . . . That was the last real laugh a lot of my buddies had . . . in their short lives."

The 1st Marine Division shipped out for Peleliu in the last week of August. Company K boarded a large LST, a shallow-draft ship as big as a light cruiser, with a load of LVTs (also known as amtracs or Alligators) in its cavernous belly. It would discharge these Alligators in the waters off Peleliu, twenty men to a vehicle, from its massive bow doors, which opened like a clam. The men in the assault companies— the Marines who would hit the beach first—bunked in the rough-riding, flat-bottomed LSTs with the machines that would carry them ashore. The rest of the division rode in more comfortable troopships.

The trip to Peleliu—2,100 miles away—took three weeks in the excruciatingly slow LSTs. It was insufferably hot below deck, but the seas were smooth all the way and the men sat on the deck sunning themselves, reading, playing poker, or writing mother. The enlisted men knew nothing about the island with the "nice sounding name, Pel' e loo" other than that it had a big airfield that Douglas MacArthur wanted knocked out to protect his flank when he returned to the Philippines. The Old Breed's coldly aloof commander, Major General William Rupertus, told them this would be a "rough but fast" mission, taking only three, maybe four days. Which meant, a skeptical sergeant mused, "we'll have to kill every little yellow bastard there."[4]

After chow on the evening of the landing, Sledge and a friend leaned on the rail of the slow-rocking ship and talked about what they planned to do after the war, trying their mightiest to appear unconcerned about the next morning. "As the sun disappeared below the horizon and its glare no longer reflected off a glassy sea, I thought of how beautiful the sunsets always were in the Pacific. They were even more beautiful than over Mobile Bay. Suddenly a thought hit me like a thunderbolt. Would I live to see the sunset tomorrow? My knees nearly buckled as panic swept over me. I squeezed the railing and tried to appear interested in our conversation."

Sledge excused himself and went below to check his combat pack. Everything was in order. Inside was "a folded poncho, one pair of socks, a couple of boxes of K rations, salt tablets, extra carbine ammo (twenty rounds), two hand grenades, a fountain pen, a small bottle of ink, writing paper in a waterproof wrapper, a toothbrush, a small tube of toothpaste, some photos of my folks along with some letters (in a waterproof wrapper), and a dungaree cap."

His other equipment and clothing included a carbine, an entrenching tool, a steel helmet, a green dungaree jacket and pants, ankle-high "boondockers," light canvas leggings, two canteens, a compass, two clips of ammunition, the regulation Ka-Bar knife in a leather sheath, a larger, meat-cleaver-style knife his father had sent him, and, for good luck, a bronze Marine emblem fastened to one collar.

When his head hit the pillow that night, he thought of home and wondered if he would die tomorrow. "I concluded that it was impossible for me to be killed, because God loved me." His heart racing, he fell asleep whispering the Lord's Prayer.

THE LANDING

In the thin light of early morning, he had a breakfast of steak and eggs and headed with his company for the tank deck of the LST. The toilets were so crowded that some men didn't have the chance to empty their bowels. To boost morale, gung ho Marines were putting on camouflage paint—"war paint," they called it. "Puts them in the mood," an officer told K Company's commander, George P. Hunt, a former newspaperman who would write a riveting account of his part of the upcoming battle, *Coral Comes High*.

Hunt was with Chesty Puller's 1st Regiment, and his company had been given the toughest assignment on D-Day. They were to storm the Point, a Japanese fortification that had been built into the soft coral rock of a small peninsula that jutted out into the sea on the far left of the landing area. If that position was not taken, the enemy would have a free field of fire down the entire length of the beach, and the landing would likely be a massacre.

On the tank deck, the Alligators' engines were rumbling, filling the hold with stomach-turning diesel exhaust, despite the huge fans whirling overhead. When the signal was given, the big bow doors separated and Sledge's amphibious tractor, following others, rumbled down the sloping ramp and settled into the sea "like a big duck." Just ahead, in the rolling blue-green water, was the Alligator carrying George Hunt. A veteran of Guadalcanal and New Britain, Hunt was scared because he knew what to expect. A greenhorn, Sledge was scared because he didn't know what to expect.

As the Marines passed the patrol boats and rocket ships, the sailors shook their fists and yelled, "Go get 'em, you Marines!" To settle their nerves, the men in one of Hunt's landing boats began singing "Give My Regards to Broadway." "Just before we hit the beach we were all singing it at the top of our lungs," a Marine Sergeant said later. "It sure made us feel good." [5]

The men had been ordered to keep their heads down, but Sledge peeked over the high gunwale "and saw several amtracs get hit dead on by screaming shells and watched in horror as the bodies of Marines were blown into the air." Those men that were still alive began walking in to shore and were cut down by machine gun fire.

"The noise from the battleships and the Corsairs [Navy fighters] and the dive-bombers was so incredible it was indescribable. You couldn't even yell to the man right next to you and have him hear you. As we moved into position we could see and feel the power of the sixteen-inch salvos fired from the battlewagons right over our heads. Every time they exploded, trees and debris were hurled high into the air. It wasn't hot yet and the sky was blue and the sun was out and I was scared to death, and so was everybody else. The main thing that concerned me was I was afraid I was going to wet my pants.

"I looked at the island and all I could see was a sheet of flame backed by a huge black wall of smoke . . . as though the island was on fire. And I thought, my God, none of us will ever get out of that place."

Back on the troopships, the men lined the rails and shouted, "Burn! Burn!" as tiny Peleliu, only six miles long and two miles wide, vanished in flame and smoke and monstrous clouds of coral dust. "We'll be off here by tomorrow," one Marine yelled.[6]

It was the same reaction as at Tarawa. Hardly a Marine could believe there was an enemy soldier alive after such a shelling. But the Japanese were dug in better than they had been at either Tarawa or Saipan. In a cave built deep in one of the island's coral ridges, a Japanese defender wrote in his diary, "We will defend Peleliu! We are imbued with the firm conviction that even though we may die, we will never let the airfield fall into enemy hands. Our morale is sky high."[7] But so was the Marines'. "Over the gunwale of a craft abreast of us I saw a marine, his face painted for the jungle, his eyes set for the beach, his mouth set for murder, his big hands quiet now in the last moments before the tough tendons drew up to kill," wrote Tom Lea, *Life*'s leading war artist in the Pacific.[8]

For more than two months, Lea had lived aboard the carrier *Hornet*, chronicling that ship's role in operations in the South Pacific. This was his first battle experience with the Marines. In their combat packs, he and two other correspondents each had a can of beer. They agreed to have their own little celebration on the beach if they made it there.

There were 10,500 Japanese soldiers and sailors on the island, about 6,000 of them members of the Kwantung Army, veterans of brutal fighting in Manchuria. Their commander, Colonel Kunio Nakagawa, had brought in mining and tunneling engineers to militarize the natural coral caves of Peleliu, which were built into a central spine of hills that ran up the northern half of the island. Sliding steel doors covered the entrances to the caves with the biggest guns, and many of the interlocking caves had electricity, ventilation systems, telephone and radio communications, and hidden exits. The largest of them held a thousand men and a number of the caves were five and six stories deep. The caves were ideally located for defense, in a 300-foot-high mountain of jagged coral, with sheer cliffs, overlooking the flat area at the center of the island, just off the beach, where the airfield was located. It was "a series of crags," Private Russell Davis described it, "ripped bare of all standing vegetation, peeled down to the rotted coral, rolling in smoke, crackling with heat and . . . stained and black, like bad teeth."[9] The natives called this menacing coral mass the Umurbrogol. The Americans would call it Bloody Nose Ridge. Taking it would cost more American lives than were lost in the assault on Omaha Beach.*

Aerial intelligence had failed to sight this high ground, for it was covered at the time with dense tropical growth. But the tremendous naval fire had blasted off the vegetation, exposing the coral ridges that began just north of the airport. There in the caves, "with plugs in their ears and hate in their hearts, they waited," Lea wrote. "Through terrifying bombing and shelling they waited for the marines to start across the 675-yard reef to the beach. . . . Then they opened up."[10]

As Sledge's landing craft approached the beach, it hit a coral shelf and the engine stalled. Shells fell all around it, creating towering water geysers, and machine gun bullets pelted the steel sides of the Alligator. "When the first shell came over, I knew my place was back home with mother."

The Alligator began running again, and as the Marines came up on the sand, the lieutenant pulled out a bottle of whiskey and shouted, "This is it boys."

"Just like they do in the movies! It seemed unreal."

Racing ashore a few yards, Sledge sought cover with members of his company. The Marines landed three regiments abreast, the 1st, 5th, and 7th Marines. Most of Puller's 1st Marines, on the left flank, attacked the lower hills of Bloody Nose Ridge and were stopped cold, with heavy casualties. Hunt's K Company, meanwhile, went straight for the Point and took it after a vicious firefight. But holding it would be a lot harder than taking it. Sledge's 5th Marines landed in the center and headed inland through low scrub vegetation toward the airport. The 7th Marines landed on the far right. After knocking out entrenched enemy positions on the southern end of the island, they were to loop north and reinforce Puller.

Tom Lea, with the 7th Marines, found it impossible to do any drawing or

---

*The total number of Americans killed or wounded in the Peleliu operation, 9,615, exceeds, by some counts, the total number of British, Canadian, and American losses at Normandy on June 6, 1944.

AFRICAN-AMERICAN SUPPLY COMPANY PINNED
DOWN ON THE BEACH AT PELELIU (USMC).

sketching on the beach. "My work there consisted of trying to keep from getting
killed and trying to memorize what I saw and felt under fire. On the evening of
D-plus-one I returned to a naval vessel offshore where I could record in my sketch
book the burden of this memory." At his home in El Paso, Texas, Lea transformed his
hastily executed pencil sketches into searing color portraits of men at war, which
were reproduced in the pages of *Life*.

Lea came across the reef on a Higgins boat. The reef was "barricaded with concrete posts and railroad-track ties, all heavily entwined with barbed wire. There were
necklaces of underwater mines around every possible landing point." And the Japanese had "planted inverted 500-lb. aerial bombs and naval torpedoes with special fuses

as mines and booby traps. Minefields stretched from the water to 50 yards inland in a pattern which insured explosives every 20 feet."[11] When his boat ground to a stop on the rugged coral, Lea splashed through the shallow surf and fell flat on his face, lying there wet and terrified as he watched a mortar tear a Marine to pieces, his head and one leg sailing into the air.[12]

Lea fell into a shell hole as another mortar came rocketing down on him. "Lying there . . . I saw a wounded man near me, staggering in the direction of LVTs. His face was half bloody pulp and the mangled shreds of what was left of an arm hung down like a stick, as he bent over in his stumbling, shock-crazy walk. The half of his face that was still human had the most terrifying look of abject patience I have ever seen. He fell behind me, in a red puddle on the white sand."[13] That shattered Marine became the subject of Lea's famous painting *The Price*. It was different from anything Lea had done before. Most of his work up to Peleliu had a sharp documentary quality, with almost no tension or bloodshed. *The Price* is so gory, so brutally grotesque, it makes you want to turn away. Peleliu changed Tom Lea. *The Price* "is a monument," wrote the novelist James Jones, "to the blood and death that all of us, even those who have been there, prefer not to see or think about when we are away from it."[14]

Lea followed the 7th Marines into the burned and mangled jungle just inland from the beach, where he found cover with other Marines in a long trench. There, he and his two friends punched holes with their knives in their three beer cans and drank a toast to the Marines on Peleliu. "The beer was hot, foamy and wonderful."

It was just before noon and the sun had burned through the overcast of the early morning. Throughout the battle, temperatures would hover around 100 degrees, reaching 115 degrees on some days, and water was in short supply in the early part of the invasion. "Sweat ran in streams from under our helmets which, without cloth covers, were burning to the touch. Our dungarees, wet with sweat, stuck to our legs and backs. The sand under our clothes scratched like sandpaper," Lea wrote.[15]

Just behind the trench, in a large bomb crater surrounded by splintered trees, an improvised aid station had been set up. No hospital tent had been erected. That would have invited enemy fire. In the center of the crater a doctor was performing surgery, while corpsmen administered to the walking wounded. "The padre stood by with two canteens and a Bible, helping. . . . He looked very lonely," Lea wrote, "very close to God, as he bent over the shattered men so far from home. Corpsmen put a poncho, a shirt, a rag, anything handy, over the grey faces of the dead and carried them to a line on the beach, under a tarpaulin, to await the digging of graves."

Toward evening, the men near the trench started to dig in for the night. Their entrenching tools were useless against the bone-hard coral. All they could do was find a hole or a slight depression and pile up stones and debris around it for cover. As they worked, they could be heard muttering. "It's the ferking night time I don't like, when them little ferkers come sneakin' into your lap." [16] When they finished, they cleaned their rifles and sharpened their bayonets.

Up the beach, to the left, Sledge's 5th Marines had moved in close to the airstrip, where they repelled a tank attack with bazookas, mortars, and their own hard-punching Sherman tanks, annihilating thirteen small, thin-skinned tanks and a company of infantry that moved across the airfield behind them. This was a carefully coordinated counterattack, not a banzai charge, the first indication the Marines had that the enemy might fight differently on Peleliu than they had at Tarawa or Saipan.

Still further up the beach, on the extreme left of the line, part of George Hunt's decimated K Company was holding the fortresslike Point in primeval, hand-to-hand fighting, cut off from the rest of the Marines on Peleliu and encircled by the best of Nakagawa's Manchuria veterans. They would be isolated and under incessant attack until they were relieved thirty hours later. Puller and the rest of the 1st Marines could not get to them. They were pinned down by fire from the caves of the Umurbrogol, just to the north of them. (After the war, the Marine Corps built an exact model of the Point at its Quantico training facility to teach new officers how to assault a "doomsday" defense.)

That evening, as he fell into a "restless doze," brushing aside the land crabs that had crawled on his face, George Hunt wondered, "Could I still find my way around New York?—almost unbelievable to see Fifth Avenue again, to buy a newspaper at Whelan's, ride the Eighth Avenue subway and the Staten Island Ferry . . . and feel the stampeding, pulsating, brawling, uproarious spirit of the city—then I must have slept." [17]

Along the beach, as the sun went down, men ate candy bars, drank warm water from canteens, and had their last cigarette before the "smoking lamp" was extinguished. Then the island blackness closed in on them. Most expected it to cool off, but it didn't; and they sat and fried in puddles of their own sweat. Waiting. When the counterattack came in Lea's section of the beachhead, it began with a flurry of small arms fire and the high-pitched screams of enemy soldiers. Then came the mortar shells, smashing down all around them, the Marine howitzers answering every few seconds. [18] Star shells lit up the sky and the whole beachhead came alive. But again, there was no suicidal assault, just nerve-rattling mortar and artillery fire.

"To me, artillery was an invention of hell," Sledge recalled. "After each shell I was wrung out, limp and exhausted." As the fight for Peleliu wore on, and the shelling intensified, there were a number of times when Sledge thought he was going to go out of his mind.

BLOODY NOSE RIDGE

Toward first light, after the shelling stopped, Marines climbed out of their primitive shelters with big grins on their smoke-smeared faces, feeling they had beaten the odds, at least for a night. "We wiped the slime off our front teeth and lighted cigarettes," wrote Lea. As they prepared themselves for battle, Lea and the Marines saw what the enemy had done that night. The nearest dead Japanese were about thirty yards in front of the trench. They had infiltrated the Marines' lines, wearing the helmets of dead Marines, and sneaked into foxholes and "cut throats. They had been slashed or shot by Marines in hand to hand fighting in the darkness and there were bodies now in the morning light." [19]

At 8:00 A.M. Sledge's 5th Marines prepared for an assault on the crushed gravel airfield. The Marines already held two sides of the field, but the Japanese had their heavy guns concentrated on the coral mound overlooking the north side of the field, just west of where Chesty Puller was trying to break through. Planes, tanks, and howitzers would spearhead the advance, followed by the foot soldiers; and the assault would be made under the full force of that other enemy on Peleliu—the blistering sun, heat waves, visible to the eye, rising up from the furnacelike coral.

Hundreds of Marines had already shriveled and passed out from heat exhaustion and their bodies lay all about, "paralyzed in grotesque shapes." [20] The 5th Marines would need water if they hoped to carry out the attack. Just as the men in Sledge's unit started putting on their gear, a supply detail came up with five-gallon water tanks. "Our hands shook, we were so eager to quench our thirst," Sledge recalls. But the water looked like "thin brown paint" in his canteen cup, and when he first drank it he had to spit it out. It was full of rust and oil and it gave off a vile smell. A supply officer had transported this water to Peleliu in fifty-five-gallon drums that had previously been filled with diesel oil. The drums had supposedly been steam-cleaned but someone had botched the job. There was nothing anyone could do now; it was drink oily water or die. Some of the men doubled over and retched.

Four infantry battalions were ordered to cross the airfield at a trot, straight into the enemy's strength. "We moved rapidly in the open, amid craters and coral rubble, through ever increasing enemy fire," Sledge remembers. "The shells screeched and whistled, exploding all around us.

"I clenched my teeth, squeezed my carbine stock, and recited over and over to myself, 'The Lord is my shepherd . . .'

"The ground seemed to sway back and forth under the concussions. . . . Chunks of blasted coral stung my face and hands while steel fragments spattered down on the hard rock like hail on a city street. Everywhere shells flashed like giant firecrackers.

"Through the haze I saw Marines stumble and pitch forward as they got hit. . . . I gritted my teeth and braced myself in anticipation of the shock of being struck down at any moment. It seemed impossible that any of us could make it across."

When Sledge made it to the northeastern side of the field, and found cover in some low bushes, he was "shaking like a leaf. I looked at one of the Guadalcanal veterans and he was shaking as bad as I was." Sledge almost laughed with relief.

Some men bled to death on the fire-swept airfield; there was no way anybody could get to them in time. The Marines were told to keep moving and not to stop and help the wounded. But an African-American Marine in one of the ammunition companies picked up a white Marine from Mississippi and carried him all the way to the aid station.

That night Sledge's unit moved through the mangrove swamps near the airfield and dug in for the night. It was impossible to get even five consecutive minutes of sleep because of the intensity of the enemy infiltration. "We never used the night," said Marine Benis Frank. "I can only think of two night operations, one on Iwo Jima and one on Okinawa, that were successful. We owned the daytime for the most part, but the Japanese owned the night." [21]

By now it was clear to almost every Marine on the island that the Japanese were not fighting as they had on Saipan and Tarawa, where they had massed their strength on the beachhead and tried to stop the Marines at the waterline. That tactic had failed everywhere. Colonel Nakagawa had contested the landing with one full battalion, inflicting over 1,100 casualties on D-Day, but he had placed most of his troops in caves in the limestone ridges north of the airfield and waited for the Americans to come to him. Beginning with Peleliu, the Japanese would rely on a preplanned defense-in-depth strategy, luring the Americans toward their strong points and unleashing hurricanes of fire from positions that neither naval nor air bombardment could reach. Japan could not win the war this way, but it could hope to make it so hideously costly that the American public would demand an end to the bloodshed without insisting on unconditional surrender.

Peleliu's ungodly landscape was a perfect laboratory to test the new defense-in-depth tactics. Once the airfield was taken, the Marines had to secure it by going north into the Umurbrogol, a wild terrain that resembled a series of reefs that had reared up from the ocean floor, five parallel, razor-sharp ridges extending for two miles up the island. "The ruggedness of the terrain," said Sledge, "was almost indescribable. . . . There were these sheer canyons, the sides at ninety-degree angles, and they would be firing at us from two and three mutually supporting caves. It had a surrealistic appearance because the contours were all at crazy angles, and there was no smooth surface to any ridge."

Enemy terrain and tactics took their heaviest toll on Chesty Puller's 1st Marine Regiment. Puller tried to bull his way through nearly impregnable enemy positions on Bloody Nose Ridge, suffering unsustainable casualties. He was a stubborn and fearless fighter, known to take long chances, but there was an almost manic quality to his aggressiveness on Peleliu, perhaps because he had just lost a brother, a fellow Marine, on Guam. He was supported by the equally unbending General Rupertus. When the overall commander of the operation, General Roy Geiger, offered to land an Army regiment being held in reserve to support Puller, Rupertus flatly refused. He distrusted the Army; the Marines would get the job done. To compound the problem, both Rupertus and Puller were hurt. Rupertus had broken an ankle in a training exercise and his injury prevented him from getting to the front to see how badly things were going. Puller aggravated a leg wound he suffered at Guadalcanal and had to be carried around on a stretcher.[22]

Major Ray Davis's 1st Battalion lost 71 percent of its number, including all the officers in the rifle companies except one; and that man, Captain Everett Pope, had a hair-raising escape from death that won him a Medal of Honor. "We were finished as a fighting force," recalls Davis, "and the survivors were numb." Davis blames Rupertus and Puller, but the entire Peleliu campaign, he says, represented "a total failure of intelligence."[23]

After taking the airport, Sledge's regiment fought for a day or so in the hills next to the 1st Marines and heard their complaints, witnessed their morale sagging. "We had lost too many good men," George Hunt writes, "how long could it keep up?"[24]

At this point in the battle, Sledge's regimental commander, Colonel Harold

"Bucky" Harris, flew over the Umurbrogol in a scout plane to see what the Marines were up against. He then went to Puller and Rupertus and told them they could never take the coral mountain by frontal assault because "the contours of the ridges were like Swiss cheese, full of caves, situated in mutually supporting positions." He recommended that they pull back and move north, where the cave defense system was weaker. Attacking from north to south, using siege tactics, they could root out the Japanese, one position at a time, with artillery, tanks, and newly developed long-range flamethrowers mounted on armored vehicles. When Rupertus came close to accusing Harris of cowardice, saying he was using too much ammunition and not enough men, Harris shot back, "General, I'm lavish with my ammunition and stingy with my men's lives." At that moment, the tent flap opened and in came General Geiger, who looked directly at Harris and said, "That's the most sensible thing I've ever heard. You can't take positions with dead marines."[25]

Geiger overruled Rupertus. On the ninth day of the battle a regiment of the Army's 81st Division, the Wildcats, relieved the shot-up 1st Marines, who had taken more casualties than any Marine regiment in the war up to this point. Trying to force the impossible, and do the job entirely with Marines, Puller and Rupertus nearly destroyed one of the best regiments in the Corps.

"You the 1st Marines?" a correspondent asked as Puller's leathernecks came off the line. "There ain't no more 1st Marines," came the reply from somewhere in the ranks.[26]

As the exhausted remnants of the 1st Marines walked off to a "safe" area near the sea, George Hunt watched some of his men find beds for themselves on the coral, while others carried their dead comrades to the beach, where "they laid them down respectfully in a straight row. There were no sheets to cover them."[27]

INTO THE UMURBROGOL

Twenty days later Sledge's regiment would be relieved, its ranks almost as decimated as those of the 1st Marines. This was after it went into the Umurbrogol to reinforce the 7th Marines. It was sent there after all the vital positions on the island had been taken: the airfield, the commanding ridge above it, and all of the island south, east, and north of Umurbrogol Mountain, including the neighboring island of Ngesebus. There would be no more frontal assaults from the south. Instead, the Marines and the Wildcats would follow Harris's more cautious plan. "We moved

AMERICAN CORSAIR BOMBING JAPANESE POSITIONS IN
THE UMURBROGOL, PELELIU, PALAU ISLANDS (USMC).

much faster, took more positions, and killed just scores of Japs because we could flush them out of the caves with direct fire from artillery, tanks, and flamethrowers," recalls Sledge. Even so, the cave fighting in the Umurbrogol was primeval, a struggle between the hunters and the hunted, the Americans above ground and the Japanese below.

The landscape had been blasted free of vegetation and scarred white by a steady storm of phosphorus shells, the explosions covering the Americans with coral dust. "When it would rain the dust, being lime, would harden, and we would move our arms and the pieces of coral would crack and fall off our dust-hardened dungarees," says Sledge. They became a living part of that war-ruined terrain and stank almost as badly as it did. The heat and the fear made them sweat, and the smell of their bodies was nauseating even to themselves. Worse, it blended with the odor of their dead. "In the tropics, when men were killed in the morning they would begin to bloat and stink pretty badly by night," Sledge recalled in a conversation long after the war.

WE WOULD COVER OUR DEAD WITH ponchos, from head to toe, and put them on stretchers behind the company area. But the dead Japs were lying all over the place in the ridges. There was no place to bury them in that coral. So they just bloated and rotted. Maggots tumbled out of their mouths and eyes, and big blowflies swarmed around the bodies. The flies would also get after our food and nothing scared them away. . . . You had to pick them off your K rations. Often we had to eat within two or three feet of a dead Jap, and he'd be pretty rotten. And the flies that were on the dead Jap would land on our canteen cups and sometimes fall into the coffee. We didn't have a lot of coffee, so we just pulled the flies out and drank it.

There was another problem. Typically, when a man who was under fire had to defecate he used a grenade canister or ration can and threw it out of his foxhole, covering it up with dirt the next day. If you were not under fire you could go back a little way off the line and dig a small hole. But there was no soil in the limestone hills of Peleliu, so there was this terrible odor from feces. Most of us got severe diarrhea and that added to our sanitary problems. The odor was absolutely vile. You felt you would never get the stench of dead and rot and filth out of your nostrils. And at night the land crabs would come out and swarm over the dead Japs. Then shells would come in and blow big chunks of the rotting corpses all over the place.

Worse than the filth was the fatigue. "The fatigue a combat infantryman is exposed to is absolutely beyond description. . . . [After a couple of weeks], we were literally shuffling around like zombies."

They began to weaken mentally as well. The entire time Sledge was on Peleliu he did not recall a single second when there was not a gun firing. There was no front line; the entire island *was* the front. That wore men down and made them feel helpless and vulnerable. "When buddies were killed or wounded, many of us just simply cried."

The men soon realized they had been sent into a death trap. In most Storm Landings—with the prominent exception of Tarawa—the Marines usually outnumbered the enemy by about three to one. But on Peleliu there were 9,000 Marines in infantry units fighting nearly 11,000 Japanese. As casualties mounted, cooks, bakers, drivers, and supply men, including African-Americans from the ammunition and supply companies, were given rifles and thrown into the fight. And every man in a rifle company, even the company commander, had to serve as a stretcher-bearer at one

1ST MARINES IN THE UMURBROGOL, PELELIU (USMC).

time or another. This was dangerous duty. "The Japs," says Sledge, "absolutely opened up on stretcher-bearers with everything they had. You cannot imagine the cold hatred we had of people who shot at us as we were taking out our wounded and were unable to fire back. Historians say we hated the Japs because we were racists. Racism had nothing to do with it. It was the way they fought."

Every day, soldiers and Marines witnessed signs of the unyielding ferocity of the enemy. Late in the fight, Sledge spotted the bodies of three dead Marines in a shell hole. They were badly decomposed, but this was to be expected in the tropics. As he looked closer, however, he was stricken with horror and revulsion—and rage such as he had never felt before. One man was decapitated. His head and severed hands rested on his chest and his penis had been stuffed into his mouth. The second man had been gruesomely mutilated in the same way. The third Marine looked like he had been chopped up like a steer in the Chicago stockyards.

This was "savagery beyond necessity," Sledge wrote later, and it changed the way he fought. He began killing without regret or remorse, routinely shooting dead and wounded enemy soldiers after seizing a position "to make sure they were dead. Survival was hard enough in the infantry without taking chances being humane to men who fought so savagely."

George Hunt put this differently. "If it hadn't been for [the Japanese] we would never have been on this goddam island in the middle of no place with all these rocks, the blasted heat and no water or chow. . . . We hated them, and we would kill them and keep killing them or we would be killed." [28]

In the Umurbrogol, there was probably more Japanese infiltration than anywhere else in the Pacific. The enemy slept in the caves all day and slipped out at night, singly or in twos and threes. The Americans, waiting in their shallow foxholes, had a password, one the Japanese could not pronounce clearly. If a garbled reply came back, the fight was on. The infiltrators would toss grenades and charge, screaming and swinging a saber or a freshly sharpened bayonet. "The sounds of the fights in the foxholes were ungodly," Sledge recalls. "Grunts and curses and screams. The fighting was savage, Neanderthal . . . Its purpose was to inflict casualties and to wear us down, which it did." As Benis Frank remarked: "It was good so many of us were so young. Only a young man could fight all day and all night." [29]

Sometimes the Japanese infiltrated in order to kill Americans wounded by shellfire earlier in the day. Sledge lost friends in these raids, which he considered yet another loathsome form of warfare, one that provoked an equal savagery in some of his comrades. Marines and Army infantry stripped Japanese corpses, looking for souvenirs—sabers, pistols, flags, hara-kiri knives, even gold teeth, which they cut out with their knives, sometimes before the wounded victim was dead. "Time had no meaning; life had no meaning. The fierce struggle for survival in the abyss of Peleliu eroded the veneer of civilization and made savages of us all," Sledge wrote in his memoirs. "We lived in an environment totally incomprehensible to the men behind the lines—service troops and civilians."

In a break in the fighting, Sledge saw a dead Japanese soldier squatting on the ground in front of his machine gun. The top of his head had been blown off, cleanly severed as if a power saw had done the job. "I noticed this buddy of mine just flippin' chunks of coral into the skull. . . . It rained all that night and the rain collected inside his skull. . . . Each time [my buddy's] pitch was true, I heard a little splash of rainwater in the ghastly receptacle. . . . There was nothing malicious in his action. This was just a mild-mannered kid who was now a twentieth-century savage. . . .

"We all had become hardened. We were out there, human beings, the most highly developed form of life on earth, fighting like wild animals."

The fighting stopped for Sledge on October 30, 1944, when his broken regiment was sent back to Pavuvu, his own Company K having suffered 64 percent casualties. The Army's Wildcats were left to finish the job, and it would take them another six hard weeks. On the night of November 24, Colonel Nakagawa, having carried out his instructions to bleed the Americans—killing or wounding 9,615 soldiers and Marines—burned his colors and shot himself in a cave in the shell-blasted Umurbrogol. Only a handful of his men were still alive. They melted into the coral ridges and did not surface and surrender until a year and a half after the war. To take Peleliu and two nearby islands, Angaur and Ngesebus, cost one American casualty and 1,589 rounds of ammunition for each Japanese defender killed.

The image that best captures the agony of Peleliu is Tom Lea's *Two-Thousand-Yard Stare*. It is the portrait of a young Marine that Lea saw in a sick bay he passed by on his way off the island. "I noticed a tattered marine standing quietly by a corpsman, staring stiffly at nothing. His mind had crumbled in battle, his jaw hung, and his eyes were like two black empty holes in his head." [30] When Lea painted him, he put him against the background of Bloody Nose Ridge. Lea's notes tell the man's story: "Last evening he came down out of the hills. Told to get some sleep, he found a shell crater and slumped into it. He's awake now. First light has given his gray face eerie color. He left the States 31 months ago. He was wounded in his first campaign. He has had tropical diseases. There is no food or water in the hills, except what you carry. He half-sleeps at night and gouges Japs out of holes all day. Two thirds of his company has been killed or wounded but he is still standing. So he will return to attack this morning. How much can a human being endure?" [31]

The Japanese defense of Peleliu did nothing to halt the American advance on the home islands, nothing to weaken American resolve to fight to the finish. Neither did taking Peleliu put America closer to winning the war. Peleliu received almost no news coverage while it was being fought and today it is a forgotten battle. All attention was on MacArthur's invasion of the Philippines and Eisenhower's drive from the tangled country of Normandy, where the Allied armies broke through tremendous German resistance in midsummer, to the borders of Germany, where they stalled that autumn in front of the Siegfried Line, the menacing belt of fortifications at the western gates of the Nazi fatherland. But Peleliu, as Sledge says, must not be forgotten. One of the most murderously fought battles in all of history, it is a lasting reminder of the debasing consequences of unrestrained war, fighting without letup or conscience.

As Eugene Sledge's ship pulled away from Peleliu, with fighting still raging in the smoking canyons of the Umurbrogol, he felt the island pulling him back, as if it were some tremendous magnet. He was terrified his regiment would be ordered to return at the very last minute to stop some unexpected counterattack or some threat to the airfield. But perhaps he felt the pull of the place because he had left some part of himself there, never to be retrieved. It wasn't innocence, but it was everything he had known as youth.

That was nothing, however, compared to the unbearable price his 1st Marine Division paid for a worthless strip of coral in one of the most remote places on earth.

CHAPTER 6

The Return

O N SEPTEMBER 15, 1944, THE MORNING the Old Breed went over the reef at Peleliu, General Douglas MacArthur's troops landed on the strategically important island of Morotai, northwest of New Guinea, taking it easily. This gave MacArthur a forward air base to hit Leyte, the midrib of the Philippines. All the while, Bull Halsey's Task Force 38 hammered the Philippine island of Luzon, along with Formosa and Okinawa, shattering Japanese airpower in the area.* MacArthur was now ready to strike.

The invasion plan brought together the two great Pacific offenses—MacArthur's forces advancing from the South Pacific up the coast of New Guinea and Nimitz's forces advancing from Tarawa across the Central Pacific. The U.S. Third Fleet, commanded by Halsey, was the most awesome naval force ever assembled. It

---

* After Halsey completed his work with MacArthur in the South Pacific, Nimitz alternated him with Spruance as commander of the main naval striking arm in the Pacific. This system allowed for a quickened pace of operations, with one commander always at sea while the other planned future operations. With Spruance in command, the Fifth Fleet retained its name. Under Halsey, it became the Third Fleet. Under Halsey, Spruance's Fast Carrier Task Force 58 became Task Force 38.

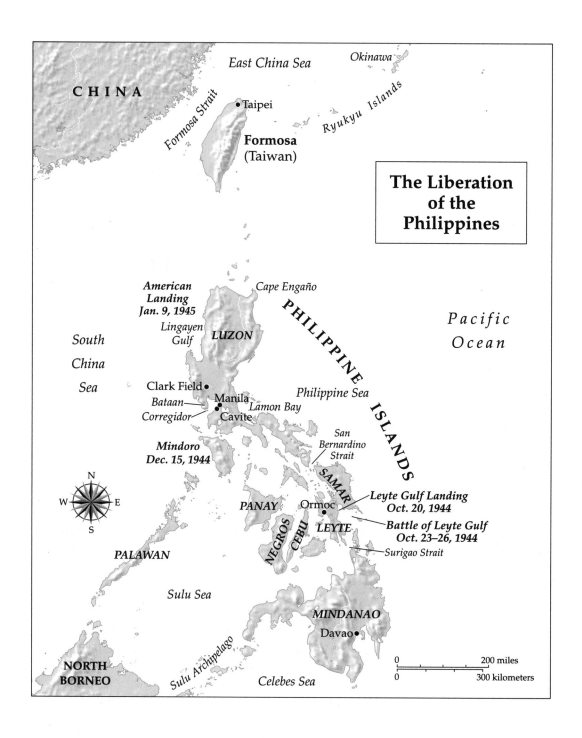

The Liberation of the Philippines

CHINA

East China Sea

Okinawa

Formosa Strait

Taipei

Formosa
(Taiwan)

Ryukyu Islands

Pacific
Ocean

South
China
Sea

American
Landing
Jan. 9, 1945

Cape Engaño

PHILIPPINE ISLANDS

Lingayen
Gulf

LUZON

Clark Field

Philippine Sea

Bataan
Corregidor

Manila
Cavite

Lamon Bay

Mindoro
Dec. 15, 1944

San
Bernardino
Strait

SAMAR

Leyte Gulf Landing
Oct. 20, 1944

PANAY

Ormoc

LEYTE

NEGROS

CEBU

Battle of Leyte Gulf
Oct. 23–26, 1944

PALAWAN

Surigao Strait

Sulu Sea

MINDANAO

Davao

N
W   E
S

PALAWAN

NORTH
BORNEO

Sulu Archipelago

Celebes Sea

0   200 miles
0   300 kilometers

would act as a shield, keeping the Japanese navy away from the assault force—MacArthur's Sixth Army, 200,000 men strong under Lieutenant General Walter Krueger. Providing close support, and putting the troops ashore, would be the job of "MacArthur's Navy," Vice Admiral Thomas C. Kinkaid's smaller Seventh Fleet of old battleships, small escort carriers, and troop transports.

The Americans landed on Leyte on October 20, 1944. Just after the first waves hit Red Beach, General MacArthur, wearing his Philippine field marshal's cap, sunglasses, and freshly pressed khakis, stepped into knee-deep water and walked toward the beach, two and a half years after he had left Bataan. Standing in a rainstorm, holding a microphone, he made an announcement: "People of the Philippines, I have returned. . . . Rally to me. Let the indomitable spirit of Bataan and Corregidor lead. . . . For your homes and hearths, strike! For future generations of your sons and daughters, strike! In the name of your sacred dead, strike!"

General Tomoyuki Yamashita, the Japanese commander on Leyte, said that had he known MacArthur himself was coming ashore he would have formed a suicide squad and killed him.[1]

THE BATTLE OF LEYTE GULF

More men went ashore on the first day of the Leyte invasion than landed in Normandy on D-Day. Although any thought of the Pacific D-Days brings up an image of assaulting Marines, the U.S. Army, under MacArthur, made more landings (some thirty of them before the Philippines), put more troops into battle, and took greater casualties than the Marine Corps in America's epic Pacific offensive.

Meeting unexpectedly light resistance, Krueger's troops swept inland, captured a strategic airfield, and put bulldozers to work preparing an airstrip long enough to handle the medium bombers and long-range fighters of George Kenney's Air Force. But before this airstrip was completed, the navies of Imperial Japan and the United States met head-on in the greatest sea battle ever fought.

For Japan, the Battle of Leyte Gulf was to be the decisive engagement of a war that had turned disastrously against it. It was Japan's last chance to protect its economic lifeline through the South China Sea to its southern resource empire. It was the Emperor, not his military leaders, who decided to make Leyte, not Luzon, the major battle for the Philippines. "Contrary to the views of the Army and the Navy General Staffs, I agreed to the showdown battle of Leyte thinking that if we attacked at Leyte and America flinched, then we would probably be able to find room to negotiate."[2]

It was a horrible strategic mistake. The calamitous naval and infantry losses on Leyte and in Leyte Gulf made the later defense of Luzon almost impossible. But going into the battle, the navy was confident. It had lost most of its carrier strength, but its commanders thought its formidable battleship and cruiser forces could deliver rapid and shattering blows. When the American invasion force hit Leyte, the Japanese set in motion a huge, highly complex counteroffensive. The key to it was a diversionary move, one that counted on Admiral Halsey's notorious aggressiveness. Admiral Jisaburo Ozawa's carrier force, with the decks of the flattops almost empty, would lure Halsey's fleet away from the Leyte beaches. At that point, two strike forces of battleships and cruisers would steam into Leyte Gulf, one from the north through San Bernardino Strait, the other from the south through Surigao Strait. This giant pincer movement would converge on the Leyte beachhead and annihilate the smaller American fleet that was covering the beachhead, isolating the troops that had already landed. It was a desperate gamble—an oceanic banzai charge.

Vice Admiral Takeo Kurita's attack force, the strongest to be deployed, was the

GENERAL DOUGLAS MacARTHUR RETURNS TO THE PHILIPPINES. VICE ADMIRAL THOMAS C. KINKAID IS STANDING TO MacARTHUR'S RIGHT (SC).

first to arrive in the Philippines. Two American submarines, *Darter* and *Dace,* sighted it heading for the San Bernardino Strait on the morning of October 23 and closed in for the kill, sinking two heavy cruisers, one of them Kurita's flagship. But they could not stop the gigantic fleet, which included five battleships, among them the world's two biggest warships, *Musashi* and *Yamato.* Switching his flag to *Yamato,* the shaken but implacable Kurita headed for San Bernardino Strait.

When Halsey got word of the fast-approaching Japanese fleet, he launched his Hellcat fighters against it in what turned into a furious, day-long air battle. The Japanese got the worst of it. One of their land-based bombers destroyed the light carrier *Princeton,* but Kurita lost the massive *Musashi,* which was ripped apart by nineteen torpedo and seventeen bomb hits and finally rolled over and sank, taking with her half her crew of 2,300 men. Even more damaging was the loss of 150 planes, nine of them to fighter ace David McCampbell, punishing evidence of overwhelming American air superiority in the Pacific. As night approached, Kurita broke off the engagement, not wanting to risk *Yamato* and his other heavy ships, all of which were pounded in the narrow San Bernardino Strait.

As Kurita steamed west to get beyond range of Halsey's carrier planes, Halsey received a report on the afternoon of October 24 that Ozawa's decoy fleet had been spotted 300 miles to the north. He set out after it at dawn the next day, with his entire Third Fleet, seeing the enemy carriers as his most important prey. In one of the most controversial decisions of the Pacific war, he failed to leave even a single picket destroyer to guard San Bernardino Strait. Nor did he tell Kinkaid that he was leaving the pass uncovered. Later, Halsey would say that he was confident Kurita had no more fight in him. He was almost right. Kurita had begun to withdraw, but goaded by his fellow commanders, who questioned his resolve, he reversed course and moved to strike the Leyte beachhead. As he passed through San Bernardino Strait on the night of October 24–25 to join the attack force heading up from the south through Surigao Strait, the Japanese believed they were about to win the most momentous naval victory of the war. They might have, had not the American commanders pulled off what Halsey called "one of the prettiest ambushes in naval history."[5]

As darkness fell on the 24th, Admiral Kinkaid's flotilla of PT boats took station just outside Surigao Strait, where Ferdinand Magellan had sailed into the Philippines in 1521. His destroyers lined the thirty-five miles of the strait itself. At the end of the narrow passage Kinkaid placed six old battleships in a line. Five of them had been sunk or damaged at Pearl Harbor, repaired, modernized, and sent to avenge themselves. The cruisers were with them.

About midnight, a PT boat signaled that the Japanese were approaching the strait. In the darkness, the PTs got two hits but the Japanese steamed on, in double column, tearing through the passage at twenty knots. The destroyers held their fire; battleships and cruisers were silent, hidden by the darkness, in the dead calm sea.

About 3:00 A.M. on the 25th, Rear Admiral Jessie B. Oldendorf, commander of Kinkaid's six battleships, ordered "Commence firing!" The destroyers steamed toward the enemy ships and fired their torpedoes. Incandescent flashes lighted Surigao Strait as the torpedoes struck home. The cruisers, ranged on opposite sides of the trap, opened fire on the Japanese caught between them. Colored recognition lights flashed as the confused Japanese, thinking their own ships were attacking them, tried to weather the storm of steel and flame. The lights gave the American cruisers splendid targets—until both the Japanese ships and the U.S. destroyers laid down smoke screens. The one U.S. destroyer crippled by Japanese fire lurched in the smoke, while the others withdrew and opened fire with their hard-hitting five-inch batteries.

Confusion failed to alter the enemy's determination: the ships plunged on through Surigao Strait, firing wildly and inaccurately. This gave Admiral Oldendorf an opportunity presented to few naval commanders. He "crossed the T" of the Japanese battle line—an action where one fleet advancing in a column forms a vertical bar and thus can fire only its forward-pointing guns, while the attackers form a horizontal bar (the top of the T) and bring their broadsides to bear, annihilating the opposition.

One after the other the Japanese ships reached a narrow part of the strait and turned, presenting perfect targets. The six American battleships, only twelve miles away, did not even have to shift the range of their radar-controlled guns. Ship after Japanese ship became a torch in the night. The cruisers and destroyers sank the remainder as they fled, leaving only wreckage and long streaks of flaming oil. The southern half of the Japanese pincer was broken. "Silence followed," wrote Admiral Samuel Eliot Morison, "to honor the passing of the tactics which had so long been foremost in naval warfare." All the great naval actions of the past three centuries, including Trafalgar and Jutland, "had been fought by classic line-of-battle tactics. In the unearthly silence that followed the roar of Oldendorf's 14-inch and 16-inch guns in Surigao Strait, one could imagine the ghosts of all great admirals, from Raleigh and De Ruyter to Togo and Jellicoe, standing at attention to salute the passing of the kind of naval warfare that they all understood. For in those opening minutes of the morning watch of 25 October 1944, Battle Line became as obsolete as the row-galley tactics of Salamis and Syracuse."[4]

Early the next morning, Rear Admiral Clifton Sprague, in charge of a flotilla of small escort carriers and destroyers, sighted the tall masts of Kurita's battleships coming over the western horizon, heading for Leyte Gulf, where the beaches were stacked with ammunition, food, and military hardware. Sprague's escort carriers—lightly armed, converted merchant ships carrying only eighteen to twenty-six planes—were directly in Kurita's path, but were no match for the four battleships and seven cruisers that hove into view.

Kinkaid, and later Nimitz, at Pearl Harbor, sent urgent messages to Halsey asking for help, but Halsey broke off action with Ozawa too late to help Sprague. Realizing he was on his own, Sprague launched every plane he had against the steel Goliaths boring in on him. The Japanese fleet steamed straight on, paying little attention to the four destroyer escorts and three destroyers that laid down smoke screens, darting in and out, matching their small fire against the thunderous volleys of the battleships, in what Admiral Kinkaid called the "most daring and most effective action" of the entire war.[5] Heavy Japanese cruisers sank one American escort carrier and hit others with crushing fire, while battleships put down two destroyers and one destroyer escort. But just as Kurita seemed on the brink of a great victory he turned and headed back toward San Bernardino Strait after losing his third heavy cruiser from air and destroyer attacks.

"At 0925 my mind was occupied with dodging torpedoes," Sprague recalls, "when near the bridge I heard one of the signalmen yell, 'Goddamit, boys, they're getting away!' I could not believe my eyes, but it looked as if the whole Japanese Fleet was indeed retiring. However, it took a whole series of reports from circling planes to convince me. And still I could not get the fact to soak into my battle-numbed brain. At best, I had expected to be swimming by this time."[6]

In the smoke and chaos of battle, Kurita believed, not unreasonably, that he was facing carriers from Halsey's fleet, for he was engaging over 400 fighters and torpedo planes, the dauntless airmen making dry runs after running out of ammunition. Kurita was also convinced, after intercepting and misreading Kinkaid's messages to Halsey, that Halsey was fast approaching with more heavy carriers, and that he would block San Bernardino Strait. Sprague's escort carriers, their destroyer screens, and their brave aviators had stopped what Admiral Morison describes as "the most powerful gunfire force which Japan had sent to sea since the Battle of Midway."[7]

After mauling the Japanese carrier fleet, Halsey steamed back to the waters off Leyte. His vanguard arrived at 1:30 P.M. on the 25th, and his planes joined those of the Seventh Fleet in harrying the fleeing enemy. One more carrier was sunk, and on that evening a submarine made a final kill, a heavy cruiser, completing the destruction of almost the entire Japanese naval force. The official score stood: four carriers, three battleships, ten cruisers, and eleven destroyers sunk—in actual tonnage, more than a quarter of all Japanese losses since Pearl Harbor. After the three-day Battle of Leyte Gulf, the Japanese navy was finished.

But just as naval history's last great surface conflict was concluding, the enemy pulled a wildly unexpected move. After Kurita retreated, several wounded U.S. escort carriers were hit by a new and terrifying weapon: the kamikaze corps. Kamikaze, which means "divine wind," refers to the typhoons that twice destroyed the fleets of Mongol invaders of Japan in the thirteenth century. The new suicide planes, armed with heavy bombs, damaged three vessels and sank one.

"Then in succeeding weeks they attacked our ships in Leyte Gulf," Admiral Kinkaid recalls. "Every day I could see the faces from the skippers down to the lowest seamen, getting longer and longer because they just couldn't stop the kamikazes. . . . As they approached, one plane would drop behind, as though there was something wrong with the engine; as the larger group went over the ships, all the antiaircraft would be trained on them, and then the plane that had dropped behind would come in in a dive. The kamikazes had a lot of tricks like that. . . . They did a great deal of . . . damage."[8]

After the Battle of Leyte Gulf both King and Nimitz were convinced that Halsey had made an unforgivable mistake in leaving open San Bernardino Strait. Another commander might have been removed, but Halsey was too important to the cause, and he had MacArthur's complete support. Overhearing a group of Navy men take Halsey to task at an officer's dinner for "abandoning us" while he went after the decoy fleet, MacArthur slammed his fist on the table and roared, "That's enough! Leave the Bull alone! He's still a fighting admiral in my book."[9]

THE FIGHT FOR LEYTE

On Leyte, MacArthur's troops made slow progress against enemy forces in the vast and wild interior. Yamashita had planned to meet the Americans in force on Luzon, not here. But bowing to the Emperor's decision, he improvised and fought a masterful defensive battle.[10] He pulled in reinforcements from neighboring islands, increasing his garrison from 23,000 to almost 70,000 troops. And these ferociously dedicated soldiers contested nearly every inch of ground in the lakelike rice paddies and precipitous mountains of Leyte. The battle was waged in the most wretched natural conditions imaginable. During the fighting, Leyte was hit by three typhoons and an earthquake.

Artillery officer Linwood Crider, twenty-three years old at the time, describes the nearly two-month-long battle for Leyte—like Peleliu, one of the largely forgotten struggles of the Pacific war:

I WAS A YOUNG ARTILLERY OFFICER and, although I had been in the South Pacific for a while, I had not participated in an operation of this magnitude. The artillery group that I was assigned to was part of the XXIV Corps Artillery. For the Leyte operation we were to provide support to the 96th and 7th Infantry Divisions. . . .

Leyte is a little over 100 miles in length and forty-five miles at its widest point. . . . We entered Leyte Gulf during the night of October 19 and . . . landed on the eastern side of the island just north of the little town of Dulag.

We landed almost unopposed and secured a beachhead. . . . Our landing had been so easy I thought perhaps we were being lured into some kind of trap. . . .

For the next three days we moved south and then I started to earn my money. First of all, the rains came. It rained between thirty and forty inches the first month we were there. Later on the rains increased. It rained over sixteen inches in one day. With the water came lots of mud. It was a special kind of mud. On the surface it was very slick, but once you sank in, it seemed to have an unusual adhesive quality. This mud also did not smell good, probably because it contained a large amount of rotting organic matter.

The worst part came at night. That's when you had to dig a hole to sleep in. Even though you quickly covered the hole with a poncho the water seeped in. And with the water came the leeches. It wasn't unusual to find a dozen of these little bloodsuckers on you in the morning. . . .

On the night of October 24 . . . we began to hear distant cannonading and could see the flash of big gun fire being reflected off low-lying clouds. . . . The firing increased until it was almost a continuous rumble. It now seemed apparent that a significant naval engagement was taking place off the southeast coast of Leyte. The sound of this gunfire continued until about 0200 the next morning. We had no way of knowing its outcome. . . . The next day we learned [from a downed Navy pilot] that "Kinkaid had kicked their ass."

During the next few days we continued the push to the west. . . . There is a ridge of mountains running down the center of Leyte that goes up to about 4,500 feet. This is extremely rugged terrain. It is covered with dense tropical growth. When you drop an artillery shell into growth like this it seems to get totally lost. . . .

The whole month of November was a miserable time. [Other Army units] had secured the north end of the island but had run into the same problem that we did when trying to push down the west coast to Ormoc. Ormoc was the major town on the west coast and it was through here that the Japanese reinforcements were being brought in from other islands in the Philippines.

The Japanese strategy for the defense of Leyte had also changed during this period. Their initial strategy was to save their best for the defense of Luzon, which was politically more significant than Leyte. They now decided to throw everything available into the defense of Leyte. Air strikes from Luzon were in-

creased and the first kamikaze attacks on the supply ships in Leyte harbor were initiated. The Japanese called this new offensive the "Wa Operation." . . .

It was in our section that [they] launched . . . the Wa Operation. Their objective was to recapture all of the airstrips on eastern Leyte and to bring their planes to these strips to support this offensive. What a stupid thing to do. These airstrips were a sea of mud and therefore worthless. . . .

[During this offensive] an incoming mortar round [hit our position.] I knew immediately that the company commander and platoon sergeant were dead. My left eye filled with blood so I had a problem assessing any further damage. I lay there for a minute, sort of numbed by what had happened. It was getting dark. I then became aware of someone trying to move me. My left leg hurt and was bleeding. A medic cut my pant leg and found a piece of shrapnel sticking in my fibula. He pulled it out and put on a compress to stop the bleeding.

Just when I was thinking that my situation wasn't that bad, I felt a pain in my lower abdomen. The medic took a quick look with a flashlight. I had been gutshot. . . .

I was quite sure I was going to die. Morning did come though and I was still alive. Three others were not. I somehow got loaded onto the back of a weapons carrier and made the bumpy ride to the battalion aid station. The doctor took a quick look at me and tagged me to go to the field hospital. . . .

My seventh day I was allowed to go back to my unit for "light duty." It was now approaching the middle of December. The 77th Division had assaulted Ormoc and taken it. The Japanese on Leyte were now cut off from receiving outside support from the other islands in the Philippines. . . .

I had about a dozen letters from my parents and my fiancée. . . . We had decided to wait until after the war to get married. I read the last letter from her first. Her opening paragraph began, "When you read this I'm sure you'll understand." . . . Here I lay on some far, distant battlefield and all the while she was with another man. She said since she hadn't heard from me for such a long time she assumed that I had lost interest in her. . . .

On the 15th of December General MacArthur declared that Leyte was secured and the fighting had ended. It's too bad he wasn't there to see what was going on because the fighting wasn't over. There were still thousands of Japanese soldiers on Leyte and they did not plan to surrender. It wasn't until [March 1945] that the Japanese on Leyte were neutralized. [Between Christmas Day and the end of the campaign the Americans killed more than 27,000 Japanese.]

By mid-January . . . we got some good news. We were no longer part of MacArthur's command and therefore would not be going to Luzon. Our destination was Okinawa, another place I had never heard of.

For his service in World War II—and the Korean War—Linwood Crider received twelve military decorations and awards, including a Purple Heart, a Bronze Star, and a Presidential Citation. "All my awards were for merit," he says today. "I got none for valor. I am not a hero."[11]

Sixty-five thousand Japanese soldiers died to hold Leyte, killing or wounding 15,500 Americans. Many of these boys breathed their last to take and hold terrain in central Leyte that was unsuitable for the construction of airfields. Steel mesh for runways sank or shifted dangerously in the soft soil, making the Leyte operation one of the most bungled intelligence efforts of the Pacific war. Inadequate air support led to further, and unnecessary, casualties, turning Leyte into an in-close infantry slugfest.

AMERICAN MORTAR SQUAD ON LEYTE (SC).

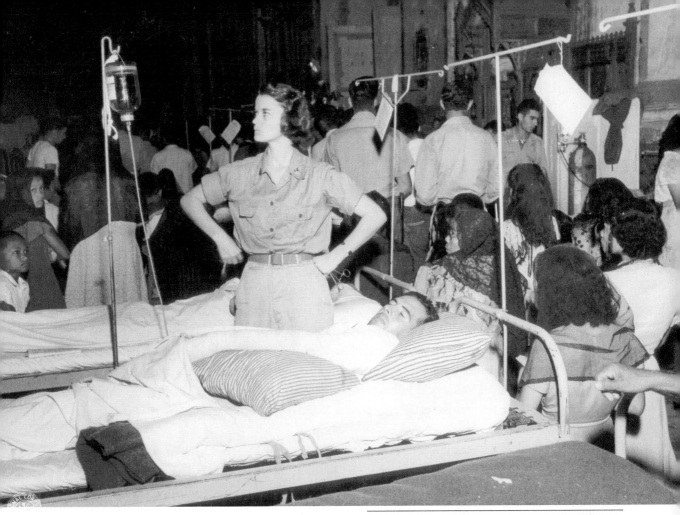

Many of the Americans fell in the weeks after MacArthur, in a publicity stunt typical of him, declared the island secured, to the amazement of Crider and other GIs. The historian of the 11th Airborne describes what MacArthur cavalierly called a mop-up operation. "Through mud and rain, over treacherous, rain-swollen gorges, through thick jungle growth, over slippery, narrow, root-tangled, steep foot trails, the Angels [as 11th Airborne troops called themselves] . . . pushed west to clear the Leyte mountain range of its tenacious defenders. It was bitter, exhausting, rugged fighting—physically, the most terrible we were ever to know." General Robert Eichelberger, commander of the U.S. Eighth Army, which relieved the Sixth Army on Leyte on Christmas Day, remarked that "if there is another war, I recommend that the military, and the correspondents . . . drop the phrase 'mopping up' from their vocabularies. It is not a good enough phrase to die for." [12]

Thousands of Japanese soldiers, weakened to the point of death by hunger and disease, fought on until the following April.

LIBERATION

Before the Americans left Leyte their dead and wounded were replaced by new draftees whose average age was nineteen. They went to Luzon to liberate 18 million Filipinos, the first large Christian population they had encountered in the Pacific.

The landing was made in Lingayen Gulf, north of Manila, on January 9, 1945, on the very spot where General Homma's troops had come ashore on the fifteenth day of the Pacific War. Despite furious attacks by waves of kamikazes, which sank or damaged forty ships of the invasion armada on its way to the beachhead, MacArthur landed a force of 68,000 men by nightfall. It would be the biggest American land engagement of the Pacific war and one the Japanese could not win, having lost so many troops, planes, and ships in trying to stop MacArthur on Leyte. "Now it is their turn to quake!" MacArthur declared. [13]

In all, MacArthur would bring 280,000 men to Luzon. Lying in wait for them but scattered widely on the island were 287,000 Japanese under General Yamashita, the largest enemy army the Americans faced in the Pacific. The stage was set, said *Life* magazine, for "the first large-scale slugging match with the Japanese army." [14]

Yamashita knew that massed American naval, air, and ground power made resistance at the beaches futile. His only option was to fight a protracted and bloody delaying action. "In Singapore, when I negotiated the surrender there with [General Sir Arthur] Percival, the only words I spoke to him were, 'Yes or no?' I intend to ask MacArthur the same question." [15] The "Tiger of Malaya" withdrew most of his forces to mountain strongholds in the east, opening the way for MacArthur's drive to Manila. Yamashita would sacrifice the capital to win the battle in the badlands.

The first big fight carried Krueger's forces across the Agno River, over low hills paralleling the gulf, and out onto the great plain leading to Manila, 110 miles southeast of Lingayen. Here tanks could operate on open terrain and fine roads.

On January 28, a band of handpicked men from the Army's 6th Ranger Battalion made a daring raid deep into Japanese-held territory on a prison camp at Cabanatuan. With the aid of Filipino guerrillas, the Rangers freed 513 American and

British POWs, including many survivors of the Bataan Death March. MacArthur would soon learn that only a third of the men he had left behind in Luzon had survived. After seeing the ghastly condition of the prisoners at Cabanatuan, and learning from his intelligence officers that other POWs and internees were dying of starvation, MacArthur called in the commander of the 1st Cavalry Division, Major General Verne D. Mudge. "Go to Manila," he ordered. "Go around the Nips, bounce off the Nips, but go to Manila. Free the internees and Santo Tomás."[16] Santo Tomás was the camp where 3,700 American men, women, and children, including the Army nurses of Bataan and Corregidor, had been interned for almost three years.

Mudge assembled two small "flying columns" of infantry and armor, a "modern version of a mounted cavalry unit," and sped for the capital, with Marine Corps dive-bombers covering his advance.[17] Along the way, jubilant Filipinos waved and shouted at them, handing them flowers, eggs, and beer. Forty-eight hours later, on the evening of February 3, they reached the city limits. The *New York Times* reported their entrance into the city:

> THE FIRST TWO FORCES HAD TO fight their way from house to house, in the face of fires and demolitions and through mined streets, to the north bank of the Pasig River, which cuts the city in two. After they crossed the stream in a fleet of amphibious trucks and moved into southern Manila, they were met with steady machine-gun and mortar fire from upper floors and from concrete pill-boxes placed at important intersections by the Japanese, who were still clinging to "Intramuros," the old walled section of the city on the Pasig's lower bank. . . .
>
> Immediately on their entrance into the capital, a flying squadron of cavalry-men sped to the gates of the Santo Tomás internment center where 3,700 persons, mostly women and children, were being detained. The troopers pushed through machine-gun nests and sniper fire up to the camp grounds and then fought from room to room to clean out the Japanese. Other forces, meanwhile, moved against burning Bilibid Prison, where 1,100 war prisoners and civilian internees were saved from flames.[18]

"Tanks were crashing at the gate," one of the Bataan nurses described the liberation of Santo Tomás. "I happened to be in the front building with a room above the front entrance. Tanks rolled to the front door." But in the darkness, no one could tell whose tanks they were. Then a soldier pulled himself out of one of the steel monsters and said simply, "Hello, folks." This was it. These were Americans. Pandemonium broke loose. Hysterically happy prisoners mobbed the soldiers of the 1st Cavalry. "The men in the tanks looked like giants to us because we were all so emaciated and thin," said Army nurse Martha Dworsky. "We were all laughing and crying, hanging out the windows, shouting and screaming and waving. It was a wild scene of joy and happiness," another nurse recalled.[19]

With the liberators was a figure familiar to the prisoners. "Carl Mydans. My God! It's Carl Mydans," cried a woman inmate as the *Life* photographer turned a flashlight on his face to identify himself.[20] Mydans had covered the battles of Bataan and Corregidor, and he and his wife, Shelley, a writer for *Life,* had been captured and interned in Santo Tomás for more than nine months before being sent to Shanghai, where they were freed in 1943 as part of a prisoner exchange. "I was picked up bodily," Mydans dispatched his editors on the morning after the liberation of Santo Tomás, "full camera pack, canteen belt, and all, and carried on the hands of the internees over their heads."[21]

Outside the main building, Mydans found a sight he had dreamed about many times. "In the brilliant light . . . stood three Japanese in officers' uniforms, ringed by soldiers pointing guns at them." The next day, he learned that every one of the prisoners was suffering from malnutrition. Most of them were so emaciated he did not recognize them. And they had been indoctrinated into a state of docility. "Even with

ENTERING MANILA (LRP).

husky welcoming Americans on the main gate, the internees would not venture past the swale fence which marked the out-of-bounds area."

On Sunday morning the American flag was raised over Santo Tomás. The whole camp shouted and cheered as the flag went up. Then someone started singing "God Bless America" and everyone joined in. "I have never heard it sung as it was sung that day," said Mydans. "I have never heard people singing 'God Bless America' and weeping openly. And they have never seen soldiers—hard-bitten youngsters such as make up the 1st Cavalry—stand unashamed and weep with them."

Later on, an American sergeant seemed confused when, leading the Japanese prison administrators away from the camp, a group of recently released children shouted to him, "Make them bow. Make them bow." [22]

By early February, MacArthur had more troops on Luzon. Landings had been made at Subic Bay on the west and at Nasugbu on the south. From both points, Allied forces were racing inland. By February 4, two American columns, including the 11th Airborne, led by General Robert Eichelberger, were within fifteen miles of Manila, MacArthur's spiritual home, the city where his mother had died, where he had courted his wife, and where his son, Arthur, had spent the first four years of his life. "We were ready for the dash on Manila," General Eichelberger recalled. "I pressed forward with the infantry, and my headquarters was set up in what had once been the annex of the Manila Hotel. It was a bare and looted building, but the view was just the way I remembered it. And just as beautiful.

"I could see the city of Manila gleaming whitely in the sunshine. I could see Corregidor, and the hook of the Cavite peninsula, which curves into Manila Bay. . . . It was strangely like a homecoming. But soon tall plumes of smoke began to rise in Manila, and at evening the tropical sky was crimsoned by many fires. The Japanese were deliberately destroying the magical town which had been traditionally called 'the Pearl of the Orient.' " [23]

The Americans drove in from three sides—the 1st Cavalry Division from the east, the 37th from the north, and Eichelberger's forces from the south. The 1st Cavalry got into the city without much trouble, but the 11th Airborne ran into 12,500 of the 16,700 Japanese sailors and marines that were guarding Manila and had to fight its way into the city, suffering heavy casualties. Earlier, Generarl Yamashita had declared Manila an Open City and ordered the commander of its defense garrison, Rear Admiral Sanji Iwabuchi, to withdraw his forces and join him in the mountains of northern Luzon. But Iwabuchi ignored that order, brought in big guns from damaged

AMERICAN NURSES LIBERATED FROM SANTO TOMÁS, MANILA (SC).

ships in the harbor, set up artillery pieces, rockets, and mortars, and staged a suicidal resistance from buildings designed to withstand earthquakes and typhoons.[24] "Manila was burning. The whole downtown section was smothered in roaring black billows of smoke," *Yank* correspondent H. N. Oliphant described the opening hours of the battle for the city. "The Jap shells were coming in. A sprawling wooden structure across the street got a direct hit. A Filipino girl stood beside us shaking her head. She said her father and baby brother were inside the burning building.

"A pretty, light-skinned woman, dressed in a kimono, was standing across the street. She scolded a little boy, who was pulling at her kimono. She pushed the child and yelled, 'Get away from me, you little Jap bastard!' "[25]

It was probably her own child, his father Japanese, and she did not want to be seen with him for fear of being branded an enemy collaborator. One American soldier, Fred Nixon, was walking along a street with a priest when they passed a procession of men carrying small coffins. "Father Rogers told us that the caskets contained the bodies of Filipino children whose fathers were Japanese. When it looked like we were winning, their families killed them so that they would not appear to be Japanese collaborators. He said the church could not condone the killings, but the children deserved a Christian funeral." [26]

These women feared reprisals for unspeakable acts of barbarity committed against their people by the Japanese. When Lester Tenney escaped for a short period from Camp O'Donnell after the Bataan Death March, he went into the hills with a small band of Filipino guerrillas. From a hilltop overlooking a village, he witnessed a group of Filipino women being tortured by the Japanese. "The women were tied, with their legs spread, to the stilts that supported their cottages. The Japanese put sticks of dynamite into their vaginas and started asking them questions that we couldn't hear. Then they lit the dynamite and within a matter of three minutes there were loud explosions and I could actually see the parts of bodies flying through the air." [27]

In some of the worst fighting of the war, building-to-building urban warfare akin to that at Stalingrad, a city of 800,000 people was almost completely destroyed, the most ravaged Allied capital after Warsaw. Nearly 100,000 Filipino civilians were killed in this urban holocaust, many of them in a succession of diehard reprisals by Iwabuchi's doomed defensive garrison. "Hospitals were set afire after the patients had been strapped to their beds. The corpses of males were mutilated, females of all ages were raped before they were slain, and babies' eyes were gouged out and smeared on walls like jelly," wrote historian William Manchester. [28]

The Japanese fought to the last man from the sewers of the city, where they were annihilated by American troops with grenades and flamethrowers. After walking through his ruined city, the Filipino journalist Carlos Romulo wrote: "Wherever I went I felt like a ghost hunting its way in a vanished world." [29] When MacArthur returned to Manila at the end of February to reestablish the civilian government, he was emotionally overcome by the plunder and slaughter and could not complete his speech. He ended instead with the Lord's Prayer.

THE LOS BAÑOS RAID

Three weeks after the liberation of Santo Tomás, MacArthur ordered an attack on a Japanese internment camp at Los Baños, forty-two miles southeast of Manila, where over 2,100 American and European civilians and POWs were slowly starving.

"It was a complicated problem," said General Eichelberger, who took part in the planning of the raid:

LOS BAÑOS WAS ON THE SOUTHERN tip of shallow Laguna de Bay, and thus some fifty miles behind enemy lines. It was estimated, and accurately, there were between eight and fifteen thousand enemy troops available for counterattack within four hours march of the camp. Past history had given us reason to fear that the Japanese camp guards, if they knew attack was imminent, might execute their prisoners and thus clean the slate. . . .

Trusted guerrilla spies were sent into the area. Five days before the operation they brought back a gentleman named Peter Miles, who had recently escaped from the camp and gone into hiding. Miles had been an engineer in the Philippines before the war, and his careful information was invaluable. Miles drew up an exact map of the camp. . . .

All of the planning was highly secret, and few of the troops involved knew anything about their mission until they were plucked from their positions near Fort McKinley under cover of darkness and moved to the positions from which they would make their attacks. Fifty-nine ungainly [amtracs] . . . moved noisily into Parañaque from the north. Nine C-47 planes . . . landed on Nichols Field [in Manila] and picked their way hopefully along the pitted runways. A company of paratroopers moved to Nichols Field and slept under the wings of the planes.

[Joseph Swing, commander of the] 11th Airborne, had planned, for the sake of surprise and safety of the internees, one of the oddest expeditions in military history. It was to include a ground force advance, an amphibious expedition, and a parachute drop. A great deal of faith, too, had to be placed on a reconnaissance platoon [of American soldiers and Filipino guerrillas, led by Lieutenant George Skau]. They departed in bancas [small boats] two days before the operation and, after reaching the southern shore, went into hiding.[30]

Luis M. Burris, commander of Dog Battery, an artillery company with the 11th Airborne, was with the amphibious tractors. He had been told that intelligence reports indicated that the Japanese planned to kill the prisoners thirty minutes before the scheduled attack on the camp. "A mistake of seconds can mean disaster for the prisoners," he told his men. A cousin of one of his men was in the camp. They started off for Los Baños at midnight and headed into landlocked Laguna de Bay for the seven-and-a-half-mile trip. The skippers of the amtracs were all amateurs, and most

GIs WITH FILIPINO GUERRILLAS (SC).

of them were confused and scared, unsure they could navigate the lake, on a moon-less light, by compass. Burris tells the story from this point:

AT THE ORDER OF "CRANK UP," a noise like a bellowing bull, came out of each of those fifty-nine diesel exhaust pipes. The roar could be heard for ten miles. None of us had considered the noise of the amtrac convoy. . . . If this noise alerted the Japanese, would they have time to react? . . . One thing we could assume was that our secrecy was blown right out of those amtrac tail pipes.

We didn't need further proof, but large fires crackled on the shoreline where entire villages cheered us. At a distance of half a mile we saw villagers dancing and waving flaming sticks as if the war was over. They had to know about the raid many hours before in order to have gathered wood for the fires. . . . Were we blundering into a trap? . . . Our adrenaline was pumping so fast we were in-toxicated.

As dawn broke, they began to search the skies from the shoreline of the lake for the paratroopers, who were to be dropped right into the camp.

NOTHING WAS THERE. WHAT HAD GONE wrong? Without the jumpers, could we get into camp before the guards shot the prisoners? Had Skau's platoon been able to get to their positions . . . ?

Then some specks were steadier and grew larger. We realized they were our planes. . . . Lieutenant John Ringler popped the first chute, followed by another. Then the whole sky was full of silk, spilling out of nine transports. We could hear rifle fire of the infiltrators on signal of the first parachute opening.

The amtracs hit the sand, and we headed, as fast as we could go, toward the center of the camp.

As they did, the reconnaissance platoon began killing Japanese sentries, and the paratroopers began mowing down the startled camp guards, who had just started doing their morning calisthenics. The job of the men in the amtracs was to round up the prisoners and get them back across the lake to safety. Burris continues the story:

THE FIRST AMTRAC, WITH . . . MY PARTY, came to a halt in the center of the camp. Prisoners were all out of their barracks milling about in confusion.

It took a short time for them to realize we were Americans. The uniforms had changed so much over the several years they had been locked up. Then came the surge of emotion for prayers answered. Prisoners just stood with arms to the heavens or hands over their faces covering the outpouring of tears. Some were on their knees praying for gratitude. . . . Many of the adults knew of the planned execution, but kept the information from the children and others who would be too upset.

A hardened criminal would have cried.

A group of 2,147 prisoners is a lot of people. They all thought the ordeal was over with no reason to hurry. They already had about as much emotion as they could stand at one time. There was no point in trying to scare them with the idea of 10,000 Japanese troops just over the hill.

We told the prisoners to throw what clothes they needed into two bags and start walking toward the beach.[31]

The amtracs carried the old, the sick, and women with children to the lake, a mile and a half away; everyone else walked. From the lakeshore, all internees were taken by the amtracs to a town across the bay. "When we got to the beach, the Japanese started to fire," recalls Margaret Nash, a Navy nurse who was holding a newborn infant in her arms. "I covered the baby with a great big hat and I lay down on the sand over her. Later I ran across the beach with her and got into another amtrac."[32]

The entire operation lasted barely four hours. Among those liberated were 1,589 Americans, including Margaret Nash and eleven other Navy nurses. Only two American soldiers were killed and two wounded. The entire Japanese garrison of 250 was killed. "It was said to be the most perfect combat operation of World War II," Burris recalled proudly. "Its success depended on teamwork and not on individual heroism."

Japanese troops converged on Los Baños the following day and slaughtered every Filipino who had not fled to the hills. Upward of 1,500 died.[33]

Following the fall of Manila, MacArthur sent airborne and amphibious troops to capture the tunneled rock fortress of Corregidor, where General Jonathan "Skinny" Wainwright had made his valiant stand in April 1942. On February 26 the last Japanese defenders blew themselves up inside Corregidor's labyrinthine tunnels. Four days later, and three years after his hasty departure, MacArthur stood on Corregidor and gave the order: "Hoist the colors and let no enemy ever haul them down." As Carl Mydans snapped his photograph, MacArthur turned to Lieutenant General Richard K. Sutherland and said, "This is home. I am home at last."[34]

The Japanese continued their resistance on Luzon. More American soldiers fought on Luzon than in either North Africa or Italy, and they and their guerrilla supporters, over 100,000 of them, died in great numbers from enemy gunfire and disease. South of Manila, a strong enemy defensive line was shattered on March 17, trapping some Japanese in caves and forcing others to retire into the remote Sierra Madre Mountains—a malaria-infested region, much of it never thoroughly explored by Westerners. Although hard fighting was to continue in northern Luzon for the rest of the war, great parts of the Philippines were now firmly in American hands, as MacArthur, in arrogant defiance of the Joint Chiefs—who wanted him to concentrate on subduing Luzon and preparing for the invasion of Japan—mounted nearly a dozen major amphibious assaults in the central and southern parts of the archipelago. In the general's view, these were liberation landings, in fulfillment of his pledge to free all Filipinos from the grip of their tyrannical masters. The landings were strategic masterworks, executed with minimal casualties, but they did nothing to shorten the war.[35]

Even Luzon was a strategically inessential objective in the opinion of some of MacArthur's sternest critics inside the military, an unnecessary battle won at fearsome cost. Sixth Army suffered almost 38,000 casualties in the battle for Luzon, and the American and Australian navies lost 2,000 men, mostly to kamikaze attacks. The Philippines were to be used as a staging area for attacks on Japan, but with the B-29s beginning to lay waste to Japan from the Marianas and the naval blockade of the home islands tightening, the Philippine campaign, some Navy and Air force leaders argued, should not have been approved.

General Eichelberger has another view. "If we were to undertake an armed invasion of Japan—and all planning, necessarily, in 1944 looked forward to that objective—we needed the deep-water harbors, the great bases, and the excellent training areas available in those islands, which, in the main, had a friendly and loyal population. We had no knowledge of the atomic bomb; indeed, it was not until almost a year later that the first atomic bomb was exploded experimentally in New Mexico. Up until then even the scientists weren't sure it would work."[36]

On August 25, 1945, almost two weeks after his government capitulated, ending World War II, General Tomoyuki Yamashita—still holed up in the vastness of northern Luzon—chose surrender over suicide in the hope that his arrest for war crimes would save the lives of his officers and men. The stoic warrior did not expect justice; nor did he get it. A revengeful MacArthur personally drew up the charges against his greatest adversary in the Pacific and had him tried in Manila, along with General Masaharu Homma, who had been in overall charge of the prisoners on the Bataan Death March. Barbaric atrocities had been committed on the steaming road to Camp O'Donnell and in the burning streets and churches of Manila. But there was no direct evidence that either commander ordered his troops to act as they did. But with the mood in ravaged Manila, that did not matter. The tribunals were "kangaroo courts," in the words of William Manchester, MacArthur's biographer. They "flouted justice" with MacArthur's approval and perhaps at his insistence.

The military's weakest case was the one against Yamashita. The dozen correspondents who heard the testimony polled themselves and unanimously found for the defendant.

Both generals were convicted by panels of Army officers and sentenced to death by hanging. After a personal appeal for clemency from Homma's wife, MacArthur reduced his sentence to one more befitting a soldier, death by firing squad. Yamashita went to the scaffold. Before he did MacArthur ordered that he be "stripped of uniform, decorations and other appurtenances signifying membership in the military profession."[37]

Yamashita and Homma were executed, separately, in the same courtyard in the town of Los Baños, where Catholic Masses were being offered for families in the community that had been massacred in one of the occupier's most monstrous reprisals.

The Japanese lost a staggering 400,000 men in the defense of the Philippines, from Leyte to Luzon. At the end of the fighting on Leyte, American soldiers found a letter from a Japanese soldier to his family:

"I AM EXHAUSTED. WE HAVE NO food. The enemy are within 500 meters of us. Mother, my dear wife and son, I am writing this letter to you by dim candlelight. Our end is near. . . . hundreds of pale soldiers of Japan are awaiting our glorious end and nothing else. This is a repetition of what occurred in the Solomons, New Georgia and other islands. How well are the people of Japan prepared to fight the decisive battle with the will to win?[38]

The B-29s

THE PLANE

The French journalist Robert Guillain was in Tokyo on March 3, 1945, when he heard the news that MacArthur's forces had liberated Manila. "No Japanese," he wrote later, "would yet let himself say the forbidden words Nippon maketa—Japan is beaten—but one could see the thought lurking behind the wooden faces."[1] More than the fall of the Philippines, however, the firebombing raids that began a week later from the Marianas shattered hope on the home front that the war could be won.

On the morning of October 19, 1944, one day before MacArthur landed in the Philippines, Captain I. J. Galantin, skipper of the submarine *Halibut*, approached the clear green waters of Saipan with his pack of underwater raiders. Galantin had last seen Saipan in January when his submarine was nearly sunk trying to attack an enemy ship inside the island's anchorage. Nine months later, *Halibut* was greeted in Tanapag Harbor by a Navy band and some familiar faces. "The harbor had been transformed into a bustling replenishment site for our submarines with the tenders *Holland* and *Fulton* on station."

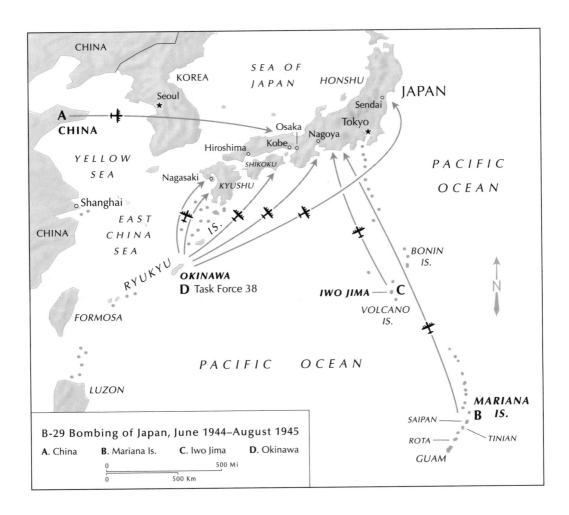

CHINA

KOREA

SEA OF JAPAN

HONSHU

JAPAN

Seoul

Sendai

A CHINA

Tokyo

Osaka

Nagoya

Kobe

Hiroshima

SHIKOKU

YELLOW SEA

Nagasaki

KYUSHU

PACIFIC OCEAN

Shanghai

EAST CHINA SEA

RYUKYU IS.

CHINA

FORMOSA

OKINAWA D Task Force 38

IWO JIMA — C

BONIN IS.

VOLCANO IS.

PACIFIC OCEAN

N

LUZON

MARIANA B IS.

SAIPAN

ROTA —

TINIAN

GUAM

B-29 Bombing of Japan, June 1944–August 1945

A. China **B.** Mariana Is. **C.** Iwo Jima **D.** Okinawa

0   500 Mi

0   500 Km

The once pristine island had been devastated by modern machine warfare. There was only one major building left standing on all of Saipan, the Navy port director's headquarters, but Galantin had never seen a busier place. It was a nonstop construction site. "New roads were being bulldozed; foundations were being poured; steam shovels and cranes groaned and screeched; huge piles of lumber grew as we watched. Everywhere soldiers and Seabees were at work with what seemed an equal number of indigenous laborers. Nightfall brought little change; powerful lights drowned the shadows until the hot sunlight poured once more over the eastern hills."[2]

The Seabees, with teams of forced Japanese labor, were transforming Saipan and neighboring Tinian and Guam into the main Pacific base for both the United

States Navy and the Army Air Forces, building from jungle and shattered coral three major military cities on the Pacific highway to Tokyo. On every inch of usable space, they were hammering and bulldozing by day and night, constructing roads, hospitals, commissaries, Quonset huts, chow halls, pipelines, storage tanks, barracks, warehouses, chapels, wells, palm-thatched officers clubs, and, on Guam's highest peak, splendid residences for the Pacific theater commander and the island commander. From their wide porches, these Navy luminaries would have unimpeded views of Apra Harbor, a four-mile-long anchorage that would soon be the second busiest war port in the world, behind Antwerp. One of the two airstrips being built on flat and green Tinian would be the largest in the world.

Wearing blue pants and up-tilted baseball caps, their sweating backs shining in the scorching sunlight, Seabees were hauling, blasting, and packing down what would eventually be enough coral to fill three dams the size of Boulder Dam. Before the war, the Seabees, whose name derived from the initials, CB, for Construction Battalion, had been sandhogs, steelworkers, dam-builders, dock-wallopers, and lumberjacks. "[These] are the men who built America's cities, dammed her rivers, strung her wires and dug her sewers," said their chief, Admiral Ben Morcell. Since the Pacific war was primarily an air and sea struggle, fought over "a limitless, unprepared battlefield," it involved more construction than any nation had previously contemplated.[3] And the Marianas was the Seabees' biggest job yet. The islands were to be turned into a vast airdrome and anchorage for the bombing and blockade of Japan.

The Seabees were Navy men, so the Navy got the best living facilities on the islands. When Army Air Force personnel began arriving around the time the *Halibut* did, they had to camp out in borrowed tents along their uncompleted jungle airstrip, in open places that they hacked out of sugarcane fields with axes and entrenching tools. Invited to lavish dinner parties at the hilltop houses of the admirals, Air Force commanders entertained in their tents with canned rations; and every day at dusk, pilots and navigators could be seen lingering outside Navy and Marine officers clubs, hoping to get invited in for a drink.

The Air Force arrived on Saipan in such a hurry and with such extravagant expectations that it had no time to build anything that resembled an amenity. At this point in the war, it was the only branch of the service—with the only weapon—capable of striking the industrial heartland of Japan; and it was under pressure to set up operations and be over target Tokyo by early November.

The Seabees had begun building an airfield long enough to accommodate the B-29s while the battle for Saipan was still being fought. The first Air Force engineering crews would not arrive until later that summer and were assigned a few acres of half-cleared sugarcane fields. Through the miserable rainy season, the Seabees and the engineers built servicing and maintenance installations for the B-29s and their crews, which were still on training exercises back home. Working in the furnace heat, officers and enlisted men battled flies, mosquitoes, dengue fever, and diehard Japanese soldiers who were still holding out in the island's deep coral caves. With these "pioneers" was a longtime staff writer for *The New Yorker*, St. Clair McKelway, now serving as staff press censor and public relations officer for the 21st Bomber Command of the Twentieth Air Force, to which the B-29s in the Marianas were assigned.

Later in the war, while he was on leave in the States, McKelway attended a preview of an Army Air Forces film called *Target Tokio*, and watched again, as he had in person, the landing on Saipan of the first B-29, Brigadier General Haywood S. "Possum" Hansell's *Joltin' Josie*. One of the Air Forces' top strategic thinkers and a former bombardment commander in the air war over Germany, Hansell had just been appointed head of the 21st Bomber Command. "What got me," McKelway wrote after seeing the film of that October landing, "was the movement and noise of the vast mob of people who had been waiting for the airplane for some hours and who, as it landed, moved toward it across the base with the happy, fluttering movement of a crowd going into a baseball park. . . . They had been waiting for this moment, actually, for days and weeks and even months. . . . The sound track for the movie was good and accurate—the noises made by a joyful bunch of men—but it didn't pick up one voice in that crowd which I still remember, the voice of a grease-monkey staff sergeant who shouted over and over, above the racket, as the B-29 people moved across the coral rubble toward the new landing strip and the idling B-29, 'Look at 'er, look at 'er, look at 'er!'"[4]

The B-29 was a gigantic leap forward in aviation technology. It was the longest, widest, heaviest airplane in the world, bigger, faster, and more formidable than its famous predecessor, the B-17 Flying Fortress. Its 2,200-horsepower engines were the most powerful yet in aviation history. It carried the biggest bomb load of any plane built, ten tons, four tons more than the B-17. Its top speed of 357 miles per hour was fifty-five mph faster than that of the B-17. And its range of 3,800 miles with a full bomb load was double that of the Fortress. It was a sixty-ton destruction machine ca-

pable of flying more than sixteen hours nonstop when fully loaded. Unlike all other aircraft, it had pressurized crew compartments, and a pressurized tube—a crawl space—connecting the front and rear sections of the plane. At altitudes up to 40,000 feet, in minus fifty degree temperatures, its eleven-man crew flew in comfort, without cumbersome heated flying suits and oxygen masks. And this Cadillac of the skies had a revolutionary remote-controlled firing system. "In earlier planes, each gunner manually controlled and aimed just one set of guns," explained Major Charles W. Sweeney, one of the first test pilots. "With the B-29, a single gunner could control several turrets with one sight and be able to direct all the fire on a single target."[5] It was truly "a super fortress, a super plane," recalls Captain Harry George. "Shirtsleeve atmosphere. Flush rivets. Powerful engines. Big. New type of bombsight. Altitude pressurized. We loved it. It was just a beautiful, beautiful plane."[6]

The crews who serviced it, as well as those who flew it, had an almost reverential affection for the plane. "The B-29s are silvery, without camouflage paint of any kind, and the [ground] crews laboriously smooth out tiny wrinkles on the exteriors and polish the silver skins far beyond necessity," wrote St. Clair McKelway. "Any night in the Marianas, you can find B-29 crew members fooling around a perfectly airworthy B-29, fussing with it as an older generation used to fuss with the new car out in the garage after dinner."[7]

The B-29 had been in development since before Pearl Harbor, and the government would spend more money on it than on the Manhattan Project. The plane was initially plagued by mechanical problems, the most persistent being a nasty tendency

A B-29 TAIL GUNNER (USAAF).

for the engines to overheat and catch fire. Test pilots were killed, so, initially, nobody wanted to fly it. Air Force chief Hap Arnold asked General Carl "Tooey" Spaatz, head of American air operations in Europe, to send him the best bomber pilot he had to help make the B-29 operational, and Spaatz sent back Colonel Paul Tibbets of Columbus, Ohio. Tibbets had led the Eighth Air Force's first strategic bombing raid of the war in August 1942 from a tiny airfield in the English Midlands. Working with aeronautical engineers in the States, Tibbets—who soon became known as "Mr. B-29"—had the plane battle-ready in early 1944.

It still had bugs, but they would have to be worked out in combat. Arnold wanted the Superfortress in the fight as soon as possible. It was mass-produced too late to be deployed in Europe, where all the runways would have had to be lengthened and strengthened. But Arnold was convinced that this tremendous instrument of war could finish off Japan without an invasion of the home islands, making the case, in the process, for the creation of a separate Air Force—independent of the Army—after the war. To ensure that he had complete control over the use of the bomber, Arnold pressed for the establishment of a new Army Air Force, the Twentieth, under his command. He got his wish, and the first B-29s were sent to India in the spring of 1944. From India they flew over the Hump—the Himalaya mountains whose jagged peaks rose to almost 30,000 feet—to bases in the Chengtu Valley in western China, where they conducted raids against coke plants, steel mills, and oil facilities in western Japan, Formosa, and Manchuria. But these China airstrips, built by local laborers who smashed stones with primitive hand tools, were out of range of Japan's great industrial cities.

On June 15, D-Day on Saipan, the China-based B-29s made their first attack on Japan, against a steel mill on Kyushu. Sixty planes reached the target, but only one bomb hit the plant. Seven bombers were lost, six of them as a result of mechanical problems and weather. Later high-altitude daylight missions were equally ineffective. More bombs landed in rice paddies than on steel furnaces and too many planes were lost. Another problem was logistics. Since the Japanese controlled the main ports of China, "we had to fly in all our own gasoline and bombs," recalls Wing Commander James V.

GENERAL CURTIS LeMAY (NA).

Edmundson. "It took roughly fifteen trips over the Hump to get enough gasoline and bombs to fly one sortie to Japan."[8]

In an attempt to turn things around, Hap Arnold sent in General Curtis E. LeMay, one of the top guns from the Eighth Air Force, the main American striking arm in the bomber war against Hitler's Fortress Europe. At age thirty-eight, he was the youngest two-star general in the Army Air Forces and had been almost single-handedly responsible for improving bombing performance in the toughest air theater in the world, where the Eighth Air Force was taking more casualties than the Marines in the Pacific. A beefy, stern-jawed disciplinarian who bluntly spoke his mind—he was jokingly nicknamed "The Diplomat"—LeMay was a large, imposing man whose round face was frozen in a perpetual scowl. But, unknown to most of his men, that was a symptom of Bell's palsy, which partially paralyzed the facial muscles at the corners of his mouth. His exterior toughness hid a ferocious dedication to the air crews who served under him in both Europe and Asia. He was a fanatic about discipline because he was convinced that discipline under fire saved lives. And he didn't believe in screaming to get results; he spoke so softly he could hardly be heard from a few feet away. "His speaking style—barely audible sentence fragments murmured through clenched teeth—reinforced his aura as a borderline sociopath," recalls one of his pilots. And his "smoldering gaze" gave the impression that "running a bombing campaign wasn't quite stimulating enough for him, that he wouldn't mind taking apart a few Quonset huts with his bare hands."[9]

LeMay improved crew performance, if not bombing results, but from the time he arrived in China in August of 1944, he realized that his operation was doomed. "It didn't work," he said later. "No one could have made it work. It was founded on an utterly absurd logistics basis."[10] No air armada that had to feed its own fuel to itself over treacherous mountains could hope to be successful.

The only reason bases had been built in China, LeMay felt, was that "our entire Nation howled like a pack of wolves for an attack on the Japanese homeland."[11] Hap Arnold knew that the future of the B-29 was in the Marianas, and he had pressed the Navy to push up the timetable for their conquest. In the Marianas, Nimitz's ships would be able to meet the bomber's prodigious supply requirements, and from there the plane could reach the concentrated six-city complex around Tokyo that housed more than half of all Japanese industry and 20 percent of the country's population.

As soon as Saipan was taken, China operations began to be phased out. By November, there were over 100 B-29s on Saipan and Hansell targeted the Japanese aircraft industry, hoping to destroy enemy air defenses in preparation for an American invasion of the home islands. Possum Hansell would first hit the Musashi aircraft engine factory, in a suburb of Tokyo, destroying it, he anticipated, with pinpoint precision, his bombardiers using the Air Force's top secret Norden bombsight, the most accurate bomb-guiding device in the world. Brigadier General Emmett "Rosie" O'Donnell, commander of the only bombardment wing on Saipan at the time, flew in the lead plane, *Dauntless Dotty*, on this mission. His pilot was Major Robert K. Morgan, one of the first pilots in the Eighth Air Force to complete twenty-five missions, the required tour of duty in that theater, flying the *Memphis Belle*, the plane made famous by Hollywood director William Wyler's wartime documentary of the same name. After returning to the States with his crew for an Air Force publicity tour, Morgan had volunteered for duty in the Pacific.

One hundred and eleven of Hansell's silvery raiders took off on November 24, a spectacular Pacific morning, to a target 1,300 miles away. It was an unprecedented mission. No aircraft had ever been asked to fly into battle with such loads over so great a distance, and the entire run up to Japan and back—thirteen to eighteen hours of air time—was over unfriendly waters. Merely getting off the ground could be a hair-raising ordeal. If one engine quit "you probably wouldn't make it to the end of the runway," recalls a B-29 crew member. "One night we didn't fly a mission and we were down at the Quonset hut site and looked up and I could practically read a newspaper five miles from the base because of the planes burning at the end of the runway. There were four of them down there, burning up gasoline and bombs." On returning to base, pilots had to put down these long-bodied monsters, each of them half the size of a football field, on specks of coral in the limitless Pacific, often in fast-forming tropical storms and in massively overcrowded air traffic patterns.

But Hansell was a pioneer in formulating the doctrine of strategic bombing from what the Air Force called Very Long Range, and he was confident he could train his crews to get excellent results with their million-dollar machines.[12] His cocky crews, who had already begun calling themselves the Saipan Hunting Club, were in high spirits, proud to be part of the first bombing raid on Tokyo since Jimmy Doolittle's in the spring of 1942, when America was losing the war. "That beautiful silver, gorgeous thing was just cruising through [the Japanese defenses]," recalls the pilot of *Joltin' Josie*, the plane Hansell had hoped to fly, leading the mission, but was ordered not to by Hap Arnold. "My airplanes were tucked in [the formation], looking like champs. And here were those poor frustrated Japanese firing with everything they had. I just thought to myself, 'Wow there is no way that these people can beat us. There is no way that we can't beat them. We are too good for these people.'"[13]

That month the Saipan Hunting Club celebrated the grand opening of its clubhouse, a Quonset hut with a long bar and a few tables and chairs. "The drink of choice that night," says Robert Morgan, a legendary imbiber, "was Purple Passion, a concoction of 180-proof grain alcohol and grape juice, and light on the grape juice, please." Two days later, the date of their next mission, "the hangovers had begun to wear off a little." [14]

One of the fliers in the Saipan Hunting Club was a twenty-six-year-old published poet named John Ciardi, a gunner who had just arrived on the island. "One of my teachers," he wrote in his Saipan diary, "used to say that the best possible job for a writer was in the Fire Department—action in concentrated doses with long spells of musing leisure between. This life fits the requirement. I would like, though, to get over a target—even Tokio." [15] Ciardi would not get his wish until December 3, but more than a thousand other crewmen in 111 planes went up with Rosie O'Donnell and Robert Morgan on November 24. They would encounter challenges that autumn afternoon that no one had anticipated.

FEAR

Approaching Tokyo, everyone worried about the flak and the fighters. The flak was heavy but inaccurate, and the Japanese planes that came up after them fought cautiously and were fat targets for the bombers' overwhelming firepower. It was the weather—the Siberian jet stream and heavy cloud cover—that caused most of the problems. "Over Japan, at 30,000 feet, the winds were from 150 to 200 miles per hour," says pilot John Jennings. "So if you were coming into the wind, you were going probably thirty, forty, fifty miles an hour over the target. You were over the target so long they could shoot the heck out of you.

"All right, so we could turn around and come in downwind. That was the answer. No. Now you're going over 300 miles per hour [sometimes up to 500 miles per hour] and the Norden bombsight couldn't figure out when to drop those things. So . . . we were getting nowhere."

The Norden bombsight failed to compensate for these demon winds, which played havoc with the bombs, and the clouds were so thick that only twenty-four of the 111 planes dropped bombs in the vicinity of the aircraft factory. The bomber fleet lost only one plane to the Japanese, but in losing it the surviving crews witnessed the depths of the enemy's desperation. The downed B-29 was struck by a stripped-down Japanese fighter that managed, without the extra weight of its guns, to reach the altitude of the B-29s. "No one who saw it was sure why it occurred," Robert Morgan remembers. "Some believed it was on purpose, a kamikaze attack, others claimed the Zero had been crippled by gunfire and collided with the Superfort accidentally." [16] If it was a deliberate ramming attack, it was the first of many, and they would grow more intense with each raid. Inspired by the kamikaze fliers, the fighter pilots would come boring in on the American bombers at closing speeds of up to 600 miles per hour. Most of them would be blown out of the sky by the bombers' gunners before they could make lethal contact with the B-29s, but "we lost considerable planes, wings knocked off, engines knocked out . . . even the noses shattered," says bombardier Ed Keyser. "After the first raid, nothing came at us from behind," recalls John Ciardi. "The Japanese lined up across the sky and came in to ram. They would all swarm on the B-29 and finish it off." [17]

Another of the enemy's weapons was Iwo Jima, the largest of Japan's Volcano Islands, which sat squarely astride the B-29 routes, almost exactly midway between the Marianas and Japan. The big bombers had to fly a fuel-consuming dogleg around Iwo Jima, but the Japanese could still pick them up on their radar and radio ahead to the Tokyo air defense system, giving it a two-hour warning. Fighters using Iwo's two airstrips were also a problem. "They could pick you off coming and going," says Edmundson. "You could be limping back from a bombing raid [with a busted-up plane], trying to squeeze your gas to have enough to get back to Tinian, and these guys would come sailing in on you and jump you out of Iwo."

Precision bombing from the long coral runways of the Marianas never worked the way Hansell had hoped it would. Subsequent missions over Tokyo, and over the Mitsubishi Aircraft Engine Works in Nagoya, Japan's third largest city, were only marginally more effective than the first Tokyo raid. The Japanese radio ridiculed Hansell's precision bombing, calling it "Blind Bombing." But for the first month or so, crew morale was surprisingly high. "I was cockeyed proud of the crew," John Ciardi wrote after his first mission. "This is the pilot's air corps, but it takes eleven men to fly a 29. And eleven men have to lose their fear and be sure of themselves before a crew can function. We functioned." [18]

The men were not blind to the moral dimensions of their work. "We were in the terrible business of burning out Japanese towns," Ciardi observed after the war. "That meant women and old people, children. One part of me—a surviving savage voice—says, I'm sorry we left any of them living. I wish we'd finished killing them all. Of course, as soon as rationality overcomes the first impulse, you say, Now, come on, this is the human race, let's try to be civilized.

"I had to condition myself to be a killer. This was remote control. All we did was push buttons. I didn't see anybody we killed." [19]

Although Ciardi believed in the war against Japan, he thought of himself as a poet, not a soldier. And as he flew more missions, he began to experience doubts that he could continue to do his war work. He started to have "sudden chemical anxieties." He was scared, scared in advance of every raid, and he couldn't dial down the fear.

He developed little routines to try to settle himself. "Whenever my imagination runs cold and damp I go out and look at a B-29 for five minutes and I'm cured. It's . . . a beautiful thing to look at, and it's pointed the right way." But the fear grew worse with every raid, and he began to try to rationalize it. "I find myself thinking that it's foolish to stick my neck out over Japan when my real usefulness and capability as a person and as a unit of society is in writing what needs to be written well. . . . I'd frankly bow out if I knew how to. I could go to Col. Brannock tomorrow and say I quit and be busted down to private [and be put on permanent garbage detail]. But I can't let myself and won't. All the same I know I'd grab at any reasonable excuse to save face. . . . If I do get killed it will be because I lack the courage to quit."[20]

FIRE STICKS

In January 1945, Curtis LeMay replaced Haywood Hansell and changed bombing tactics. He experimented with firebombing, with mixed results, and had the planes go in lower, at 25,000 rather than 30,000 feet, to allow the navigators to see the target better and to cut down on mechanical breakdowns by putting less strain on the engines. Flying this low, the B-29s could also get underneath the jet stream winds and drop their incendiaries more accurately. The men objected. They saw that extra 5,000 feet as their "margin for life." At 30,000 feet, the enemy fighters had difficulty getting to them and the flak was far less accurate. "This 25,000 ft. business is bad stuff. . . . Losses are going to be heavy," Ciardi confided to his diary. "This man I have never seen will very likely be what kills me." That night Ciardi wrote a letter home to be mailed "in case I didn't come back."[21]

Curtis LeMay had arrived on Saipan with a reputation as a "cigar-chomping miracle worker," but his bombing tactics were as unproductive as Hansell's.[22] "We were still going in too high, still running into those big jet stream winds upstairs. Weather was almost always as bad," LeMay confessed later.[23] In early March, under pressure from Hap Arnold to launch a maximum mission against Japan, he changed tactics radically. John Ciardi described the new approach: "He said, Go in at night from five thousand feet, without gunners, just a couple of rear-end observers. We'll save weight on the turrets and on ammunition. The Japanese have no fighter resistance at night. They have no radar. We'll drop fire sticks."[24]

These were small cylinders—weighing six pounds—filled with napalm, an insidious new weapon of warfare developed by Standard Oil and DuPont in 1944. Napalm was gelatinized gasoline that created running rivers of fire, ferociously hot fires that were nearly impossible to put out by conventional means. And napalm stuck to anything it came into contact with: animate or inanimate. It would be shatteringly effective in Tokyo, LeMay reasoned, where 90 percent of the structures were built of

wood or heavy paper. Stripping the planes of guns and gunners and going in low would save on fuel. Extra gas tanks for the high-altitude missions were stored in the bomb bays. No extra tanks meant extra incendiaries.

The fire sticks were stored in large cylinders, which were packed together in bundles, "Molotov flower baskets," the Japanese would call them. When these clusters were dropped, they broke apart above the target, filling the sky with dozens of containers of napalm. Each stick would ignite on contact, setting a small fire, and thousands of these small fires would merge, creating a city-consuming conflagration.

But Curtis LeMay wanted to do more than start a big urban fire. He wanted to start a firestorm—a thermal hurricane that kills by heat and suffocation, as flames suck oxygen out of the atmosphere. He wanted to create a holocaust.

There were precedents. In late July 1943, Britain's Royal Air Force launched a succession of night raids against the great German city of Hamburg, killing at least

45,000 people—most of them women, children, and the elderly—and leaving 400,000 survivors homeless. It was suffering and loss never seen before in a bombing raid. In ten days, more civilians were killed in Hamburg than would be killed in Great Britain by German bombs during the entire war. And most of them died in the firestorm created by the bombs, not directly under the bombs. The brains of fire victims fell from their burst temples and tiny children "lay like fried eels on the pavement. Even in death," said a witness, "they showed signs of how they must have suffered—their hands and arms stretched out as if to protect themselves from that pitiless heat."[25]

Then on the night of February 13–14, 1944, Air Marshal Arthur Harris's bombers, with some help the following day from the American Eighth Air Force, started an equally vicious firestorm in Dresden, in eastern Germany. The hurricane of fire incinerated the center of the city, killing between 30,000 and 40,000 civilians, many of them refugees fleeing the Red Army, which had begun its final, furious drive on Berlin that January. The writer Kurt Vonnegut, Jr., a German prisoner of war in Dresden, survived the fire in the meat locker of a slaughterhouse. When he and his fellow prisoners were led out of the shelter the next day, Dresden was "like the moon now," Vonnegut would write later, "nothing but minerals." The prisoners noticed "little logs" lying on the pavements. "They were people who had been caught in the fire storm."[26]

Hoping to strike the first of a terrible succession of blows that would end the war, Curtis LeMay planned to ignite an even greater fire in flammable Tokyo.

"We thought he was crazy," Newell Fears, a B-29 flier, describes the reaction of the crews to LeMay's orders to go in at low level, half as high as Mount Fuji, a marking point for earlier high-altitude raids. The men thought they would be suicide missions. As the 334 bombers were being gassed and readied in the fading afternoon light of March 9, 1945, the fliers who were not going to Tokyo that night went down to the flight line to say farewell to their friends, certain that many of them were not likely to return.

On the morning of March 10, John Ciardi recorded in his diary a decisive change in the air war against Japan:

THE BOYS ARE JUST BACK FROM a razzle-dazzle play over Tokio. They left a general conflagration behind them. . . .

The planes hit at 3 A.M. All ours got through. Reports are inconclusive, but it must have been terrific. . . . While Tokio burns—there's another one called for tomorrow night [against Nagoya].

Shortly after this, a personnel officer read a recent issue of *The Atlantic Monthly* with some of Ciardi's poems in it. They needed someone at headquarters to do public relations work, and he was called in and put in charge of awards and decorations. A week or so later, his former crew was killed over Tokyo when their plane was hit and blew up in midair. "It was luck—and poetry—that saved me," Ciardi would say years later.[27]

Knox Burger, a correspondent for *Yank* in Saipan, describes that first low-attitude Tokyo fire raid, which he witnessed from one of the B-29s:

ONE NIGHT IN MARCH 1945 SOME 300 B-29s, loaded with incendiaries, flew up to Japan from the Marianas to burn out the heart of Tokyo. They set fires which leveled 15.8 square miles of the most densely populated area on earth. By the next morning at least 100,000 people were dead and more than 1,000,000 were homeless. It was probably the worst fire in history.

Subsequent incendiary attacks devastated most of Tokyo, but in this first

OFF TO THE EMPIRE (USAAF).

raid, which was without precedent in air war, more people died than had been accounted for on any other mission thus far in the war. . . .

The target . . . was a mass firetrap of flimsy frame houses and shops which housed a big percentage of the population in Tokyo. . . . Several large factories turned out parachutes and airplane parts, but the real economic strength of the area lay in the thousands of domestic industries that had sprung up with war. Not many of the householders had refrigerators or electric stoves—drill presses were installed instead. And a lathe had come to be a common back-room fixture.

On March 9 a strong wind had been rattling the shaky panes in the doors and windows all day. For the past few nights single B-29s had appeared over the sky, without dropping any bombs but flying very low and setting off a riot of searchlights and antiaircraft fire. A lot of people on the ground had the uneasy feeling that something was due to happen. . . .

The first ships [of the raiding party] were 12 pathfinders whose job it was to light up the outer reaches of the target area for the main force. They were met by searchlights, accurate, intense flak, and strong headwinds.

Then the rest of the B-29s came in.

They were met by terrific flak. . . .

Crewmen looked out at searchlights aimlessly fingering the smoke clouds, picking up a ship, losing it again, picking up another momentarily. There were some fighters up, but most of them refused to close in and shoot. They couldn't see the B-29s blacked out over the target.

The long sky-train droned over the bay for three hours, pouring millions of incendiaries inside roughly patterned circles laid out by the pathfinders. During the first half-hour it was like flying over a forest of brightly lighted Christmas trees. The bombs flickered like faraway candles. Then the fires spread and merged. At the end it was like flying over a super-blast-furnace.

Heat thermals from the fires raging on the ground hurled the bombers thousands of feet upward in a few seconds. Gusts from the inferno were so powerful that crewmen rattled around inside the ships like bones in a dice cup. Floor-boards were uprooted. Because of the low altitude, the ships had not been pressurized, and the smoke and soot and smell seeped into the cabins.

The B-29s created large-scale havoc. From 7,000 feet crewmen could see the framework of big buildings in which fires had burned away the roofs and illuminated the window holes. They could see whole blocks like this, and the general impression was of a huge bed of red-hot and burned-out embers.[28]

What was it like to fly over this boiling sea of flames, every bomber feeding it with 20,000 pounds of gasoline and chemicals? Here are the observations of some of the men who were on that mission and the missions that followed it, in lightning succession, against other urban targets, five missions in all—a five-city blitz over a ten-day period.

Captain Charlie Phillips's plane approached the coast of Japan just after midnight, after the pathfinders had marked the target, drawing a huge flaming X with large napalm bombs on ten square miles of the city. The first wave of planes set the fire with larger incendiaries; later waves fed it with smaller ones. When Charlie Phillips first sighted Tokyo, it was already in flames. The fire looked to him like the scourgelike forest fires he had seen in California.

Phillips recalls:

NO ONE HAD ANY LIGHTS SHOWING. It was completely dark. If you got picked up by a searchlight, you were so well illuminated that you couldn't see out of the airplane. You'd have to fly on instruments. But most of us went in and came out in the dark.

We had designated targets. We were responsible for our own bombing, unlike daylight missions, where the lead bombardier would make the Norden bombsight run in his aircraft and all of the rest of the bombardiers would drop their bombs as they saw the bombs leave the bay of his plane. On those missions, we would bomb with concentrated destructive power because we were in a very tight formation, our wings overlapping.

The night bombing was completely different and it was horrifying to the crews because of the danger of collisions. When you send 300 airplanes up there with no lights and you didn't know where anybody is, it's serious. You couldn't see other aircraft. You just had to grit your teeth, hold your heading, drive on it, drop the bombs, and make a big, steep turn out of there and head for home.

What surprised us was the terrible turbulence we ran into. Not being the first planes in, we flew into a dirty gray cloud reaching up to 40,000 feet. As we entered that cloud we ran into a huge updraft. [My] plane was tossed about like a leaf in a fall windstorm and it was hard to keep the wings level. You could not

A Japanese Baka bomb (USAAF).

see a horizon, so you had to do instrument flying to keep the airplane on a level keel. And there was a monstrous thermal updraft that increased airspeed. I noticed that we were fifty miles an hour over the redline speed. When we talk about the redline airspeed, that's when the guarantee runs out. That's when the wings might come off. The turbulence might tear the plane apart. So I pulled the power back to idle and slowly got the airspeed reduced to below that redline.

We went into the fire cloud at 7,800 feet but came out at 14,000 feet, because of this monstrous updraft.

"Those thermal waves would bounce your plane clear around," observed radio operator George Gladden. "I had my flak suit on and my chair was bolted to me with the seat belt and when the wave hit it jerked the bolts out of the bottom of that thing and I was stuck against the ceiling with a chair tied to me."

"The turbulence was so bad our aircraft was flipped over on its back, and it was a terrific fight to get it back upright," recalled Captain Harry George. "[Then] we looked out and saw Tokyo burning. You could smell it at this low altitude. The smell of it was putrid.

"On the right hand side I [saw] another plane alongside of us about a half a mile out. It was, I learned later, [a small, single-seat] Jap suicide plane—a Baka bomb—with a ton of TNT on the warhead. It didn't have any landing gear. It was dropped from a twin-engine bomber in the sky and it drew a bead on one of our planes. Luckily it didn't hit it.

"The incendiary bombs were in 2,000-pound clusters and each of them was small. We had twenty clusters in the bomb bays. When a cluster was dropped it would blow apart about 3,000 feet over the target. And as soon as the [thirty or so] little bombs in the clusters hit the ground they would start things burning. They were filled with napalm. If you threw water on them, they would burn more fiercely. You couldn't stop 'em from burning."

"Our biggest concern was getting caught in a searchlight," said David Farquar, a gunner with the 6th Bomb Wing. "The searchlights would crisscross the sky and as soon as they would focus on a plane you were a target for fighters, because once they had you in one searchlight fifteen or twenty searchlights would be on you. There was no place to hide, and you're blinded by the light. . . . Once you're in the lights your chances of making it through are very slim."

"Looking down out of the window of the plane was like looking into what I think hell would be like," said Lieutenant Fiske Hanley. "We could smell human flesh burning at 4,000 feet."

"This blaze will haunt me forever," one pilot said to himself as he made the sign of the cross. "It's the most terrifying sight in the world, and, God forgive me, it's the best." [29]

"I didn't hate these people I was incinerating. I'd been in the war a long time and, damn it, I was tired of hating," Robert Morgan recalled years later. "But that didn't lessen my resolve to fly a perfect mission. And a perfect mission that evening over Tokyo meant killing a lot of innocent people. The problem was I hated the Japanese leaders, the guys who bombed Pearl Harbor and got us into this ugly war. And to bring them down we had to do some awful nasty things to people who maybe didn't deserve it.

"I will never forget the sickening smell of those roasting bodies, an odor carried up to us by violent updrafts. I later learned that some fliers gagged and vomited from this stench, and that a few had passed out." [30]

St. Clair McKelway was with Curtis LeMay at his headquarters on Guam during the night of the first Tokyo fire raid. "He had told the rest of his staff to go to bed if they wanted to, that he was going to sit this one out. . . . LeMay was . . . in the operations-control room, whose walls were covered with charts, maps, [and] graphs. . . . He was sitting on a wooden bench smoking a cigar. 'I'm sweating this one out myself,' he said. 'A lot could go wrong.'" [31]

LeMay had not informed Hap Arnold, back in Washington, about the strike until the day before his planes took off, insuring that his commander could not stop the radically risky mission. He had gambled, against the advice of his advisors, that the Japanese did not have the kind of low-level flak that the Germans did, which was deadly accurate at 5,000 to 7,000 feet. If they did, he'd lose a lot of crews, and perhaps be stripped of his command. "This was General LeMay's idea; it was his show; and he wanted to lead it," says Robert Morgan, as he had led some of the great raids against Nazi Germany. [32] He would have done so had he not been briefed about the atomic bomb. No one who knew about "the big firecracker" was permitted to fly over Japan and risk getting shot down, captured, and questioned.

There was something else on the general's mind. "No matter how you slice it, you're going to kill an awful lot of civilians," he told himself. "But, if you don't destroy the Japanese industry, we're going to have to invade Japan. And how many Americans will be killed in an invasion of Japan? Five hundred thousand seems to be the lowest estimate. Some say a million."[33]

LeMay told McKelway he couldn't sleep:

"I USUALLY CAN, BUT NOT TONIGHT. . . . In a war," he said, "you've got to try to keep at least one punch ahead of the other guy all the time. . . . I think we've figured out a punch he's not expecting this time. I don't think he's got the right flak to combat this kind of raid and I don't think he can keep his cities from being burned down—wiped right off the map. . . . If this one works we will shorten this damned war out here."

He looked at his watch. "We won't get a bombs-away [report] for another half hour," he said. "Would you like a Coca-Cola? I can sneak in my quarters without waking up the other guys and get two Coca-Colas and we can drink them in my car. That'll kill most of the half hour."

We drove the hundred yards to his quarters in his staff car and he sneaked in and got the Coca-Colas. We sat in the dark, facing the jungle that surrounds the headquarters . . . [until] the bombs-away message from the first B-29 formation over Tokio came in. It was decoded and shown to him. "Bombing the primary target visually," it told him. "Large fires observed. Flak moderate. Fighter opposition nil." . . . Then the bombs-away messages from other formations began coming in fast. After the first three, they all reported "Conflagration." . . .

"It looks pretty good," LeMay said . . . "But we can't really tell a damn thing about results until we get the pictures tomorrow night. Anyway, there doesn't seem to have been much flak. We don't seem to have lost more than a few airplanes." [They lost twelve B-29s.] He shifted his cigar and smiled. . . .

The following night, around twelve, we had the pictures. . . .

The staff officers' five or six jeeps swept up to LeMay's tent like so many cowboys' horses, the officers driving them leaped to the ground, and we all got to the General's bedroom just as the photo-interpretation officer walked in with the pictures under his arm. LeMay [was] in pajamas. . . . The photo-interpretation officer spread the pictures out on a big, well-lighted table and LeMay . . . walked up to it and bent over them.

There was about one full minute of silence. "All this is out," LeMay then said, running a hand over several square miles of Tokio. . . . "This is out—this—this—this. . . ." We crowded in for a better look. "It's all ashes—all that and that and that," said [another officer], bending over the pictures.[34]

In less than three hours, LeMay's B-29s dropped almost a quarter of a million bombs on Tokyo, burning to bare ground sixteen square miles of the city, an area equivalent to two thirds of Manhattan Island. There was more destruction than any documented fire in history, including the combined earthquake and fire of 1923 in Tokyo. Knox Burger's estimate in *Yank* of the number of people killed—at least 100,000—used to be considered high, but recent studies validate it, and put the number of injured at about one million. Next to Hiroshima, where approximately 130,000 people were killed by the atomic blast, this was the most destructive air attack of the entire war.[35] And the human cost of the raid would have been far greater had not over a million and half people already evacuated Tokyo.[36]

Before March 10, only about 1,300 people were killed in all the B-29 raids on Japan. So this raid had as cataclysmic an impact on the Japanese people as did the later, atomic bombing of Hiroshima. For the people in Tokyo that night, nothing in their history or their imaginations could have led them to believe that this was a man-made act. For the first time in the history of humanity, technology approached nature in its destructive capacity.

Knox Burger, who went to Tokyo after the surrender and interviewed victims of the fire, describes the panic and devastation inside the city:

SOME PEOPLE, FOLLOWING THE DIRECTIONS GIVEN them by police and civilian fire wardens, stayed by their homes and formed bucket brigades, or transferred their families and their valuables into air-raid shelters beside the houses. Whole families were roasted as the flames engulfed these shelters, and wooden doors and supports burst into flames of terrific heat.

Others, several hundred thousand others, with clothes and children piled on their backs, straggled off toward the rivers, the bay, or an open space—whichever happened to be the closest. The wind acted like a lid on the fire, keeping the heat low and forcing the flames to spread out instead of up. Smoke

and sparks were everywhere, and white-hot gusts came roaring down narrow streets.

As soon as the big, fluffy coverings on their backs caught fire or a kimono or a jacket started to smolder, the wearers would rip them off. Many people who hadn't had a chance to douse themselves with water were stark naked by the time they reached safety. And safety that night was a sometimes thing. People crowded across firebreaks, hoping the broad lanes had halted the fire's spread, but the fire ranged on both sides, so people had to fall back into the avenues themselves. They lay down in the center of the streets as far as possible from the flames on each side. The next morning, vehicles couldn't pass because of the litter of corpses. Waves of heat had swirled across the firebreaks, and people burned to death without being touched by flame. Other blasts of pure heat killed people as they ran.

The wind seemed to blow the fire in all directions. A wave of flame would follow the people out of a block of houses like a breaker on the beach. Then, in front of the people, it would catch a load of incendiaries, and they would be walled in. Many times the flames, lashed by cross-drafts, reversed their field. All that night the general direction of the flight across the lowlands surged one way and then another as new fires started and the ground wind shifted. . . . The fire commissioner of the Fugawa district, perhaps the worst hit of all, said, "Everything burned so quickly it was like a bad dream. We couldn't stand up against the wind."

By dawn the wind had died and most of the fires had burned themselves out. . . . The next day was clear and cold. What had been the marrow of one of the world's most congested cities was a bed of ashes. Here and there a building burned, orange against a pall of smoke and dust that overhung the city. Blackened bodies lay strewn among the embers. Charred telephone poles stood along the streets, their tips glowing like cigars. For acres the only structures that rose above the horizon were an occasional double-decked storage vault, some schools, and a few gutted factories. A forest of chimneys stood like sentinels, marking the sites where other factories had stood.

The survivors sat or stood looking stupidly at the monstrous flatness. They were too exhausted for anger or bitterness, too stunned to comprehend what had happened. Their throats and eyes ached from smoke and wind; almost all of them had painful burns. People got in line in front of aid stations and rice-distribution centers almost automatically. There was very little noise. Occasionally a brick wall would tumble.

The police took charge of the dead, collecting corpses in piles and burning them. The piles gave off a blue-white smoke, heavy with the stink of death.[37]

Even those who had managed to get out of their tinderbox neighborhoods to the fetid canals that coursed through the Tokyo flats died. Those in the deeper water were boiled alive. Those in the shallow places, buried in muck up to their mouths, were later found dead; not drowned, but suffocated by the burning air and smoke.

LeMay called it a strategic raid, an attack on Japanese war industries. As he wrote after the war:

IT WAS THEIR SYSTEM OF DISPERSAL of industry. All you had to do was visit one of those targets after we'd roasted it, and see the ruins of a multitude of tiny houses, with a drill press sticking up through the wreckage of every home. The entire population got into the act and worked to make those airplanes or munitions of war . . . men, women, children. We knew we were going to kill a lot of women and kids when we burned that town. Had to be done.[38]

Morality aside, this was not "strategic bombing." The Japanese had the right word for it: slaughter bombing. Did "moral considerations" affect his decisions to firebomb cities? LeMay was asked by an Air Force cadet after the war. "Killing Japanese didn't bother me very much at that time. It was getting the war over that bothered me. . . .

"I guess the direct answer to your question is, yes, every soldier thinks something of the moral aspects of what he is doing. But all war is immoral and if you let that bother you, you're not a good soldier."

Then he added, tellingly: "I suppose if I had lost the war, I would have been tried as a war criminal. Fortunately, we were on the winning side."[39]

As soon as LeMay got the damage assessments for Tokyo, and the estimates of his own losses, twenty-seven Superforts, he ordered more raids. "It would be possible, I thought, to knock out all of Japan's major industrial cities during the next ten days."[40]

Charlie Phillips flew all five of these missions and afterward wrote to his wife that he had never been more exhausted in his life. "It was wam bam. We flew to Nagoya [Japan's third largest city], to Osaka [Japan's second largest city with a population of 3.5 million], to Kobe [Japan's major port and shipbuilding center, with a population of a million], back to Nagoya again, all in ten days' time." In ten days, LeMay burned out half of the built-up area of four of Japan's biggest cities, and killed at least 150,000 men, women, and children. A comparison with the bomber war against Germany points up the magnitude of LeMay's so-called achievement. In a mere five raids, he caused more physical damage than Allied bombers inflicted on the six most heavily hit German cities of the war, and 41 percent of the total destruction suffered by German cities during the entire war. This was done with less than 1 percent of the total tonnage dropped on Germany during the war and with minimal losses. In the five missions, he lost a total of only three bombers to enemy flak, none to fighters, and nineteen to mechanical failure.[41]

"Then," says LeMay, "we ran out of bombs. Literally." Later, he gave an accurate assessment of the murderous efficiency of his raids. "The ten-day blitz of March was a turning point. The morale of the Japanese people began a steady decline, never to rise again. Industries ceased to exist, or operated at greatly reduced rates. The panic-stricken people began an exodus from the major cities. The rate of absenteeism in the war industries recorded an alarming rise. . . . Fire, not high explosives, did this. And we possessed no more fire with which to speed the capitulation."[42]

When the Navy brought more bombs to the Marianas, thousands of tons of scalding chemicals, the city-burning campaign resumed and intensified. Now LeMay bombed by day and night, at low and high altitudes, because there was soon nothing to fear. Japan's air defense system had been obliterated. "We had nothing in Japan that we could use against such a weapon. . . . We felt that the War was lost," said Prince Naruhiko Higashikuni, commander of Japan's home defense headquarters.[43] After the war, Japan's Prime Minister, Admiral Kantaro Suzuki, told United States bombing assessment experts: "I myself, on the basis of the B-29 raids alone, felt that the cause was hopeless."[44]

Historian Michael S. Sherry argues that "for many Japanese, the March 10 raid and the ones to follow it triggered the plunge into a mood of desperation even more than did the apocalyptic events of August."[45]

Nine days after great parts of the capital were turned into rubble and ash, the Emperor inspected the city by car. An aide noted victims "digging through the rubble with empty expressions on their faces that became reproachful as the Imperial motorcade went by. . . . Were they resentful of the emperor because they had lost their relatives, their houses and belongings? Or were they in a state of utter exhaustion and bewilderment?"[46] The answer is probably both, and many of those closest to the Emperor began to be concerned about the possibility of a popular uprising against the Imperial regime. They need not have worried. "Until the very end," as Hirohito's principal biographer writes, "most Japanese people . . . remained steadfast in their resolve to obey their leaders and to work and sacrifice for the victory that they were constantly told was coming."[47]

On June 15, LeMay ended his campaign against six of Japan's seven largest cities. (The fourth largest city, Kyoto, the ancient imperial capital, was spared by order of Secretary of War Stimson.) In the six cities of Tokyo, Osaka, Nagoya, Yokohama, Kobe, and Kawasaki over 126,762 people were killed—according to conservative estimates—and a million and a half dwellings and over 105 square miles of urban space were destroyed. In Tokyo, Osaka, and Nagoya alone the areas leveled (almost 100 square miles) exceeded the areas destroyed in all German cities by both the American and British air forces (approximately seventy-nine square miles).[48]

But Curtis LeMay was far from finished. From mid-June until the end of the war, he concentrated on burning out small- and medium-sized Japanese cities, hitting thirty-nine of them on nine nights. In all, the Americans bombed sixty-six cities (including Hiroshima and Nagasaki), destroying 178 square miles (43 percent) of their living space. By comparison, Allied bombing destroyed seventy-nine square miles of Germany's urban space. In Germany, the hardest hit city was Berlin. It lost ten square miles of its built-up area; Tokyo lost nearly six times that much. As historian Kenneth P. Werrell points out, the total destruction of Tokyo, Nagoya, and Osaka exceeded the total destruction of all German cities. One quarter of Japan's city dwellers (8.5 million people) were forced to flee their homes, and the bombing, including the atomic bombs, killed an estimated 330,000 people, about half the number that perished under the bombs in Germany.

The cost to the United States was light by the cold calculus of modern war. In the bombing campaign against the Third Reich, the Anglo-American air forces lost over 20,000 bombers and 158,546 flying personnel. In the far shorter bombing campaign against Japan, the Twentieth Air Force, flying from the Marianas, lost 414 bombers in battle. Just over 1,000 men were killed and another 1,700 or so were listed as missing in action.[49]

The fliers who had hotly contested LeMay's initial decision to go in low suddenly became his strongest supporters. "It turned out to be the greatest strategic decision that LeMay ever made. It's what really turned the tide and put us in control of the Japanese," says John Jennings. "LeMay was tough and uncompromising—and more than a little frightening in his steely resolve," says Robert Morgan, "but in my opinion he was easily the greatest Army Air Force general of the war, and one of the greatest of all American generals. It took us fliers on Saipan a while to realize this but then it all became clear: this maniac, as we called him at first, knew how to beat the enemy. And he beat him by taking big chances, not big losses. His fliers appreciated that."[50]

Harold Tucker, a B-29 gunner, believes, as LeMay did, that if the fire raids had continued, "we may not have had to drop the atomic bomb. We could have just burned them out."

Some of these men were stirred by revenge. Not having met the Japanese face-to-face in combat, they did not have Eugene Sledge's visceral hatred of the enemy, but they had lost friends in the war and were aware of atrocities committed by the Japanese in the Philippines and elsewhere. But it was love, not vengeance, that kept them in the fight, a passionate loyalty to the men they flew with. This and a desperate desire to end the war as quickly as possible, and by any means possible, so they could get back to their "real lives." The crews weren't motivated by "patriotism," John Ciardi said forty years after the war. "I think it was a certain amount of pride. The unit was the crew. You belonged to eleven men. You're trained together, you're bound together. I was once ordered to fly in the place of a gunner [on another crew] who had received a shrapnel wound. I dreaded that mission. I wanted to fly with my own crew. . . . I did not want to run the risk of dying with strangers."

But Ciardi is quick to add that he knew why he was in this war. "As an American, I felt very strongly I did not want to be alive to see the Japanese impose surrender terms." [51]

While these American fliers killed, they did not think of themselves as killers. "We had to kill to end the war," says pilot Harry George. By starting a war of aggression, and then refusing to surrender when there was no hope of victory, the Japanese militarists were responsible for the incineration of babies and grandmothers, Harry George and other B-29 crewmen insist. "We knew. We heard about the thousands of people [we killed], the Japanese wives, children, and elderly. That was war. But I know every B-29 air crewman for the next two or three years would wake up at night and start shaking. . . . Yes, [the raids] were successful, but horribly so."

Most of these men saw the war as the journalist Russell Brines did. Brines had lived in Tokyo; he knew the people, spoke the language. And he had been a prisoner of the Japanese. In a best-selling book, *Until They Eat Stones*, published in 1944, he explained what the Americans were up against in the final year of this war:

"WE WILL FIGHT," THE JAPANESE SAY, "until we eat stone!" The phrase is odd; now revived and ground deeply into Japanese consciousness by propagandists skilled in marshaling their sheeplike people. . . . [It] means they will continue the war until every man—perhaps every woman and child—lies face downward on the battlefield. . . .

American fighting men back from the front have been trying to tell America this is a war of extermination. They have seen it from foxholes and barren strips of bullet-strafed sand. I have seen it from behind enemy lines. Our picture coincides. This is a war of extermination. The Japanese militarists have made it that way.[52]

Only one Medal of Honor was conferred on a B-29 flier during the entire war. The recipient was Staff Sergeant Henry Eugene "Red" Erwin of Bessemer, Alabama, a hard-muscled former steelworker who was in the habit of calling his wife, whom he wrote to every day, "Cupcake." His act of heroism will have to stand for other brave men who, unfairly, were not decorated. St. Clair McKelway tells his story:

ERWIN'S B-29 WAS LEADING A FORMATION to Japan on one of the first incendiary raids. He had been given the additional duty of shoving phosphorus bombs down a chute near the rear end of the forward crew compartment. These bombs were being used on that mission to spread smoke over a certain area of Japan and thereby aid the other airplanes to make an effective rendezvous. One of Erwin's phosphorus bombs was faulty. It began to sputter and smoke as he put it into the chute. The sputtering phosphorus flew into his face, ate part of his nose away, and blinded him. The stuff splattered on his clothes, on his hands, inside his shirt. . . . The airplane quickly filled with smoke and fumes, and the pilot lost control of it. It went into a spin. Erwin knew what to do and he did it. A phosphorus bomb weighs about twenty pounds. Erwin pulled the sputtering bomb out of the chute, picked it up in his bare hands, and started carrying it to the nearest opening—the pilot's windows. From where he was, this was a distance of about twenty feet. He couldn't see, so he felt his way along the passage with his shoulders, holding the bomb in his hands.

In a B-29 certain crew members have tables to work on during a flight, tables which, when raised, cut off this passage. The navigator's table was raised when Erwin got to it. The navigator didn't know what was going on, for he was blinded by the smoke and fumes, as was everybody else in the airplane, and was sitting with his back to the table, having swung around in his swivel chair. Erwin felt the table against his thighs. He held the bomb then for a few seconds in one hand, resting it against his chest, and with the other unlatched the table and lowered it so he could get by. All the time the bomb was sputtering and burning, throwing white-hot phosphorus all around. Erwin carried it to the front of the compartment. The pilot and co-pilot had opened their windows, trying to get rid of the fumes and smoke. Erwin threw the bomb out the co-pilot's window. Then he walked a few steps back toward his post, near the other end of the compartment, and fell.

The pilot managed to bring the airplane out of its spin three hundred feet above land a few seconds after that [and headed back to safety]. . . . The rest of the crew did what they could for Erwin. His face was burned all over and his nose was half gone. The flesh around his eyes was raw, his skin was blistering, and it seemed certain to his comrades that he would never see again. His hands were burned to the bones. His shirt and pants were afire when the crew got to him and the skin under his clothes was burned away.[53]

Five weeks later, in a Navy hospital on Guam, a general pinned the Medal of Honor on the bandages that covered Red Erwin's entire body. The crew, whose lives he saved, gathered around his cot during the brief ceremony. Erwin breathed and was fed through a tube, but his eyes were all right. The rest of him was patched together by plastic surgeons back home.

THE BLOCKADE

The bombing raids were still going when St. Clair McKelway returned to New York on leave in June 1945. "I see by the New York papers that LeMay is throwing his B-29s at the Japs in different ways, with different tactics," he wrote. "Flying low and only at night, specially trained B-29 squadrons have mined the harbors of Japan's main islands, strengthening the naval blockade, and preventing the Japs from moving their war industries to Manchuria before they are entirely wiped out on Honshu."[54]

These missions had begun in late March 1945, and came at the culmination of a devastatingly successful campaign against enemy shipping by American submarines. The mining campaign was intended to bottle up Japanese harbors and major waterways, chiefly Shimonoseki Strait, between the southern island of Kyushu and the island of Honshu, the main channel from Japan's Inland Sea to the Sea of Japan and the Asian mainland. Most of the Japanese shipping that had survived naval air and submarine attacks had to pass through this strait to reach the great ports of the Inland Sea. Mining operations, first suggested by the Navy and grudgingly supported by LeMay, were designed to cut off imports—including food and vital raw materials—from Japanese-occupied Asia; prevent the flow of supplies to Japanese armies in the Pacific; and disrupt coastal shipping. It was called Operation Starvation.

The men who carried out this dangerous operation, the crews of the 313th Bomb Wing, describe it:

"The Inland Sea's outlet was the Shimonoseki Strait, which was comparable to our Panama Canal. All traffic that flowed from the four major Japanese islands to the Asian mainland went through it. We had to cripple it," observes Robert Rodenhaus. "General John C. Davis was the commanding general of the 313th Wing. He chose my plane, *The Lucky Strike*, to lead the planes that went in. We were number one."

"Japan was perfect for mining," explains John Jennings. "It had very shallow waters. The Navy provided the mines. Some were 1,000 pounds, some 2,000 pounds, and they would be dropped from 5,500 to 7,500 feet at night with parachutes." There were three types of mines: magnetic, pressure, and acoustic, and they were almost impossible "to sweep," adds Fiske Hanley. "They lay on the bottom of these shallow waterways and would listen for noises, or feel for pressure, or for the magnetic influence from a ship. They were set so they might go off on the first ship to go over them or the tenth. They were devilish things."

Many B-29 crewmen considered the mining missions their most dangerous duty. "We were conned immediately from both sides with searchlights," Rodenhaus continues his story. "Powerful [radar-directed] searchlights. They were demoralizing. They are psychologically wrenching, because they illuminate completely the interior of the airplane. You gotta wear dark glasses, and as you travel they are passing you from one searchlight battery to the next. You're never out of their sight." As John Jennings says, "the mining missions are where we lost most of our planes and people."

Over 12,000 mines were laid, 2,100 of them in the Shimonoseki Strait. By the end of the war, these mines had sunk or disabled 650,000 tons of Japanese shipping. As early as May 1945, however, mining operations had blockaded every Japanese shipping lane, virtually cutting off communications between Japan and the Asian mainland. Submarines, meanwhile, had severed communication between Japan and its southern resource colonies, and LeMay's B-29s had destroyed a good part of Japan's industrial war machine. By the end of May, the lethal combination of burning and blockade had closed the huge ports of Nagoya, Yokohama, and Tokyo.

The Japanese also used mines, to defend their shores against the expected American invasion. Finding these minefields and plotting them was one of the most harrowing and least known operations of the war. Marty Schaffer, a Navy enlisted man from Allentown, Pennsylvania, served on the submarine *Polaris* in the waters off Japan in the last year of the war:

THE JAPANESE MINES WERE ANCHORED TO the ocean floor, just jiggling there, swinging on a chain. Our job was to plot them, using sonar. When we went in to plot them, "silent running" was announced over the PA system. That meant four knots on the propeller screws, real quiet. Everyone who wasn't on duty went to their bunks, sometimes for ten hours—and waited in absolute silence, in the dark, listening to the eerie "ping, ping" of the sonar. When we picked up a mine you would hear an echo. Then everybody would tense up. Sometimes I'd try to read to steady the nerves, but that didn't work. I'd sometimes fall asleep but that was bad, because I'd have these terrifying dreams of the boat getting blown apart by a mine.

The most awful thing was the sound of the chains. You could hear the chains, or cables, that held those mines scraping the side of our boat, and that was hair-raising. Any second, you thought—kabang! you're blown to bits. I'll never forget that sound, that nerve-rattling scraping. I can still hear it. I don't call myself a veteran. I call myself a survivor.

Sometimes we weren't down very far, and the sea was so rough it would toss our boat around. And there were loose mines floating around, mines that had been torn loose by monsoons or storms. We always worried about running into those. We'd go after them when we came topside to recharge our batteries. We had a yeoman who was a sharpshooter, a good old boy. The other kids would try to get the mines with machine guns, but he'd say, "step aside, lads," and with one shot would hit the detonator and explode the mine.

When I think about it now, we were in a hell of a mess when we went into those fields. Minefield plotting became so tight that you actually had to back out of the minefield. There wasn't enough room to turn around. But nobody on the boat ever broke down or panicked. It was the training, the tough training we went through, and the screening. We were an elite service, all volunteers, and everyone did his job.[55]

Submarines participated in nearly every type of Navy operation in the war, including setting up, with Navy destroyers and long-range patrol planes, a search-and-rescue lifeline for B-29 crews, like Charlie Phillips's, that had to ditch in the Pacific or parachute into its dangerous waters. Submarines alone rescued 247 downed airmen in the last three months of the war.

But with Japan more dependent on ocean shipping than any other major power, the main job of the silent service was commerce raiding. From the day Pearl Harbor was attacked, it was a campaign of unrestricted submarine warfare against Japan, with no warning given to enemy ships, armed or not. Navy code breakers spearheaded the effort. They deciphered the Japanese shipping codes, which gave the location of every convoy in the Pacific, and guided submarines to these easy targets. By the end of the war, it was, as Marty Schaffer said, "like shooting fish in a barrel," for there was no Japanese navy or air force to contend with.[56]

It had not always been this easy. In World War II, one out of every seven men in the submarine service was lost at sea. With only 2 percent of the Navy's ships and personnel, the U.S. submarine service accounted for more Japanese shipping sunk than all other arms of the services put together. By 1945 Japan's five great Pacific ports handled less than one eighth of their 1941 trade; and three quarters of the Japanese fishing fleet was destroyed. In the summer of 1945, Japanese planners doubted that the country could feed itself into the next year.

According to Vice Admiral Charles A. Lockwood, Jr., commander of the Pacific Fleet submarine force, American submarines sank a total of 1,256 Japanese ships, 167 combatant ships, including four carriers, and over 1,000 tankers, transports, and cargo ships. Eight million tons of Japanese merchant marine shipping was sunk in the war, over half of it by American submarines, and most of the rest by bombers and underwater mines. Most critically, the submarine service cut off oil supplies from Southeast Asia to oil-starved Japan and created desperate shortages of food and essential raw materials, including rubber, coal, lumber, iron ore, and nitrates for explosives. In the end, blockade would be far more damaging to the Japanese war economy than LeMay's fire raids, which struck an urban economy that was already fatally wounded. But before the war against shipping strangled its economy, Japan, "a maimed but still vicious tiger," amassed the strength for one final, furious struggle on the islands of Iwo Jima and Okinawa.[57]

FOR THE B-29s

On a night in May 1945, B-29 co-pilot Harry George was on a fire raid over Tokyo:

THE SEARCHLIGHTS LOCKED IN ON US. . . . Then the flak hit and the plane started to rock. The engineer behind me said, "I'm losing number one." Then he said, "Now I'm losing number three." Then the interphone went dead. No conversation at all. I used the emergency interphone and asked for a crew report. We had four men in the rear waist compartment. I waited probably ten seconds. Not a sound. Then all of a sudden the tail gunner reported he was okay. But no word from the waist compartment. So I took off my flak suit and went back there to see what happened.

I got to the tunnel—there was thirty-five feet of narrow tunnel—and I went in with my parachute on. That made it tough for me to get through, and I started to think, "If we go down and I'm caught in this tunnel . . ."

When I got through and stuck my head out at the other end it was an awful sight. Our left gunner was badly wounded. His jaw had been shot away by flak. He had lost the whole calf of one leg. The other gunner had a flak wound in his leg. The radar man, God bless him, was giving first aid. We had a top gunner there who also had a couple of small flak wounds. . . .

As I started to help these guys, we started back to Iwo Jima, which we had captured from the Japanese a couple of months before. That was three good hours away. We went through weather. We only had two engines. The bomb bay doors were hanging open. Couldn't get 'em closed. Finally got back to Iwo. The place was covered with fog. We couldn't get back to Tinian, another three and a half hours, so we just said we'd circle and wait. The control command at Iwo Jima said our best bet was to ditch the airplane near the beach and we said, "No, we will not ditch because our gunner will not survive a ditching." We had given him three pints of plasma and morphine. He thought he was going to die.

Then the engineer said, "We're about to run out of gas." So we had to try to land. It was light by this time, about nine o'clock in the morning. They directed us around the top of Mount Suribachi and down through the clouds. We got down to about fifty feet and didn't see the runway. All we saw was a cemetery and we didn't want to go there, so we pulled up around again trying to line up again over the island, which was only seven miles long. . . .

On the third pass around, the engines started cutting out. We were about out of gas. We just had enough to pull to 1,200 feet and we rang a bell for the crew to bail out. The bombardier had gone back and they were going to dump the badly wounded gunner, Dick Neil, out the back with his ripcord tied to a rope that was tied to the plane. But even though his jaw was gone, he was able to say he would get tangled up. He said, "I'll pull it." And so he bailed out and pulled his own ripcord. He landed about 500 yards from a MASH [mobile army surgical hospital] unit and they saved him.

The rest of us—all ten of us—bailed out and landed on the island, except the commander, Gus, who went into the water. A Navy boat went out to find him in the heavy fog, and they only found him because he was blowing that police whistle that's attached to the Mae West [his inflatable life jacket].

I landed in a big foxhole, a bomb shell hole. Then this big Marine comes sliding down in that volcanic dust . . . and he says, "Are you all right?" And I said, "Boy, am I glad to see you Marines!"

That was one of the reasons Marines had been ordered to take Iwo Jima—to help the bomber boys. After Iwo Jima was secured in late March, about 2,400 B-29s, many of them shot-up and fuel-starved, would make unscheduled landings on or near the island.[58] Lives were saved. But the cemetery that Harry George's crippled plane flew over, the largest American burial ground in the Pacific, contained almost 6,800 graves. In the sulfuric ash of barren Iwo Jima, the Marines fought their bloodiest battle ever, suffering more than 26,000 casualties.

Uncommon Valor

THE FINAL BATTLES

In the early fall of 1944, Captain William Sanders Clark of Cleveland, Ohio, was stationed with the Marines on Saipan. He had fought to take the island from the Japanese, knowing it would become a base for the B-29s, and now he eagerly awaited their arrival. "None of us had ever seen a B-29," he wrote in his war diary, "so all hands were on the lookout for the first one." Sanders was there when *Joltin' Josie* touched down, and he was there when Possum Hansell's crews took off on their first bombing raid against Tokyo.

"In our officers club we talked with B-29 crews who had been over Tokyo. We envied these fellows and also greatly admired them. During these early raids there were a lot of Marines who would have paid money to go along on a bombing mission. However, the losses of bomber personnel rose steadily and this early enthusiasm waned. The 3,000-mile bombing run from Saipan to Tokyo and back was [one of] the most dangerous in the world. For several months there was nothing but the enemy on Iwo Jima. The only place that planes could set down in case of trouble was in the sea!

Destroyers, search planes, and submarines did a magnificent job of rescue work but the toll of casualties continued to mount. It was this condition more than anything else that made the conquest of Iwo a military necessity." [1]

That was not quite true. The decision to invade Iwo Jima had actually been made before the first B-29 took off from Saipan. On October 3, 1944, the Joint Chiefs of Staff approved Chester Nimitz's plan to avoid taking Formosa and go straight for the kill, seizing the islands of Iwo Jima, about 700 miles south of Tokyo, and Okinawa, the largest of the Ryukyu Islands, which is only 350 miles from Kyushu, the southernmost main island of Japan. The Iwo Jima landing was scheduled for February 19, 1945; Okinawa's L-Day, or Love Day, as it was called in military code to prevent confusing it with Iwo Jima's D-Day, would be only six weeks later, on April 1. Unknowingly, the high command had chosen the sites for the last great battles of World War II.

Okinawa, a large island with excellent harbors and airfields, would be an ideal staging base for an assault on the home islands. And Iwo Jima was seen as much more than a possible refuge station for distressed B-29s. The main reason for taking it was to provide air fields from which P-51 Mustangs could escort LeMay's Superforts to Japan. Just after arriving in the Marianas in January 1945, LeMay met with Admiral Raymond Spruance, commander of the Iwo Jima fleet operation, and told him straight out. "Without Iwo Jima I couldn't bomb Japan effectively." Spruance had been having some last-minute doubts about the wisdom of taking the strongly defended island, rather than bombing and bypassing it, as he had Truk, in the Caroline Islands, but his conversation with LeMay gave him reassurance. [2]

Taking Iwo Jima would also allow the Navy to put a much needed air rescue station on the island, 800 miles further north from the Marianas, for distressed B-29s returning from the long over-water run from Japan. And it would stop enemy air raids on B-29 bases in the Marianas. [3]

In October 1944, Japanese fighter-bombers flying from fueling stations on Iwo Jima had begun a series of "vengeance raids" on Saipan. "Their first raid came as a real surprise," William Clark recalls. "Toward dusk, several Japanese planes suddenly swooped low over Isley Field and proceeded to bomb and strafe the parked Superforts. The enemy pilots were audacious and were only fifty feet above the runways. They [took us by] surprise and left the field littered with burned and blasted B-29s."

On later night raids, batteries of crisscrossing searchlights picked up enemy planes as they flew in tent-high over Isley Field. Clark and his fellow Marines, who were camped near the airfield, had "ringside seats" for these aerial duels. "We would cheer wildly and shout, 'Get the yellow bastard, don't let that goddamned son-of-a-bitch get away.' Every man on the ground felt that he could help the gunners' aim with a little profanity."

In December 1944, the Japanese destroyed more B-29s on the ground in the Marianas than were lost in the air over Japan. This helped to persuade Admiral Nimitz—who was also having second thoughts about invading Iwo Jima—that the operation had to go forward.[4]

The battles of Iwo Jima and Okinawa "sound like oft-repeated tunes," James Jones wrote in his history of the war. "So familiar by now that the reader can just about chant them in unison with me. . . . The sequence of landings, moves inland, fierce resistance, head-on attacks, final splitting of the defenders into isolated pockets—they were like the choreographed movements of some classic military ballet." But each of the two battles had its own "diabolical hardship" that set it off from each other and from all previous Pacific struggles.[5]

At Iwo Jima, it was an end-of-time environment of volcanic rubble and ash and the way the enemy used it to create a killing field like none other in history. It was the Marines' costliest battle ever. In one month, they suffered one third of the total number of deaths they would incur in all theaters in World War II. The eight-square-mile island cost the Americans—Marines, Navy, and Army—28,686 casualties, including 6,821 killed. It was the first time in the Central Pacific campaign that the enemy inflicted more casualties on an American invasion force than it sustained itself.

Okinawa's extra hardships were its size, its large Japanese population, and the unprecedented waves of kamikaze attacks—by air and sea—that would kill or wound almost 10,000 sailors. For three months, Okinawa was the scene of the greatest air-naval-land battle in history. The Americans suffered over 49,000 casualties, more than 110,000 Japanese soldiers were killed, and 150,000 to 170,000 noncombatants died. Okinawa was a horrifying foretaste of what an invasion of the Japanese mainland would cost—for both sides.

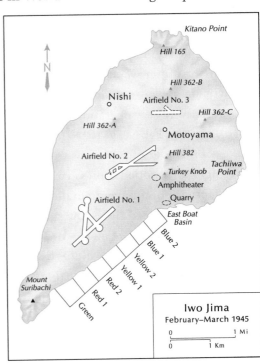

Iwo Jima
February–March 1945

0 _____ 1 Mi

0 _____ 1 Km

The assaults on Iwo Jima and Okinawa took place with the war in Europe nearing its end, as the Allies began closing in on Berlin, the Russians from the east and the Anglo-American armies from the west. And the fighting on Okinawa went on for seven weeks after Germany surrendered on May 7, 1945. Americans at home watched these two epic struggles closer than they had ever watched events in the Pacific. These battles would determine how much longer this death-dealing war would last. We today, of course, know it ended in August of 1945, but at the time Americans feared that it could go on for another two to three years. For combat-battered veterans stationed in Europe, nervously reading about developments in the far-off Pacific, this was almost too cruel to contemplate.

IWO JIMA

On a harsh, rainy morning in late January 1945, William Sanders Clark left Saipan's Tanapag Harbor with an invasion convoy headed for Iwo Jima. Like almost every man on board he knew little about the mission ahead. Back on Saipan, he and other Marines had talked to bomber crews who had been "softening up" the target. They saw no signs of life on the island. "All you'll need is about one regiment to walk ashore and bury the dead," a B-29 pilot assured them.[6] But the commanders who planned the operation were clearly worried. The Navy's photo reconnaissance confirmed their worst fears. The preliminary bombing had merely driven the dug-in defenders deeper underground. What had initially seemed to Nimitz and Spruance a relatively easy operation would be a bloodbath for the assault troops.

On February 16, three days before D-Day, Admiral Richmond Kelly Turner, commander of what was the largest Navy-Marine landing operation up to that time, held an emotional press conference on his flagship, USS *Eldorado*. Granite-featured Harry Schmidt, commander of the three Marine divisions that would make the assault, predicted the island would be taken in ten days. It would be a small campaign between two large ones—Luzon and Okinawa. "But everyone [knew] we would lose a lot of men," recalled Robert Sherrod, who was there that day. "We knew the underground defenses of this little island were as nearly impregnable as man could devise, and that seventy-four straight days of bombing had not knocked them out."

"Iwo Jima is as well defended as any fixed position that exists in the world today," Admiral Turner informed the reporters assembled in his palpably tense briefing room. Then Colonel Thomas Yancey, the chief intelligence officer, spoke. "Iwo is

625 miles north of Saipan and 660 miles south of the Japanese empire. It is of the greatest importance to the enemy. It is small: five miles long and two and one-half miles wide at its widest point. Mount Suribachi on the southern tip is a volcano, 554 feet high. About one third of the island is airfields and revetments, one-third cane fields and scrub growth, one third is barren. The beaches we will land on are volcanic ash, the northern two thirds of the island is a plateau whose height goes up to about 350 feet." The invasion beaches were between the plateau and the volcano, at the southern end of the island's eastern side.[7]

A crusty Marine described the island with greater economy. "Think of a [large] bad-smelling pork chop burned black. . . . That was Iwo Jima."[8]

When Yancey completed his briefing, a member of General Schmidt's staff outlined the plan of attack. This had already been given to all officers in the amphibious force, and William Clark described it accurately in the memory book he kept during the battle. "The 5th Division was to land near the base of Mount Suribachi. Its mission was to secure the volcano, thus denying the Japs perfect positions from which to subject our landing beaches to severe enfilade fire. When this was accomplished, it was to turn north and drive up the west side of the island. The 4th Division [to which Clark was attached as a radio operator] was to land near the center of the island. [Our] mission was to cut directly across the island, capturing Motoyama Airfield No. 1. This was the primary enemy airstrip. This accomplished, the division was to make a right pivot and drive up the east side of the island. The 3rd Division was to be a floating reserve to be used only in case of emergency."

With the Japanese dug-in, it would be a "frontal assault," the reporters were informed, a slugging match, yard by yard, with no room for maneuver or strategy. At least one of the generals was "misty-eyed," and the reporters filed out of the briefing room with what Sherrod describes as "the sort of the pit-of-the-stomach emotion one feels when he knows that many men who love life are about to die."[9]

At night, in the rank-smelling holds of the rusted troopships, with all doors and hatches sealed tight, the Marines "spoke more flatly, and with less whimsical woodrapping, of the expectation of death than any assault troops I had ever been with before," reported *New Yorker* correspondent John Lardner. "I did not see a man . . . who expected anything but a bloody and disagreeable time of it." They had been told that it would by tough, that the island was "too small to provide room for maneuver." As one Marine major kept telling his men over and over again, " 'You can't run the ends up there. . . . Every play is between the tackles.' "

Thousands of these men were veterans of other hotly contested island assaults, and these earlier campaigns had had taken a toll on them, on their bodies as well as their minds. "In the Army," Lardner explained, "shock troops are a small minority supported by a vast group of artisans, laborers, clerks, and organizers. In the Marines there are practically nothing but shock troops. For such troops, in time, no matter how well trained and competent, a saturation point is bound to come."[10] Men bound for the battle openly wondered whether Iwo would be it for them, not the place where they "bought it"—death was always expected—but where they broke down and could fight no more, letting down themselves and their brother Marines.

First to hit the beaches were the frogmen. Navy underwater demolition teams swam into the landing areas two days before D-Day, covered by the fire of a dozen gunships, backed up by destroyers and cruisers. In an interview given long after the war, frogman Andy Anderson describes the work of the men who were known as "half-fish and half-nuts":

I'LL NEVER FORGET WHEN WE FIRST arrived in the waters off Iwo on D-minus-three and stood on the deck and looked at that island. It was the most godforsaken place I'd ever seen, with the rising smoke and haze and that frightening-looking volcano. It flashed through my mind that this would be a great place to film a Dracula movie. We all thought, "Why do we want that miserable piece of real estate?"

Our job was to swim in to the invasion beaches, locate mines and detonate them, identify other beach obstacles, and bring back samples of the sand to see if our landing vehicles could operate on that brown volcanic ash. The operation had to be done in daylight to be sure we got all the mines. At a thousand yards, the gunboats—converted LCI [Landing Craft Infantry] ships—fired their rockets and we raced by them in speedboats and were dropped into the water 700 yards off the beach. Five pairs of swimmers went in at 100 yards apart.

Our first shock was the temperature of the water. When you hit that water at fifty-eight degrees it was a real character builder. We had no rubber suits or scuba tanks. They weren't used until the Korean War. We were the naked warriors; that's what they called us. We went in with swim trunks, a pair of fins, a mask, a knife, a slate and pencil, and blasting caps for detonating mines, which we kept in condoms to keep the powder dry. We strapped the condoms to our belts. In fact, we used so many condoms in training back in Florida that the Navy sent down a morals officer to look into the situation.

We painted our bodies with grease that was mixed with silver paint, to give

us camouflage. When we got close to the beach, an awful lot of enemy fire was coming at us. I rolled over in the water and looked back and all those gunboats that were supposed to be giving us cover had been either sunk or disabled. When the Japanese mortar shells came down they actually popped us up, almost out of the water. And we could look down in the water and see the shells that missed us, spiraling to the bottom. But bobbing out there, with silver paint on, we were hard targets to hit.

When we almost reached the beach we saw an abandoned boat with a sniper in it. He kept popping up and shooting at us. My swim partner was a young Irish kid with a hot temper and he stood up, shook his fist, and shouted, "Why don't you come down here and fight like a man." I screamed at him, "Matt, get your tail down or it's going to get blown off." On the beach, all I remember is looking up and seeing this sixteen-inch stuff exploding out of these cliffs and the tremendous return fire of our ships. It was terrifying, and the noise was deafening.

After we got our sand samples and other information we swam back to the rendezvous point with the speedboat. Going back you didn't know whether to zig or zag as the shells came in on the left and then the right, one after the other, till they pulled us out of the sea.

Part of our mission that day was to get the Japanese to fire on us, so we could locate their big beach guns, which were hidden in cliffs and hills. We fooled them. They thought we were the first wave of the invasion force. That night Tokyo Rose went on the radio and congratulated the valiant defenders of Iwo Jima for repulsing the American invasion. But all we did was force them to make a mistake by firing on us. The next day the Navy pulverized those beach guns, saving lives on D-Day.

Our operation was successful in other ways. We didn't find any mines or obstacles and there were no sandbars. It was well graded for bringing up LSTs. We didn't have to do any demolition and only two swimmers were killed in the whole operation, one after he got back on the boat. [Two hundred sailors, however, were killed or wounded on the disabled gunboats.]

As soon as we were pulled out of the water, we were debriefed. Then a chart of the beach was made and sent to the Marines.[11]

That night, after singing religious hymns on the deck to settle himself, William Clark "slept better than I had slept before many a college exam." Morning broke bright and clear; high clouds, calm seas—a perfect invasion day. After watching the third and final day of the greatest naval bombardment of the Pacific war, Clark boarded a boat to guide in the first waves of assault vehicles. After this he became a kind of water cop, keeping boats moving to and from the thickly congested beach. "This gave me an opportunity to view the whole attack."

Out at sea, John Lardner transferred to a ship closer to shore to watch Clark and the first wave head in. His first trial was the wet, loose web of rope that hung from the side of the troop carrier. "Even young Marines have been killed on these descents when the sea has been rough," he wrote, "and for those over thirty-five the endless sequence of nets, Jacob's ladders, bouncing gangways, and lurching boats is a hazard and nightmare."

After maneuvering down the ropes, Lardner boarded a small boat with Colonel Thomas Wornham, a regimental commander of the 5th Marine Division, and headed through the choppy seas to Wornham's control ship. It was anchored at the line where the first wave of assault troops "formed up in their amtracks and began their long, slow, bobbing run for the beach." The men in the boats were "a fierce and stirring sight as they passed us to disappear in the valleys of the water between us and the beach. I stood watching them as well as I could from the rail of the control ship beside a regimental messenger, a Navajo Indian named Galeagon, and we spoke of how most of the shock troops we could see, their hands and faces greased dead white for protection against possible flame barriers, sat up very straight and looked intently ahead." [12]

The first assault waves came ashore at nine o'clock, right on schedule. It was a surprisingly easy landing. The toughest part was scaling the steep terraces of soft volcanic ash that rose up in front of the men as they walked out of the surf, each Marine carrying sixty or more pounds of equipment. Reaching the top of the dunes on their bellies and scanning the horizon, the Marines found what looked to be an abandoned island. "Where's the reception committee?" asked Private Louie Adrian. [13] Three hours later, with the beach jammed with men and equipment, Adrian got his answer.

The Japanese used monstrously large mortar shells, "flying ashcans" the Marines called them, which blew parts of men and machines as high as a hundred feet in the air. Landing that afternoon, Private First Class Thomas H. Begay, a full-blooded Navajo, said the beach was the "scariest damn thing" he had ever seen. "I got numb . . . all over my body. No feeling, I was scared as hell, I mean scared. Even though I'm walking, I feel like I'm standing in one place. And that place was like wrecking yard. They had things blown to pieces, it's like traffic jam. . . . There was piles of bodies, and wounded ones. . . . I grow up that day. I age about two years right on that beach, got my Ph.D. about war." [14]

The enemy zeroed in from Mount Suribachi and from the cliffs and hills north of the beachhead, and nearly everywhere they put a shell it hit a man or a machine. "No man who survived that beach knew how he did it," said Joe Rosenthal, the Associated Press photographer who would take the most famous picture of the war on Iwo Jima. "It was like walking through rain and not getting wet." [15]

That evening, Captain Clark, working close to the beach, watched the Marine tractors, the only vehicles

MARINES ON A THIRTY-MINUTE RUN TO THE BEACHES OF IWO JIMA AT THE FOOT OF MOUNT SURIBACHI (USMC).

D-PLUS-ONE ON IWO JIMA (USMC).

capable of negotiating the soft ash with little trouble, scurrying "back and forth like a bunch of ants. Some of our fellows carried badly needed supplies right to where the fighting was in progress. These cumbersome vehicles were choice targets for Jap gunners and mortarmen." It was a job, in the pitch black of night, requiring "daring and cool courage," the tractors' only guide being a blinking flashlight held by a Marine officer who directed the unloading of ammunition and other supplies. Much of this work was being done by African-American Marines with the ammunition and depot companies, eleven of whom were wounded, two fatally.

John Lardner had landed later in the day with the fourteenth wave and experienced some of the worst of the mortar assault. "At Iwo, as at Anzio, there quickly developed two fronts—the battle front forward and the shelling front on the beaches, where our supply and reinforcement lines were wholly dependent on boats and amphibious vehicles that were being stalled and pounded by surf and wind. And in the case of Iwo, the Marines depended also on motor or human convoys, which were slowed by drifting volcanic sand." The Japanese had high ground over the supply beaches and pounded them mercilessly. "The mortar shell . . . travels in a high, lobbing trajectory and throws its fragments over a wide radius when it explodes. It makes for tearing, disfiguring wounds and disfigured dead." Everywhere Lardner looked, he saw "slashed and mangled bodies."

As he slogged forward through the thick, shifting sand, his breathing "sharp and painful," he heard the "whine and bang of mortar shells dropping and bursting" all around him. At one point, after stopping for forty minutes, his body pressed against the sand, he realized that "there is such a thing as wishful pinned-down thinking," and that "it can become a more dangerous state of mind than any other in an area that is being shelled. A man tends to cling to his trench, even if it is in the center of a target, when the sensible thing is to [move forward]." It took Lardner almost twenty minutes more to adjust his nerves and move ahead, struggling all the while to fight "overpowering intimations of mortality." [16]

Around five o'clock that afternoon, Robert Sherrod was about to board a landing boat to head into the beaches when he ran into his friend Keith Wheeler of the *Chicago Times*. Wheeler was returning from the island to write his D-Day story. "There's more hell in there than I've seen in the rest of this war put together," he told Sherrod. "I wouldn't go in there if I were you, it's plain foolishness. The Nips are going to open up with everything they've got tonight." Sherrod shook his head and headed in. When his Higgins boat crunched ashore, he found it almost impossible to dig a foxhole in the loose volcanic ash. "It's like diggin' a hole in a barrel of wheat," a Marine next to him shouted.

By this time, the 5th Division had cut across the tail of the pork-chop-shaped island, isolating Suribachi from the rest of Iwo Jima, and General Schmidt had 30,000 Marines ashore, against about 21,000 Japanese defenders.

Learning from the failures of Tarawa, the Navy had fired a rolling barrage in front of the advancing Marines, giving the Japanese no time to reoccupy emptied positions. And carrier planes flew in low, strafing and bombing. But aside from the beach and a small portion of Motoyama Airfield No. 1, the Japanese owned the rest of the real estate, and no place on it was beyond the range of their heavy guns. After the remainder of the assault force, over 40,000 men, landed over the course of the next week, Iwo Jima would be one of the most heavily populated eight square miles on earth.

When Sherrod arrived on the beach, the mortar fire had quieted down and he was even able to catch a little sleep. But just after 4:00 A.M. the Japanese opened up with everything they had. "The first big mortar shell hit only a few yards from my foxhole, and it sounded like the break of doom. . . . All night the Japs rained heavy mortars and rockets and artillery on the entire area between the beach and the airfield. Twice they hit casualty stations on the beach. . . . The corpsmen were taking it as usual." [17]

Squad leader Albert J. Ouellette landed with two doctors and forty corpsmen. "Before the day was out, one doctor was killed when he lost both legs, and only two corpsmen were left," he recalls. "All the rest were dead or wounded." [18]

Navy corpsman Stanley E. Dabrowski landed under heavy fire near Mount Suribachi. "I had a carbine and a .45. Unlike the Army in Europe, we were armed. That was because of our experience on Guadalcanal. At that time corpsmen still wore Red Cross brassards on their arms and a red cross on their helmets. They were the first ones to be knocked off." Even after that, the Japanese, spotting the medical kits that corpsmen carried on both shoulders, focused their fire on them.

On landing, Dabrowski and his team of corpsmen picked the deepest shell hole they could find and set up an emergency aid station. "Evacuation of wounded was extremely hazardous. The stretcher-bearers were under constant fire. . . . When we started experiencing heavy casualties, it was almost impossible to comprehend. Because of the heavy artillery and mortar fire there were a lot of traumatic injuries, traumatic amputations. . . . No arms, or both legs. And then there were abdominal injuries, torn-out intestinal tracts. Often I was beside myself trying to decide what to do with these people. . . .

"Sometimes these young men would be covered by a poncho and lying on a stretcher. And I'd say, Hey, Mac, how are you doing? Pretty good, doc. What's the problem? Oh, my left arm got it. So you'd lift the poncho and you'd see a stump." [19]

When the firing let up at daylight, Sherrod walked back to the beach. He saw only a dozen or so dead Japanese. "The Jap plan of defense was plain," he wrote in his first story from Iwo Jima. "Only a few men would defend the beaches. The mortars and machine guns from the hillside caves . . . would stop the landing."

By the second morning, there were 2,400 casualties among the landing force, and most of them had "died with the greatest possible violence. Nowhere in the Pa-

A Marine hands a cigarette to a wounded Japanese soldier half buried in a shell hole, after knocking away a grenade that was near his hand. The embittered local conscript gave the Marines information about Japanese defenses on Mount Suribachi (Lou Lowery/USMC).

cific war have I seen such badly mangled bodies," wrote Sherrod. "Many were cut squarely in half. Legs and arms lay fifty feet away from any body."[20] The velocity and intensity of the mortar and artillery fire on the compacted battleground was the reason nearly 8 percent of the Americans wounded on Iwo Jima would die of injuries, as against the overall World War II number of 3 percent.

On that rainy second day, with the wind off the ocean blowing the volcanic dust in their faces, the Marines got a close look at the piece of bleak Pacific cinder they had been sent to take. The pre-invasion bombardment had annihilated the island's vegetation. Between Suribachi on their left and the sloping wasteland of black crevices and cliffs on their right, there was nothing but a flat field of volcanic ash. Flies and mosquitoes were so thick in places men dared not open their mouths, and orders went out not to drink the sulfur-contaminated water. Big "slit-faced" bats soared out of smoking caves on shell-scarred Suribachi and clouds of black sulfur gas flared up through piles of steaming rocks, giving off the smell of rotten eggs. Iwo Jima means "Sulfur Island" in Japanese, and it was the sulfur deposits that had originally drawn prospectors. On at least one occasion, Marines could feel the whole island shaking. "It was as if the very earth itself was alive," recalls William Clark. "At first we were deathly afraid that the entire beach was mined and it would soon erupt. However, successive tremors made us realize that volcanic action was still taking place."

But it was the barren and blasted landscape that provoked the greatest concern. "There was no cover and concealment as we had practiced in our training exercises," says Captain Lawrence Snowden. "There wasn't anything to hide you."[21] When men walked in soft ash up to their knees, and pulled one leg out, it left no imprint. The only marks in the tundra of sand and ash were huge craters created by the naval shelling. Hundreds of them gave the place a lunar appearance. And like walking on

IWO JIMA'S MOONSCAPE (USMC).

the moon, it was as if no one had been there before. There were Marines who fought on Iwo Jima for the entire six-week campaign who never saw a living enemy soldier. "It was an eerie landscape," says Marine Fred Hayner. "While you couldn't see them, you had a feeling that the Japanese had you always in their sights."[22]

As at Peleliu, the battle was fought in two dimensions: the Marines were *on* Iwo Jima, the Japanese were *in* it. Robert Sherrod had not been to Peleliu, so he had no idea what the Marines were in for. After the third day, he filed a cautiously optimistic report. "It seems certain that we will take Iwo Jima at a smaller cost in casualties than Saipan's 16,000. Probably no large percentage of the Jap defenders have yet been killed, but henceforth the Japs will kill fewer Marines and the Marines will kill more Japs."[23] As Sherrod admitted later, "I did not then know the real underground strength of Iwo, nor the capabilities of its defenders."[24]

Iwo Jima had been turned into the world's greatest underground citadel. "[When the invasion comes] every man will resist to the end, making his position his tomb," announced the man who masterminded its defenses, General Tadamichi Kuribayashi.[25] Iwo Jima was of more than strategic value to Japan. It was home territory, administered as part of the Tokyo Prefecture; the mayor of Tokyo was the mayor of Iwo Jima. Anticipating an American invasion before one was planned in detail, the Japanese had begun bolstering the island's defenses after the Americans landed on Saipan. The assault on Peleliu gave them an additional six months to turn Sulfur Island into a subterranean death trap, defended by veterans of the Kwantung Army. Emperor Hirohito, the Son of Heaven, had taken a personal interest in preparing the island's defenses, sending Kuribayashi, the commander of his Palace Guards, to defend it. Kuribayashi was iron-spirited and aggressive, the most formidable adversary the Marines would face in the Pacific war. He was from a distinguished samurai family and fought like a true professional warrior.

The general brought hard discipline to Iwo Jima, abolishing the consumption of alcohol and evacuating all civilians, including his officers' "comfort girls," young women forcibly recruited from Korea and Manchuria. He then brought in Korean slave laborers, military engineers, and demolition experts, and supervised the construction of a phantasmagoric warren of interwoven caves and gun galleries inside Suribachi and under the rock-strewn badlands at the northern end of the island. His cave defenses were stocked with weapons, fuel, and rations, and all had myriad secret entrances and exits. They were mutually supporting, and if one position was threatened, his men could easily sneak through tunnels to the next—above, below, or behind the original position, surprising the Marines with exterminating counterfire.

A MARINE SNIPER ON THE SLOPES OF SURIBACHI (USMC).

Over the entrances to these tunnels and caves Kuribayashi built double-layered concrete blockhouses and pillboxes, which were concealed by volcanic ash. Only the gun muzzles were exposed. Suribachi itself had seven levels of tunnels, connecting almost 1,000 gun galleries.

Kuribayashi respected his enemy. Serving in the Japanese embassy in Washington before the war, he had traveled around the United States and was impressed by its industrial prowess. "The United States is the last country in the world that Japan should fight," he had written his wife.[26] Preparing for the American assault, he told his men what to expect and how to die. A list of "courageous battle vows" was posted in every underground position: "Each man will make it his duty to kill ten of the enemy before dying; until we are destroyed to the last man we shall harass the enemy with guerrilla tactics."[27]

He would fight as Colonel Kunio Nakagawa's forces had at Peleliu. American intelligence had a name for it, "the cornered rat defense." The Japanese would hole up and wait for the Americans to come to them, bleeding them in a battle of attrition. A dying officer who was found on the ground at Iwo Jima was heard to say over and over, "wait for them, wait for them, make them come to you."[28] But while Kuribayashi learned the lesson of Peleliu, American commanders ignored it, paying scant attention to their own intelligence reports. That is why they had been surprised on the beaches, first by no resistance, then by the nature of the resistance—flaming metal rather than fighting men.

On D-plus-two, the 28th Marines of the 5th Division began the assault on Mount Suribachi. From this combination fortress and watchtower the enemy was pouring down fire on the beaches, and artillery spotters were siting targets for guns all over the island. It had to be taken out, and quickly. And the key weapons for taking it were Sherman medium tanks armed with Mark I flamethrowers capable of spewing burning napalm 150 yards.

Sergeant Bill Reed, a correspondent for *Yank*, recounts the opening of the battle for "Hot Rocks," as the Marines called Suribachi:

FOR TWO DAYS THE MEN WHO landed [at the foot of the mountain] were pinned to the ground. Murderous machinegun, sniper, and mortar fire came from a line of pillboxes 300 yards away in the scrubby shrubbery at the foot of the volcano. . . . Men lay on their sides to drink from canteens or to urinate. An errand between foxholes became a life-or-death mission. . . .

Towering over them was Mount Suribachi, a gray unlovely hulk with enemy pillbox[es] . . . in its sides. Marines . . . grew to hate the mountain almost as much as they hated the Japs who were on it. Reaching the summit was almost as much of a challenge as destroying the men who defended it.

The supporting air and naval fire did much. . . . But when it came to the specific four-foot-square machinegun emplacements and the still smaller snipers' pillboxes there was little the offshore and air bombardment could do except silence them for a few minutes. Everyone knew that in the end the troops would have to dig them out.

The foot troops made their drive on the third day. They were aided by a naval and air bombardment so terrific that the Tokyo radio announced that the mountain itself was erupting. They were also aided by their own artillery and rocket guns, landed with superhuman effort the previous day in spite of a choppy ocean and the enemy's guns.

But the foot troops were aided most by the tanks that advanced with them and lobbed shells into the stone-and-concrete revetments that blocked the way of the foot troops. The Japs were afraid of our tanks—so afraid that they ducked low in their shelters and silenced their guns when they saw them. . . .

As soon as the tanks had passed or had been blown up by mines, the Japs came out of their holes and attacked our men from behind with machineguns and mortars. . . . The enemy had hundreds of pillboxes and emplacements connected by a network of tunnels. When the Japs were driven from one pillbox, they would disappear until the Marines advanced to another, and moments later they would appear at their old emplacements, lobbing grenades at our men who had just passed.

By early afternoon of D-plus-two the Japs at the foot of Suribachi had been silenced. However, everyone knew there were Japs still around . . . [in] their shelters. . . .

There were also many Japs who were dead. They were dead in every conceivable contortion of men who met death violently. Their arms and legs were wrenched about their bodies and their fists were clenched and frozen. Those who had been killed by flamethrowers were burned to a black darker than the ashes of Suribachi or scorched to a brilliant yellow. Their clothes had been burned off, and the heat vulcanized their buttocks together with ugly black strips. It was good to see these sights after having been pinned down to [the beach] for two terrible days.

There were dead Marines too. Some platoons had been entirely stripped of their officers and noncoms. Some had lost more than three-fourths of their men since morning. . . . But the worst of the battle for Suribachi was over. Our men had fought their way in under the guns higher up on the mountain.[29]

That night, half of the small enemy force of 300 that was still inside the mountain made a breakout, trying to reach their comrades on the northern side of the airfield. Not more than twenty made it. The following morning, February 23, a patrol led by Lieutenant Harold G. Schrier began the ascent of the still dangerous mountain. Its job was to secure the summit. "Just before we set out, Colonel Chandler Johnson, our battalion commander, handed Harold Schrier a small American flag," says Charles W. Lindberg, one of the two flamethrower men in the platoon, a Marine respected for his almost inhuman composure under fire. "He said, 'If you get to the top, raise it.' I remember he used that word, if.

"Staff Sergeant Lou Lowery, a photographer for *Leatherneck* magazine, went with us."[30]

That morning the fleet had been notified of the mission and told to withhold all fire on Suribachi. Sailors stood by their silenced guns, watching the ascent through binoculars. The volcanic ash and broken rock on the steep path made it tough going, and the men slipped and slid. "We all expected trouble, but not a shot was fired at us," says Lindberg. When they reached the crater's rim, two of the Marines claimed the mountain for their country in their own way: by urinating on it. Then some of the men found a fragment of old pipe, shot a hole through it, and tied the flag to it. "Towards ten thirty, we found the highest point we could and we raised it." As the men gathered around the flag, Lou Lowery recorded the event with his camera. "Then things broke loose down below," says Lindberg. "Our troops started to cheer and our ships whistled and blew their horns. I was so proud. It's a feeling I'll never forget."

The cheering grew louder when the beachmaster turned up the volume of his public address system and announced that the flag was flying on Suribachi. That entire area of the island erupted with noise, the cheers and whistles of the Marines accompanied by the sirens and bells of the fleet. "Talk about patriotism!" says Coast Guardsman Chet Hack. "The uproar almost shook the sky."[31]

The men on the summit didn't have time to celebrate. "Just after we had the flag up, all of a sudden from our right side some shots were fired," Lindberg recalls.

MOUNT SURIBACHI. THE FIRST FLAG GOES DOWN AS THE SECOND FLAG GOES UP (USMC).

"Some Japs were running out of caves, one of them swinging a broken saber, and we drove them back into their hiding places. . . . Then we went around the crater and burnt out some other holes and threw some explosives into whatever caves we could. By about one thirty, we had the mountain secured. . . .

"I found out later that they had changed the flag. I didn't pay any attention to it."

After the first flag went up, Colonel Chandler Johnson sent a runner to the beach to get a larger flag. He was worried that Secretary of the Navy James Forrestal, who was with the invasion fleet, would want the flag on Suribachi for himself. "It was the first American flag to fly over Japanese home territory in World War II. Johnson wanted to preserve that flag [for the battalion]," says Lindberg. Johnson's man got a larger flag, eight feet by four feet eight inches, from the communications officer of an LST, who had picked it up in a salvage depot at Pearl Harbor. Johnson handed the flag to nineteen-year-old Rene Gagnon and told him to get it to the top of the mountain as fast as he could. When Gagnon reached the summit, Sergeant Mike Strank, who had climbed Suribachi with him, took the flag from him, handed it to Schrier, and announced, "Colonel Johnson wants this big flag run up high, so every son a bitch on this whole cruddy island can see it." [32]

When Tarawa veteran Norman Hatch, the 5th Marine Division photo officer, had learned that a larger flag was going up he sent two of his men, Sergeant Bill Genaust, a movie cameraman, and Private Bob Campbell, a still photographer, to the top of Suribachi to cover it. The diminutive Associated Press photographer Joe Rosenthal joined them. As the three photographers ascended Suribachi they ran into Lou Lowery, who was on his way down, and apparently was not aware there was going to be a second flag raising. "You guys are a little late," he said, "the flag is up, but it's a helluva view up there."

When they reached the rim of the crater about noon, a couple of Marines were attaching a flag to a twenty-foot iron pipe they had found in a pile of rubble. Schrier ordered the replacement flag raised at precisely the moment the original flag was lowered. Six men raised the flag: Mike Strank, Rene Gagnon, Ira Hayes, Harlon Block, Franklin Sousley, and Navy corpsman John Bradley. When the flag started to go up, Rosenthal was talking to Genaust, but then stopped and shouted, "There it goes!"

"Out of the corner of my eye, as I had turned toward Genaust, I had seen the men start the flag up. I swung my camera, and shot the scene," Rosenthal remembered. Campbell got a different still shot, one of the first flag going down while the second one went up. And Genaust caught the replacement flag going up with his color movie camera.

Rosenthal feared there might have been too much movement for him to have taken a good picture. A few minutes later, he took a second shot, a posed picture with a group of Marines crowded around the replacement flag cheering and raising rifles and helmets high.

Colonel Johnson got the original flag and secured it in the battalion safe. The replacement flag flew on Suribachi for three weeks, before it was torn to shreds by the wind. And the country got one of the most famous photographs ever, and one of the finest. It became the most widely reproduced still shot of all time. An engraving of it appeared on a three-cent postage stamp, a painting of it was used in the most successful bond drive of the war, and after the war, the sculptor Felix de Weldon spent nine years on a 100-ton bronze statue based on it that commands the entrance to Arlington Cemetery.

The story of Joe Rosenthal's photograph has been mired in myth and misrepresentation. To this day, some people still believe, despite several excellent books on the flag raising, that Rosenthal staged his photograph. Rosenthal himself added to the confusion. Nine days after taking the picture, he walked into press headquarters on Guam and a correspondent walked up to him.

"CONGRATULATIONS, JOE," HE SAID, "ON THAT flag raising shot on Iwo."
"Thanks," I said.
"It's a great picture," he said. "Did you pose it?"
"Sure," I said. I thought he meant the group shot I had arranged with the Marines waving and cheering, but then someone else came up with the [flag raising] picture and I saw it for the first time.
"Gee," I said. "That's good, all right, but I didn't pose it. I wish I could take credit for posing it, but I can't."
One of the correspondents had overheard only the first part of the conversation and he wrote that Rosenthal had posed it, that it was a "phony."
"As I left for home," says Rosenthal, "I had the fear that, through no fault of my own, I was in the doghouse. When I arrived in San Francisco, however, I found that I was now a celebrity." [33]

When Rosenthal's packet of pictures had been sent by mail plane to Guam to be developed, the Associated Press photo editor picked up a glossy print of the flag raising, whistled, and said, "Here's one for all time!"[34] He radioed the image to AP headquarters in New York, and it made every front page in America.

The picture arrived at exactly the right time and with just the right message. The war in Europe was almost over, but news from the Pacific was discouraging. Americans had already died in godforsaken places that people back home had difficulty finding on a map: Kwajalein, Saipan, Peleliu, Tarawa. And at Iwo Jima they were dying in horrifying numbers, and for what? Were these awful little islands worth it? (In 1944, the Navy had come up with a secret plan to shoot shells filled with poison gas onto Iwo Jima, taking it without losing a single American life, but Roosevelt had scotched that plan, insisting that poison gas only be used as a last-ditch retaliatory measure.)[35]

At the same time, the conservative press was excoriating Nimitz for his costly Storm Landings, demanding that the President turn over the Pacific war to MacArthur, whose forces were taking big swathes of enemy territory with proportionally fewer casualties than Nimitz's Marines. Americans were impatient; they were exhausted; and they could not see the end to this war with an enemy that seemed to have a collective death wish. "The Pacific war is gradually getting condensed, and consequently tougher and tougher," wrote Ernie Pyle. "The closer we go to Japan itself, the harder it will be. . . . To me it looks like soul-trying days for us in the years ahead."[36] As Americans read this on February 24, 1944, their spirits must have dropped. Ernie Pyle, the man they trusted to tell the truth, had actually said "in the years ahead."

The next day, Americans at home opened their Sunday morning newspapers and there, spread out before them on the top of front page was Rosenthal's photograph of six American warriors putting up that wonderfully big victory flag. Maybe Ernie Pyle was wrong. Suddenly, the end of the war seemed in sight. The message of the photograph also matched the wartime mood. Here were "six Americans, all for one, working together in victory and valor, and above them, Old Glory," as the writer Hal Buell has observed. "Finally, for the first time, a clear, simple statement from the Pacific gripped the United States."[37]

No major paper carried Lowery's photograph or mentioned the first flag raising. There was only one flag raising, the one captured for all time by Joe Rosenthal. Second only to the one that flew over Fort McHenry on the night Francis Scott Key wrote "The Star-Spangled Banner," this became the most famous American flag that ever flew. To the men on Iwo Jima it was the flag that didn't count. But to Americans back home that replacement flag was the only flag they wanted to hear about. They weren't looking for truth, after all; they were praying for encouragement.

The morning that the first flag went up there were still thirty days of combat ahead. The 28th Marines had paid a stiff price for Suribachi, and now the regiment moved north, with almost every assault unit on the island, into the teeth of Kuribayashi's defenses. One of the first Marines to be wounded in the drive north was Charles Lindberg. After he was evacuated from the island and read the reports in the papers about the flag raising he found it difficult to suppress his anger. "It just didn't

A CHAPLAIN FROM THE 5TH MARINE DIVISION CELEBRATES MASS ON MOUNT SURIBACHI (NA).

make sense to me that something like that could happen. We went up the mountain and we raised the flag. We took the enemy off the top of the mountain. Somebody comes up four hours later and puts up another flag and they're national heroes."

By the morning of the fifth day, over 5,000 Marines had fallen—three for every two minutes of action on Iwo Jima. And now the Americans faced an obstacle greater than Suribachi—the barren stone plateau to the north of the airfields, where Kuribayashi had constructed his most imposing defenses, including his own underground headquarters. On D-plus-six the Marines moved northward, three divisions strong (the "emergency" 3rd Division had been put ashore right after D-Day). They now had the enemy outnumbered by at least three to one, but by going underground the Japanese nullified the Americans' prodigious firepower. "For all our technical skill, we had on Iwo no method and no weapon to counteract the enemy's underground defense," wrote Sherrod. "The Japs made us fight on their own terms." [38]

A team of Marine Corps correspondents described the attempt to smash through these defenses at a place called "The Wilderness":

WHEN THE 24TH REGIMENT'S 2ND BATTALION reached . . . "The Wilderness" . . . they spent four days on the line, with no respite from the song of death sung by mortars among those desolate and gouged shell holes. The Wilderness covered about a square mile inland from Blue Beach 2, on the approaches to Airfield No. 2, and there was no cover. Here stood a blasted dwarf tree; there a stubby rock ledge in a maze of volcanic crevices.

The 2nd Battalion attacked with flame throwers, demolition charges, 37-millimeter guns, riflemen. A tank advancing in support was knocked out by a mortar shell. After every Japanese volley, Corsair fighter planes streamed down on the mortar positions, ripping their charges of bombs into the Wilderness. But after every dive was ended, the mortars started their ghastly song again.

Cracks in the earth run along the open field to the left of the Wilderness, and hot smoke seeped up through the cracks. Gains were counted in terms of 100 or 200 yards for a day, in terms of three or four bunkers knocked out. Losses were counted in terms of three or four men suddenly turned to bloody rags after the howl of a mortar shell, in terms of a flame-thrower man hit by a grenade as he poured his flame into a bunker. . . .

The Japs were hard to kill. Cube-shaped concrete blockhouses had to be blasted again and again before the men inside were silenced. Often the stunned and wounded Japs continued to struggle among the ruins, still trying to fire back. . . . A Marine assaulting a pillbox found a seriously wounded Jap trying to get a heavy machine gun into action. He emptied his clip at him but the Jap kept reaching. Finally, out of ammunition, the Marine used his knife to kill him.

Forty-eight hours after the attack began, one element of the Third Division moved into the line under orders to advance at all costs.

Behind a rolling artillery barrage and with fixed bayonets, the unit leaped forward in an old-fashioned hell-bent-for-leather charge and advanced to the very mouths of the fixed Jap defenses. Before scores of pillboxes the men flung themselves at the tiny flaming holes, throwing grenades and jabbing with bayonets. Comrades went past, hurdled the defenses and rushed across Airfield No. 2. In three minutes one unit lost four officers. Men died at every step. That was how we broke their line.

Across the field we attacked a ridge. The enemy rose up out of holes to hurl our assault back. The squads reformed and went up again. At the crest they plunged on the Japs with bayonets. One of our men, slashing his way from side to side, fell dead from a pistol shot. His comrades drove his bayonet into the Jap who had killed him. The Japs on the ridge were annihilated.

And now behind those proud and weary men, our whole previously stalled attack poured through. Tanks, bazookas, and demolition men smashed and burned the by-passed fortifications. In an area 1,000 yards long and 200 deep, more than 800 enemy pillboxes were counted.

The survivors of this bold charge covered 800 yards in an hour and a half. Brave men had done what naval shelling, aerial bombardment, artillery and tanks had not been able to do in two days of constant pounding. What was perhaps the most intensively fortified small area ever encountered in battle had been broken.[39]

Iwo Jima would have been tougher to take without the help of the Navajo "code-talkers," who had been serving in the Pacific since Guadalcanal. The Navajo language has no alphabet, and in 1941 was known to no more than forty non-Navajo in the world, none of them Japanese. The Marine Signal Corps recruited 420 of the 3,600 Navajo who served in all branches of the military. It trained them as radiomen and had them develop a highly secret metaphoric code, which included hundreds of words of their own invention for military terminology like machine gun and bazooka. The code was never written down—it had to be memorized—and it remains one of the few unbroken codes in military history. (The Army recruited Comanche

Indians for the European theater and used them on the Normandy beaches and in the drive to the Rhine.) "We named the airplanes 'dive bombers' for *ginitsoh* (sparrow hawk)," says Cozy Stanley Brown of Chinle, Arizona, "because the sparrow hawk is like the airplane—it charges downward at a very fast pace. . . . We usually used the harmful animals' names that were living in our country for the alphabet. . . . We were well taken care of. The generals would not allow other soldiers to come near us. . . . We were not supposed to take order[s] except from high [officers] we were assigned to."[40]

The code-talkers were generally split up into two-man teams, "one on either end of a field telephone or walkie-talkie so they could transmit coordinates for artillery or air strikes, relay information on enemy positions, and provide other valuable intelligence without the Japanese being able to decipher the information," explains one of their historians.[41] On Iwo Jima's impossible terrain, where secure communication between ground troops and supporting tanks, artillery, planes, and ships meant life or death, the code-talkers relayed almost a thousand messages without an error, including the one announcing the flag raising on Suribachi. "They told us that being a code-talker, we can't make mistakes," says Thomas Begay. "Has to be perfect. Because if we make a mistake, say the wrong word, could kill a lot of our men."[42] The code-talkers gave the Marines on Iwo Jima something the enemy did not have—a rapid, reliable, and absolutely secure system of communication. Most of the messages were sent in the fury of combat, and three code-talkers were killed.

"Why do you have to go?" Navajo mothers asked their sons who volunteered for the Marines. This is "the white man's war."[43] Cozy Stanley Brown provided one answer. "My main reason for going to war was to protect my land and my people because the elderly people said that the earth was our mother," and it was being dominated by foreign countries. "There are Anglos and different Indian tribes living on the earth who have pride in it. . . . I believe what we did was right, and it was worth it. We protected many American people, also the unborn children, which would be the generation to come. . . .

"I brought one of the enemy's scalps home," he declares with a warrior's pride. "The Squaw Dance was performed on me for the enemy scalp that I brought home with me."[44]

When Motoyama Airfield No. 1 was secured and cleared of mines, transports flew in from Guam to evacuate the badly wounded and to bring in cases of whole

blood. Twenty-three-year-old Norma Crotty from Cleveland, Ohio, was on one of the first R4D cargo planes to land on Iwo Jima.

TWELVE OF US NURSES HAD BEEN flown from Honolulu to Guam, where we lived in hospital tents. We were there only a few days when our chief nurse said we were going to fly to Iwo Jima to bring back patients to the hospital on Guam. We didn't know much about the place, and we were astonished to hear that we would be flying into a combat area.

We left Guam about four o'clock in the morning and tried to sleep a little bit on the plane. When we approached Iwo, the pilot woke us up, and we looked out and saw the whole fleet in the water around this tiny island, ships of all kinds firing away, and you could see the smoke coming up from the island. It was impressive. I felt like I was living in a newsreel.

When we landed we ran to the aid station, which was nothing but a big tent, a sandbag tent. Iwo was almost indescribable. There was tremendous noise and dirt and it was all gray sand, which I found out later was volcanic ash, nothing green, no vegetation whatsoever. It was cool and the island smelled, and there were smashed planes and equipment all over the place, and big bulldozers at work. It was so far removed from any experience I ever had.

The patients were on the ground. With the help of the doctors we picked out the worst cases and took them to the plane. The worst things you would see were burns, and men who were torn up by shrapnel. We had some men who were flamethrowers and their tanks had blown up, and it was horrible—the pain, the terrible pain. On the four- to five-hour trip back, we worked with corpsmen—there were no doctors—to stabilize the men and monitor their condition, checking for bleeding, giving them plasma, and feeding them sliced peaches in little paper cups, which we would sit on their chests. It was like they were swallowing little goldfish.

We gave them morphine occasionally, but we didn't have oxygen, or water to wash our hands. We worried about that, going from patient to patient without being able to wash our hands. The men, about thirty of them, were on stretchers and they were stacked up three and four high on the plane, and it was cold and drafty. Generally there was only one nurse and one corpsman on every plane. We were on our own.

The fellows were so much younger than us, seventeen or eighteen years old, and some of them looked younger than that. Like little boys. And they wanted their mothers, and we sort of became their mothers and comforted them. They were all very courteous and appreciative of anything we did. As much as we did for them medically, I think it was the comforting that was most important to them, and to us. Mostly, they wanted to talk to us, and they enjoyed watching us comb our hair and put on lipstick. They'd ask us to do that. The feeling of closeness to these boys I didn't have again until I had children.

What was touching to me was that so many of them were replacements, right out of high school. And now a lot of them were ruined for life.

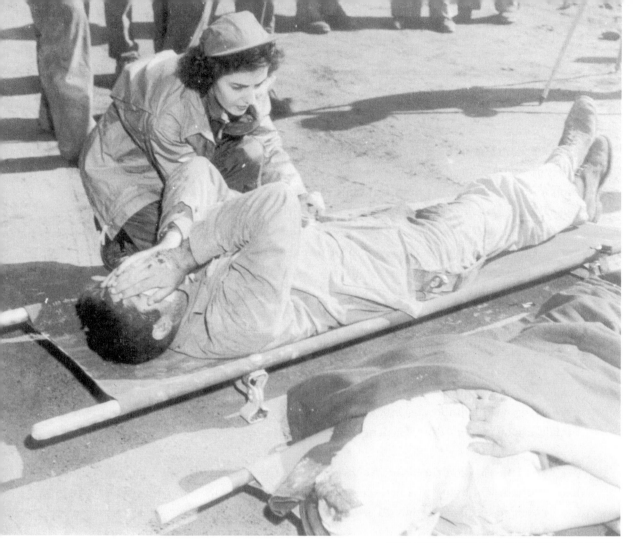

The thing that matters most to me now, fifty years later, are the friendships I made with the eleven other nurses I worked with on those trips between Guam and Iwo. We stayed very close through the years. You must remember that women and girls back in the 1940s hardly left their mothers. It was quite a thing to be away, without any family support, on your own. That meant a lot, because then you knew through the rest of your life you could do just about anything that you put your mind to, that nothing could stop you. You knew you were in control. That was the good thing we got out of our war experience.[45]

Almost 2,500 wounded men were airlifted out of Iwo Jima. Not one patient was lost on the flights to Guam.

On March 4, a Sunday, the Marines around the airfield got an unexpected visitor. The fuel-starved B-29 named *Dinah Might*, on its way back from Japan, skidded to a stop at the end of a runway less than half the size of the one it had taken off from in the Marianas. "As the silver craft came to a stop at the northern end, shellfire began hitting near it. The Japanese wanted that B-29 badly," says Iwo veteran Richard Wheeler. "But *Dinah Might* swung around and taxied out of range toward Suribachi. Hundreds of Seabees and Marines cheered their throats dry as the sixty-five-ton plane stopped and cut its engines." The hatch opened and four or five of the fliers "jumped down and fell to their hands and knees and kissed the runway," another Marine recalls. "What a contrast! Here were men so glad to be on the island they were kissing it. A mile or two to the north were three Marine divisions who thought the ground . . . [was] not even good enough to spit on." [46]

The silver bomber had a faulty fuel valve, and thirty minutes later it was airborne again, soaring out to sea. "If anything was needed to tell the Marines why they were dying on this unholy island," wrote correspondent Keith Wheeler, "the successful landing of *Dinah Might* furnished the demonstration." [47]

Then there were the dead. At this point in the battle, William Clark was still back at the beach, living in a foxhole, working with the supply companies. The fighting had ended in his sector but all around him was the smell and physical presence of death. "Directly offshore from our bivouac area lay a pontoon barge which held several rows of white-clad figures laid in stretchers. These were the mortal remains of men who had died aboard hospital ships and had been towed into shore awaiting burial. There was no time to tender them this decency. For days the barge rocked back and forth on the waves and one by one the bodies would slip overboard. . . . Some were washed ashore; others went to sea."

On the beach, burial detachments were at work. "Anyone who thinks that death on the field of battle is a hero's end should be made to watch a burial party picking up the remains of some poor devil whose luck had run out," says Clark. "We kid ourselves into calling this man a hero. Calling him a hero does not bring life into this limp mass of flesh. Such a man as this was sacrificed by the stupidity of mankind which made such an end possible."

By D-plus-fourteen, many of the Japanese cross-island defenses had been broken and Kuribayashi had only about 3,500 battle-ready troops left. On the high ground in the center of the island, Marines of the 3rd Division had driven a wedge into the northern third of Iwo Jima still held by the Japanese. This wedge was exploited in fighting that took the attackers through a "jungle of stone"—wild lava ledges, smoking sulfur pits, chasms, cliffs, caves, boulders. Four days later the breakthrough to the sea was accomplished and the Japanese force was split. Turning southward, Marines cleaned out the eastern pocket in cave warfare, and it was on the northernmost tip of the island, at Kitano Point, that Kuribayashi reputedly was killed leading his men in a final attack, although his body was never found.

On March 14, General Schmidt declared the island officially occupied by the forces of the United States, and the Army was brought in to finish the job. But the battle really ended on March 25, D-plus-thirty-four, when the last enemy stronghold was taken in a place called Death Valley. A week before this, Admiral Nimitz had issued a statement that summed up the fight. "On Iwo island, uncommon valor was a common virtue." [48] That was nice to hear, but it was thin consolation for the battered and bleeding Marines, among them the company that had raised the flag on Iwo Jima. Easy Company had landed with about 235 men and received seventy replacements. By the battle's end, it had suffered 240 casualties, more than 100 percent of its original number. Among the dead were three of the Marines who had raised the second flag on Suribachi: Mike Strank, Harlon Block, and Franklin Sousley, and one of the photographers who immortalized the act, Bill Genaust.

On March 17, Prime Minister Kuniaki Koiso, speaking by radio, called the fall of Iwo Jima "the most unfortunate thing in the whole war situation." He was quick to add, however, that the nation would fight to the last man "to shatter the enemy's ambitions." [49]

As if to bear out that threatening prophecy, a remnant of Kuribayashi's men mounted one final attack in the early morning hours of March 26, the day after the Americans had declared the battle over. "About 300 of them took off straight down the center of the island," recalls Fred Hayner. "They went right down the airfields and they caught a group of young pilots who had come in with P-51s to escort the B-29s over Tokyo and Yokohama. These fellows, along with some Seabees and Marine construction units, were sleeping in tents or on the ground and the Japanese killed about fifty of them." [50]

Some of the dozing airmen had their throats cut before they had a chance to hear the alarm. "The ensuing battle, which lasted into the daylight hours, was confused and wild," writes Richard Wheeler, "with hand grenades exploding, rifles and machine guns crashing, and men on both sides shouting and cursing and lamenting in pain and terror. The Seabees employed their training as infantrymen, the Army brought up flame tanks, and the Marines first formed a defense line and then counterattacked. With the Marines was a shore-party unit made up of blacks who had seen no previous action, and they performed splendidly." [51]

One of the dead Marines was Lieutenant Harry L. Martin. He earned the Medal of Honor that morning, the last of twenty-seven to be earned by Marine and Navy combatants in the Battle of Iwo Jima.

The dangerous "cleanup" operation went on into the summer, conducted by the 147th Regiment of the U.S. Army, which killed another 1,600 Japanese. "On moonlit nights," a Japanese cave survivor wrote after the war, "I was particularly sad. Watching the moon, I counted the age of my son or thought of my wife's face." [52]

Only about 1,000 Japanese were captured. The remains of thousands of their comrades still lie in the rocks and caves and shifting ash of desolate Iwo Jima.

On April 7, 119 P-51 Mustangs took off from Iwo Jima to escort a fleet of Curtis LeMay's Superforts on a daylight raid on Tokyo. As it turned out, however, the six fighter squadrons stationed on the island were neither effective nor needed, as they were in bomber runs over Nazi Germany. The brutal nine-hour trip to Japan and back, in the punishing winds over the home islands, was too great even for the long-distance Mustangs, which suffered a rash of mechanical and navigational breakdowns. And Japan was never able to put up enough defending aircraft to seriously bother the formidable Superforts. For the reminder of the war, only ten escort missions were flown from Iwo Jima. But to argue, as one historian does, that this made the storming of Iwo Jima a "horrific" mistake, is to see history from hindsight, not as it was lived. [53] At the time the Iwo Jima operation was planned, B-29s were just arriving in the Marianas, and no one expected that they would not need heavy fighter coverage. Both Haywood Hansell and Curtis LeMay had been bomber commanders in Europe, where they saw their crews decimated on long-range, unescorted missions until the Mustang arrived in England in late 1943 and turned the tide of the air war.

Before leaving Iwo Jima, William Clark attended the dedication ceremony of the 4th Division cemetery. The Marines had begun setting up this burial field on the third day of the battle, and the first bodies had arrived three days later. "From that point on, the number of bodies collected was much more than we could handle in any one day," observes Lieutenant Gage Hotaling, a Navy chaplain assigned to the Graves Registration Section. "At one time, we had four hundred or five hundred bodies stacked up, waiting for burial. . . . I am not a smoker, but I found that the only way that I could go around and count bodies was to smoke one cigarette after another. . . . I was addicted to smoking for twenty-six days. . . .

"Once we had bodies lined up, I would give a committal to each one, with Marines holding a flag over the body. And I said the same committal words to every Marine, because they were not buried as Protestants or Catholics or Jews. They were buried as Marines."[54]

The cemetery was dedicated on March 15. Sergeant Bob Cooke, a combat reporter and former Scripps-Howard columnist, described the services. "The Catholic altar was a pile of water cans, the Protestant, the radiator of a jeep. The communion rail was a mound of black volcanic gravel. . . . Yet not in any of the world's great cathedrals or churches was there more sincere reverence. Men ignored heavy shells overhead. Clouds of dust from tanks and bulldozers swept the area. But the chaplain's vestments, the altar cloth, and cross gleamed through the pall of the battlefield."[55]

As the band played the Marine Corps Hymn, William Clark sang along with the other survivors of this epic Pacific battle. "Never in my life had I beheld such a sobering experience. Before me stretched row upon row of new white crosses and headboards. I stood there looking at the somber scene and in my mind formed a question, Why? Why must men be such fools? No war can possibly be won when so much human suffering must be endured."

Okinawa

THE FINAL BATTLE

In February 1945, Eugene Sledge and the 1st Marine Division were at their rest camp on Pavuvu preparing for another island blitz, what would be the last and largest of the more than 100 Pacific D-Days. In the evenings, after training exercises, they gathered around radios and listened to news reports of the desperate fighting on Iwo Jima. To many of them, it sounded "like a larger version of Peleliu." It was also a foretaste of what they would confront on their next landing, where the Japanese would employ the defense-in-depth tactics of Peleliu and Iwo Jima with appalling effectiveness.

Sledge and the other enlisted men had no idea where they were headed next. Their first hint was a map they were shown, without names on it, of a long, narrow island about 300 miles south of the Japanese mainland. A few days later, a friend "came excitedly to my tent," Sledge recalls, "and showed me a *National Geographic* map of the Northern Pacific. On it we saw the same oddly shaped island. . . . It was called Okinawa."

The Old Breed sailed from Pavuvu on March 15, while fighting still raged on Iwo Jima, and on the other side of the world Eisenhower's columns poured into Germany. They were bound for Ulithi Atoll, about 260 miles northeast of Peleliu, where their convoy would join the assembling invasion fleet. They arrived there six days later, anchoring in the spacious, necklace-shaped lagoon, with its crystal-clear water.

Ulithi was the biggest dividend of the Peleliu campaign. While the Old Breed were suffering and dying in the smoking coral of the Umurbrogol, the Army's Wildcats had captured this long atoll, with its 110 square miles of anchorage, without firing a shot or losing a man. Ulithi, not worthless Peleliu, was turned into the marshaling yard for the tremendous armadas that would be hurled against Iwo Jima and Okinawa. "We lined the rails of our transport and looked out over the vast fleet in amazement," Sledge remembers. "It was the biggest invasion fleet ever assembled in the Pacific, and we were awed by the sight of it." [1]

This was only part of an amphibious force that was larger than the one that had assaulted the Normandy beaches on June 6, 1944.[2] From San Francisco to the Philippines, from Hawaii to Guadalcanal—from eleven ports in all—nearly 1,500 vessels, carrying over half a million men—soldiers, Marines, sailors, and airmen—and covering thirty square miles of ocean, would converge at Okinawa at approximately the same time, in what would be one of the logistical miracles of modern warfare.

Spearheading the assault was an amphibious landing force comprised of 183,000 men, backed by another 115,000 support troops and the mightiest assemblage of warships in history: forty large and small carriers, eighteen battleships, five heavy cruisers, close to 200 destroyers and fifty submarines.* Their mission was to take the island and turn it into the England of the Northern Pacific, an assembling point, airbase, and anchorage for the even greater invasion fleet that was expected to strike the

---

*The Normandy armada included 110 big-gunned warships—six battleships, twenty-three cruisers, and eighty-one destroyers.

No precise figures are available for the number of Allied fighting men that landed in Normandy on the first day of the invasion. Stephen E. Ambrose sets the figure at 175,000, while a number of other historians put it at somewhere near 153,000, which I think is about right. These figures include the 23,000 troops landed by parachute or glider.

While the size of the ground forces available on the opening day of the Normandy and Okinawa operations was roughly equivalent, the buildup in Normandy dwarfed that at Okinawa, where the Americans fought essentially with what they brought with them on April 1. By contrast, after a week, some 430,000 men had been brought across the English Channel to the French coast. After a month, the number had grown to over a million. This makes Overlord indisputably the largest amphibious invasion in history.[2]

EAST CHINA SEA

IE SHIMA

MOTOBU PENINSULA

OKINAWA

Mt. Yaetake ○ Nago

PACIFIC OCEAN

USMC III

TENTH

XXIV

Yontan Airfield
Kadena Airfield

EASTERN ISLANDS

Naha

Naha Airfield

Shuri Line

Shuri

OROKU PENINSULA

Okinawa
April–June 1945

0   5 Mi

0   5 Km

Japanese homeland, only 350 miles to the north, later that year.

While Sledge and his friends were admiring the ships at anchor, they saw what turned out to be an awful omen. Anchored near them was "a terribly scorched and battered aircraft carrier. . . . A Navy officer told us she was the *Franklin*. We could see charred and twisted aircraft on her flight deck, where they had been waiting loaded with bombs and rockets to take off when the ship was hit. It must have been a flaming inferno of bursting bombs and rockets and burning aviation gasoline. We looked silently at the battered, listing hulk until one man said, 'Ain't she a mess! Boy, them poor swabbies musta caught hell.' "[3]

They had. Seven hundred and ninety-eight of *Franklin*'s crew were dead and 265 more were wounded, many of them horribly burned. No ship in the entire war suffered more damage and managed to stay afloat, although it never returned to combat. "It seemed to us beyond human belief that the shattered *Franklin* could have made port," wrote Robert Sherrod, who had flown to Ulithi from Guam for what everyone thought would be the last and largest battle of the Pacific island campaign. Unknown to Sledge and his pals, *Franklin*, and a number of other ships in Marc Mitscher's Task Force 58 had been hit by Japanese kamikazes while conducting raids against airfields on Kyushu.

Beginning in mid-March, Mitscher's pilots destroyed almost 500 enemy planes, preventing the decimated Fifth Air Japanese Fleet from tearing into the troopships of the American invasion armada on L-Day. The cost was steep. Four carriers, *Enterprise, Intrepid, Yorktown,* and *Wasp,* were damaged (the *Wasp,* seriously) by kamikazes and conventional aircraft. But none suffered as badly as the *Franklin.* In the early morning of March 19, just as the carrier's fueled and armed Helldivers, Corsairs, and Avengers were preparing to launch, a lone, low-flying Japanese bomber emerged from the soupy overcast and made a direct hit on *Franklin*'s wooden flight deck with two heavy bombs.

The action was wildly confusing that morning, with the enemy planes flying so close to the carriers and their escorts that men at the guns had no idea whether they were being attacked by kamikazes or conventional dive bombers. But it didn't matter. "Sailors who survived that terrible fight," recalls Mort Zimmerman, a signalman on an LCI that laid smoke screens to camouflage the fleet, "lived in mortal fear of the Jap suicide planes for the rest of the war." [4] So did the American high command. "Any mention of suicide planes was taboo," Sherrod recalls. "In our news stories we simply had to ignore one of the most lurid stories of the war, or of any war." [5]

SAILORS ON LEAVE ON ULITHI ATOLL (USN).

Nimitz would not remove these restrictions on the press until April 13. He did this less than an hour before President Roosevelt died of a stroke at his retreat in Warm Spings, Georgia, so the kamikaze threat went to the back pages of the American papers—but only for a few days.

During the week they were anchored at Ulithi, the Old Breed went ashore on the palm-covered islet of Mogmog for what Sledge called some "recreation and physical conditioning." Another Marine more accurately described the day as a raucous beer blast. Mogmog was a sixty-acre "recreational island" capable of accommodating over 15,000 sailors who had been at sea for weeks or months. On Mogmog they could swim, play baseball and basketball, and drink—beer for enlisted men and blended whiskey for officers at their segregated "lounges," where they had exclusive access to the company of visiting Navy nurses, and where they were entertained by African-American Navy bands.

After calisthenics, the officers of the 1st Marine Division broke out warm beer and Cokes, and Sledge and some of the guys played a game of pickup baseball. "Everybody was laughing and running like a bunch of little boys," Sledge recalls. William Manchester, who was there with the 6th Marine Division, describes a different scene. "Each of the . . . U.S. fighting men heading into the battle was to be allowed . . . all the

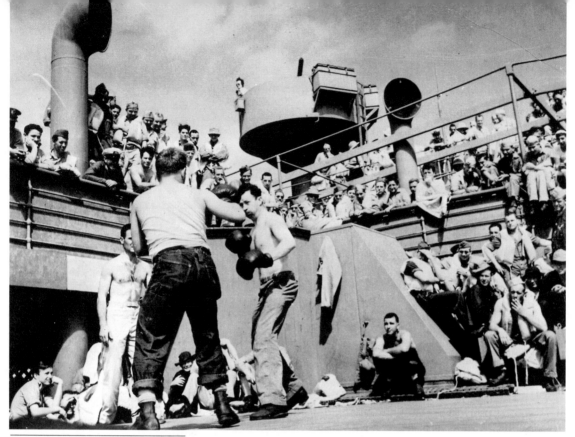

BOXING MATCH ON DECK (LRP).

beer he could drink while PA systems belted out songs popular at home. It was a thoughtful gesture. Unfortunately, the picnic wasn't left at that. A recreational officer thought red-blooded American boys deserved another outlet. It was his idea to issue us sports equipment so we could burn up all that energy accumulated during the long voyage here. It didn't work quite as expected. He had no notion of what it meant to be psyched up for combat. We quickly got loaded and called . . . for madder music and stronger wine. When none was forthcoming, we destroyed most of the sports gear, and the hardchargers among us began hitting people over the head with Louisville Sluggers. The officer was furious, but his threats were as futile as a clock in an empty house. What could he do? Deprive us of the privilege of getting shot at?"[6]

At island closing time, 6:00 P.M., the men jammed Mogmog's single jetty for the short ride back to their ships. Onboard, the fights continued, with sailors and Marines throwing each other overboard and having to be fished out by the neutral Coast Guard.

Back on the troopships, company commanders met with their men to give them their final briefings for Operation Iceberg. This time there was no promise of a short battle. "This is expected to be the costliest amphibious campaign of the war," an officer told Sledge's company. "We can expect 80 to 85 percent casualties on the beach." Standing on the fantail of the assault transport *George C. Clymer*, with his men gathered around him in a tight semicircle, Lieutenant William Manchester unrolled a map of Okinawa, a place almost none of the men had heard of until the last week or so. Americans with a sense of history remembered it as the island Commodore Matthew Perry had landed on in 1853 on the journey that ended Japan's 200-year-long isolation from the rest of the world. The Commodore had planted the American flag on a hill adjacent to ancient Shuri Castle, a center of pre-Japanese culture where both Sledge and Manchester would experience some of the severest fighting of the war. Perry signed a treaty with the regent of Okinawa. It declared that "whenever citizens of the U.S. come to Luchu [Okinawa] they shall be treated with great courtesy and friendship [and] shall be at liberty to ramble where they please without hindrance."[7]

Okinawa is a big island, sixty miles long and two to eighteen miles wide. The north is hilly and thickly forested; the south is rolling farmland, broken by a series of steep ridges and cliffs near Shuri. Here the Japanese concentrated their defenses. General Mitsuru Ushijima's forces, working furiously for 100 days under the direction of Colonel Hiromichi Yahara, Ushijima's operations officer, had built fortifications of great scope and strength. The Okinawans buried their dead in elaborate concrete tombs that dotted the landscape, and the 110,000 defenders—about 24,000 of them Okinawan conscripts—also planned to use these as shelters and fire points. This would give the defenders both concealment and the high ground; and with five times the number of the troops that defended Iwo Jima, an excellent chance of bleeding the Americans badly, while the kamikazes pounded their fleet. At Okinawa, as combat correspondent John Lardner pointed out, the Japanese would fight two suicide battles: "the violent, quick suicides of the kamikaze forces," and "the equally certain suicide of a strong, armed land force, dug into fine positions behind big guns, with no hope whatever of reinforcement or escape."[8]

Tokyo conceded defeat before the battle began. This was to be a delaying action designed to give the barbarians a foretaste of what taking the home islands would entail. But to the men on the other side, victory hardly seemed foreordained. For one thing, the Americans had not yet figured out the enemy's plan for opposing the landings. What most concerned Vice Admiral Richmond Kelly Turner, commander of the amphibious force, was the depth and ferocity of the opposition on the beaches. Having no idea what to expect, he had to be ready for a Tarawa-like resistance, right at the waterline.

He might also have been concerned about the commander of the land forces, Army Lieutenant General Simon Bolivar Buckner, Jr., son of the Confederate general who had surrendered Fort Donelson to Ulysses S. Grant. Fifty-eight-year-old "Buck" Buckner was one of the most respected leaders in the American Army, a West Point graduate and a former commandant at the Point, a charismatic instructor in the service's highest staff colleges, and the commander who had cleared the Japanese out of the Aleutian Islands. An outwardly confident man, he looked every inch the leader: tall, hard-muscled, and robustly handsome, with thick white hair and sharply chiseled features. Turner found him easy to like, but Buckner was all-Army in the way he fought and Admiral Turner was a Marine at heart. He feared that Buckner would move with a deliberateness bordering on caution, using heavy artillery fire and a continuous flow of reinforcements to take ground a yard at a time, in an effort to wear down the enemy without suffering intolerable casualties. Turner favored the Marine way of fighting—going in fast and light, taking big risks in order to win in a flash and move on to the next objective. At Okinawa, fewer men would be lost this way, he reasoned, than by the Army method of digging in and pounding the enemy at a distance, tactics that would expose Buckner's own troops, which included Turner's beloved Marines, to the enemy's heavy guns, emplaced in high, concealed positions.

Admiral Turner also worried about the fleet, which had to stay and provide air cover and gun support for the ground forces. A ponderous infantry offensive spelled deadly danger for the blue jackets battling the kamikazes.

And while Buckner might be a big brain and a brave man, this was the first time he would lead a full army into combat, the new and tremendously formidable Tenth Army, with a landing force, including reserves, of eight divisions, five Army and three Marine.[9]

The plan for L-Day, April 1—Easter Sunday—was for Buckner to land four divisions—two Army, the 96th and the 7th, and two Marine, the 1st and the 6th—on beaches just south of the island's midriff. They would be preceded by the greatest naval bombardment in history, almost 45,000 rounds of shells, 33,000 rockets, and 22,500 mortars.[10] The immediate objective was the seizure of Yontan and Kadena airfields, not far from the beachhead. Once the airstrips were in American hands, the GIs would swing south, into the most densely populated area of the island, while the Marines wheeled northward into wild, weakly defended Motobu Peninsula.

Admiral Nimitz was more concerned about this invasion than any previous one.

He expected the fleet to be hit hard by both kamikazes and conventional aircraft from the hundred or so enemy airfields within range of Okinawa. "This is the biggest thing yet attempted in the Pacific," declared the naval intelligence officer at the briefing Robert Sherrod attended on the command ship *Panamint*, "all the forces available in the Western Pacific are involved except those in the Philippines and the Aleutians." This included the B-29 units in the Marianas. Curtis LeMay had been pressured by Nimitz to suspend his fire raids against Japanese cities in order to bomb the enemy's fighter fields.

The American command expected the fiercest land resistance in the southern part of the island, where "we know there are caves by the thousands, and pillboxes, bunkers, and trenches. . . ," the intelligence officer on the *Panamint* pointed out, "Okinawa will be the first heavily inhabited enemy island we have invaded. The population is about 450,000, and we have no reason to believe they are any different people from the mainland Japanese. We expect resistance to be most fanatical."[11]

The Japanese garrison *would* fight with suicidal defiance, but most of the civilian population would try to stay out of harm's way. Japan had not officially claimed the island until 1879, and the Okinawans, who were not ethnically Japanese, were treated as second-class citizens of the empire. It was difficult for them to see this war as theirs. Still, fed by Japanese propaganda, they lived in mortal terror of the American devils, who, they feared, would torture, rape, and kill them in great numbers. "We spent the last week of March like criminals on death row," recalled an Okinawan conscripted into the defense force. "The instrument of execution was there . . . all ready for us. . . . It was the American fleet instead of an ax or noose."[12]

As Sherrod and forty or so other correspondents boarded landing ships the next day, Coast Guard Commander Jack Dempsey, the former heavyweight champion of the world, was there to see them off. "Keep your head down," someone shouted at Ernie Pyle, who would land with the Old Breed. "Listen, you bastards," Pyle shot back at the reporters standing near him. "I'll take a drink over every one of your graves." Then he swung around, put up his fists, and asked the champ if he wanted to go a few rounds.[13]

The landing was one of the most pleasant surprises of the war.

John Lardner was assigned to the 4th Marine Regiment, Marine Raiders with a record of reckless bravery going back to Guadalcanal. "These boys of mine are very good, and they love to kill Japs," Colonel Alan Shapley, their leader, told Lardner. "This will be a very tough show, but the boys are full of shooting." On L-Day, "these boys full of shooting rode into the beaches in the amtracks, erect and fierce as always in their white war paint and steeled against the withering fire they had been prom-ised for weeks."[14] Hitting the sand, they met an empty landscape with not a Japanese in sight. Hardly pausing, they tore ahead for their L-plus-three (fourth day) objective, Yontan Airfield.

"We were in a Higgins boat," Eugene Sledge recalls L-Day, "and when an am-trac came to pick us up and take us into the beach the driver told us he had just taken some troops ashore and there was no opposition, nobody was fired at. We couldn't be-lieve it. It was the first good news we had heard during the war and everybody started singing 'Little Brown Jug,' and we sang it all the way into the beach. When the tailgate went down we just walked out, formed up, and moved inland to cut the island in half."

Another surprise was Okinawa itself. "We had been warned about terrible ter-rain, jungle rot, and an infestation of the world's deadliest snakes," says Sledge. "But the island was pastoral and handsomely terraced, like a postcard picture of an Orien-tal landscape, and hardly anyone ran into the habu snakes whose bites were supposed to be fatal. The island looked like a patchwork quilt, with little farms and fields and rice paddies, all surrounded by low stone walls. The weather was cool, about sixty-five degrees, and there was the wonderful smell of pines, which reminded me of home. It was such a beautiful island; you really could not believe that there was going to be a battle there."[15]

As they moved inland over the next few days, Sledge found the Okinawans friendly and easy to like, but Pyle, a notorious cultural chauvinist, described them as "filthy," "rather stupid," and "pitiful" in their poverty.[16]

From a mountaintop, a Japanese officer watched 60,000 American troops splash ashore and seize two important airfields. Where were the clouds of suicide fliers his leaders had told him would be sent to flame the barbarians' invasion fleet? Japanese air commanders had spotted the approach of the American armada but were unable to mount serious opposition that day from bases on Formosa and Kyushu that had been badly damaged by Spruance's carrier planes and LeMay's B-29s. And bases on nearby islands for hundreds of enemy suicide boats—light motor craft with 300-kilo-gram charges in their bows—had been reduced to dust by Navy Hellcats and Army assault units. "As I observed the landing operations, I was convinced this was a com-plete defeat," the Japanese officer recalled. "The soldiers felt the same way. But we thought it was our destiny to share the fate of the island, and so held on to our pride."[17]

By 10:00 A.M. Shipley's Rangers had a crap game in progress at undefended Yonton Airfield. Hearing a loud noise, the men looked up and saw an unsuspecting Japanese fighter plane about to make a landing. Seconds after he taxied to a stop his plane was riddled with holes. He jumped out of the cockpit with his revolver drawn and was instantly cut down. "I'm sorry the boys were so damn impulsive," Shipley told Lardner. "He would have been a good prisoner." [18]

"Where is the enemy?" every American wondered those first days on Okinawa. Had the Japanese played an elaborate April Fool's joke on them? "I may be crazy but it looks like the Japanese have quit the war, at least in this sector," Richmond Kelly Turner radioed to Admiral Nimitz. Nimitz replied: "Delete all after 'crazy.'" [19]

While the Old Breed cleaned out pockets of resistance at the center of the island and two Army divisions moved south against the first line of Japanese defenses, Manchester and the 6th Marine Division drove north into the steep, densely wooded hills and ravines of Motobu Peninsula. "There was no role here for mechanized tactics; tanks were useful only for warming your hands in their exhaust fumes," Manchester described the six-day-long battle for Motobu Peninsula; "This was more like French and Indian warfare." [20] In hand-to-hand fighting with bayonets and knives, the Marines captured Motobu Peninsula and then subdued the rest of the thinly populated northern part of Okinawa.

While fighting in the north, the Marines learned of the death of Franklin Roosevelt. He was the only President the younger men had ever known, but most of the talk was about his successor. "Who the hell is Harry Truman?" one soldier spoke for thousands like him who felt their fates were suddenly in his hands. [21]

Six days later, on April 18, Ernie Pyle was killed on the small island of Ie Shima, four miles off Motobu Peninsula. He was accompanying the 77th Army Division on an amphibious operation to take the island's airfield when a jeep he was riding in was hit by a burst of machine gun fire. Pyle fell unhurt into a roadside ditch. There was another burst and a bullet pierced his helmet and entered his left temple. He died instantly. When his body was recovered, his hands still clutched the ragged knit cap he carried at all times.

When Pyle had been assigned to the 6th Marine Division, many of the men did not recognize the small, frail, balding man with the stubby white whiskers and the frayed woolen cap. But when they learned who he was, they invariably asked him what he thought of the Pacific war. Pyle would smile wearily and say, "Oh, it's the same old stuff all over again. I am awful tired of it." [22]

The last time Sherrod saw him was April 9, when they were in a room aboard the *Panamint*, writing dispatches on typewriters provided by the Navy. Sherrod told

ERNIE PYLE ON OKINAWA (NA).

him he was heading home in a few days, and Pyle said he was going back, too, in a month or so. "I'm getting too old to stay in combat with these kids. I think I'll stay back around the airfields with the Seabees and the engineers in the meantime and write some stories about them." He had made his last landing, he said. Nine days later, Sherrod was in Hawaii when he heard that Pyle had been killed. "I never learned which doughboy of the Seventy-seventh Division persuaded Ernie to change his mind and go on the Ie Shima invasion. . . . But Ernie rarely refused a request from a doughboy." [23]

After northern Okinawa was secured on April 20, the victorious 6th Marine Division "expected a respite, hot chow, and a few days in the sack. We didn't get any of them," says Manchester. They had been hearing "ominous rumors of stiffening resistance in the south. GIs were encountering unprecedented concentrations of Japanese artillery fire. Progress was being measured in yards, then feet. . . . It was Peleliu and Iwo all over again, but to the nth degree." The Japanese strategy was now revealed. "Looking back, I can't imagine how we could have been so ignorant," says Lieutenant General Victor "Brute" Krulak, operations officer for the 6th Marine Division.

General Ushijima *had* played a cruel April Fool's joke on the Americans. Abandoning the beaches and most of the north, he concentrated his forces along three menacing defensive lines in the south, the strongest of them the Shuri Line, which

Manchester called "the war's great Gethsemane." He used every hill and ravine as his ally, hiding his troops and artillery—the most powerful artillery the Japanese had available in the Pacific war—in a sixty-mile network of caves and tunnels, subterranean defenses far deeper and more extensive than those on Iwo Jima. He had already lured Army units into his trap and was butchering them. Now the Marines were rushed south to reinforce them. Wedged together on a terrain-constricted battlefield, Marines and Army infantry and a determined enemy would wage one of the most terrible struggles in the history of organized warfare.

With American ground forces bogged down in a close-quarter slaughter, the Japanese unleashed a new weapon on the enemy fleet—not individual kamikaze attacks, but massed suicide raids of up to 300 planes. These were called Kikusui, or "floating chrysanthemums." "Ultimately they failed," Manchester writes, "but anyone who saw a bluejacket who had been burned by them, writhing in agony under his bandages, never again slandered the sailors who stayed on ships while the infantrymen hit the beach." [24]

TREASURES OF THE NATION

By the late spring of 1945, Japan's situation was so grave, with Iwo lost and the Americans on Okinawa, that its military rulers turned to a desperate scheme, codenamed Ten-Go, to protect the most vulnerable points of its rapidly deteriorating defense perimeter. Almost 5,000 aircraft based on Formosa and the home islands were assigned to one-way missions against the American fleet. As Japan-based reporter Robert Guillain noted, the military leaders committed "the nation's total air power to an all-out battle. It was not even a question of winning or dying, but of dying in any case and winning if possible." [25] It was state-sanctioned and -encouraged suicide. [26]

Most of the planes were reliable but outmoded Zeros; however the Japanese did use the Baka bomb that the B-29 crews confronted in the skies over Japanese cities. At Okinawa it was employed against ships. Piloted by one man and launched like a glider from the underside of a two-engine bomber, it contained in its nose a ton of TNT. It was powered by three rockets and could dive on a vessel at a speed of up to 550 miles per hour, making it almost impossible to hit once it was launched. "The small size and tremendous speed of Baka made it the worst threat to our ships that had yet appeared, almost equivalent to the guided missiles that the Germans were

A KAMIKAZE HEADED FOR THE BATTLESHIP *MISSOURI*. THE PLANE BOUNCED OFF A GUN MOUNT AND CAUSED ONLY MINOR DAMAGE TO THE SHIP (NA).

shooting at London," wrote Admiral Samuel Eliot Morison.[27] But before it was launched, the Baka bomb's weight slowed down the mother ship and impeded its maneuverability, making it an easy target for American interceptors.

Most of the kamikaze raids at Okinawa were made in daylight by waves of planes that attacked continuously, inflicting more casualties in ships and personnel than in any previous battle fought by the American Navy. "It is absolutely out of the question for you to return alive," the suicide pilots were told. "Your mission involves certain death. . . . Choose a death which brings about the maximum result."[28]

The suicide pilots, called "treasures of the nation," were abysmally trained, but they were a cross section of the country's educated elite. Most of them were college students in the humanities who had recently been called into service. These "hero-gods of the air" were not the mindless fanatics, hopped up on saki, that many American sailors believed them to be. With few exceptions, they flew to certain death for what they considered unselfish causes—patriotism, family honor, and unflagging loyalty to the Emperor. They were willing to die to protect loved ones back home from an unimaginably destructive American invasion. If Iwo Jima gave Americans concern about the costs of an invasion of Japan, Curtis LeMay's fire raids on the cities of the empire revealed to the Japanese people the terrible power of an avenging enemy that could only be stopped, they believed, by the most desperate measures.

Here are parts of two typical letters written by young suicide pilots:

> My dear parents,
>
> The Japanese way of life is indeed beautiful and I am proud of it, as I am of Japanese history and mythology, which reflect the purity of our ancestors and their belief in the past. . . . And the living embodiment of all wonderful things from our past is the Imperial Family, which is also the crystallization of the splendor and beauty of Japan and its people. It is an honor to be able to give my life in defense of these beautiful and lofty things.[29]

> Please do not grieve for me, mother. It will be glorious to die in action. I am grateful to be able to die in a battle to determine the destiny of our country.[30]

On April 6 and 7, 355 kamikazes, along with 345 conventional dive-bombers and torpedo planes, flew from hastily repaired airfields and hit the great fleet assembled in the waters off Okinawa, in what was the first and largest of ten massive attacks. On that same day, American submarines spotted an enemy naval force coming out of the protection of the Inland Sea and heading for Okinawa. The flagship was *Yamato*, the biggest battleship afloat, escorted by a light cruiser and eight of Japan's latest and largest destroyers. The sleekly proportioned dreadnought, bearing the ancient name of Japan, was on a suicide mission, carrying only enough fuel, by same accounts, to get to Okinawa. After inflicting maximum damage on the enemy's amphibious force, she was to beach herself and use her enormous guns as artillery support for the armies on Okinawa.

The men on board expected to die. When *Yamato* slipped out of the Inland Sea and headed for Okinawa, the crew had gathered on deck and sang a battle anthem:

> *Across the Sea, corpses in the water,*
> *Across the mountain, corpses in the field.*
> *I shall die for the Emperor.*
> *I shall never look back.*[31]

Yamato was also an expensive decoy. Sailing without air cover, she could be expected to draw great numbers of Hellcats, Avengers, Corsairs, and Dauntlesses that might otherwise be used against the suicide bombers. Admiral Mitscher summoned nearly 300 planes for the slaughter, and wave after wave of them tore into *Yamato* until she exploded tremendously and capsized, taking down with her most of the crew, about 3,600 men. The Navy interceptors also sank the escorting cruiser, *Yahagi*, and four destroyers, while losing only twelve fliers.[32]

It was the Imperial Navy's last great sortie of the war but it helped half of the kamikazes to get through to the American fleet, which had been joined by the Royal Navy's Pacific Fleet. In one of the fiercest air duels in naval history, the Japanese lost almost 400 planes to American fighters and withering antiaircraft fire, but they inflicted grievous damage, sinking eleven ships, including three destroyers. Altogether, Japan would mount 900 attacks on the fleet, mass raids as well as individual sacrificial sorties, from early April until the middle of June, when it began to run out of both pilots and planes, the remainder being husbanded for the "final battle" in the home islands.

A ring of early warning radar picket stations was the fleet's first line of defense. Small destroyers and other light vessels, including minelayers, gunboats, and landing craft, were placed on the outer perimeter. They picked up incoming enemy planes with their radar and vectored circling carrier aircraft to them. It was these smaller ships, heavily armed but thinly plated, that took the brunt of the Japanese air attacks. Rarely was a destroyer on picket duty for more than five hours without being hit by enemy bombers. Admiral Matome Ugaki, commander of Japan's 5th Air Fleet, ordered his fliers to "get the destroyers. Without their radar warning of our approach, we will enjoy great success."[33]

Inside the radar picket were the larger destroyers of the gunfire support screen. They had rapid-firing antiaircraft guns with nasty five-inch shells. Kamikazes flew directly into "as formidable an assembly of gun power as could be found perhaps anywhere in the war," in the opinion of Rear Admiral M. L. Deyo, commander of the naval force protecting the beachhead. Still, they made a "high percentage of hits," says Deyo. "Two hits out of seven [attempts.]"[34]

The blows they delivered, while serious, were rarely mortal—not a single aircraft carrier or battleship was sunk in the waters off Okinawa. But a number of destroyers took a fatal beating.

In the first and largest Kikusui attack, the destroyer *Newcomb*, part of the gunfire support screen, was assaulted in lightning succession by three kamikazes, two of

them scoring direct hits. Then a fourth one smashed into the forward stack, "spraying the entire amidships section . . . which was a raging conflagration, with a fresh supply of gasoline," wrote her skipper, Commander I. E. McMillian.[35] Lieutenant Leon Grabowsky of the destroyer *Leutze* risked his ship to try to save *Newcomb*. Correspondent Evan Wylie describes the heroic efforts of both crews, beginning his story just before a fifth kamikaze missed *Newcomb* and slammed into *Leutze:*

AT ALMOST COLLISION SPEED, [*LEUTZE*] SWEPT up alongside the *Newcomb*. There was a grinding crash . . . as the two ships came together. The men jumped across and made the ships fast. Fire hoses were snaked across the rails. Powerful streams of water leaped from their nozzles and drove the flames back from the prostrate men. Rescue parties rushed in and dragged them to safety.

The suicide boys were not through. Another plane was roaring in, headed straight for the *Newcomb*'s bridge. Looking up, Joseph Piolata of Youngstown, Oh., saw the other destroyer firing right across the *Newcomb*'s deck. The gunners did their best, but the *Newcomb*'s superstructure hid the plane from their sights. On both ships the men watched helplessly. This was the kill. The *Newcomb* could never survive another hit.

But the battered, burning can still had fight in her. Incredulously the men of the *Newcomb*, crouched on her stern, struggling in the water, lying wounded on the deck, heard their ship's forward batteries firing. There was no power, but the gunners were firing anyway—by hand.

The gunnery officer stood at his station shouting the range data to the men in the forward five-inch turrets. In the No. 2 turret Arthur McGuire of St. Louis, Mo., rammed shells with broken, bleeding fingers. . . . The Jap had the *Newcomb*'s bridge in his sights. . . . But the burst from McGuire's gun caught him and blew him sideways. The hurtling plane missed the bridge by a scant eight feet, skidded across the *Newcomb*'s deck and plowed into the other destroyer.

With a gaping hole in the afterdeck and the portside a tangled web of broken lines and wildly sprouting fire hoses, the *Leutze* drifted slowly away.

Without water to fight the fire still raging amidships, the *Newcomb* was doomed. But the destroyer's crew contained some obstinate people. Donald Keeler of Danbury, Conn., was one of them. . . . When it became evident that all the power was gone he joined the crowd on the stern just in time to hear that the after ammo-handling rooms were burning and the magazines were expected to go any minute.

Keeler elected to fight the fire. His only hope lay in a "handy-billy," a small, portable pump powered by a gasoline engine. . . .

Groping around in the blistering heat, Keeler found the handy-billy. Carefully he wound the rope around the flywheel, held his breath and yanked. The engine kicked over and kept going. Now Keeler had water. He and [three other sailors] . . . got the fire under control. Then they dragged the pump forward.

The No. 3 handling room was a roaring furnace. Steel dripped like solder from overhead. . . . Flames shot from the ammo hoists like the blast of a huge blow torch. It looked hopeless, but Keeler shoved the hose in the doorway. No sooner had he done so than a wave came over the side and doused the pump. The chattering handy-billy spluttered and died. Keeler rushed back to the pump. Again he wound the rope around the flywheel, gritted his teeth and yanked. "I think I even prayed that second time," he said. "But the damn thing popped right off, something it wouldn't do again in a million years."

The men went back into the handling room. They kept the hose in there, taking turns. The magazines didn't blow up.

Up forward sailors were trying to fight the fire with hand extinguishers. A withering blast of heat drove them back. Their life jackets were smoking; their clothing was afire. The *Newcomb*'s doctor, Lt. John McNeil of Boston, Mass. . . . found one of the crew battling the flames with hair ablaze, half blind from the blood dripping from the sharpnel wounds in his face and forehead. With difficulty [he and another man] . . . dragged him off to the emergency dressing station in the wardroom. Many of the pharmacist's mates were out of action. Men with only first-aid training helped McNeil mix blood plasma for the burn cases.

Early Sayre of Roseville, Oh., was trapped on the stern unable to get his casualties forward. He was working on a fracture when someone tugged on his sleeve. "Blue Eyes has been hit bad. Looks like he's bleeding to death."

Blue Eyes was the youngest member of the crew. He had come aboard claiming eighteen years, but the men had taken one look at him and decided he must have lied to get in. Now he lay on the deck, blood spurting from a vein in his neck. Sayre had no instruments. He knelt down beside Blue Eyes and stopped the flow of blood with his fingers. He stayed there while the second plane came in and hit the other destroyer twenty feet away. He stayed there for almost an hour longer until they could come and take Blue Eyes away and operate on him and save his life. But Early Sayre had saved it already.

The rest of the Japs had been driven off. It was beginning to get dark when a ray of hope came to the exhausted men of the *Newcomb*. Keeler's volunteer fire department seemed to be holding the fires. Perhaps now they could save their ship. But the wave that had stopped the handy-billy was followed by another and another.

The *Newcomb* was sinking. The weight of the water that the hoses had poured into her after compartments was dragging her down. The rising water moved steadily forward. It reached the after bulkhead of the forward engine room. If it broke through, the *Newcomb* was done for. And the bulkhead already was leaking. . . .

In the forward engine room the damage-control party shored up the bulging bulkhead [and] . . . the *Newcomb* stopped sinking.

Now the blinkers flashed in the darkness. Other destroyers were coming alongside. Over their rails came men with fire hoses and pump lines, doctors and pharmacist's mates with plasma and bandages. Tugs were on the way. The fight was over.

The *Newcomb*'s men had answered the question: Just how much punishment can a destroyer take?[36]

Both destroyers had to be scrapped. Forty-seven men were killed or missing, and many of the wounded were grotesquely burned. After receiving treatment, some of them "looked like mummies under their bandages, breathing through a tube and being fed intravenously while their bodies healed."[37]

An American aircraft carrier was the dream target of every suicide pilot. On May 11, Admiral Mitscher's flagship, *Bunker Hill*, her deck crowded with planes waiting to take off, their tanks filled with highly volatile aviation gas, their guns loaded with ammunition, was hit almost simultaneously by two kamikazes. The horribly crippled ship lost 396 men and was put out of commission after fifty-nine consecutive days at sea. Reporter Phelps Adams was nearby, on the bridge of the carrier *Enterprise*, when enemy planes came tearing out of the low-hanging clouds:

BEFORE GENERAL QUARTERS COULD BE SOUNDED on this ship, and before half a dozen shots could be fired by the *Bunker Hill*, the first kamikaze had dropped his 550-pound bomb and plunged squarely into the midst of the thirty-four waiting planes in a shower of burning gasoline.

The bomb, fitted with a delayed action fuse, pierced the flight deck at a sharp angle, passed out through the side of the hull and exploded in mid-air before striking the water. The plane—a single-engine Jap fighter—knocked the parked aircraft about like ten-pins, sent a huge column of flame and smoke belching upwards and then skidded crazily over the side.

Some of the pilots were blown overboard, and many managed to scramble to safety; but before a move could be made to fight the flames another kamikaze came whining out of the clouds, straight into the deadly anti-aircraft guns of the ship. This plane was a Jap dive bomber. . . . A five-inch shell that should have blown him out of the sky, set him afire and riddled his plane with metal, but still he came. Passing over the stern of the ship, he dropped his bomb with excellent aim right in the middle of the blazing planes. Then he flipped over and torched through the flight deck at the base of the island [the ship's central command tower]. . . .

BUNKER HILL HIT BY TWO KAMIKAZES WITHIN THIRTY SECONDS (NA).

The entire rear end of the ship was burning with uncontrollable fury. It looked very much like the newsreel shots of a blazing oil well, only worse—for this fire was feeding on highly refined gasoline and live ammunition. . . .

The carrier itself had begun to develop a pronounced list, and as each new stream of water was poured into her the angle increased more dangerously. Crippled as she was, however, she ploughed ahead at top speed and the wind that swept her decks blew the flame and smoke astern over the fantail and prevented the blaze from spreading forward on the flight deck and through the island structure. Trapped on the fantail, men faced the flames and fought grimly on, with only the ocean behind them, and with no way of knowing how much of the ship remained on the other side of that fiery wall.

Then, somehow, other men managed to break out the huge openings in the side of the hangar dock, and I got my first glimpse of the interior of the ship. That, I think, was the most horrible sight of all. The entire hangar deck was a raging blast furnace, white-hot throughout its length. . . .

Up on the bridge, Capt. George A. Seitz, the skipper, was growing increasingly concerned about the dangerous list his ship had developed, and resolved to take a gambling chance. Throwing the *Bunker Hill* into a 70-degree turn, he heeled her cautiously over onto the opposite beam so that tons of water which had accumulated on one side were suddenly swept across the decks and overboard on the other. By great good fortune this wall of water carried the heart of the hangar deck fire with it.

That was the turning point. . . . After nearly three hours of almost hopeless fighting . . . the battle was won and the ship was saved. . . .

Late today Admiral Mitscher and sixty or more members of his staff came aboard us to make this carrier his new flagship. He was unhurt—not even singed by the flames. . . .

As he was hauled aboard in a breeches buoy across the churning water that separated us from the speedy destroyer that had brought him alongside, he looked tired and old and just plain mad. His deeply lined face was more than weather beaten—it looked like an example of erosion in the dust-bowl country—but his eyes flashed fire and vengeance.[38]

After the fire was put out, the flight deck of *Bunker Hill* looked like "the crater of a volcano." That night corpsmen prepared 396 bodies for burial at sea.

Three days after Mitscher transferred his flag to *Enterprise,* a kamikaze smashed into it and it was lost for the remainder of the war. The admiral had to transfer his flag to the *Randolph.* Having had two flagships shot from under him in four days, Mitscher said, "Any more of this and there will be hair growing on this old bald head."

The hospital ship *Comfort,* its lights ablaze and its deck marked with a huge

Red Cross, was severely crippled. Three British carriers were also hit, but suffered little damage because they had steel decks. The American carriers were fitted out with light wooden decks to give them added speed and maneuverability. "When a kamikaze hits a U.S. carrier, it's six months' repair in Pearl," said an American officer. "In a Limey carrier, it's 'Sweepers, man your brooms.'" [39]

Admiral Mitscher told reporters that the kamikazes "don't worry us very much." But Robert Sherrod "knew the sailors were worried, and so was I." [40]

The Japanese flew 1,900 kamikaze sorties against the Okinawa fleet, in addition to the 5,000 to 6,000 sorties by conventional aircraft. In these raids, both massive and intermittent, and in attacks on their bases, they lost an astounding 7,830 planes, by official American estimates.* But they sank thirty-six American ships and damaged 368 others, including thirteen carriers, ten battleships, and five cruisers. The 9,731 officers and men killed or wounded at Okinawa—over 4,900 of them killed—represented one seventh of the Navy's total casualties in World War II. The Navy suppressed these horrifying casualty figures for a month after the conclusion of the battle. [41]

"When the kamikazes started to come in the rule was never fire until one of them came directly at you. Don't provoke the guy," recalled Mort Zimmerman.

THEY WOULD COME IN AT YOU in such numbers and so low that you could see the expressions on the faces of the pilots from the deck of the ship. Some destroyer crews would lower their guns into the water and throw up these huge walls of water, and when some of the older planes hit them they would just disintegrate.

It was awful to see the guys who got burnt in the fires these planes set off. They looked like charcoal logs.

I saw a destroyer escort that was on picket duty come into harbor and it was so beat up that the highest-rated man on the ship was a chief. Water was pouring out of the hull, everything above deck was charred and shattered, and from bow to stern I counted ninety bunk bottoms, dead guys wrapped in bunk bottoms. And I wondered how many other guys had gone over the sides. You could not believe what this ship looked like. Later they beached it and put up

---

*These high figures are probably the result of the double counting of kills by pilots and gunners. The true figure is probably closer to 3,000 combat losses.

DEAD SAILORS WRAPPED IN CANVAS BUNK BOTTOMS (NA).

a sign that said, essentially, "Look at this thing. This is what you are fighting against."

Close to shore, we also encountered Japanese suicide swimmers. They would swim out in the morning, under the fog, dive beneath a ship, and blow it and themselves up. So every morning, beginning at daybreak, we would put out watches and fire on anything that moved in the water. I was a bad shot, so I used a Thompson submachine gun. Anything I saw I sprayed.

Waiting for a kamikaze raid was sometimes worse on your nerves than the actual raid. Because once those sons-of-bitches started coming in there was no time to worry or think. Then it was a game of survival, and almost all your instincts were on high alert.[42]

Radar and radio communications allowed the Navy time to prepare for the larger kamikaze attacks and to alert the crews. "But this practice had to be stopped," said reporter Hanson Baldwin. "The strain of waiting, the anticipated terror, made vivid from past experience, sends some men into hysteria, insanity, breakdown."[43] Admiral Halsey would later write that the kamikaze was "the only weapon I feared in the war."[44] Yet even on the biggest kamikaze raid of the war, on April 6–7, the Americans had more ships in the water than the Japanese had planes in the air.

A picture released by the Navy after the Battle of Okinawa tells the larger story. It is called *The Fleet That Came to Stay.*

SLAUGHTER ON THE SHURI LINE

As the kamikazes continued to terrorize the American fleet, Army infantry units, reinforced by the 1st and 6th Marine Divisions, made excruciatingly slow progress against the Shuri Line, which extended across the island, with Naha, Okinawa's capital, on the west, the commanding heights of Shuri Castle in the center, and the hills around Yonabaru on the east coast. As the battle of brute attrition wore on into May, Admiral Nimitz grew increasingly irritated with General Buckner. Nimitz complained to the general that his methodical method of fighting was causing the Navy to lose "a ship and a half a day." But even when assault-trained Marines were brought in, the enemy line held, and Buckner, backed unexpectedly by Nimitz, jettisoned a proposal for a risky amphibious landing behind the Shuri Line.

"We poured a tremendous amount of metal in on those positions," recalls a Marine commander. "Not only from artillery but from ships at sea. It seemed nothing could possibly be living in that churning mass where the shells were falling and roaring but when we next advanced, Japs would still be there, even madder than they had been before." [45]

As the battle raged, troops and conscript laborers continued work on Colonel Yahara's interlocking network of deep, heavily fortified caves. From these hidden positions on the faces of hills, cliffs, and sharply pitched ravines the Japanese resorted to "sleeping tactics," putting heavy artillery and mortar fire on the enemy trapped below them on flat fields and farms, and coming out only at night in small infiltration parties, as they had at Peleliu and Iwo Jima. "Counting both sides, the [Shuri Line] represented an extraordinary concentration of 300,000 fighting men and countless terrified civilians, on a battleground that was about as wide as the distance between Capitol Hill in Washington and Arlington National Cemetery," writes William Manchester. "In the densest combat of World War I, battalion frontage [the width of the front line covered by a battalion] had been approximately eight hundred yards. Here it was less than six hundred yards. The sewage, of course, was appalling. You could smell the front long before you saw it; it was one vast cesspool." When Manchester caught his first glimpse of the front, from a high hill overlooking it, his thoughts flowed back to the photographs his father, a World War I veteran, had shown him as a boy. "This, I thought, is what Verdun and Passchendaele must have looked like. The two great armies, squatting opposite one another in mud and smoke, were locked together in unimaginable agony. . . . [And] there was nothing green left; artillery had denuded and scarred every inch of ground." [46]

Throughout the month of May, the Marines launched attack after bludgeoning attack against the western end of the ten-mile-long Shuri Line, while the Army did the same against the eastern side. Much of the battle was fought in driving rain and knee-deep mud. "Our division [the 6th] entered the southern battle lines on May 1,"

wrote Raymond Sawyer, who had left home in 1941, at the age of fifteen, to join the Marines, lying about his age to an overeager enlistment sergeant. "We joined our 1st Marine Division near the bluffs above the Asa Kawa River [on the right flank of the Shuri Line, above Naha]. The next forty days would witness the most intense fighting encountered in the South Pacific." [47]

The toughest obstacle was Sugar Loaf Hill, a mound of coral and volcanic rock, less than 100 feet high, that was the anchor of the Shuri Line. It stood about one mile from General Ushijima's command center in a tunnel under Shuri Castle and at that time it was the bloodiest battlefield in the world. [48] The battle for the hill took place from May 13 to May 17. During those four days Sawyer's Marines reached the top of Sugar Loaf twelve times but was unable to hold the summit in hand-to-hand combat, despite heavy artillery support.

The Japanese had more and better artillery on Okinawa than in any previous island campaign, but so did the Americans. The shock and carnage was almost unendurable for the men on both sides. "The ground swayed and shook from concussion as shells erupted all around and steel fragments tore through the air and through men's bodies," Eugene Sledge recalled. "When the shells finally stopped we were all shaking. You could not hold your rifle steady." [49] The never-ending artillery fire produced a higher number of neuropsychiatric casualties than in any other Pacific battle. Hundreds of men simply went crazy.

In was no better for the GIs on the other end of the Shuri Line. *Life* photographer W. Eugene Smith, a veteran of thirteen Pacific actions and twenty-three bombing missions, was nearly killed by mortar fire while putting together a photo essay on "the working day" of Terry Moore, a foot-slogging Private First Class of the 7th Division. They were on a muddy ridge together when the artillery and mortar fire started coming in on them. "They had us zeroed in and we just lay and took it," wrote Smith.

TERRY LAY A FEW YARDS AWAY. I adjusted my camera, judged the footage and waited. I wanted to show Terry under close mortar hits, it was part of his day. The trouble with taking photographs when the air is full of lead is that you have to stand up when anyone with any sense is lying down and trying to disappear right into the earth. I got to my feet. . . .

The next thing I remember was a spiral ringing in my ears and I knew I was regaining consciousness. I knew I had been hit but I did not hurt. I felt warm

EXHAUSTED SOLDIERS ON THE SHURI LINE (SC).

and cozy. I heard the cry, "Medic, medic over here, the photographer." I had a surge of happiness: I could hear. . . . I rolled over on my left elbow and warm blood came gushing from my mouth and face, but I could see. Another surge of happiness. . . . But then I saw [that] the index finger [of my left hand] was hanging by a cord. . . .

I could not swallow and I choked as I breathed. The blood gurgled in my throat at each breath. I had a moment of fright, overwhelming fright. I could not breathe. . . .

Then consciousness again: the face was Terry's and the voice was Terry's. . . .

"Take it easy, Smitty." He was holding my smashed hand. . . . Then I realized I couldn't talk. I just gurgled. But Terry understood.

With Terry's help, Smith made it to the road, where he was placed into a supply jeep. He was losing a lot of blood. " 'Move fast through the villages,' I heard some one say. 'Artillery.' I prayed, 'Oh please God, no more artillery.' "[50]

Smith was evacuated to a hospital on Guam and underwent several surgeries before he was able to use a camera again. He wrote the text for his story of Terry Moore from a hospital bed, and it appeared with his photographs in *Life*. Not shown in the picture story was the badly blurred photograph of the explosion that nearly killed him. Smith took it less than a second before he was hit. He left it out because it had nothing to do with Terry.

While Raymond Sawyer and the 6th Marine Division were still assaulting Sugar Loaf Hill, Eugene Sledge's Company K moved onto a barren, muddy ridge called Half Moon Hill, a key supporting position for Sugar Loaf Hill, just to the right (west) of them. They had relieved a company of 6th Marine Division that had taken morale-depleting casualties. "They could not remove their dead because of the thousands of Jap shells unleashed on the area," Sledge writes. "The day we moved onto Half Moon, torrential rains began and did not slacken for ten days. Tanks bogged down and all our attacks had to stop, so we occupied the Hill amid death and heavy shellfire. Almost every shell hole in the area had a dead Marine in it, and they were all infested with maggots. The rain washed the maggots off the dead and into our foxholes. . . .

"The Japs were attacking every night, and we were killing them in our lines every night. In the Pacific, decay is rapid. We threw mud on the dead bodies with our entrenching tools to hold down the swarms of big flies and maggots. The next day . . . a few shells came in and blew the corpses apart. There were body

parts lying all over the place; we called it 'Maggot Ridge.' If we went down the ridge
and slipped and fell, we slid all the way to the bottom. When we came to our feet,
the maggots were falling out of our dungaree pockets, our cartridge belts and everything else." And "many of us who fell," Sledge says, "were covered with our own
vomit."

With rain pouring down on them, with mud caked in their throats, with decaying bodies all around them, with flies swarming in their food, with the landscape
butchered beyond belief, and with amoebic dysentery breaking out among the com-

pany, "[we] believed we had been flung into hell's own cesspool." Beginning on Okinawa, and continuing for the next twenty years, Sledge was afflicted by terrifying nightmares.

On Okinawa, the dream was always the same. "The dead got up slowly out of their waterlogged craters . . . and with stooped shoulders and dragging feet, wandered around aimlessly, their lips moving as though trying to tell me something. I struggled to hear what they were saying. They seemed agonized by pain and despair. I felt they were asking me for help. The most horrible thing was that I felt unable to aid them." [51]

Adding to the men's torment was their complete ignorance of how the battle was going elsewhere, not just in this gully or on that ridge—and their feeling, as more and more of their friends died, that death had become "a kind of epidemic." As the divisions were bled down, veteran Marines like William Manchester started to see, to their despair, dozens of seventeen-year-old boys, fresh out of boot camp. If he were to die, Manchester wanted to die among raggedy-ass Marines like himself, not these anxious-looking kids who had barely begun to shave. [52]

"What kept you going," Sledge says, "was the fact that you felt like you had to live up to the demands of your unit and the buddies that were depending on you." [53]

Manchester believes it was all that and more. "To fight World War II you had to have been tempered and strengthened in the 1930s Depression by a struggle for survival—in 1940 two out of every five draftees had been rejected, most of them victims of malnutrition. And you had to know that your whole generation, unlike the Vietnam generation, was in this together, that no strings were being pulled for anybody; the four Roosevelt brothers were in uniform, and the sons of both Harry Hopkins, FDR's closest advisor, and [Senator] Leverett Saltonstall. . . . served in the Marine Corps as enlisted men and were killed in action. . . .

"You also needed nationalism, the absolute conviction that the United States was the envy of all other nations." And you needed to believe in certain core values. "Debt was ignoble. Courage was a virtue. Mothers were beloved, fathers obeyed. Marriage was a sacrament. Divorce was disgraceful. . . . [And] you assumed that if you came through this ordeal you would age with dignity, respected as well as adored by your children. . . .

"All this led you into battle, and sustained you as you fought, and comforted you if you fell, and, if it came to that, justified your death to all who loved you as you had loved them.

"Later the rules would change. But we didn't know that then. We didn't know."[54]

As the 6th Marines continued to hurl themselves against Sugar Loaf Hill, a reporter from *Time* described one of their assaults: "There were fifty Marines on top of Sugar Loaf Hill. They had been ordered to hold the position all night, at any cost. By dawn, forty-six of them had been killed or wounded. Then, into the foxhole where the remaining four huddled, the Japs dropped a white phosphorus shell, burning three men to death. The last survivor crawled to an aid station."[55]

The Marines tried every tactic, every weapon they had, but the courageous enemy seemed to get even stronger. The Americans could tell by their morning examinations of the Japanese dead that the enemy wasn't ready to give up. The corpses looked healthy and well fed, the uniforms almost brand-new.

On May 8, the troops on the Shuri Line learned that Hitler had committed suicide in his Berlin bunker and that Germany had surrendered. "No one cared much," admits Sledge. "We were resigned only to the fact that the Japanese would fight to total extinction on Okinawa. . . . Nazi Germany might as well have been on the moon."[56]

By sundown on May 17, the 6th Marine Division had almost given up hope of taking Sugar Loaf Hill. They were worn down and nearly out of ammunition. But they stayed and prevailed. Elements of the Tenth Army, including Sledge's unit, had taken the hills that flanked Sugar Loaf, threatening to envelop Ushijima, and the next morning Manchester's 29th Marines, with new tanks, captured the summit and held it. After smashing through the Shuri Line, the Americans pursued the Japanese army as it retreated to a strong line of ridges on the southern end of the island.

In fifteen days of fighting on the Shuri Line the Japanese had lost nearly 50,000 soldiers. The Marines lost almost 3,000 men, killed or seriously wounded, roughly the same as at Tarawa. The Army took even greater casualties during the same period. As historian George Feifer writes in *Tennozan*, his searing account of the Battle of Okinawa, "Gaining control of the 'pimple of a hill' . . . [was] by some measures the hardest single battle in the Pacific War and hardest for Americans anywhere in World War II."[57]

While Sledge's 1st Marine Division fought the rear guard that had been left on Shuri Heights, Raymond Sawyer's regiment marched south on May 22 to join other units of the 6th Marine Division in the capture of Naha. On the morning of June 5,

THE STEEPLE OF A CATHOLIC CHURCH BELOW SHURI CASTLE
PROVIDED A SNIPER'S NEST FOR THE JAPANESE (USMC).

while engaged in a firefight near the city, Sawyer was knocked unconscious by the blast of a 60mm mortar shell. He woke up in a cave that had been set up for emergency surgery and learned he had shrapnel wounds all over his body. A surgeon from his hometown of Woburn, Massachusetts, sewed up his abdomen and sent him to a hospital plane, to be flown to Guam for additional surgery. On June 25, 1945, in a brief ceremony at the fleet hospital on Guam, Admiral Nimitz presented him with the Navy Cross for heroism on Sugar Loaf Hill.

Back on Okinawa, on June 2, William Manchester suffered a superficial gunshot wound, the million-dollar wound that was the dream of almost every fighting man. He was out of the war, temporarily, in a well-run field hospital, eating hot food on clean plates and listening to Jack Benny on the radio. But when he learned that his 6th Marine Division was going to bypass Naha and make an amphibious landing behind Japanese lines he went AWOL and made the successful landing with them.

Early the next morning, he was standing around with some friends when he heard a familiar shriek. Seconds later, an eight-inch shell landed yards away from them. One of his buddies disintegrated, flesh, bones, and blood flying everywhere. When Manchester woke up on the ground he was blind (temporarily) and deaf (with both eardrums ruptured) and his body was punctured by shards of shrapnel and pieces of his dead friend's bones. He was left for dead, but a corpsman found him, gave him two shots of morphine, and arranged for his evacuation to Saipan.

Pursuing the enemy south of the Shuri Line, the Tenth Army was forced to do a lot of "cave flushing." Working in small teams, sometimes with tanks equipped with long-range flamethowers, infantrymen would call into a cave, often with bullhorns, demanding that the occupants come out with their hands high. If the occupants refused, the cave blowers dropped fifty-five-gallon drums of napalm into the mouth of the cave, ignited them with phosphorus grenades, and mowed down every enemy soldier who tried to escape. To avoid death by fire and suffocation, some Japanese soldiers crawled into the deepest reaches of caves and pressed live grenades to their bellies. Civilians hid with soldiers in these caves and uncounted thousands of them were buried alive.

If the Japanese soldiers agreed to come out with their hands up, they were sometimes shot anyway. Americans did not trust their intentions. A surviving Japanese officer recalls that "when Americans urged Japanese soldiers to come out of their caves, they would put hand grenades under their armpits. Outside, they'd get as close as possible to the Americans, throw the grenades and try to fly back into the caves."

Some enemy soldiers put on Okinawan kimonos and hid grenades or small demolition charges under them. This caused innocent citizens to be killed by nervous American soldiers who shot anyone who moved suspiciously. One devoutly religious Marine found it "pretty hard at first" to accept that "our people were shooting human beings who weren't necessarily military. But after I saw what their people— including civilians—did with their hands up, I worried about us, not them. I wanted to leave Okinawa alive!"

To the Japanese and Okinawans, the flamethrower was the most terrifying weapon in the American arsenal. But the men carrying them were as frightened of the enemy as the enemy was of them. A flamethrower man had ninety-five pounds of lethal firepower strapped to his back. One bullet in the tank meant instant incineration. And because of the weight of the tank, he could not crawl or lie flat if fired upon; nor did he carry a rifle. "You couldn't see them in [their hiding places], but

A DEMOLITION SQUAD PREPARES TO BLOW UP A
JAPANESE CAVE (SC).

they could see you—a perfect bull's eye without a rifle," recalls Evan Regal, a farm
boy from upstate New York. "Every time I had to walk up to a hole, I was scared out
of my mind because I was a sitting duck." Casualties among flamethrowers were far
higher than for riflemen. "I stepped over hit flamethrowers like logs," said one infantryman.

Regal describes a typical cave-flushing operation: "You pulled the triggers—
there were two—just as soon as you thought your flame could reach them. In it went
and all hell'd break loose. You heard the shuffling and the screaming and almost always some would come running, their hair and clothes on fire, for the riflemen to
pick them off. . . . Napalm stuck to their skin like jelly glue even when they ran out,
and we used napalm most of the time on Okinawa. . . .

"You have utterly no compassion for their screams because you've seen so many
of your own cut down and you know it can be you the next second; if you give them
the slightest chance, they'll put a bullet between your eyes. . . . All you care about the
Japs is that they fry fast."[58]

For civilians, the battle south of the Shuri Line was a wholesale slaughter. Up
to 100,000 noncombatants died in the month of June. As the Japanese troops retreated,
the terrified civilian population went with them, filling the roads and villages with

an almost indistinguishable mixture of combatants and noncombatants. So they were killed in nearly equal numbers, "grandfathers, grandmothers, mothers with children on their backs, scurrying along, covered in mud," in the words of one refugee.[59]

Those not killed by random American fire died of disease, starvation, and a score of other war-related causes, including suicide. As at Marpi Point, many jumped from high cliffs into the shallow surf. The Navy tried to stop them, and tried to rescue those who were pinned to the bottom of the cliffs, terror-stricken at the sight of the American naval guns glaring at them. "Those who can swim, swim out!" Navy translators in a rescue boat shouted to a group of Okinawans standing in the breakers. "Those who can't swim, walk toward Minatogawa! Walk by day. Don't travel by night. We have food! We will rescue you!"

"They actually did!" recalls Miyagi Kikuko, a sixteen-year-old member of an

A FLAMETHROWER ATTACKS A HIDDEN ENEMY POSITION (SC).

Okinawan student defense group who was trapped with her friends in the churning surf. "They took care of Okinawans really well, according to international law, but we only learned that later. We thought we were hearing the voices of demons. From the time we'd been children we'd only been educated to hate them. They would strip the girls naked and do with them whatever they wanted, then run over them with tanks. We really believed that. . . . So what we had been taught [by the Japanese] robbed us of life. . . . Had we known the truth, all of us would have survived. . . . Anyway, we didn't answer that voice."

The next day three of Miyagi Kikuko's friends were killed by random American fire and ten classmates gathered in a cliffside cave and pulled the pin of a hand grenade they had been carrying. "When the firing stopped I . . . stepped out over the corpses," she recalls. "The automatic rifles of four or five American soldiers were aimed right at me. My grenade was taken away. I had held it to the last minute."

Miyagi Kikuko was fed and taken to a camp in the north, where she was re-united with her mother and father. "Mother, barefoot, ran out of a tent in the camp and hugged me to her. 'You lived, you lived!'"[60]

In the Battle of Okinawa at least a third of the island's population of almost 490,000 died, and nearly every town and burial tomb was turned into smoking rubble. Few people suffered as greatly in modern warfare as the Okinawans. Their losses in property and lives show how horrible an invasion of the Japanese home islands would have been for civilians, whether they resisted or not.

In early June, Eugene Sledge's 1st Marine Division was sent south to assault the western anchor of the enemy's final defensive line at Kunishi Ridge, a sheer coral cliff laced with caves and gun emplacements. As Sledge approached Kunishi "its crest looked so like Bloody Nose [Ridge] that my knees nearly buckled. I felt as though I were on Peleliu and had it all to go through again." The week-long battle for Kunishi finished off the Japanese on Okinawa, and on June 20 Sledge's battalion was one of the first American units to reach the southern tip of the island. They stood on a hill overlooking the sea and felt a surge of accomplishment. "This was different from Peleliu. We could see its meaning."[61]

The next morning, Sledge went with his company's corpsman to assist some Marines who had been attacked by two Japanese officers wielding samurai sabers. One of the officers lay dead on the ground when Sledge arrived at the scene. "Nothing remained of his head from the nose up—just a mass of crushed skull, brains, and bloody pulp. A grimy Marine with a dazed expression stood over the Japanese. With a foot planted firmly on the ground on each side of the enemy officer's body, the Marine held his rifle by the forestock with both hands and slowly and mechanically moved it up and down like a plunger." Sledge winced each time it struck the "gory mass" that had been the man's face. Then he and a friend took the sick, war-shattered Marine by the arms and led him away. He went unresisting, almost like a "sleep-walker." Sledge helped the corpsman drag the broken body of the enemy officer to a gun position and roll it down a hill.

On June 21, 1945, the Tenth Army declared the island secured, after eighty-two days of fighting. What followed for Sledge and Company K was worse, they thought, than the battle. They were ordered to clean out diehard Japanese defenders and to bury the enemy dead in their area. "It was," Sledge says, "the ultimate indignity," digging graves for the men who had been trying to kill them for the last seven weeks.[62]

When they were finally sent back up north Sledge began to look for old friends. He didn't find many. Only twenty-six Peleliu veterans who had landed with the company survived the fight.

It was the bloodiest campaign of the Pacific war. Total American combat casualties were 12,510 killed or missing in action (4,675 Army, 2,928 Marines, and 4,907 Navy)—almost twice that of Iwo Jima—36,613 wounded, and a slightly lower number of nonbattle casualties, including pychiatric cases, accidents, and illnesses. In all, American losses were nearly 73,000, only slightly less than the number of trained defenders they fought. The American Army counted 107,539 enemy dead, but thousands of others were sealed in caves, never to become statistics. On Okinawa, the Japanese lost more men than the American armed forces—Marines, Army, Navy, and Coast Guard—lost in the entire Pacific war.[63] And more people—combatants and noncombatants—died than were killed in the atomic attacks on Hiroshima and Nagasaki combined.[64]

The butcher's bill would have been higher, and the battle longer and more difficult, had it not been for the logistics miracle pulled off by the U.S. Navy. Seriously wounded men—over 150 of them a day—were evacuated by air and sea to Guam. This translated into a mortality rate among the wounded that was half that of other Pacific battles, roughly 2.8 percent, the rate of the European theater. Medical personnel on the island had available to them whole blood that was donated in the United States, flown to the West Coast under refrigeration, shipped to Guam in thirty-six hours, and transshipped from there to Okinawa. In all, the Tenth Army used more than 15,000 gallons of whole blood. Unless a man was very badly hit, his chances of survival were excellent.

The Japanese, by contrast, had to treat their wounded on the firing line or in dark, stinking hospital caves, where drugs were perilously scarce, medical supplies medieval, and infection from dirt and vermin rampant. And those that died were denied a proper burial because of unrelenting American artillery fire. The enemy dead were either left on the battlefield, stacked in caves, or placed in shallow holes.

Excellent logistics also allowed American soldiers and sailors to prevail in a battle far from their main bases, 6,200 miles from San Francisco and 4,000 miles from Pearl Harbor. Fuel, bombs, and ammunition were shuttled into the area from Ulithi and the Marianas, two great fleet tankers sailing from Guam every day. And supply ships brought in the myriad items required for the invasion force to absorb and deliver tremendous punishment without a serious drop-off in morale: 2.7 million packs of cigarettes, 1.2 million candy bars, over 24 million pieces of mail, and more critically, 854 replacement planes and 207 replacement pilots, an effort alone that required four escort carriers shuttling weekly from Ulithi and Guam and seventeen more steaming to and from the American West Coast and the Marianas.[65]

Okinawa was the only major battle in the Pacific in which the commanding officers of both sides died. Ushijima committed suicide, and Buckner was killed by enemy artillery fire near the end of the fight. A sizable number of prisoners were captured, 7,401. Although about half of them were conscripted Okinawans, this was evidence, perhaps, of growing disillusionment among recent conscripts in the Japanese army. Even so, far greater numbers committed suicide or fought on when death was a certainty. Their disregard for death rested, not in hope, but in the despairing conviction that, with defeat inevitable, their lives must be sacrificed to protect family, homeland, and Emperor.[66]*

Few American soldiers who participated in the death struggle on Okinawa believed that the Japanese army could be beaten short of utter annihilation. Reporters who covered the action agreed. "People out here attach more importance to the Kamikaze method of attack as an illustration of the Japanese state of mind than as a weapon of destruction," wrote *New York Times* correspondent W. H. Lawrence. "Considered carefully, the fact that literally thousands of men, many of them young and in their prime, will go out alone on missions of certain death to achieve results that even at best would not be commensurate with the sacrifice, is certainly not one calculated to breed optimism."

The brutal eighty-two-day campaign had convinced the soldiers and Marines that Lawrence interviewed that the war with Japan "may well last for years, instead of months, as some optimists hope," and that it could be won only "by ground action. Large-scale bombing and fleet action unquestionably will reduce the enemy's power of resistance, they believe, but when his soldiers and sailors hole up in caves, as they

---

*In an astute study of MacArthur's psychological warfare campaign in the Southwest Pacific, *You Can't Fight Tanks with Bayonets: Psychological Warfare Against the Japanese Army in the Southwest Pacific* (Lincoln: University of Nebraska Press, 1998), Allison B. Gilmore argues that the morale of Japanese soldiers fighting MacArthur began to drop once they perceived Japan's military situation deteriorating fatally. But as historian Richard B. Frank argues, "translating depressed morale into a greater rate of battlefield surrenders, much less a national surrender . . . is another matter." Gilmore reports that 7,297 Japanese were captured on Luzon. But the Japanese had 287,000 troops there. "This makes the rate of battlefield surrenders just 2.5 percent," Frank writes, "which is virtually indistinguishable from the 1 to 3 percent rates in the ferocious battles elsewhere." Frank, *Downfall*, 71–72.

did on this island, they can be flushed out and killed only by foot soldiers supported by tanks and flamethrowers."

Nor did the American fighting men who won our greatest victory in the Pacific see any strong evidence of the Japanese soldier losing his will to resist. "The record number of prisoners taken in the final days of this campaign can be considered only a minor gain for our psychological warfare efforts when it is measured against the unabated fanaticism with which the enemy fought," wrote Lawrence. Considering this, "hope for quick victory dims.

"There are too many crosses in the seven Division cemeteries on Okinawa for anyone to say that disposing of the Japanese is a one-handed job, requiring only a 50 percent home-front effort, now that Germany is out of the war." [67]

In early July rumors started to run through the ranks that the troops on Okinawa would hit Japan next. As Sledge said, "No one wanted to talk about that." [68]

The Setting Sun

BURMA

When American troops invaded Okinawa in April 1944, the Japanese army in China was bogged down in the greatest guerilla war of the century, carrying out well-organized "annihilation campaigns" against guerrillas and their village supporters, extermination operations that killed over two and a half million noncombatants. Only if killing was winning did they hold the upper hand. In every other Asian theater the Imperial Army had either been defeated or backed up on its heels. "The Japs in this area are on the run," Marvin Kastenbaum, an American GI, wrote his family from Namhpakka, Burma, "and where I was sitting yesterday, I could see the famous Burma Road."[1]

The turning point in Burma had come in August 1943. At the Quebec Conference, Roosevelt and Churchill decided that the time was propitious for a counteroffensive against Chinese-held Burma. Lord Louis Mountbatten was named supreme commander in Southeast Asia and Vinegar Joe Stilwell, who had led a heroic retreat from Burma in the spring of 1942, was given command of Chinese and American ground forces. With the Japanese controlling the Burma Road, Stilwell's most urgent task was to reopen a supply line to China. He had already established an air transport system over the Hump to supply Chiang Kai-shek's Chinese Nationalist Army from India. By the end of 1943, the American "Humpsters," flying underpowered cargo planes through some of the most wretched weather in the world, were delivering more supplies to China than had ever gone over the Burma Road.

This allowed the Chinese to tie down over a million Japanese troops that could have been deployed in the Pacific against MacArthur and Nimitz. "Strong winds, with speeds sometimes exceeding one hundred miles per hour, created mountain waves and vertical sheers that could overturn an aircraft, send it rocketing upward for thousands of feet or plunge it downward into the mountains. According to the season, thunderstorms, torrential rains, hail, sleet, snow, and severe icing held sway," recalls an American flier. "Bring me men to match my weather," was the Humpster's motto. If pilots survived hits by Japanese Zeros they parachuted into unfathomable jungle, a fifteen-minute fall from 17,000 feet. Those not picked up by rescue teams, among them the American reporter Eric Sevareid, walked out of "tiger country" with the help of upcountry headhunters.[2]

THE HEAD OF A JAPANESE SOLDIER HANGS FROM A TREE ALONG THE BURMA ROAD TO LASHIO IN NORTHERN BURMA, FEBRUARY 1945 (NA).

Late in 1943, American engineers and 15,000 American troops—60 percent of them African-Americans—began building a new road to connect Ledo, Assam, in eastern India, with that part of the Burma Road still in enemy hands. But first the Japanese had to be cleared from northern Burma. British Major General Orde Wingate and his raiders, called Chindits, after the statues of dragons that guard Burmese temples, had already begun this operation, crossing from India through Japanese lines and wrecking airfields, blowing up bridges, and dynamiting railways. Wingate's Chindits were second-line troops—nearly all of them married men from the north of England, aged twenty-eight to thirty-five. Wingate told them they had to imitate Tarzan. "For six sweltering months in the Indian jungles he trained them in river crossing, infiltration tactics and long forced marches with heavy packs, until they were the toughest of shock troops," wrote Charles Rolo, a war correspondent for *The Atlantic Monthly.* On returning from the raid one private remarked: "The whole job was a piece of cake compared to the training."

The Chindits lived on rice, vultures, jungle roots, and grass soup, and kept in touch with one another by carrier pigeons, birdcalls, and messenger dogs. Elephants carried their mortars and folding boats; carts drawn by oxen were stacked high with machine guns and boxes of grenades. Supplies were dropped in by air. Looking like some desert prophet with his long beard and a blanket draped over his shoulders, Wingate drove his raiders mercilessly, reminding them that their security lay in speed.[3]

Wingate's raiders and their American prototype, Merrill's Marauders, organized by Brigadier General Frank D. Merrill, harried the enemy in northern Burma while Stilwell fought down from China to protect the construction of the Ledo—later named the Stilwell—Road. Meanwhile, the Japanese went on the offensive in March 1944, attacking across the Indian border at Imphal, the main base of Lieutenant General William Slim's Fourteenth Imperial Army. They ran into unexpectedly strong resistance, and the British were soon counterattacking, aided by vengeful Burmese hill men. The miserably supplied Japanese invasion army was destroyed and a starving remnant limped back into Burma. Fifty thousand of the 80,000 elite troops that had begun the confident push into India died. British losses were equally appalling. But in 1944 the Japanese were in full retreat down the road they had come up in 1942, the road to Mandalay, to Rangoon, and to Tokyo.

In the closing months of 1944, Stilwell's army, now commanded by Major General Albert C. Wedemeyer, who replaced Stilwell as Chiang Kai-shek's chief of staff, cleared the way for the opening of the Stilwell Road. This epochal engineering achievement rose as high as 4,500 feet through the Patkai Mountains and passed through untouched wilderness. "The work was done principally by black combat engineers," recalls one of the African-American truck drivers on the Ledo Road. "I take my hat off to those guys, talk about cliff-hangers, and in bulldozers, no less. They took the turns out of the road and made curves."[4]

On January 28, 1945, the first convoy, consisting of fifty African-American and fifty Chinese drivers, drove over the Hump and crossed into China.

Over the next four months the Allies launched a coordinated offensive. Three armies converged on the Japanese in Burma: the American-trained Chinese from the north, General Slim's Fourteenth Imperial Army from the center, and three divisions of Indian and African troops from the south. Before these overwhelming forces Mandalay fell on March 20 and Rangoon on May 3. After liberating Burma and inflicting over 300,000 casualties on the Japanese army, General Slim began planning the liberation of Malaya and Singapore, an enormous operation that the end of the war would thankfully make unnecessary.

HELL SHIPS AND DOG CAGES

As Japanese power crumbled in Southeast Asia and the Central Pacific, and as military conscription drained Japan's industrial workforce, the government began shipping great numbers of prisoners of war to the home islands. There they worked as laborers in shipyards, steel mills, coal mines, and other vital sectors of the economy. These industrial slaves were transported by sea in the steaming overcrowded holds of merchant vessels, where thousands died of starvation, disease, and suffocation. The death toll rose alarmingly in late 1944 when Allied warships and planes gained domination of Japan's shipping lanes in preparation for the invasion of the Philippines. The Japanese refused to mark the ships that carried its prisoners of war, and these slow-moving, lightly armed vessels were easy prey for Allied submarines and fighter planes. Over the course of the war, approximately 21,000 Allied POWs died at sea, about 19,000 of them killed by friendly fire. By comparison, about 20,000 Marines died in the entire Pacific war.[5]

The *Arisan Maru*, torpedoed by an American submarine, took down with it over twice as many American POWs as died on the Bataan Death March, almost 1,800. No combatants in the war suffered and died more horribly than did the prisoners on these hell ships. And driven insane by their conditions, prisoners sometimes killed one another.

Sergeant Forrest Knox was one of ninety-nine men from the small town of

DEATH SHIP POWs (SC).

Janesville, Wisconsin, to be captured by the Japanese after the surrender of Bataan. In September 1944, as MacArthur's armies prepared to land in the Philippines, Knox was working with an 800-man crew on airfield construction at a camp near Manila. He worked barefoot, in a G-string and straw hat, digging ditches and draining mosquito-infested rice paddies with shovels made out of thin sheet iron. He was losing his eyesight and all feeling in his legs, he had malaria and hookworm, and he weighed barely ninety pounds. He had managed to keep only two things from the Bataan Death March, a toothbrush and a filthy neck towel, which had kept him from dying from heat stroke. As Admiral Halsey's planes pounded the airfields around Manila, he was moved with prisoners from other camps to Bilibid, a compound in Manila, where he ran into some old buddies from his Janesville National Guard tank unit. They and approximately a thousand other prisoners were to be shipped to Japan in the stinking hold of a rusty freighter called the *Haro Maru*. It was a place that soon became, in Forrest Knox's words, "a madhouse."

THEY PUT 500 OF US IN one hold and 500 in the other. . . . After the ship was loaded, tugs pulled us away from the dock and moored us to a buoy in the harbor. Tropical sun on a steel deck. Body heat from 500 men packed together. All around men began passing out. They just slid down out of sight, where men stepped or stood on them. . . .

As a guy goes crazy he starts to scream—not like a woman, more like the howl of a dog. . . . It must have been 120 or 125 degrees in that hold. The Japs' favorite trick was to cut off our water. It was bad enough in other places when they did this, but there, in this oven, when they cut it off, guys started going crazy. People running, people screaming. An American colonel was on deck. There was always some Americans topside who were used to raise and lower the honey buckets and food tubs. The Japs told the colonel to tell us to be quiet. He shouted down, "Be quiet or the Japs will completely cover over the hatch with canvas." . . .

With the temperature we were in, if they'd closed off that little air we got, I don't know how many of us would have been alive by morning. I had picked up the habit of wearing a small sweat towel around my forehead. . . . The next guy that went by screaming they caught and killed. . . . He was strangled with my little towel. A guy that had worked in a mental institution in Pennsylvania knew how to do it. Several others were also killed [strangled or beaten to death with canteens]. The crazy ones . . . howled because they were afraid to die—but now the ground rules changed. If they howled, they died. The screaming stopped. . . . The Japs didn't cover the hatch.

"No one was ever punished for these deaths," says Private William R. Evans, who was in the hold with Knox, "and the Japs didn't give a shit."[6]

The last of the death ships to leave the Philippines was the passenger-cargo vessel *Oryoku Maru*. It pulled away from the Manila docks on December 13, carrying 1,619 POWs in her holds, along with over 2,000 Japanese merchant seamen and civilians, who were quartered above deck. All but thirty of the prisoners were Americans.

"We were jammed in the holds," recalls Lieutenant Melvin Rosen, a young American artillery officer. "There was no place to lie down; some people couldn't even sit down, and everybody had diarrhea. The floorboards were full of human waste and vomit, and the stench was unbearable. The temperature was over 100 degrees, and people started going mad that first night, screaming for water and air. Some guys drank their own urine, and it drove them crazy." Others scraped the sweat off the steel sides of the ship and tried to drink it. "One person near me," says Private First Class Lee Davis, "cut another person's throat and was holding the canteen so he could catch the blood."

About fifty men died that first night, an unknown number of them strangled or beaten by other prisoners. Others were killed trying to stop them, in their frenzy, from murdering fellow Americans.

The next morning the ship was bombed and strafed by Navy planes as it headed north, hugging the shore. The killing was above deck. More than 300 Japanese died and hundreds more were injured seriously. Waiting for the cover of night, the ship's crew offloaded the passengers to the site of a former U.S. naval base, leaving only the guards, the gun crews, and the prisoners on the battered *Oryoku Maru*. That night, thirst-crazed men turned into "human vampires," says Major John M. Wright, "biting men and sucking blood in their mad lust for liquid in any form."[7]

Toward morning it got quiet, as most of the exhausted prisoners passed out, sleeping fitfully in their own vomit and urine. Then the dive-bombers returned.

"They put a 500-pound bomb in the hold with us," recalls Colonel Maynard Booth, "and there was a terrible bloody mess. Arms and legs and blood and guts were flying all over the place, and one guy who got blasted to pieces landed right on top of me. About 200 guys were killed, and the whole ship was on fire. Then it got real quiet. And as you heard people groaning, the Japs ordered us to swim to shore, which was only a couple of hundreds of yards away. I stayed on the ship and went up into the cabins and got life preservers and put them on our wounded, and heaved these men over the side of the ship. Then I bailed out with my life preserver and started swimming. Japanese onshore were machine-gunning us, but most of us managed to make it."

"When we got to shore," says Melvin Rosen, "they herded us into an old tennis court surrounded by a chicken-wire fence and gave each of us a tablespoon and a half of raw rice and a little water. That was our diet for the next five days. After that we were taken on trucks to a town we had passed through on the Bataan Death March, San Fernando, Pampanga."

"They said they were going to take our wounded to the hospital," recalls Booth. "They were beat up real bad and the Japs didn't have any medicine. They loaded fifteen of them on the back of a truck like they were sides of beef and went down the road two or three miles, kicked them out into a ditch, and [beheaded] them, as we found out later."

The 1,333 prisoners that survived were jammed into boxcars and taken to a small port on northern Luzon. "We were lined up and packed into two Jap freighters," says Captain Marion "Manny" Lawton. "The *Enoura Maru* housed almost 1,000 of us. The rest were loaded on the *Brazil Maru*."

"The *Enoura Maru* was a freighter that had just unloaded horses for the Japanese horse artillery," says Booth. "There was horse manure on the floors and we were so hungry we picked the bugs out of it and ate them and crawled on the floor looking for barley that the horses hadn't eaten." As the two hell ships headed for Formosa, rice was lowered to the men in tubs. "The flies were like hornets coming out of their hive. When the tub got to the bottom you couldn't see the rice for the flies," says Lawton. "We were so hungry it didn't make any difference." Twenty-one POWs died along the way and their bodies were tossed overboard

LIBERATED POWS IN THE PHILIPPINES (USN).

to the sharks. The ships arrived in Formosa on New Year's Eve. Just after the prisoners on the *Brazil Maru* were transferred by barge to the *Enoura Maru*, an American dive-bomber hit that ship and it sank at anchor in shallow water. Almost 300 men were killed instantly in the forward hold and at least another 250 were wounded. "The Japanese kept us down in the hold with our dead and wounded for three days, and then sent down a cargo net to load the dead," says Rosen. "After a few days, sitting in the smashed hull, we were put on the *Brazil Maru* and headed in a convoy for Japan." They left without four doctors who had died of exhaustion while assisting the wounded, using old razor blades and rusty scissors for surgical instruments.

Only about 900 POWs remained and as many as thirty of them a day died on the two-week passage to Japan. Officers and men traded their wedding bands and service academy rings to their Japanese guards for cupfuls of water and dry rice, and the fighting continued. "Let me tell you what it felt like to be hungry all the time," says Major William Adair. "It was a stomach pain. Not a great pain, but an annoying one. And it never went away while I was a prisoner. Never."

As they headed further north, they ran into snow and ice storms and men started coming down with pneumonia. A tarpaulin had been put over the hatch, but the freezing wind whipped through the hold. "When it rained, the dirty water from the deck would pour down on us. Men drank it—filthy, dirty water. The diarrhea and pneumonia just started wiping us out. We buried an average of twenty-five a day," says Lawton.

At least half of the prisoners had malaria; and the genitalia of men with beriberi swelled, causing excruciating pain. Men with dry beriberi experienced stabbing pains, like electric shocks, in their legs and feet, and almost everyone had dysentery. When they landed in northern Kyushu after a forty-eight-day journey, only 450 of the original 1,619 were still alive, and about 150 more died from maltreatment during the first week in Japan. "The Japanese weighed some of us when we came ashore," says Rosen, "and I weighed exactly eighty-eight pounds."

The prisoners were divided into groups and sent to three different camps. When Manny Lawton arrived at Camp No. 3 there was snow on the ground and the men were moved into unheated barracks. Lawton learned from a corpsman that his closest friend, Captain Henry Leitner, had pneumonia. "The next morning I looked up and there was Henry in his undershorts, nothing else on, strolling toward the door. I called to him and asked him where he thought he was going. He said, 'I'm going to get some of that snow. I'm thirsty.' I said, 'Henry, please come back. There's plenty of hot tea here.' 'No,' he said, 'I'm hot. I've got to have something cool.' His fever was burning. He strolled on out. That night he died." [8]

"Unlike a lot of the guys, I don't have nightmares today," says Melvin Rosen. "But every morning when I come down and pick up the kettle on the stove and empty the old water in it, I think of how many lives that little bit of water might have saved when we were in those hell ships." [9]

Before being transferred to Korea, Rosen was taken to a slave labor camp on Kyushu, where one of the prisoners was Lester Tenney, a fellow survivor of the Bataan Death March. This was Fukuoka Camp No. 17 in Omuta, just east of Nagasaki. It was a compound built by the Mitsui Coal Mining Company and run by the army. And it had a reputation. "This camp was as tough as they came," says Staff Sergeant Harold Feiner. "It was mean. If there was nothing else that had gone wrong, the work itself would have made it bad. We mined coal twelve hours a day, had a thirty-minute lunch break, and were given one day off every ten days." [10]

Lester Tenney had been with the original group of prisoners who opened the camp. When he was first taken underground he was ordered to build ceiling supports.

"When I asked why this was needed, one of the civilian workers told me that the mine had been shut down years before because all the coal that was safe to extract had already been removed. . . . We paid a price for doing this. . . . Even with the ceiling sagging, and only three feet high, we went in and got the coal on our hands and knees; and men got hurt doing it—from cave-ins especially. A lot of guys died in that mine."

Men mutilated themselves to get out of work. Tenney describes how it was done:

I TOOK A BIG STEEL LOCKING pin from one of the coal cars, put my hand over a piece of timber, and took that bar and smashed it into my hand as hard as I could. The pain was excruciating. But my hand started to swell up, and it looked like it was broken. I had to make it look like an accident. So I got a pickax and tore some coal down on myself and let out a yell. I showed my bleeding and swollen hand to the Japanese supervisor, but the hand wasn't broken and I had to go to work the next day. The next time, I said to myself, I'll go to an experienced bone breaker and have it done right.

We had bone crushers, guys who would break a bone with a shovel or a jackhammer for a price, usually cigarettes or rations of rice. A hand cost one ration of rice, a foot five to eight rations. You didn't get out of work for long, even with a broken leg, but it was worth it to some guys who reached the point where they felt that if they went in that mine the next day they'd die there.

Another way to get out of work was to manufacture ulcers on your feet, so you couldn't put on a shoe. Making an ulcer was simple. I took a pin and pricked twenty or so holes in my foot in a pattern about the size of a dime. Then I got some lye from the bathroom and mixed it with lye soap to make a paste. I put that paste on the bleeding area and put a bandage over it. The next morning I took off the bandage and I had a nice burn scab. I picked away at the crust with a knife and saw that I had a beautiful, fresh-looking ulcer. Every day I made it bigger, until it was the size of a half-dollar. The medics, who were Americans, let me off work for a week.[11]

There were other ways to make ulcers. Some men put battery acid from their miner's lamps on their festering sores.

"The diet of the prisoner of war was based solely on rice," reported Thomas Hewlett, an American Army doctor at Omuta, "and all the men lived in a state of chronic starvation." This led desperate men to steal food from the prison galley. Those caught were denied rice and water for days and were beaten with bamboo poles, baseball bats, and pick handles. When the guards were finished with them they would urinate in their faces. At Omuta, several prisoners were executed for stealing canned food and Red Cross parcels that were supposed to be given to them. Thirty-eight percent of the 36,260 American military personnel captured and interned by the Japanese died in captivity, a total of 13,851. By contrast, 99 percent of the 93,941 Americans captured by the Germans survived the war.[12]

For some prisoners, tobacco was as essential as food. "They would desperately trade off some of their rice for a little bit of tobacco, either cigarettes or shaved tobacco, which they made into cigarettes with the thin rice paper of the little Bibles that GIs were issued," said one prisoner.[13] Traders would go around the camp calling out, "nicotine for protein," and there were always takers. Some men smoked themselves to the point of death.[14]

Conditions grew worse in the winter and spring of 1945 when Curtis LeMay's B-29s began their fire raids against Japanese cities. "Instead of merely hitting us with their hands or fists, the Japanese used shovels, picks, and sections of steel chain," says Tenney. "They swung the chains around overhead until they reached a high speed. Then, using the chain's momentum, they inflicted brutal blows upon our bodies. . . . In one attack, my cheekbones were gashed, the skin above my eyebrow was broken, my nose . . . was smashed, and my entire chin was gushing with blood." Dr. Hewlett told him his left scapula was broken, but he was sent back into the mine because he could still shovel coal with one hand. "The beatings were bad," says Tenney, "but the more of them we got the better we felt about the war effort."[15]

The Japanese saved their cruelest treatment for downed American flyboys. On the desolate island of Chichi Jima in the Bonins, where the Japanese had an important communications post, eight captured Navy and Marine fliers were brutally executed and the officers of the garrison ate the flesh and livers of several of them at ceremonial dinners. (A ninth flier shot down over the island, Navy carrier pilot George H. W. Bush, a future President of the United States, was rescued at sea by the submarine *Finback*.)[16] In Japan, captured "B-29ers" were segregated from other POWs, usually in small torture camps run by the Kempeitai, the Gestapo-like secret military police. They were interrogated and tortured. Some were put on public trial as war criminals and executed; others were beheaded or bayoneted on the spot. One group of fliers was shot with bows and arrows and then decapitated. At another camp, three airmen were tortured and burned alive. In one of the most ghastly atrocities, eight B-29 crewmen shot down near the end of the war were offered by the army to the medical professors at the prestigious Kyushu Imperial University, who used them as specimens for vivisection experiments. Under the direction of Dr. Fukujiro Ishiyama, one of Japan's most respected surgeons, "the professors," writes historian Gavan Daws, "cut them up alive, in a dirty room with a tin table where students dissected corpses. They drained blood and replaced it with sea water. They cut out the lungs, livers, and stomachs. They stopped blood flow in an artery near the heart, to see how long death took. They dug holes in a skull and stuck a knife into the living brain to see what would happen."[17] No anesthetics were administered.

Records are incomplete, but it is likely that over 200 American fliers were killed after being captured by the Japanese military.

Flying out of Saipan, a B-29 named *Rover Boys Express* was shot down by Japanese fighters over Tokyo on January 27, 1945. Five crew members survived a terrifying explosion, and with their ordinary escape hatch damaged, parachuted out of the bomb bay. One of them was Ray "Hap" Halloran, a twenty-two-year-old navigator from Cincinnati, Ohio. Japanese civilians followed the flight of his chute, captured him, and beat him into a state of unconsciousness with wooden and metal poles. Then they stoned him with large rocks. As Halloran slipped in and out of consciousness, he looked up and saw six military police standing over him. They cut his parachute, stuffed part of it into his mouth, tied his hands and feet, beat him with the butts of their rifles, and tossed him into the bed of a truck. After a brutal interrogation at a nearby air base, he was again beaten in the chest and back with rifle butts.

THEY TOOK ME TO A SHOPPING area and made me stand and bow to jeering crowds of people. I think the purpose was to build morale among the civilians who had taken quite a beating from the B-29s. After people finished throwing stones at me, I was blindfolded again and taken to the Kempeitai torture prison in downtown Tokyo. That's where I spent the next sixty-seven days in a cage.

The cage was elevated about four feet off the floor. I was covered with blood. I was cold. And I was crying with pain. The other prisoners, Japanese conscientious objectors, complained to the guards that they couldn't sleep with all the noise I was making. So they pulled me out of my cage and took me to a doctor. He had a big tube in his hand, with a needle at the end of it. There was green liquid in the tube. The doctor said this would make me sleep. Somehow I con-

HAP HALLORAN IN CAGE AT THE TOKYO ZOO
(ILLUSTRATION BY RICHARD ROCKWELL).

vinced him not to inject me. Later I learned the greenish liquid was poison. Six
other prisoners were injected and died.

After a few days, they carried me—I couldn't walk—across a courtyard to
what we called the stables, and I was locked in another cage. It was small and
you entered through a door on the floor. They pushed you in like you were a
dog, and it really was a dog cage. I was ordered to lie in my cell with my head to
the door, and the guards played a game of punching my head with their rifle
butts.

It was cold and I had only one blanket and there was a hole in the floor for a
toilet. The biggest thing in my life was a rice ball the size of a golf ball that
they'd roll in through a small feeding slot at the base of the door. I was a big
guy and I lost over 100 pounds in prison.

Firm rule. No speaking. No noise. There was one young guy in another cage, an eighteen-year-old gunner who kept saying, "Okay, Mom, I'll be right down for breakfast." He violated the rule. He was taken out and he never made it home.

Each day, you try to hang in there. At first I tried to cope by thinking of my family but that was no good. It broke me down internally. I prayed a lot. I said, "Please God, I'm really in trouble. I need your help." No one came to help me.

I was always in darkness. The only light I ever saw was a low-wattage bulb on the ceiling of my cage. The darkness makes you go nuts. The only time I saw the light of day was from under a blindfold when they carried me out to interrogate me and beat me. But, crazily, I looked forward to the interrogations. They broke the everlasting boredom and were a chance to get out of the cavelike darkness. I missed them when they stopped.

The next thing I remember is the big Tokyo fire raid of March 10. I heard multi-engine planes at low altitude and I thought that was strange. We always flew at 30,000 feet. Then the bombs started to fall and my cage jumped; and for the next two or three hours fire was all around us. At the back of my cage was a small window. There was a black cloth covering it, but on that night I could see the red sky and the flames through the covered window. And though it had been a calm night before the bombers came, I heard the wind blowing like a tornado. I was frightened out of my mind, 'cause fire really scares me. I was convinced I was going to burn to death.

I could hear mothers and children screaming and running. The prison was right across from the Emperor's Palace and they were jumping into the moat to escape the flames and heat. But I didn't know that at the time.

The next morning an interpreter came in, a polite guy, and told me what had happened the night before, like he was trying to be informative. He spoke of bodies stacked three and four

RAY "HAP" HALLORAN (COURTESY OF RAY HALLORAN).

feet high in the streets and of thousands of bodies floating down the river to Tokyo Bay. Then he looked at me and said, "Hap, I regret to advise you that at our meeting this morning the decision was made to execute you B-29ers."

A few days later I was taken out and told to take off my shoes. I thought— death sentence. They blindfolded me, tied my hands and feet, and loaded me on a truck. They dropped me off at the Tokyo Zoo, just tossed me off the truck. Then they pulled off my blindfold, put me in a tiger cage, stripped off my clothes, and tied my hands to the bars. The purpose was to let civilians see me. "Do not fear these B-29 fliers. They are not super beings. Look at this one." I was a pathetic sight, standing there, skinny as a rail, with a long, filthy beard, shivering from the cold, with my body covered with running sores from lice and fleas. I was trying desperately to act like an Air Corps guy, you know, with dignity. It was pretty tough, but you've got to do it, maintain your dignity as best you can.

They left me at the Ueno Zoo overnight and the next day they took me to a place with some other B-29ers and a bunch of other prisoners, the Omori Prisoner of War Camp, about twelve miles from downtown Tokyo. It was on a little island in Tokyo Bay, only a couple of hundred yards out in the bay. Thank God for that little separation because the subsequent fire raids burned down everything right across from us.

At Camp Omori, Hap Halloran met Air Commander Robert Goldsworthy, who had also been tortured in a Kempeitai prison. "Sometimes I'd get so low that I wanted to quit," Goldsworthy recalls, "and Hap would buck me up. And days when Hap would get like that I'd take him off to the side and buck him up. . . . We used to say 'home alive in '45.' We knew it couldn't go on much longer because our guys were devastating Japan from the air." [18]

DECISIONS

On June 15, when General Curtis LeMay ended his incendiary campaign against Japan's six largest cities, having turned them into charred wastelands, he began his attacks on smaller cities. His crews also targeted shipping and harbors, oil facilities, and railroads. By now, the enemy's air defenses had been destroyed. "At this time," LeMay recalled, "it was actually safer to fly a combat mission over Japan in a B-29 than it was to fly a B-29 training mission back in the United States." [19]

While LeMay's "burn jobs," as he called them, obliterated Japan's urban culture, Admiral Halsey's Task Force 38 cruised at will up and down the coast of Japan, shelling port cities and military installations, including Tokyo Harbor. Navy planes ripped up airfields and burned planes on the ground; and they attacked railroad trains and passenger ferries filled with women and children, attacks the Japanese considered more reprehensible than "Devil LeMay's" napalm raids. Every Japanese citizen became a military target. "I did want every Japanese dead," John Ciardi admitted. "Part of it was our propaganda machine, but part of it was what we heard accurately. This was the enemy. We were there to eliminate them. That's the soldier's short-term bloody view." [20]

LeMay dropped leaflets as well as bombs, his own foray into psychological warfare. In bold red and black script, the leaflets warned the citizens of cities targeted for incineration to "evacuate at once!" On the other side of the leaflet were these words:

THESE LEAFLETS ARE BEING DROPPED TO notify you that your city had been listed for destruction by our powerful air force. The bombing will begin within seventy-two hours.

This advance notice will give your military authorities ample time to take necessary defensive measures to protect you from our inevitable attack. Watch and see how powerless they are to protect you. [21]

LeMay writes: "At first they thought we were bluffing. . . . There wasn't any mass exodus until we knocked the hell out of the first three towns on the list. Then the rest were practically depopulated in nothing flat." The leaflets had a crushing impact on civilian morale, producing defeatism and terror. Their government, the Japanese people realized, was powerless to protect them.

With thousands of American and British heavy bombers on the way from Europe and with 5,000 more B-29s on order, LeMay was convinced he "could bomb and burn them until they quit," avoiding a humanly costly invasion of the home islands. [22] He informed General Arnold, however, that by October he would run out of cities to burn.

On June 18, 1945, President Truman was scheduled to meet with his top military advisors. "I have to decide Japanese strategy—shall we invade Japan proper or shall we bomb and blockade?" the President wrote in his diary the day before the meeting. "That is my hardest decision to date." [23]

Truman was concerned about casualties, hoping to prevent "an Okinawa from one end of Japan to the other."[24]

At the meeting, General George Marshall presented an invasion plan, code-named Downfall. It was supported, although not enthusiastically, by the Navy and the Air Forces. Both services privately continued to believe that they could force a surrender short of an invasion, one by blockade, the other by conventional bombing. Downfall was a two-phase operation. The Americans would land on the Japanese island Kyushu on November 1 with over a quarter of a million assault troops, seize the southernmost part of the island, and build naval bases and airfields for the larger invasion of Honshu and the Tokyo Plain in March 1946, should it be necessary. The first landing was code-named Olympic, the second, Coronet. MacArthur would be in charge of the ground troops, Nimitz would command the naval forces. Olympic alone would be a combined operation larger than the Normandy invasion, requiring the entire American and British Pacific fleets, and 5,000 combat aircraft. Marshall told Truman that there would probably be 350,000 defenders on Kyushu. A precise estimate of American casualties might not have been mentioned at this meeting, but Truman had been led to believe that the number of dead Americans would probably be higher than 25,000 in the first thirty days.

Airpower alone could not bring down Japan, Marshall was convinced, even combined with a tightened naval blockade. The ground troops would have to finish the job. Truman commented that the effect of Olympic would be to create "another Okinawa closer to Japan," and approved the Kyushu operation, adding that they could decide "later" whether to proceed with Coronet.[25]

There was no mention of the atomic bomb, which had not yet been tested. But as the meeting was breaking up, Truman asked Assistant Secretary of War John J. McCloy, who had sat silently through the proceedings, for his views. Speaking with some reluctance, McCloy suggested that the threat of the bomb might provide a "political solution," making an invasion unnecessary. "I said I would tell them [the Japanese government] we have the bomb and I would tell them what kind of a weapon it is. And then I would tell them the surrender terms."[26] The Japanese, he said, should also be told that they could keep the Emperor. Truman said he would take this under consideration and hurried off.

Momentum for using the bomb—when it was ready—was already building. Reports about Japanese atrocities against American POWs were being headlined in newspapers and magazines, fueling demands for retribution. The American public—and many of Truman's advisors—were also convinced that the Japanese would slaughter all prisoners of war in the event of an invasion. They were apparently not wrong. In August 1944, the Japanese government had sent a directive to commandants of POW camps. What later became known as the "Kill-All Order" called for "extreme measures" to be taken against prisoners when the military situation became "urgent. . . . Whether they are destroyed individually or in groups, or however it is done, with mass bombing, poisonous smoke, poisons, drowning, decapitation, or what, dispose of the prisoners as the situation dictates. . . . It is the aim not to allow the escape of a single one, to annihilate them all, and not to leave any traces." [27]

The American public was also weary of war and deeply alarmed by the rising numbers of American casualties. Over 64 percent of American battle fatalities in World War II took place in the one-year period between June 1944—the month of the Normandy and Saipan invasions—and May 1945. An invasion of the home islands would mean a large-scale redeployment of troops from Europe to the Pacific and yet one more battle—the bloodiest of them all—for Pacific assault troops like Eugene Sledge. "After [Okinawa] . . . we all knew that General MacArthur was already planning our role in the next damned landing, the biggest one in history . . . right down the gut to Tokyo. None of us veterans," said Sledge, "expected to survive that epic carnage." [28]

The families of these men were as concerned as they were. That June, Marvin Kastenbaum's father had four of his sons serving in the military, and another son had just been killed in April. One son was likely to be discharged early, but Jimmie Kastenbaum was with the infantry in the Philippines, Jack Kastenbaum was in Europe, awaiting transfer to the Pacific, and Marvin had been moved from Burma to China. "The prospect that Jack and Jimmie and I would converge on Japan from three different directions had to be a cause of some concern to my father," Marvin wrote later.[29]

The invasion that never happened was a real and awful thing to American fighting men. The assault troops had been chosen and were already in training. Over 766,000 Army, Marine, Navy, and Coast Guard personnel were assigned to Olympic alone, over twice as many men as participated in the initial landings at Okinawa and Normandy combined. To support such a massive amphibious force, MacArthur and Nimitz planned to assemble the largest fleet of warships ever assigned to a single campaign. Nearly 1,000 warships would have participated in operations off the coast of Kyushu. And almost half a million Purple Hearts were being made and stockpiled for the operation.[30]

That July and August, Army intelligence intercepts reported an enemy buildup on Kyushu greatly in excess of what the Joint Chiefs had originally anticipated. Decoded messages indicated that the Japanese would have 900,000 troops on Kyushu by November and that they would be prepared to meet the Americans on the first high ground behind the beaches. Suicide squads were being trained to throw themselves on American tanks with handheld bombs capable of penetrating heavy armor, and Japanese military planners expected the 5,000 kamikazes they had held back for the invasion to destroy over 40 percent of the American fleet. The Emperor took a personal interest in developing plans for repulsing the American invasion. He attended ceremonies at court for the regiments being raised for the defense of the "divine homeland" and encouraged the formation of citizen suicide units.[31]

Intelligence sources predicted a "titanic confrontation," with possibly "unbearable" American losses—losses sufficient, perhaps, to force the Americans to back off from their demand for unconditional surrender.[32] That, not victory, had become the only realizable aim of even the most diehard Japanese militarists. This is why the defeat at Okinawa was actually encouraging to the Japanese military. On Okinawa, a badly outnumbered force, cut off from supplies and without vigorous civilian support, had held off the invaders for almost a hundred days, inflicting frightful casualties. In a statement made after the war, Major General Masakazu Amano, an architect of defensive preparations on Kyushu, declared: "We were absolutely sure of victory. It was the first and only battle in which the main strength of the air, land and sea forces were to be joined. The geographical advantages of the homeland were to be utilized to the highest degree, the enemy was to be crushed, and we were confident that the battle would prove to be the turning point in political maneuvering."[33]

When American political leaders "said that the Japanese were likely to fight to the death rather than surrender unconditionally, they were not exaggerating what the Japanese government itself was saying," writes historian Herbert Bix.[34] The paradoxical effect of the decisive American victory at Okinawa was to discourage the Americans "while inspiring the Japanese."[35]

Japan had already been defeated militarily. Now, the American objective was to force a defiant government to surrender, a government that still had the support of its people. Residents of Tokyo hurled ridicule on their conquered Axis ally for surrendering unconditionally, verbally accosting Germans on the streets and in the trains. "The Tokyo papers," Robert Guillain reports, "blamed Germany's defeat on its lack of bushido. With bushido . . . one never dies, never surrenders unconditionally."[36]

While the President and his advisors planned the final stroke against Japan, a team of nuclear scientists at a secret facility at Los Alamos, New Mexico, was hurrying world-altering work to conclusion. At the same time, a new Air Force unit was conducting highly secret training operations in the Marianas. Flying stripped-down B-29s designed to achieve maximum speed and altitude, pilots and crews of the 509th Composite Group were dropping enormous pumpkin-shaped bombs, one to a plane, on a desolate island near Tinian. Their commander was thirty-year-old Colonel Paul Tibbets, who had been chosen to head this operation because he knew the B-29 better than anyone else in the air service. A year before arriving in Tinian, he had suggested to Curtis LeMay, while the general was in the States, en route to the Marianas, that he finish off Japan with low-level fire raids. (When LeMay decided—on his own—to go in low, he may have remembered Tibbets's advice.)[37] Now Tibbets was awaiting the arrival in the Marianas of a new kind of fire that he was sure would end the war.

Commander (later Vice Admiral) Frederick L. Ashworth, who would fly on the Nagasaki mission, had picked Tinian as the base for Tibbets's operation. At the time, Ashworth was a thirty-five-year-old Navy commander working at Los Alamos for Major General Leslie Groves, administrator of the Manhattan Project, the vast scientific and industrial enterprise—unprecedented in size—created in 1942 to build the world's first atomic bombs. "I was what was known as a weaponeer," Ashworth said in a recent interview.

THERE WERE TWO OF US, BOTH Navy men. The other was Captain William "Deak" Parsons [the Manhattan Project's chief of weapons development], who flew on the Hiroshima mission. We were in charge of the bombs, since the crews knew nothing about them.

In February 1945 General Groves sent me to Guam to deliver a letter from Admiral King to Admiral Nimitz, saying that a highly secret . . . "new weapon will be ready in August of this year for use against Japan by the 20th Air Force." . . .

The letter asked Nimitz to provide the necessary support for this operation, and it also said that the bearer would search for a proper base for this operation in the Marianas.

I went back to Washington to pick up the letter. I had a money belt with a zipper on it and I put it in there, under my khaki uniform shirt. When I got to Guam, the admiral's aide escorted me to Nimitz's office and I told Nimitz that I had to deliver the letter to him with no one else in the room. After his aide left, I pulled up my shirt, unzipped this sweaty old money belt, and handed him the letter. He read it and said grimly, "Don't they know we've got a war going out here? This is February now. You're talking about August. Why can't we have it out here sooner?" Nimitz wanted it to be available for Iwo Jima and Okinawa.

I told him that this was the schedule and it was a very tight schedule. He wasn't happy with this. He thanked me and I left his office.

I went from there to Tinian, after scratching Guam and Saipan as sites for the operation. Tinian was a natural because it had the longest runway in the world. The island commander took me to a spot on the north end of the island and I thought this is the place to put it. It was isolated from the other bomber groups on Tinian and would be ideal for top secret operations.[38]

After training at desolate Wendover, Utah, the 509th began arriving in Tinian in late May. Tibbets was confident his group of 1,800 men "would do the work of two million soldiers."[39] "The 509th was totally isolated within its own compound, connected by taxiways to North Field," recalled Major Charles Sweeney, the B-29 test pilot from North Quincy, Massachusetts, who was in charge of training exercises. "The compound was enclosed by a high fence with a main gate that was guarded around the clock by armed sentries. . . . This area contained the only windowless, air-conditioned buildings in the Pacific. . . . Here the various components of the bombs would be assembled. . . . Anyone trying to gain access without proper clearance could be shot."[40]

Tibbets and Sweeney were the only members of the 509th who had been officially informed that the unit was preparing to drop an atomic bomb. "The men were only told what they needed to know to do their jobs," Tibbets says, although it is likely that the bombardiers, at least, soon figured out what they would be asked to do. Tibbets had little contact with the Los Alamos scientists and no interest whatsoever in the deep physics behind the bomb. "They told me it would explode with the equivalent of 20,000 tons of TNT. . . . All's I could say was that's going to be a damn big explosion."[41]

J. Robert Oppenheimer, director of the Los Alamos laboratory, explained to Tibbets that once the atomic bomb was released the delivery plane would have to make a dizzying 155 degree diving turn to get as far away from the point of explosion as possible. Otherwise the delivery plane was likely to be blown out of the sky. "This was difficult to do," Tibbets found out, "[without] snapping the tail off the airplane." In dry runs over the island of Rota, and later over Japan itself, Tibbets had his pilots practice these radical turns after releasing a single 10,000-pound bomb. These bombs were the shape and color of a pumpkin and the same size as the plutonium bomb that would be used against Nagasaki.* "I wanted them to get shot at," says Tibbets. "I wanted them to experience every possible emergency before they had an atom bomb and were really playing for keeps. I wanted the Japanese to see planes, flying alone, and to think they were on reconnaissance operations."

Tibbets planned to fly these "pumpkin runs" himself but LeMay insisted the Army could not risk having him fall into enemy hands, with knowledge of the bomb.[42]

Other airmen on Tinian resented Tibbets's "glory boys." They had the best living quarters on the island and flew the safest missions—and some of them bragged to friends in the other bomber groups that they were personally going to win the war. "The other guys had lost a lot of crews and they had to come in low, while we went in high where they couldn't get any antiaircraft or fighters up to us, so we were relatively safe," says airman Raymond Biel. "And we had brand-new planes and were getting the best of treatment from the government. To the other men, it didn't seem we were doing anything to end the war."[43]

On July 29, General Carl "Tooey" Spaatz arrived from Europe, via Washington, D.C., to take command of the Strategic Air Forces, which was created expressly for the atomic bomb missions. LeMay was made his chief of staff. Spaatz carried with him top secret orders drafted by Groves and approved by Truman:

THE 509 COMPOSITE GROUP, 20TH AIR Force, will deliver its first special bomb as soon as weather will permit visual bombing after about 3 August 1945 on one of the targets: Hiroshima, Kokura, Niigata and Nagasaki. To carry

---

*The Manhattan Project produced two types of atomic weapons, one using uranium (U-235), the other plutonium, which was created from uranium. The explosive power of the bombs resulted from the instantaneous release of energy upon the splitting, or fission, of the atomic nuclei in uranium-235 or plutonium.

These weapons had different detonation systems. The uranium bomb was set off by using a gunlike device that fired a subcritical slug of uranium (one not compact, or dense, enough to explode) into a subcritical core of uranium. The slug or bullet, was placed at one end of a long hollow tube similar to a gun barrel, with an explosive packed behind the bullet, and the core was placed at the other end of the sealed tube. When the bullet was fired and hit the core it produced a critical mass, setting in motion a self-sustaining chain reaction and a nuclear explosion.

The plutonium bomb was detonated by an implosion process. Plutonium was arranged inside the bomb in the form of a hollow sphere and surrounded by a sphere of conventional chemical explosives. When the fuse was ignited, the explosion of the outer sphere compressed the inner sphere of plutonium into a ball-like critical mass, the size of a baseball. A chain reaction and an explosion followed instantaneously.

military and civilian scientific personnel from the War Department to observe and record the effects of the explosion of the bomb, additional aircraft will accompany the airplane carrying the bomb. . . .

Additional bombs will be delivered on the above targets as soon as made ready by the project staff.[44]

Stricken from the atomic target list, as it had been from LeMay's list of cities to burn, was Kyoto. Nagasaki replaced it. It was a major military port in western Kyushu that was the home of the enormous Mitsubishi Steel and Armament Works and of a plant that made the torpedoes that were used against the American fleet at Pearl Harbor. Hiroshima, the primary target, was the southern headquarters and supply depot for the homeland army that would mount the defense of Kyushu. Located on the main island just across the Inland Sea from Kyushu, it had a population of about 350,000 and also contained a number of war industries.

The United States was about to commit the most destructive single act in the history of civilization. How had it come to this decision?

The world's first nuclear explosion occurred in the New Mexico desert, at a remote area of Alamogordo Air Force Base, in the early morning hours of July 16, 1945. Truman was notified immediately and received a detailed description of the plutonium explosion five days later at Potsdam, an undamaged suburb of Berlin where he was meeting with Stalin and Churchill. Groves's report was euphoric. The "awesome roar" of the bomb had been heard at a distance of 100 miles and the "searing light" from the explosion had been seen 180 miles away. "All seemed to feel," wrote Groves's deputy, Brigadier General Thomas F. Farrell, "that they had been present at the birth of a new age." But Groves concluded soberly, "We are all fully conscious that our real goal is still before us. The battle test is what counts."[45]

At Potsdam, Truman also secured a pledge from Stalin that Russia would soon enter the war against Japan. "I've gotten what I came for—Stalin goes to war August 15 with no strings on it," Truman wrote jubilantly to his wife on July 18. "I'll say we'll end the war a year sooner now, and think of the kids who won't get killed. That is the important thing."[46] With Russia on the move in East Asia, it would be impossible for Japan to bring in reinforcements from Manchuria, northern China, and Korea to help stop an American invasion.

On July 26 the Allied leaders at Potsdam issued an ultimatum calling for "the unconditional surrender of all the Japanese armed forces. . . . The alternative for Japan is prompt and utter destruction."[47]

None of the President's advisors opposed using the atomic bomb. But Secretary of War Stimson, Assistant Secretary of State Joseph Grew, and a number of others had tried to persuade Truman to eliminate the unconditional surrender clause of the Potsdam Declaration or at least modify it to allow the Japanese to keep their Emperor. They did so not to avoid dropping the A-bomb (Grew didn't know about the bomb), but to make an invasion unnecessary.

These proposals appealed to Truman's interest in saving lives, but to Secretary of State Jimmy Byrnes this was rank appeasement. Byrnes, the longtime Democratic leader of the Senate, had enormous influence on the President, a former senator from Missouri. The Germans had to accept unconditional surrender, he argued. Why not the Japanese? Byrnes was also concerned about Truman's standing with the American people. A Gallup poll taken on May 29 showed the American public overwhelmingly opposed to retaining the Emperor, whom they saw as a Hitler-like figure who had encouraged Japanese aggression. A third of those polled wanted him executed as a war criminal. Only 7 percent favored retaining him as a figurehead.

That spring, Americans learned of the Palawan Massacre. To prevent 150 American POWs from falling into enemy hands, Japanese soldiers on the Philippine island of Palawan put them into an air raid shelter, doused them with gasoline, and set them on fire with long torches. Some of the men—their bodies in flames—managed to escape the shelter, but most were cut down by gunfire and finished off with bayonets. Miraculously, a few escaped to tell their grisly story, which further inflamed anti-Japanese sentiment in the United States. Giving in to Stimson, Byrnes warned, "would mean the crucifixion of the President." [48]

Some scholars criticize the "uncompromising" nature of the Potsdam Declaration. But Truman was determined to overthrow the Imperial system, or *kokutai*, that was behind Japan's racist war of conquest in Asia, in the same way that Roosevelt and Churchill had vowed to eradicate Nazism root and branch. Japan must not be treated more leniently than Germany.

Truman intuited correctly that the Emperor was not a mere ceremonial figure, but an active advocate, until the dying days of the war, of a fight to the finish with the Americans. And historian Herbert Bix points out what Truman could not have known: that even the peace faction in the Japanese cabinet wanted to retain this authoritarian system. The entire cabinet and the Imperial court were fighting not for a constitutional monarchy, Bix argues, but "for a monarchy based on the principle of oracular sovereignty," a system that could allow them to continue to control the Japanese people. [49] It is unlikely, moreover, that an American guarantee of the maintenance of the Imperial system would have caused Japan to surrender before the Normandy invasion on terms acceptable to the Americans.[50]

On July 24, after agreeing to the wording of the Potsdam Declaration, Truman had learned from Stimson that one bomb would probably be ready by August 1. The President "was highly delighted," Stimson wrote in his diary.[51] Did he make his final decision to drop the bomb that day? We will never know. Probably, there was no one moment when he made up his mind. The only real decision he had to make was whether or not to stop the almost unstoppable momentum of events. Leslie Groves would later observe that Truman's "decision was one of noninterference—basically, a decision not to upset the existing plans."[52]

Truman knew the bomb would kill tens of thousands of innocent people, and that did not sit well with him. But he weighed this against the horrendous cost in American lives if the invasion were to go forward. He has been accused of crossing a moral threshold, but America had already crossed that ethical boundary with the firebombing of Tokyo and the saturation bombing of German cities in late 1944 and early 1945—raids aimed at transportation targets in tightly settled urban cores. "Every step in the bomber's progress since 1937," the editors of *Life* observed just after the atomic bombs were dropped, "has been more cruel than the last. From the concept of strategic bombing, all the developments—night, pattern, saturation, area, indiscriminate—have led straight to Hiroshima."[53] By this point in the war the mass killing of innocents had come to be seen as a narrowly military decision, independent of ethical considerations. There was no debate in Truman's circle over the ethics of the bomb.

Philip Morrison, a scientist who helped build the plutonium bomb and was at Tinian to assemble it, argues that the bomb "was not a discontinuity. We were carrying on more of the same, only it was much cheaper." One bomb, one city. "For that war, it was just one more city destroyed." The scientists who made the bomb, he argues, bear as much responsibility for its use as President Truman. The Army did not approach the physicists. "We went to the Army. I mean the scientific profession. Einstein, the pacifist, at its head. We beat on the doors and said, We must be allowed to make this weaponry or we're going to lose the war. Once we did that, we didn't stop. I didn't stop. I didn't work a forty-hour week. I worked a seventy-hour week . . . [making] weapons. . . .

"I was wildly enthusiastic, 'cause I was a long-time anti-Nazi and this was the war I expected and feared. I was caught up spontaneously and naively in this terrible war. It was a great crusade." The scientists he worked with realized, Morrison adds, "that the idea of dropping it was implicit in making it." [54]

On July 26, the day Truman released the Potsdam Declaration, the cruiser *Indianapolis* arrived at Tinian with the firing mechanism and uranium bullet (U-235) for the first bomb, nicknamed "Little Boy." The uranium core arrived by air shortly thereafter, along with the plutonium core for the second bomb, "Fat Man," named, for its shape, after Winston Churchill. This bomb was bigger and more powerful than Little Boy. A third bomb was scheduled to be sent from Los Alamos in late August, according to Groves's original timetable.

After delivering her top secret cargo, the *Indianapolis* headed for the Philippines. On July 30, she was torpedoed and sunk by a Japanese submarine. Only 317 of the sailors survived; most of the others died a horrible death in shark-infested waters because of a botched Navy rescue mission. "The *Indianapolis*," Leslie Groves wrote later, "was a very poor choice to carry the bomb. She had no underwater sound equipment, and was so designed that a single torpedo was able to sink her quickly." [55] (She was hit by two torpedoes.)

Although the Japanese had already attempted feeble peace overtures through Russia, Prime Minister Kantaro Suzuki, a seventy-seven-year-old admiral, publicly announced that they would "ignore" the Potsdam Declaration—"kill it with silence"—and continue to fight. The cabinet was almost evenly split between diehards who wanted to continue the war and those who wanted peace, albeit on terms favorable to Japan. No one in the cabinet was willing to accept the Allied demand for unconditional surrender. Truman gave the order to the air command at Tinian: "Release when ready but not sooner than August 2." [56]

Bad weather canceled the first flight, scheduled for August 3, but on August 5, meteorologists called for several consecutive days of clear visibility. "Now we were ready," Tibbets recalls. Two planes would fly to the target with the *Enola Gay*, the lead plane that Tibbets named after his mother. *The Great Artiste,* piloted by Chuck Sweeney, would drop instruments to record heat, blast, and radiation, and an unnamed plane with George Marquardt at the controls would photograph the blast. At a tense preflight briefing, Captain Parsons told the crews they would be delivering the most powerful weapon in the history of the world, but the words "atomic" and "nuclear" were apparently not used. Nor, of course, were the crews told that the uranium bomb had not, and could not be, tested because of the slow production of U-235.

THE FLIGHT AND GROUND CREW OF THE *ENOLA GAY* AFTER THE HIROSHIMA MISSION.
PAUL TIBBETS IS STANDING WITH HIS HAT ON IN THE CENTER UNDER THE PROP (NA).

(The uranium bomb was used because Los Alamos had exhausted its entire "immediate supply" of plutonium in the test bomb.)[57] Afterward, the men went to the mess hall for a preflight meal. It was 12:30 A.M., August 6, 1945. When Tibbets got up to leave, flight surgeon Don Young handed him a pillbox containing twelve cyanide capsules, one for each member of his crew. They were to be passed out if an emergency occurred. The crewmen could use them or not. There were no suicide orders.

As Chuck Sweeney's crew stowed their gear and prepared their airplane, Sweeney jumped into a jeep and drove over to Tibbets's plane. "The scene I encountered was surrealistic. There had to be two hundred people . . . standing in an island of intense light. Mobile generators were powering all forms of illumination: stands of high-intensity shop lights, floods, popping flashlights, and klieg lights like those you'd see at a grand opening of a movie. . . . Army photographers and film crews, MPs, technicians, senior officers, and civilians—who, I presumed, were the scientists— milled about." [58]

When Tibbets climbed into the cabin of *Enola Gay* he felt he was about to be a part of "the greatest single event in the history of warfare." [59]

With his plane overweight because of the four-and-a-half-ton bomb, Tibbets burned practically every inch of the runway before he eased back on the yoke and the *Enola Gay* rose majestically into the air. It was 2:45 A.M. Tinian time. Eight minutes into the flight, Captain William Parsons, the weaponeer, and his assistant, Morris Jeppson, crawled into the cramped bomb bay and inserted the explosive propellant powder into the bomb's gunlike firing mechanism and hooked up the detonator. The arming was done in the air because Parsons feared the plane stood a good chance of crashing on takeoff.

It was a perfect tropical night, with clear skies and a light breeze. As the *Enola Gay* approached the target six and a half hours later, after rendezvousing with the two other planes over Iwo Jima, the sun was shining brilliantly and visibility was perfect. Bombardier Thomas Ferebee released the bomb just seventeen seconds behind schedule. The plane jumped violently, 9,000 pounds lighter, and Tibbets made the dangerous diving turn he had been practicing for almost a year. "When we completed the turn, we had lost 1,700 feet and were heading away from our target with engines at full power. . . . Then everyone was quiet as a church mouse because we had nothing else to do," Tibbets recalls. They were about eleven miles from the drop point when a bright light filled the plane and a tremendous shock wave smashed into them. "The plane shook, and I yelled 'Flak!' thinking a heavy gun battery had found us." At a press conference the next day, co-pilot Robert Lewis told reporters he "felt as if some giant had struck the plane with a telephone pole." No one, not even Oppenheimer, was sure the plane would be able to withstand the shock of the blast. But after the second, and lighter, shock wave hit them Tibbets knew they'd survive. "And for the record, I announced over the intercom, 'Fellows, you have just dropped the first atomic bomb in history.' " [60]

George "Bob" Caron, the tail gunner, had the best view; and he was on the intercom describing the mushroom-shaped cloud that rose high above the city and

HIROSHIMA (NA).

seemed to be coming right at them. "We were not prepared for the awesome sight that met our eyes as we turned for a heading that would take us alongside the burning, devastated city," Tibbets wrote later. "The giant purple mushroom . . . had already risen to a height of 45,000 feet, three miles above our altitude, and was still boiling upward like something terribly alive. It was a frightening sight, and even though we were several miles away, it gave the appearance of something that was about to engulf us.

"Even more fearsome was the sight on the ground below. At the base of the cloud, fires were springing up everywhere amid a turbulent mass of smoke that had the appearance of bubbling hot tar. . . . The city we had seen so clearly in the sunlight a few minutes before was now an ugly smudge. It had completely disappeared under this awful blanket of smoke and fire.

"A feeling of shock and horror swept over all of us."

"My God!" Lewis wrote in his log.

The bomb detonated at 1,900 feet above the ground at 8:16 Hiroshima time, forty-three seconds after it was dropped. Almost in that instant, there was no city.

"I think this is the end of the war," Tibbets said to Lewis as they headed back to Tinian.[61]

President Truman thought the same. When he got the news, four hours later aboard the cruiser *Augusta* on his return from Potsdam, he grabbed the messenger by the hand and said, "This is the greatest thing in history."[62]

Caron could see the mushroom cloud for an hour and half as the *Enola Gay* sped southward from the horror of Hiroshima. The cloud did not disappear until they were almost 400 miles away. On their smooth return to Tinian, Tibbets smoked his pipe and then dozed off, the first time he had ever been able to sleep in an airplane. "When we landed, someone yelled, 'Attention!' and General Tooey Spaatz came forward. He pinned the D.S.C. [Distinguished Service Cross] on me while I stood at attention, palming the bowl of my pipe and trying to work the stem up my sleeve."[63] A crowd of exuberant airmen milled around the plane, cheering and shouting, and all the military brass in the Marianas was on hand.

At a press conference, none of the correspondents questioned the use of the atomic bomb. "These reporters had seen the war at first hand," Tibbets said later, "and, like every soldier I met, welcomed anything that would shorten the conflict."[64]

When news of the bomb was announced on Armed Forces Radio, American soldiers in the Pacific at last saw the end in sight. "We whooped and yelled like mad, we downed all the beer we'd been stashing away," recalled a Marine veteran of Okinawa. "We shot bullets into the air and danced between the tent rows, because this meant maybe we were going to live."[65]

That afternoon there was a raucous beer party at the Tinian officers club. "All work on the island had stopped, and . . . the order of the day was to get drunk," Chuck Sweeney recalls. But Sweeney was exhausted and ready to leave after an hour. As he started for the door of the big Quonset hut, Tibbets spotted him and waved him over. "Chuck, if it becomes necessary, the second one will be dropped on the ninth. Primary target will be Kokura. The secondary target will be Nagasaki." Then he paused and said, "You're going to command the mission." [66]

It would be Chuck Sweeney's first combat mission command.

"EVERYTHING INTO NOTHING"

None of the physicists on Tinian went to the party that night. "We obviously killed a hundred thousand people and that was nothing to have a party about," recalls Philip Morrison. "We knew a terrible thing had been unleashed." [67]

The bomb was horrifyingly successful. Pedestrians who were alive one second were vaporized the next, leaving behind nothing but shadows etched eerily into the concrete sidewalks. A Japanese journalist described the bomb's effects:

EVERYTHING STANDING UPRIGHT IN THE WAY of the blast—walls, houses, factories, and other buildings were annihilated and the debris spun round in a whirlwind and was carried up in the air. . . . Horses, dogs and cattle suffered the same fate as human beings. . . .

Beyond the zone of utter death in which nothing remained alive houses collapsed in a whirl of beams, bricks and girders. Up to about three miles from the center of the explosion lightly built houses were flattened as though they had been built of cardboard. Those who were inside were either killed or wounded. Those who managed to extricate themselves by some miracle found themselves surrounded by a ring of fire. . . .

About half an hour after the explosion, whilst the sky all around Hiroshima was still cloudless, a fine rain began to fall on the town and went on for about five minutes. It was caused by the sudden rise of over-heated air to a great height, where it condensed and fell back as rain. Then a violent wind rose and the fires extended with terrible rapidity, because most Japanese houses are built only of timber and straw.

By the evening the fire began to die down and then it went out. There was nothing left to burn. Hiroshima had ceased to exist. [68]

Victims walked around in shock, with burnt skin hanging from their arms and faces. When one infirmary ran out of medication, volunteers sterilized the wounds with salt water. People were so damaged, one volunteer soldier recalls, "We took a broom, dipped it into . . . salt water, and painted over the bodies."[69]

Dr. Michihiko Hachiya was the director of the Hiroshima Communications Hospital, which was 1,500 yards from the hypocenter, the point directly under the blast. He began keeping a diary the evening the bomb hit.

THE HOUR WAS EARLY; THE MORNING STILL, warm and beautiful. . . . Clad in drawers and undershirt, I was sprawled on the living room floor exhausted because I had just spent a sleepless night on duty as an air warden in my hospital.

Suddenly, a strong flash of light startled me—and then another. . . . Through swirling dust I could barely discern a wooden column that had supported one corner of my house. It was leaning crazily and the roof sagged dangerously.

Moving instinctively, I tried to escape, but the rubble and fallen timbers barred the way. . . . A profound weakness overcame me, so I stopped to regain my strength. To my surprise I discovered that I was completely naked. . . .

All over the right side of my body I was cut and bleeding. A large splinter was protruding from a mangled wound in my thigh, and something warm trickled into my mouth. . . . Embedded in my neck was a sizable fragment of glass.

Dr. Hachiya and his wife, Yaeko, who was also hurt, managed to escape the house. Just as they came to the street, a house across from theirs collapsed almost at their feet.

OUR HOUSE BEGAN TO SWAY, AND in a minute it, too, collapsed in a cloud of dust. Other buildings caved in or toppled. Fires sprang up and whipped by a vicious wind began to spread.

It finally dawned on us that we could not stay there in the street, so we turned our steps toward the hospital [only a few hundred yards away]. Our home was gone; we were wounded and needed treatment; and after all, it was my duty to be with the staff. . . .

I was still naked, although I did not feel the least bit of shame.

Dr. Hachiya collapsed in the street and sent his wife ahead of him to get help. After a while, he struggled to his feet and walked on, blood spurting from his leg wound.

I PAUSED TO REST. GRADUALLY THINGS came into focus. There were shadowy forms of people, some of whom looked like walking ghosts. Others moved as though in pain, like scarecrows, their arms held out from their bodies with forearms and hands dangling. These people puzzled me until I realized that they had been burned and were holding their arms out to prevent the painful friction of raw surfaces rubbing together. A naked woman carrying a naked baby came into view. I averted my gaze. . . . An old woman lay near me with an expression of suffering on her face; but she made no sound. Indeed, one thing was common to everyone I saw—complete silence.

Dr. Hachiya made it as far as the Communications Bureau, located in the building adjacent to the hospital. It was being used as an emergency hospital. His friends saw him outside the building and carried him in on a stretcher. As he was being treated, he looked up and saw that the hospital was on fire. He and the other patients were evacuated to a rear garden.

THE SKY WAS FILLED WITH BLACK smoke and glowing sparks. Flames rose and the heat set currents of air in motion. Updrafts became so violent that sheets of zinc roofing were hurled aloft and released, humming and twirling, in erratic flight. Pieces of flaming wood soared and fell like fiery swallows. . . .

The Bureau started to burn . . . until the whole structure was converted into a crackling, hissing inferno.

Scorching winds howled around us, whipping dust and ashes into our eyes and up our noses.

The Communications Bureau was evacuated, and after being carried out and finding his wife by the main gate, Dr. Hachiya passed out.

MY NEXT MEMORY IS OF AN open area. The fires must have receded. I was alive. . . .

A head popped out of an air-raid dugout, and I heard the unmistakable voice of old Mrs. Saeki: "Cheer up doctor! Everything will be all right. The north side is burnt out. We have nothing further to fear from the fire. . . ."

She was right. The entire northern part of the city was completely burned. The sky was still dark, but whether it was evening or midday I could not tell. . . .

The streets were deserted except for the dead. Some looked as if they had frozen to death while in the full action of flight; others lay sprawled as though some giant had flung them to their death from a great height.

Hiroshima was no longer a city, but a burnt-over prairie. To the east and to the west everything was flattened. . . . How small Hiroshima was with the houses gone.[70]

Of Hiroshima's 76,000 buildings, 70,000 were destroyed or damaged, for in this pancake-flat city there were no hills or ridges to blunt the sensational power of the blast. "Such a weapon," said one victim, "had the power to make everything into nothing."[71]

Treating the burn victims, doctors did not realize at first that they were dealing with an absolutely new thing—radiation sickness or what they would call atomic bomb disease. "People who appeared to be recovering developed other symptoms that caused them to die. So many patients died without our understanding the cause of death that we were all in despair," Hachiya observed in his diary.[72] Those who suffered only minor burns lost their hair, their gums bled, they vomited blood, they developed raging fevers, and they died. For weeks they died at a rate of a hundred a day.

No one will ever know how many people died at either Hiroshima or Nagasaki. Robert Oppenheimer had predicted a death toll of 20,000 from one bomb. At Hiroshima, an estimated 100,000 to 140,000 died almost immediately. Over the course of the next five years, another 100,000 died, according to Japanese records. Curtis LeMay would boast that "we scorched and boiled and baked to death more people in Tokyo on that night of March 9–10 than went up in vapor at Hiroshima and Nagasaki combined."[73] He is wrong. More people died in the atomic blasts.

LeMay has argued that it is no more "wicked" to kill people with atomic weapons than with conventional bombs. But that fails to account for radiation disease, one of the worst ways imaginable to die. Nuclear bombs continue killing long after they detonate; and they kill insidiously and across generations. Nuclear power is the fire that mankind has not yet learned to put out. "If a person picks up one rem it can linger in your cells all your life," said Marine veteran Victor Tolley, who was stationed in Nagasaki shortly after the bomb was dropped. "It may lie dormant and nothing may happen to me. But when I die and I'm cremated and my ashes are scattered out over some forest, that radiation is still alive. Twenty-seven thousand years from now, somebody might pick up that rem of radiation from those ashes of mine and come down sick."[74]

But LeMay *was* correct when he said "the crew who freighted the ordnance up to Hiroshima and Nagaski and dumped it, didn't know just what they really had. Nobody was sure about the destructive capacity, not even the scientists." [75]

After Hiroshima, Truman warned the Japanese leaders that "if they do not now accept our terms they may expect a rain of ruin from the air, the like of which has never been seen on this earth." [76] There was no response; the cabinet was still deadlocked. To their everlasting discredit, the Japanese ruling elite, including the Emperor, was more concerned about the destruction of its own power than the destruction of its country. At any point, now or before this, the rulers could have stopped the insane violence. In delaying, they risked not only more nuclear devastation, but an invasion that would have had catastrophic consequences for the Japanese people.

Orders had already been cut to drop the second bomb, and Truman made no effort to intervene. This was the most frightening aspect of early atomic diplomacy—there was no diplomacy. Once in place, the technology dictated the decision-making. Even Truman sensed this. "I fear that machines are ahead of morals," he wrote in his diary after learning of the first atomic test. [77]

Although a third bomb was not yet ready, Groves wanted the Japanese to believe that the Americans had an unlimited supply of super bombs and were prepared to use them. If two were dropped in quick succession, the enemy would not know what to expect. Or as one of Tibbets's fliers put it years later, "Hit 'em twice and make them think we've got a barrel full of these things at home. That was the psychology." [78]

Initial plans called for an August 11 drop day for the second bomb, but forecasters predicted bad weather for that day and the following five days. So Sweeney's mission was moved up to August 9. The target was still Kokura, with its enormous arsenal, a great source of strength for the army that was being mobilized to repel the American invasion. Since the intricate measuring instruments for the Hiroshima flight had been installed in Sweeney's plane, *The Great Artiste*, Sweeney and his crew would fly Fred Bock's B-29, *Bockscar*, and Bock's crew would fly *The Great Artiste*. This would lead to considerable confusion in reportage of the event. William L. Laurence of the *New York Times*, who would win a Pulitzer Prize for his coverage of the Manhattan Project, flew in *The Great Artiste* with Bock's crew yet erroneously reported in the *Times*, and in his later book, that Sweeney dropped the bomb from *The Great Artiste*. For years afterward, other authors repeated his error.

LeMay had assumed that Tibbets would fly this mission. But Tibbets told him, "I'm getting enough publicity. The other guys have worked long and hard and can do the job as well as I can." [79] He would regret that decision.

Victory

THE FORGOTTEN BOMB

This was "the forgotten bomb," says Navy Commander Frederick Ashworth, the weaponeer in charge of Fat Man, the plutonium bomb dropped on Nagasaki. "The Nagasaki strike was a kind of sideshow to the first one. There was no fanfare when we left and no fanfare when we got back. Yet few people realize that our mission was almost a national disaster."[1]

Chuck Sweeney wanted to fly a flawless mission, as Tibbets had done.[2] But from start to finish, the second most important bombing strike of the war was a succession of near-disastrous accidents, bad command decisions, and broken orders. The bomb was dropped a mile and a half from the designated target. *Bockscar* came perilously close to running out of fuel and ditching at sea. And the bomber nearly crashed on an airfield it was not scheduled to land on. One man saved the mission and the careers of the pilot and the weaponeer, who, together, broke strict orders about how the bomb was to be dropped, orders that had come down from the highest authority.

It all began with a typhoon off Iwo Jima.

***Bockscar* AFTER THE NAGASAKI MISSION (USAAF).**

"The night we were getting ready to go to Hiroshima, there were thunderstorms in the area, lightning all over the place, and you get a little skittish about lightning," recalls Ashworth, a coolly composed aviator who had commanded a torpedo squadron in the South Pacific earlier in the war. "That's bad news in the airplane business. Then we got word about a storm at Iwo Jima."

The three planes flying to the target, *Bockscar*, *The Great Artiste*, and an observation plane piloted by Colonel James Hopkins, were to take off from Tinian and rendezvous over Iwo Jima. But the weather forced them to take a different route and reassemble at Yakushima, a small island off the coast of Kyushu. "Because of the bad weather at low altitudes and our proximity to the Japanese mainland, the rendezvous would be at 30,000 feet instead of at 8,000, as on the Hiroshima mission," Sweeney wrote in his memoir, *War's End*. "This meant we would be flying through some turbulent weather for about five hours in complete radio silence. Then all three of us had to arrive at a tiny spot in the ocean within one minute of each other."[3]

At the preflight briefing, Sweeney's crew was told that they were to drop the bomb visually. These were the "only stringent orders that we had," Ashworth recalls. "General Groves wanted to be sure that we knew exactly where we were putting it, and radar bombing equipment at that time was notoriously inaccurate. There was a provision that if it couldn't be dropped by visual bombing with a Norden bombsight then we should bring it home."

Out on the flight deck, Philip Morrison and his team of scientists had just finished loading the "man-made meteor" into *Bockscar*.[4] The bomb bay doors were open, so Sweeney bent down to look. "There it was. . . . Ten feet eight inches long, five feet across, painted with high-gloss yellow enamel and black tail fins. It weighed 10,300 pounds, at least 1,000 pounds heavier than Little Boy. It resembled a grossly oversized decorative squash. I could see that many people had signed the bomb or left poems and messages with varying degrees of vitriol."[5]

The takeoff would be "dangerous because there was no way of rendering [the bomb] safe," Morrison notes.[6] Unlike the uranium bomb used at Hiroshima, the complicated implosion system was sealed inside the bomb. Ashworth would not be able to wait until after takeoff to arm Fat Man, as Parsons had "late-armed" Little Boy, with its gunlike firing mechanism. If the plane were to crash and burn on takeoff, as so many B-29s did on Tinian, the bomb might detonate. "You probably would not have had a full-scale detonation," says Ashworth, "but you'd have had a smaller one. With all that fuel aboard, you would have had a raging fire and the heat would have set off the explosives in the bomb, causing a cook-off, a low-level detonation, that would have torn the bomb apart, spreading chunks of radioactive plutonium all over that part of the island. This was a very serious consideration. The only thing that could be done was to reinforce all the fire-fighting and ambulance equipment on the field and hope that if it happened, we could put the fire out before anything went radically wrong."

Chief scientist Norman Ramsey was so concerned about a nuclear accident that he stood at the end of the runway with the emergency equipment so that in the event of an explosion he would be blown up and would not have to do any explaining.

The only people to see the plane off were a few Army photographers and "the boss," Paul Tibbets. Just as Sweeney was ready to take off, his flight engineer, Sergeant John Kuharek, leaned into the front of the cockpit and said, "Major, we have a problem. The fuel in our reserve tank in the rear bomb bay bladder isn't pumping. We've got six hundred gallons of fuel trapped back there."[7] Kuharek thought the problem was a solenoid and that it would take several hours to fix. Sweeney pulled off his harness and climbed out of the plane to consult with Tibbets. "Sweeney and Kuharek

THE CREW OF *BOCKSCAR* ON ARRIVAL AT TINIAN AFTER THE NAGASAKI MISSION. MISSING ARE FREDERICK ASHWORTH AND HIS ASSISTANT, LT. PHILIP M. BARNES. CHUCK SWEENEY IS ON THE FAR LEFT (USAAF).

walk up to the jeep I'm sitting in," Tibbets recalls, "and Sweeney says, 'We can't transfer fuel from our bomb bay.'

"I said, 'What do you give a damn about it. The fuel is only carried as ballast' [to balance the bomb in the forward bomb bay]. . . . With my airplane I had 1,000 gallons of fuel more than I needed."

Sweeney still looked concerned.

" 'Chuck,' I told him, 'you've lost a lot of time now. If you're waiting for me to tell you . . . to cancel the mission, I'm not going to. You're the airplane commander. You can say cancel or don't cancel.'

"He said, 'Well, we're gonna go.'

"When Sweeney got ready to walk away, I said, 'Chuck, you've already lost about forty-five minutes. Get back in that airplane, go to your rendezvous point and tell the other planes the same thing I told you at Iwo Jima [where Tibbets and Sweeney rendezvoused on the Hiroshima mission]: Make one 360 degree turn, be on my wing, or I'm going to the target anyway.' " [8]

Tibbets also advised Sweeney that if he ran into any problems on the bomb run he should consult with Kermit Beahan, the bombardier, who had plenty of combat experience in Europe. As they prepared for takeoff, with lightning streaking across the black sky, everyone was on edge. "Young man, do you know how much that bomb cost?" Admiral W. R. E. Purnell, a high official in the Manhattan Project, asked Sweeney. "About 25 million," said Sweeney. "See that we get our money's worth," Purnell cautioned.

As the plane raced down the runway at 150 miles per hour a horrible thought went through Sweeney's mind: Had the Japanese figured out the point of origin of the first flight? Were they out there, over the ocean, waiting for him? But the takeoff went smoothly and they cruised to the assembly point off the coast of Japan at 17,000 feet to try to get above the rough weather. At 5:30 A.M. sunlight started to fill the flight deck and the storm was behind them. "All seemed right," Sweeney recalls, "in our pressurized, air-conditioned, encapsulated universe." [9]

Sitting in the cabin of *The Great Artiste*, reporter William Laurence took out his notebook and began to write. "Somewhere beyond these vast mountains of white clouds ahead of me there lies Japan, the land of the enemy. In about four hours from now one of its cities, making weapons of war for use against us, will be wiped off the map by the greatest weapon ever made by man. In one-tenth of a millionth of a second, a fraction of time immeasurable by any clock, a whirlwind from the skies will pulverize thousands of its buildings and tens of thousands of its inhabitants. . . .

"Does one feel any pity or compassion for the poor devils about to die? Not when one thinks of Pearl Harbor and of the Death March on Bataan." [10]

When *The Great Artiste* reached Yakushima, *Bockscar* was waiting for it. The two planes began circling, waiting for the third ship, piloted by Colonel Hopkins. Sweeney's orders were to wait fifteen minutes and then head for the target. But he considered the observation plane vital to the mission, perhaps because the photographic equipment had malfunctioned on the Hiroshima flight. The minutes ticked away. They were flying under radio silence; there was no way to contact Hopkins. Sweeney circled for forty minutes, wasting precious fuel.

"I couldn't see what was going on," says Ashworth. "I was down below, in the navigator's compartment, just behind the flight deck. We started to circle and circle. . . . I remember Sweeney coming on the intercom and saying, 'Look, gang, we gotta do this right for Paul.' He wanted a perfect operation, like Tibbets had flown. That meant that three planes proceeded to the target. That's probably why he overrode his instructions to spend no longer than fifteen minutes at the rendezvous." In wasting gasoline, he "very nearly lost the mission right there.

"Finally, after forty-five minutes; I went up to Sweeney and said, 'Look, we've gotta get going. I don't care about the observers [in Hopkins's plane]. I want to be sure that the airplane carrying the instruments is the one that's with us. . . . Is it?' That's when he told me it *was* the instrument plane. . . .

"The other plane never showed up. We found out later that he was up at 39,000 feet while we were at 30,000 feet, where we were all supposed to be."

One error led to another. In frustration, unable to find the two other planes, Hopkins broke radio silence and asked Tinian, "Has Sweeney aborted?" The message caused consternation at Tinian. "Here was this plane," says Ashworth, "that was supposed to be with *Bockscar* and it had no idea where *Bockscar* was, with a 10,000-pound nuclear weapon on board. When General Thomas Farrell, Groves's deputy on Tinian, got word of this he was having breakfast. He immediately became sick and raced outside the officers' mess and vomited." [11]

Sweeney blames Hopkins for the delay at the rendezvous point, but Tibbets blames both Ashworth and Sweeney. Tibbets is convinced that Ashworth told Sweeney to wait for the observation plane. "Sweeney didn't have sense enough to know that that Navy commander couldn't tell him a damn thing. Sweeney was browbeaten by Ashworth. [Later] I told Sweeney to his face, 'Sweeney, you forget who was in command of that airplane. . . . You wasted your envelope.' " [12]

But Sweeney insists that he, not Ashworth, made the decision to "give Hopkins a little more time." [13] Tibbets was correct about one thing, however. This was the critical mistake of the mission. From here on, nothing went right.

At 9:45 *Bockscar* and *The Great Artiste* arrived over the Kokura arsenal. It was hazy and there were broken clouds, but Sweeney thought he had a chance to spot the target. He began the bomb run, turning the plane over to bombardier Kermit Beahan, the most qualified member of the crew. By acclamation, his fellow crew members had named their plane—the plane Captain Fred Bock was flying that day—*The Great Artiste* after this brawny, handsome twenty-six-year-old Texan, an artist with the bombsight as well as with the ladies. A graduate of Rice University, Beahan had flown in North Africa and Europe and been shot down four times. Although he developed a slight stutter after surviving a crash that killed his pilot and co-pilot, he was rock-steady under pressure. He may have been unlucky in combat, but he was good.

"[Beahan] hit those bomb bay doors and they opened up and the ship started to wobble a little because of the drag of the doors," recalls assistant flight engineer Ray Gallagher. "So now you're waiting. You've got your welder's goggles on to protect your eyes from the blast. You're waiting, bracing yourself for the ship to go up, because you're dropping 10,000 pounds of weight." Only seconds into the bomb run, Beahan said he couldn't see the aiming point. Smoke and clouds obscured it.

Two nights earlier, Curtis LeMay's B-29s had firebombed a steel mill in Yawata, just to the north, and shifting winds had begun to carry the heavy black smoke of the still burning factory over Kokura. Sweeney yelled, "No drop," and "at that," says Gallagher, "we were told 'no talking on the ship!' We didn't want the Japanese to be able to pick up anything. Complete silence." Flak was exploding all around the plane, making it buck and shiver. The enemy gunners had the right altitude and were zeroing in. Kokura, the Pittsburgh of Japan, was one of the most heavily defended cities in the empire.

Then Sweeney did something almost no combat pilot ever did: he made a second bomb run, giving the flak gunners another chance. "Oh boy!" said Ray Gallagher to himself. Ashworth admits he pressured Sweeney to make the second run. "I suggested to Sweeney, 'Why don't we go around 120 degrees and come in from a different direction, and maybe the wind will be such that Beahan can see what he's looking for.' But we still couldn't see the target. I did this, even though we had a potential fuel problem, because I knew General Groves wanted the second bomb dropped as soon as possible after the first one, to try to convince the Japanese we had more of these things and would use them. There was great pressure to get that second bomb dropped quickly."

"We're not playing here too long," Sergeant John Kuharek's voice came over the intercom, breaking the silence, "because we've got a problem with gas." But Sweeney made a third run! The flak got closer and Gallagher looked out and saw fighters climbing to intercept them. Beahan said, "I can't drop," and Sweeney closed the bomb doors. As he did, Gallagher muttered into his mike, "Let's get the hell out of here." [14]

"In hindsight, I recognize that this was a stupid way of doing it," Ashworth admits. "Sweeney was told at this briefing to make only one pass at the target. If he couldn't drop it he was supposed to take it to the secondary target, or bring it home. So here again, Sweeney was violating his instructions.

"We spent fifty minutes over the target and I finally said to Sweeney, 'We gotta get to Nagasaki, our secondary target.' That was a suggestion. It was Sweeney's decision. He was the commander of the aircraft, and he agreed." Sweeney was determined not to fly back to Tinian—humiliated—with the bomb.

Tibbets is convinced that neither Ashworth nor Sweeney wanted to return to Tinian because "they wanted to beat [me]. Well the elements wouldn't let 'em do it. They didn't have enough sense to see that. . . . I said to Sweeney later. 'You should have turned around and come back home. Nobody had the gun to your head.'

"I don't know why even Ashworth didn't make that decision to turn around and bring it back." In going to Nagasaki dangerously low on fuel, Sweeney jeopardized his own life and the lives of his crew. "We haven't talked about it in great length, but I told Chuck, 'You're the only bad mistake the 509th ever made.'"

Ashworth agrees. "We had the wrong guy flying the plane." Yet he blames Tibbets for picking Sweeney. "He had a bunch of experienced, combat-tested guys like Fred Bock. Yet for some reason, God only knows why, he chose Sweeney, who was green. It was a disastrous mistake and a shoddy operation. We were lucky we didn't get into more trouble than we did."

Yet it was Ashworth, under pressure from Groves to drop a second bomb soon after Hiroshima, who had suggested they go on to Nagasaki, knowing the plane had a fuel problem. In this way, atomic diplomacy figured strongly in what was nearly a catastrophic atomic mission.

On the way to Nagasaki, Kuharek informed Sweeney that he had only enough fuel for one bomb run if they were to make it to Okinawa, their emergency landing field. As they approached the target, the heart of the port city's downtown, there was dense cloud cover. A visual drop seemed impossible. What would they do with the bomb? Drop it in the ocean? "We couldn't take the bomb [back] with us," says Gallagher. "We were running out of gas and there was too much weight."

Back at Tinian, the generals and scientists worried that Sweeney, hours behind schedule, had crashed or been shot down.

"I was responsible to see that the bomb got off and got on the target," says Ashworth. "So I said to Sweeney: 'We'll make this approach by radar and hopefully the visual bombardier may be able to see the target when we get closer to it.'" Sweeney claims that he made that decision. That is unlikely, for Ashworth was in complete charge of the bomb. According to Gallagher, Ashworth made the decision and told Sweeney, "I'll back you." Sweeney didn't balk; this is what he wanted to do.

Having come this far—having gotten this deeply into trouble—neither man felt he had any other choice. They didn't want to jettison the bomb in the ocean or disconnect the firing circuit and crash-land at sea with the bomb in the bomb bay, losing it in the ocean. "We were violating orders," says Ashworth, "but in tight situations like this the man in charge has to make a decision on the spot. You simply have to step up and do it. I thought making a radar drop was the right thing to do. You can't just wring your hands. Our mission was drop the bomb on one of two targets and the second target was right below us. I wouldn't have jettisoned the bomb under any circumstances. We needed to get two off, back to back, to force a capitulation."

Now it was up to Kermit Beahan. "On his shoulders," Ashworth said later, "rested one half of the Manhattan Project's finances, namely a billion dollars that had been put into making this plutonium bomb that had to be dropped someplace."

The crew was told to prepare for a radar run. It was still overcast; no one could see the city. Thirty seconds before the bomb's release, the bomb bay doors snapped open. Twenty seconds later Beahan spotted a thin break in the clouds and hollered, "I can see it, I can see it, I've got it!" Sweeney answered, "You own it." [15] Immediately, the radar run was stopped and Beahan "took over, set up the bombsight and dropped the bomb," says assistant co-pilot Fred Olivi. "So actually, we did in the end follow orders." But they had come within seconds of violating them.

Beahan said later that he had studied the target thoroughly before the mission and knew he was somewhere over the industrial area of Nagasaki. "It was not," says Ashworth, "a blind drop, as Olivi claimed later."

"There she goes!" someone said on *The Great Artiste*, which was about a mile and a half in back of *Bockscar*.

"Captain Bock [piloting *The Great Artiste*] swung around to get out of range; but even though we were turning in the opposite direction, and despite the fact that it was broad daylight in our cabin, all of us became aware of a giant flash that broke through the dark barrier of our arc-welder's lenses and flooded our cabin with intense light," William Laurence wrote.

"We removed our glasses after the first flash, but the light still lingered on, a bluish-green light that illuminated the entire sky all around. A tremendous blast wave struck our ship and made it tremble from nose to tail. This was followed by four more blasts in rapid succession, each resounding like the boom of cannon fire hitting our plane from all directions.

"Observers in the tail of our ship saw a giant ball of fire rise as though from the bowels of the earth, belching forth enormous white smoke rings. Next they saw a giant pillar of purple fire, 10,000 feet high, shooting skyward with enormous speed."

Less than a minute later the purple fire reached the altitude of the planes. "It was no longer smoke, or dust, or even a cloud of fire. It was a living thing, a new species of being, born right before our incredulous eyes." [16]

Back in *Bockscar*, Ray Gallagher shouted to Sweeney over the intercom, "the mushroom is coming toward us! It's right under us!" That got everyone's attention because the scientists had emphatically told the crews to steer clear of the radioactive cloud. "When Sweeney became aware of it," says Fred Olivi, "he dove the aircraft down and to the right with full throttles, to pull away from the oncoming mushroom cloud. For a while I couldn't tell whether we were gaining on it, or it was gaining on us. . . . But then we began to see that we were pulling away and we escaped the radiation."

The cloud kept rising "in an elemental fury" to a height of almost 60,000 feet.[17]

The mood in *Bockscar* was relief, not elation. Beahan had gotten rid of the bomb. "If Beahan doesn't accomplish the release," Ashworth said later, "we're in a disaster situation. There would have been a board of investigation if we had bombed by radar, and we might even have missed Nagasaki, because radar bombing was notoriously inaccurate. That would have caused a national embarrassment and might even have prolonged the war. If Beahan hadn't done his job, Sweeney would never have become a general and Ashworth would never have become an admiral."

But now the pilot and the weaponeer had another problem: they had no idea of where, exactly, the bomb had landed. Beahan had gotten one quick look at Nagasaki before releasing his cargo. But Fat Man turned the city into a boiling inferno of fire and smoke, reducing ground visibility to zero. "To be able to tell headquarters back in Tinian precisely where it had gone was impossible," Ashworth admits. "I sent Tinian a coded strike report saying just that we had hit Nagasaki, but added, 'Conference recommended before any news release.' This shook them up at Tinian, I learned later. But this was the first time they had heard from us. We were running over two hours late and, before this, they had no idea where we were or what we were doing."

When they left Nagasaki, Sweeney asked Kuharek, "What are your readings for gas?"

"You've got two hours."

"What's your time from here to Okinawa?" Sweeney asked navigator Jim Van Pelt.

"You've got two hours."

Sweeney instructed radio operator Abe Spitzer to start putting out calls to the air-sea rescue teams. Spitzer got no response. With the mission running hours behind schedule, Navy rescue teams had probably left their prearranged positions, assuming that *Bockscar* was on its way safely back to Tinian. No one would be waiting for them if they had to ditch at sea.

By the time they sighted Okinawa they were flying on fortune and fumes. Sweeney repeatedly called the tower at Yontan airfield, but couldn't get a response. Losing patience, the volatile Irishman ordered the crew to fire the emergency warning flares. "Red and green flares were fired out in an arc, bursting away from the airplane." There was no answer from the field. "Mayday, Mayday," Sweeney shouted into the mike. "I yelled back toward Olivi and Van Pelt, 'Fire every goddamn flare we have on board.'" The color-coded flares went out, nearly every color in the rainbow, each color signifying a different type of problem: "aircraft out of fuel"; "prepare for crash"; "heavy damage"; "dead and wounded on board." That got their attention on the ground, and the crew could see planes peeling away from runways and emergency equipment racing toward the edge of the airstrip.

Sweeney told the crew to brace themselves for "a rough one." He was going in without clearance—into the busiest airfield in the world. And it was hard to see because the plane was filled with gray smoke from the flare guns. A B-24 was taking off just where *Bockscar* was heading and the two planes almost collided in midair. "We were hot," says Olivi. "We were going in about 160 miles an hour and when we hit the ground it must have been at least 150."

When *Bockscar* touched down halfway down the runway it bounced into the air almost twenty-five feet, and "veered violently to the left toward a line of B-24s parked wingtip to wingtip along the edge of the runway." But Sweeney muscled the plane under control with the help of its specially installed reversible propellers. Just barely missing the row of B-24s, the big bomber came to a screaming stop at the end of the island. As it rolled onto a taxi strip, one of the engines quit. Sweeney killed the other engines and slumped back in his seat. "Total silence fell over the compartment. No one made a sound." Emergency vehicles came racing toward them, sirens blaring. Sweeney opened the nosewheel door. A rescue worker stuck his head in. "Where's the dead and wounded?"

"Back there," said Sweeney, pointing to the north, toward Nagasaki.[18]

Kuharek later measured the fuel. They had seven gallons left, about one minute of flight time.

As soon as they landed at Okinawa, Ashworth had to quickly figure out where the bomb had hit so he could make a report to Tinian. "The instrument-carrying airplane landed on Okinawa shortly after we did," he recalls, "and strangely who should arrive shortly thereafter but the third plane that had never joined us. It had gone on to Nagasaki and done some observing after the bomb was dropped. So I got the three pilots together, and Beahan, and I spread out a target map on the hood of a jeep, right on the runway. After we talked it over, it became obvious that the point of detonation was the industrial Urakami River Valley, which was a mile and a half from the center of the city, our aiming point, and directly over the huge Mitsubishi Steel and

Armament Works. That was good enough for me." This long industrial valley was separated from the downtown by a ridge of hills, which contained the blast and saved tens of thousands of lives. By missing the intended target by almost two miles, Beahan had turned to cinder and ash one of Japan's stupendous industrial complexes, employing some 40,000 workers.

Ashworth and Sweeney commandeered a jeep and had the driver take them to a communications center, but "the guy manning it said, 'I'm too busy, get out of here,'" Ashworth recalls. So they went over to General Jimmy Doolittle's tent and Ashworth told a staff officer, "We have just dropped an atomic bomb on Nagasaki and need to inform Tinian." Doolittle's aide told them they had better see the general first. Doolittle had just transferred the headquarters of Eighth Air Force from England to the Pacific, in preparation for the invasion of Japan. He was all business. There would be no messages sent until they told him what they had hit. Ashworth pulled the target map out of his leather pouch. "Doolittle looked at it for a while and said, 'You know, General Spaatz will be far happier that it went off over there than if it had over the city, because there will be far fewer casualties.' Then he let me send my detailed letter message. After this, we returned to the plane. It was refueled and we flew back to Tinian. On the way we heard on Armed Forces Radio that the Russians had entered the war against Japan."

There was no word of the surrender of Japan, however. That got some of the men thinking that they might be flying another of these missions very soon. They flew the rest of the way in a somber mood, smoking cigars, drinking pineapple juice, and listening to the tunes of Glenn Miller and Tommy Dorsey.

At 10:30 P.M., *Bockscar* landed on Tinian, twenty hours after taking off. No one was there to greet them except their ground crew and one photographer—and Paul Tibbets, standing at a distance with a high-ranking Navy officer. (In a recent revision of his memoirs, Tibbets claims he had gone to bed, but that seems unlikely. Sweeney says he was there, and Tibbets would have wanted to attend the post-flight briefing.)

The next morning, Tibbets thought he would have to make a difficult decision: "what, if any action should be taken against the airplane commander, Charles Sweeney, for failure to command." But LeMay made the decision for him. After a press conference on Guam, in which nothing came out about the problems the crew experienced, LeMay called together Sweeney and Tibbets. "You fucked up, didn't you, Chuck?" LeMay confronted him. Sweeney did not respond. LeMay turned to Tibbets and told him that an investigation into the conduct of the Nagasaki mission "would serve no useful purpose." [19] So a cloak of official secrecy was thrown over the operation.

That evening, in a meeting in the Imperial Library, the militants in the Japanese cabinet were still arguing for a continuation of the war, for a suicidal battle on home soil. But the double blow of the second bomb and the Russian invasion of Manchuria gave Emperor Hirohito the leverage he had been recently seeking. He feared—as did the moderates in the cabinet—that the people might eventually revolt against the regime if it allowed the war to continue for much longer. He wanted to end the war, not to save his subjects from further suffering, but to preserve his own authority and that of the Imperial system. We must "bear the unbearable," he told the cabinet in the early hours of August 10.[20]

Later that morning, President Truman received Japan's "conditional" acceptance of the Potsdam Declaration. Japan would surrender, but only if the Emperor retained his sovereignty. To this Truman consented, over Secretary of State Byrnes's strong objections, with the stipulation that the Emperor would submit to the authority of the Supreme Allied Commander in Japan. The Emperor would stay, but the institution was now under the control of the United States, which was quite different from recognizing the Emperor's power as a condition of surrender. As Truman wrote in his diary, if the Japanese people want to keep the Emperor "we'd tell 'em how to keep him." [21]

While the Japanese considered this counterproposal, Truman suspended all B-29 bombing raids and further use of the atomic bomb. "Our production facilities were operating at such an accelerating rate," Groves wrote later, "that the materials for the next bomb would be ready for delivery to the field momentarily." During this period, seven "pumpkin" raids were made on Japan "in preparation for further atomic attacks, if they should become necessary." And General Groves's people at Los Alamos and Tinian remained in a state of high readiness to prepare additional bombs immediately should peace talks break down.[22]

After receiving no word from the Japanese for three days, Truman had Marshall order an all-out bombing attack on August 14. It was the most awesome air display of the war; more than 2,000 planes participated. "On the third day, we got orders for a maximum effort," Fred Olivi recalls. "Everything that could fly was supposed to fly against the Japanese empire. Our crew participated in that raid in a plane called *Straight Flush*. Other aircraft from islands closer to Japan got to the empire first so I think the bombs we dropped were the last bombs that were dropped on Japan."

When Chuck Sweeney and his crew returned to Tinian, after dropping a "pumpkin" on the Toyoda Auto Works at Koromo, the booze was flowing and bedlam had broken out on the island. Japan had surrendered. World War II was over. It was August 15 in the Marianas. Back in the United States, across the International Dateline, it was still Tuesday, August 14, 1945.

"I had occasion to meet some of Doolittle's fliers at an air show after the war, and one of them signed their book for me," recalls Fred Olivi. "It says 'from the first to the last.' They were the first to bomb Japan and we were the last."

In New York City a crowd estimated at two million jammed Times Square and the surrounding area in the biggest celebration in the nation's history. The "din," said the *New York Times,* was "overwhelming." [23]

It was victory, but at what a cost! An estimated 60 million people died worldwide, almost forty million of them civilians. New research indicates that as many as 27 million Russians died. China lost at least fifteen million people, Poland six million, Germany over four million, Japan over 2,700,000, among them 1,270,000 members of the armed forces killed in the years between Pearl Harbor and the surrender. (The number of Japanese killed was approximately 3 to 4 percent of the country's 1941 population of 74 million.) Millions of innocents died in calculated acts of violence and annihilation. In the bombing of England, Germany, and Japan, 1.3 million people perished, more than half of them women. The Germans, the Russians in Germany, and the

A NAVAL CONSTRUCTION BATTALION CELEBRATES
THE END OF THE WAR (NA).

Japanese in China murdered political and racial enemies in staggering numbers. And to defeat Fascist and Fascist-style regimes, the Allies lost twice as many fighting men as the Axis, among them 405,399 Americans, including over 100,000 in the Pacific.[24]

Although there was no Pacific equivalent in monstrous scale to the Holocaust, the Japanese military committed tens of thousands of atrocities against citizens and soldiers that fell under its control. Worst of all were the experiments of Unit 731, the top secret Manchurian center of the Japanese army's extensive experiments in bacteriological warfare. Several historians have documented the gruesome research conducted on live prisoners by the scientists of Unit 731, under the direction of General Shiro Ishii, a medical doctor. Experimenters drilled holes into live bodies and removed entrails; limbs were "frozen until they gave off a sound like a plank of wood when struck; eyeballs [were] forced out by the application of massive pressure to the head; bodies [were] reduced to a fifth of their weight by dehydration; knives [were] inserted into the various organs of living subjects to see which produced the quickest death; malnutrition and frostbite [were] carefully simulated, with all their agonies; Chinese civilians, Russian 'spies,' Manchurian 'bandits,' [and] American and British prisoners of war [were] infected with germs of every kind." These were sprayed onto their bodies, injected into them with needles, shot into them with bullets, or transmitted by fleas and rats that were released into the prisoners' compounds. When prisoners refused to eat food contaminated with potassium cyanide, they were machine-gunned. The bodies of the victims of these experiments were burned, and when they didn't burn thoroughly, were put into a pulverizing machine. After the war, Japanese engineers blew up the buildings and burned all the incriminating evidence.*

*Even before the war was officially over, Japanese commanders of prison camps and bacteriological warfare experiments destroyed documentation of their villainy, making it difficult to prosecute and convict them. But a number of them received what they deserved at some fifty local military tribunals that were convened all over Asia, and later in the Soviet Union. The Allies made a distinction between "major" war criminals—military and political leaders involved in what was seen as a "conspiracy to wage wars of aggression," beginning in Manchuria—and "minor" criminals, those charged with specific atrocities. In all, roughly 5,700 Japanese were indicted for these minor, or Class B and C, war crimes. Nine hundred and eighty-four convicted war criminals received death sentences (920 were actually executed) and approximately 3,500 were sentenced to prison terms. Many of those who committed some of the most heinous crimes were impossible to track down, and researchers and officials who were part of the notorious Unit 731 received secret immunity. The Americans, who controlled the trials, exempted them, including Dr. Ishii, from prosecution for turning over their research to U.S. Army and intelligence officials.

High-ranking Japanese officials accused of major, or Class A, crimes were tried at the

It was too much death to contemplate, too much savagery and suffering; and in August 1945 no one was counting. For those who had seen the face of battle and been in the camps and under the bombs—and had lived—there was a sense of immense relief. They had survived the greatest explosion of violence in human history, a war so terrible that even the atomic bomb was seen by some as an instrument of deliverance.**

"When the atom bomb ended the war, I was in the Forty-fifth Infantry Division, which had been through the European war so thoroughly that it needed to be reconstituted two or three times," writes historian Paul Fussell. "We were in a staging area near Rheims, ready to be shipped back across the United States . . . [to] the Philippines. My division . . . was to take part in the invasion of Honshu. . . . I was a twenty-one-year-old second lieutenant of infantry leading a rifle platoon. Although still officially fit for combat, in the German war I had already been wounded in the back and the leg badly enough to be adjudged, after the war, 40 percent disabled. But even if my leg

---

International Military Tribunal for the Far East, or Tokyo War Crimes Trial—the Pacific equivalent to the Nuremberg Tribunal. These trials were convened in the Japanese War Ministry, on the outskirts of the capital, on May 3, 1946, and lasted for thirty-one months. The eleven justices were from each of the countries at war with Japan. Altogether, twenty-five major military and civilian leaders were tried, the most famous of them General Hideki Tojo, who had failed in a suicide attempt in August 1945. The Emperor was not put on trial because General Douglas MacArthur, who virtually ruled Japan during the first years of the occupation, thought that this would provoke major resistance to the American occupation. The defendants, who were all incarcerated in Sugamo Prison, made an iron pact to keep their sovereign's name and reputation unsullied, despite robust protests from the Australian and French judges that he should stand trial, since only he possessed the final authority to declare war.

All but two of the defendants were found guilty of a criminal conspiracy to wage aggressive war, an unprecedented charge in international law, which did not attribute responsibility for acts of war to specific individuals or consider aggressive war a crime. Seven top Japanese officials went to the gallows: General Tojo, Koki Hirota, Prime Minister during the time of Japan's most vicious atrocities against Chinese civilians and soldiers, General Iwane Matsui, who commanded troops involved in the Rape of Nanking, General Akira Muto, head of the occupation of the Philippines, and three others. None was repentant; all of them dropped to their deaths shouting, "Banzai."

The other convicted high officials received prison sentences ranging from seven years to life. Few of those who went to prison served their full sentence. In 1958, the last of the prisoners were granted clemency and released.

**Had the atomic bombs not been dropped, and had Japan prolonged the war, Curtis LeMay would have continued, and greatly accelerated, his bombing campaign, turning Japan into a scorched wasteland and killing many more people than died at Hiroshima and Nagasaki.

buckled and I fell to the ground whenever I jumped out of the back of a truck, and even if the very idea of more combat made me breathe in gasps and shake all over, my condition was felt to be adequate for the next act. When the atom bombs were dropped and news began to circulate that 'Operation Olympic' would not, after all, be necessary, when we learned to our astonishment that we would not be obliged in a few months to rush up the beaches near Tokyo assault-firing while being machine-gunned, mortared, and shelled, for all the practiced phlegm of our tough facades we broke down and cried with relief and joy. We were going to live. We were going to grow to adulthood after all." [25]

In Okinawa, Eugene Sledge and his regiment received the news of the bombs and the surrender "with quiet disbelief coupled with an indescribable sense of relief. . . . Except for a few widely scattered shouts of joy, the survivors of the abyss sat hollow-eyed and silent, trying to comprehend a world without war." [26]

On August 15, when the Emperor spoke for the first time ever to his people, telling them the war was over, the American airmen in the Omori prisoner-of-war camp were going to work. "I didn't hear it and wouldn't have understood it anyway," recalls Hap Halloran. "The day the war ended for us was August 29, when the [Navy] came into Tokyo Bay."

Evacuation of prisoners held in Japan was to begin after the representatives of the Japanese government formally signed the articles of surrender on September 2. But when Bull Halsey was presented with evidence that prisoners were still being brutally treated, he sent a rescue mission to Tokyo Bay on August 29. It was commanded by Harold Stassen, the future governor of Minnesota and presidential candidate. "We saw about six landing craft with American flags flying," says POW Fiske Hanley. "It was the most beautiful sight I've ever seen in my life." Frank "Foo" Fujita, one of the few Japanese-Americans to be captured in the Pacific war, became so excited he jumped into the bay and swam out to meet them, along with about a dozen other prisoners.

"After I had made about forty yards, my strength left me and I started to sink. I was completely underwater but somehow managed to get my head up for one more breath. . . . The next thing I knew . . . the two largest hands ever created on earth . . . were pulling my frail 110 pounds out of the water. As the other landing craft picked up the rest of the swimmers, I lay on the deck too exhausted to move.

"As the boats pulled in the Omori docks, the whole camp was crowded at the little island's edge, and from somewhere American, British, and Dutch flags appeared and were being wildly waved. . . . We [were] about to be the first POWs liberated from Japan.

"All the POWs in camp were whooping and yelling as the landing party came ashore. . . . [Then] the Japanese camp commander . . . came storming to the dock and walked up to the commodore [Stassen] and . . . shouted: 'What are you doing here? The war is not over, officially. You must not do this!'"

Stassen was ready for him. "We are taking these prisoners of war out of here, starting right now! What's more, you are to have every Allied prisoner in the Tokyo area right here by tomorrow morning so that we can take them too!"

Then, said Fiske Hanley, "the meanest-looking Marines I've seen in my life climbed off those boats and surrounded the camp. They loaded us onto those landing craft and took us out to a beautiful hospital ship, the *Benevolence,* and we were in heaven. We ate till it came out of our ears." Hap Halloran shoved down eighteen Milky Way bars in two hours.[27]

"When I stepped on that hospital ship, all my senses were suddenly bombarded with new experiences," recalls Halloran's prison comrade, Robert Goldsworthy. "We lived like pigs for so long. All of a sudden there were nurses with starched uniforms, clean, smelling good. But my greatest thrill took place a few hours earlier, when I first boarded the ship. I had beriberi, my ankles were swollen. I had amoebic dysentery and I had yellow jaundice, and I weighed about eighty-five pounds. I was lifted onto the deck by two sailors and I stumbled over to the railing and looked at Omori prison camp and shook my fist and yelled, 'You bastards, I beat you.' Then I took a big deep breath of free air."[28]

That evening, all the ships of the liberation task force were lit, breaking the wartime procedure of blacking out ships at night. "It was a wonderful picture," says one Marine, "with all the ships flying large battle flags both at the foretruck and the stern. In the background was snowcapped Mount Fuji."[29]

During the next two weeks, more than 19,000 Allied prisoners were liberated. Freedom came for some prisoners a little earlier, when their Japanese guards capitulated. On the morning of August 15, Lester Tenney and other prisoners on the brink of death at Fukuoka Camp No. 17 were about to enter the coal mine when the guards told them to turn around and walk back to camp. The Japanese ordered everyone into the mess hall and passed out full Red Cross boxes. Everyone knew they were about to be freed. But when? Would it be that night? They were looking for a sign. Tenney, who spoke Japanese better than most of the other prisoners, was prodded to go out into the prison yard and greet one of the guards, without saluting or bowing. "I took the challenge. Out of the barracks I went, and I walked on the parade ground until I saw a guard. With one mighty heave of my hand, I waved at him and said, 'Hello.' He smiled at me, bowed, and said in English, 'Hello.' . . .

"The war was over!" [30]

On August 31, the most famous POW of the war, General Jonathan Wainwright, the commander Douglas MacArthur had left in charge of Corregidor, arrived in Tokyo and was taken to the Grand Hotel, where he had an emotional reunion with MacArthur.

Wainwright had just been released from a Manchurian POW camp four days earlier. "I rose and started for the lobby," MacArthur described that meeting in his memoirs, "but before I could reach it, the door swung open and there was Wainwright. He was haggard and aged. His uniform hung in folds on his fleshless form. He walked with difficulty and with the help of a cane. His eyes were sunken and there were pits in his cheeks. His hair was snow white and his skin looked like old shoe leather. He made a brave effort to smile as I took him in my arms, but when he tried to talk his voice wouldn't come.

"For three years he had imagined himself in disgrace for having surrendered Corregidor. He believed he would never again be given an active command. This shocked me." MacArthur embraced him and said, "Your old corps is yours when you want it." [31]

Two days later, a destroyer took Wainwright to the battleship *Missouri,* anchored in Tokyo Bay, flying the American flag that had flown over the Capitol building in Washington the day the Japanese bombed Pearl Harbor. Standing at a place of honor in the center of the deck with General Sir Arthur E. Percival, who had surrendered the British forces in Singapore and spent the balance of the war in a

GENERAL DOUGLAS MACARTHUR'S REUNION IN JAPAN WITH GENERAL JONATHAN WAINWRIGHT (NA/SC).

ADMIRAL NIMITZ AND GENERAL MACARTHUR ON
THE *MISSOURI* FOR THE JAPANESE SURRENDER (NA).

prison camp, Wainwright watched MacArthur sign the instrument of capitulation. MacArthur presented the first fountain pen he used to Wainwright, the second to Percival. After all the delegates signed the surrender document, the general, dressed in plain suntans, like the other American officers, spoke: "Let us pray that peace be now restored to the world and that God will preserve it always."[32]

At that moment 462 silver B-29s filled the sky, flying low over the stately, slate-gray battleship. They made a long majestic turn and disappeared in the mists hiding Mount Fuji. Standing on the deck of the *Benevolence*, Hap Halloran looked up and cried tears of happiness.

As the big leather folders containing the surrender documents were gathered, a GI was heard to say: "Brother, I hope those are my discharge papers."[33]

So the most destructive war in history came to an end. And it concluded, fittingly, in a holocaust that made it clear to every living man and woman that humanity could not survive another total war.

It was Douglas MacArthur, speaking by radio broadcast to the American people from the deck of the surrender ship, who uttered the first words of what everyone hoped would be a new era of peace.

"Today the guns are silent. A great tragedy has ended. A great victory has been won. The skies no longer rain death—the seas bear only commerce—men everywhere walk upright in the sunlight. The entire world is quietly at peace. The holy mission has been completed. And in reporting this to you, the people, I speak for the thousands of silent lips, forever stilled among the jungles and the beaches and in the deep waters of the Pacific which marked the way. . . .

"We have had," the general concluded, "our last chance. If we do not now devise some greater and more equitable system, Armageddon will be at our door."[34]

Remembering

"HOW WOULD YOU LIKE TO GO up to Japan tomorrow?" Paul Tibbets asked Chuck Sweeney at almost the very hour MacArthur was signing the formal surrender on the *Missouri*.[1] The next morning, with Tibbets at the controls, twenty members of the 509th, along with a few scientists, flew to Tokyo in a C-54 transport. They wanted to see Hiroshima but the runways were in no condition to handle their plane, so, after a brief stay in Tokyo, they flew to a field sixteen miles from Nagasaki. They were the first group of Americans to visit the area after the bomb blast—and they were not supposed to be there.

Tibbets was shocked by the terrible destruction in the Urakami Valley. "Block by block had been flattened, as if by a tornado. . . . Strangely, however . . . there were no bodies anywhere. . . . There were not many people in the streets in the heart of the city. But outside the areas where the damage was heaviest, in the major residential and business districts of the city, life was proceeding in an almost normal manner. The people were polite and didn't even seem to think it unusual that American airmen were there so soon after the long war."[2]

Sweeney walked alone to where ground zero would have been, 2,000 feet from the destroyed Mitsubishi Steel and Armament Works, in what had been a poverty-stricken community of small homes and industrial plants. Although there had been no firestorm as there was at Hiroshima, the bomb had obliterated the entire industrial valley. Of the approximately 70,000 people who eventually died in Nagasaki as a result of the bomb (about 40,000 immediately), almost all were from this area. Standing in this tremendous field of rubble and ruin Sweeney "thanked God that it was we who had this weapon and not the Japanese or the Germans. . . . But I felt no remorse or guilt that I had bombed the city where I stood. . . . My crew and I had flown to Nagasaki to end the war, not to inflict suffering." [3]

Tibbets's reaction mirrored Sweeney's. He had no animosity toward the Japanese people. He saw himself fighting against an evil system imposed on the people by a powerful military regime. That is why, he says, "I have no personal feeling of guilt about the terror that we had visited upon their land." Tibbets has never deviated from that position. [4]

"Please try to understand this," he told reporter Bob Greene forty-five years after the war. "It's not an easy thing to hear, but please listen. There is no morality in warfare. You kill children. You kill women. You kill old men. You don't seek them out, but they die. That's what happens in war." [5]

Tibbets has no patience with revisionist historians who claim the bomb would not have been used on Caucasians. "If the Germans had not surrendered, I would have flown the bomb over there. I would have taken some satisfaction in that—because they shot me up. . . . My instructions were to create an elite bombing force . . . with the understanding that, when trained, they would be divided into two groups: one to be sent to Europe and the other to the Pacific. . . . There was no Japanese target priority," he argues in his own book on the flight of the *Enola Gay*. "All our early planning assumed that we would make almost simultaneous bomb drops on Germany and Japan." [6]

Where were the dead victims of the Nagasaki blast that Tibbets failed to see on his visit to the city? Where were the wounded? The dead were vaporized or already in their final resting place. The wounded were packed into emergency centers, like the one run by Dr. Takashi Nagai, a professor of radiology at the medical school of the University of Nagasaki. Dr. Nagai had been swept into the air and injured by the atomic blast. His house was buried and his wife killed. A few days later, he carried her blackened bones to a relief center in the countryside, where he gathered together a small band of doctors, nurses, and students. They were working night and day to help the sick and dying while Sweeney and Tibbets were touring the city. Nagai and his colleagues were in the country because the bomb had destroyed the Nagasaki Hospital and Medical College. It had also killed half of the city's medical personnel.

Nagai was a devout Catholic and most of the victims he treated were from his parish church, the Urakami Cathedral, only 500 yards from the hypocenter. The area around the cathedral, the largest in East Asia, contained over half of the city's 14,000 Roman Catholics, who traced their religious roots back to the conversion efforts of St. Francis Xavier in the sixteenth century. Almost all of them were killed by the blast, which also destroyed the cathedral.[7]

After closing down his relief center in the mountains, Nagai moved to a small hut built on the site of his former house. He began a life of meditation and prayer, surrendered almost all of his earthly belongings, and dedicated his life to the desperately poor people of the neighborhood. He died in 1951, and today his home is a shrine, visited by people from all over the world. Some of them remember Nagai's dying words. "Grant that Nagasaki may be the last atomic wilderness in the history of the world."[8]

For those who lived through the worst of it, it was a war that was never over. "Instead of talking about it, most [American fighting men] didn't talk about it," said James Jones. "It was not that they didn't want to talk about it, it was that when they did, nobody understood it. It was such a different way of living, and of looking at life even, that there was no common ground of communication in it."

Long after the war, an infantryman who had fought in the Battle of the Bulge got talking to Jones at a bar. He said his platoon had taken some prisoners near St. Vith. "There were eight of them, and they were tough old timers, buddy. Been through the mill from the beginning. It was about the fourth or fifth day, and we needed some information. But they weren't talking, not those tough old birds. You had to admire them. So we took the first one off to the side, where they could see him, and shot him through the head. Then they all talked. They were eager to talk. Once they knew we were serious. Horrible? Evil? . . . We needed that information. Our lives depended on it. We didn't think it was evil. Neither did they. But how am I going to tell my wife about something like that? Or my mother?"[9]

Nor could folks back home fully understand the comradeship and love that kept Marines like Eugene Sledge together under the most awful assaults on their humanity—or the horrifying mental torture that some men experienced, pain that persisted for years after the fighting ended.

Airman Ray Halloran walked through a hell storm after the war.

WHEN I GOT HOME I WAS NOT that boy my parents saw go away. I met them, for a few hours, at the train station on my way to a hospital in West Virginia. They looked real worried. I was limping badly and they were convinced I'd lost a leg. I told them I hadn't, but I didn't want to prove it by pulling up my pants. If I had they would have seen the nasty scars from the lice and flies that had bit me in my cage. I think they could also see that, mentally, I wasn't in good shape. I was a little strange.

At the Army hospital at White Sulphur Springs, I got excellent care, but I couldn't talk to the doctors and nurses about my feelings. They didn't know what was inside me. Only the other patients did, those who had suffered in the war. We hardly ever talked about our experiences; but you looked at another patient and you knew he understood. They were the only people I could communicate with, so I was afraid to leave the hospital.

After a while, I made a try of it, took a shot at normal life. I got a job and in 1953 I got married and we adopted three children. I was okay most of the time but the nights were bad. I broke windows and did a lot of other dumb things, like running out in the streets screaming. That terrified my wife and children.

I had horrible nightmares. I dreamed I was falling through space and was trying to reach out for something. I saw fires all around me, and people beating me. I'd crawl in closets and under the bed to get away from what was happening to me. I didn't talk much about it. I thought it was my problem to solve.

I never wanted to go back to Japan—never! They had done this to me, especially the guards that beat me, like this guy we called "Horseface." I could have killed him. But then I decided to go back. I did it because I thought it would help me get rid of the nightmares. I had to get better. I couldn't go on the way I was. If I could see things that were still real inside my head—the torture prison, the city burning down around it, almost killing me, the people who beat me—see them as they are now, not as they were back then, maybe that would help me get better. My wife thought I was goofy but nothing else was working.

I had a contact. I had been in touch with one of my former prison guards, the only one in the prison who treated me like a human being. Before this, I arranged for him to come to study at the University of Illinois. There should be a reward for good people, I think. He would be the anchor I needed over there.

He and his wife met me at the airport and we had dinner at the Palace Hotel overlooking the Palace grounds, right near where I was a prisoner of the Kempeitai. This worked out well. I started feeling blood and air coming back into me. I even got up in the middle of the night and walked around the perimeter of the Palace grounds. Was I looking for the torture prison? Maybe I was.

Later I found out where it had been. At first, no one would tell me. Everyone claimed they knew nothing about it. But some people arranged to have me taken there. It was done in secret. The people in the building said I was at the wrong place. I knew they were wrong. I looked around, and then left. No one there could hurt me anymore. I started to feel better.

I traveled all over Japan on the trains. I went to a town called Shizuoka, where I met a doctor who spoke perfect English. He took me to a small mountain in the middle of the town that had been turned into a memorial. Two B-29s had slammed into one another and crashed in the town. A Buddhist monk found the mangled bodies and buried them on the mound. They were human beings, he told the angry townspeople. They deserved a proper burial. He also built a memorial for them, a simple but handsome obelisk. On the other side of the mound he had built an identical memorial for the 2,000 people of the town who had been killed during that raid.

The doctor brought along two bouquets of flowers. He handed me one. He said, "You put yours by the monument for our people and I'll put mine by the monument for your people." It was a beautiful setting, on the crest of a hill overlooking the town. We both prayed and then quietly walked down the hill, each lost in our own thoughts. We went to his home and he made me feel at ease.

After this trip, I saw Japan in a different way. I wasn't ready to change my final judgment. Nor had I conquered all my demons. But I was getting better. And now after five trips over there I have lots of Japanese friends and I can say that I have no animosity toward the Japanese people. And gradually, I've become a more settled person. I'm not normal yet. But I don't have anger in me.

I guess it's kind of selfish. I've used the people who made me sick to help me get better.[10]

PACIFIC D-DAY
INVASIONS: 1942 - 1945

The following is a list of the 126 American amphibious invasions in the war in the Pacific. It was compiled using official Army and Marine sources and was prepared in association with Martin Morgan, the research historian at the National D-Day Museum in New Orleans.

DATE	SITE	DATE	SITE
August 7, 1942	Guadalcanal	June 30, 1943	Rendova
August 7, 1942	Tulagi	June 30, 1943	Baraulu
August 7, 1942	Gavatu	June 30, 1943	Sasavele
August 7, 1942	Tanambogo	June 30, 1943	Vangunu
August 7, 1942	Florida	August 12, 1943	Baanga
August 30, 1942	Adak	August 13, 1943	Vela Cela
January 11, 1943	Amchitka	August 15, 1943	Vella Lavella
February 21, 1943	Banika	August 15, 1943	Kiska
February 21, 1943	Pavuvu	August 27, 1943	Arundel
May 11, 1943	Attu	September 13, 1943	Sagekarasa
June 22, 1943	Woodlark	October 6, 1943	Kolombangara
June 23, 1943	Kiriwina	October 27, 1943	Choiseul
June 30, 1943	New Georgia	November 1, 1943	Bougainville

DATE	SITE	DATE	SITE
November 1, 1943	Puruata	February 17, 1944	Bogon
November 3, 1943	Torokina	February 17, 1944	Engebi
November 20, 1943	Tarawa	February 17, 1944	Parry
November 21, 1943	Bairiki	February 29, 1944	Los Negros
November 20, 1943	Makin	March 11, 1944	Butjo Mokau
November 20, 1943	Butaritari	March 12, 1944	Huawei
November 20, 1943	Kotabu	March 15, 1944	Manus
November 22, 1943	Kuma	March 20, 1944	Emirau
November 21, 1943	Abemama	April 1, 1944	Koruniat
November 26, 1943	Buariki	April 1, 1944	Ndrilo
December 15, 1943	Arawe	April 3, 1944	Rambutyo
December 26, 1943	Cape Gloucester	April 9, 1944	Pak
January 2, 1944	Saidor	April 22, 1944	Aitape
February 1, 1944	Majuro	April 22, 1944	Hollandia
February 1, 1944	Calalin	April 23, 1944	Tumleo
February 1, 1944	Dadap	April 23, 1944	Seleo
February 1, 1944	Kwajalein	May 17, 1944	Wakde
February 1, 1944	Ninni	May 18, 1944	Insoemoar
February 1, 1944	Gea	May 27, 1944	Biak
February 1, 1944	Gehh	June 15, 1944	Saipan
February 1, 1944	Ennylabegan	July 2, 1944	Noemfoor
February 1, 1944	Enubuj	July 21, 1944	Guam
February 1, 1944	Ebeye	July 22, 1944	Cabras
February 1, 1944	Mellu	July 24, 1944	Tinian
February 1, 1944	Ennuebing	July 30, 1944	Sansapor
February 1, 1944	Ennumennet	September 15, 1944	Peleliu
February 1, 1944	Ennubirr	September 15, 1944	Angaur
February 1, 1944	Ennugarrett	September 15, 1944	Morotai
February 1, 1944	Roi	September 22, 1944	Ulithi
February 1, 1944	Namur	October 20, 1944	Leyte
February 4, 1944	Loi	December 15, 1944	Mindoro
February 4, 1944	Burnet	January 3, 1945	Marinduque
February 5, 1944	Bigej	January 9, 1945	Lingayen Gulf
February 5, 1944	Gugegwe	January 11, 1945	San Fabian
February 6, 1944	Ennugenliggelap	January 29, 1945	San Narcisco
February 12, 1944	Rooke	February 19, 1945	Iwo Jima
February 15, 1944	Nissan	February 19, 1945	Samar
February 17, 1944	Eniwetok	February 28, 1945	Palawan
February 17, 1944	Rujoru	March 10, 1945	Zamboanga
February 17, 1944	Aitsu	March 18, 1945	Panay

DATE	SITE	DATE	SITE
March 26, 1945	Cebu	March 29, 1945	Negros
March 26, 1945	Aka	April 1, 1945	Legaspi
March 26, 1945	Geruma	April 1, 1945	Okinawa
March 26, 1945	Hokaji	April 3, 1945	Masbate
March 26, 1945	Zamami	April 10, 1945	Tsugen
March 26, 1945	Yakabi	April 16, 1945	Ie Shima
March 26, 1945	Keise	April 18, 1945	Parang
March 27, 1945	Tokashiki	April 28, 1945	Macajalar Bay
March 27, 1945	Kuba	June 26, 1945	Kume
March 27, 1945	Amuro	July 12, 1945	Sarangani Bay

ORGANIZATION OF THE UNITED STATES GROUND FORCES, WORLD WAR II

(All numbers are approximations, as the number of men in each military unit fluctuated with the changing pace and character of the war and the number of replacements available.)

Platoon	20–50 men
Company	100–200 men in 3–5 platoons
Battalion	600–1,100 men in 3–5 companies
Regiment or Brigade	1,800–3,200 men in 2 or more battalions
Division	10,000 men in 3 or more regiments or brigades
Corps	50,000 men in 2 or more divisions
Army	100,000 men in 2 or more corps
Army Group	500,000 men in 2 or more armies

Source: Williamson Murray and Allan R. Millett, *A War to Be Won: Fighting the Second World War* (Cambridge: Harvard University Press, 2000), 580.

RANKS, OFFICERS, UNITED STATES ARMY, AIR FORCE, AND MARINES

General of the Army
General
Lieutenant General
Major General
Brigadier General
Colonel
Lieutenant Colonel
Major
Captain
First Lieutenant
Second Lieutenant

RANKS, OFFICERS, UNITED STATES NAVY

Admiral of the Fleet
Admiral
Vice Admiral
Rear Admiral
Commodore
Captain
Commander
Lieutenant Commander
Lieutenant
Sub-Lieutenant
Midshipman

ABBREVIATIONS
DLM: Donald L. Miller
EC: The Peter S. Kalikow Oral History Collection of the Eisenhower Center for American Studies, New Orleans, Louisiana, courtesy of the National D-Day Museum, New Orleans, Louisiana.

CHAPTER 1: THE RISING SUN
1. *New York Times* (April 19, 1940).
2. Michael A. Barnhart, "Japan's Economic Security and the Origins of the Pacific War," *Journal of Strategic Studies* 4 (June 1981), 106.
3. Ibid., 107.
4. Takehiko Yoshihashi, *Conspiracy at Mukden: The Rise of the Japanese Military* (New Haven: Yale University Press, 1963), 14; Daniel Yergin, *The Prize: The Epic Quest for Oil, Money, and Power* (New York: Simon & Schuster, 1991), 305.
5. Saburo Ienaga, *The Pacific War: A Critical Perspective on Japan's Role in World War II* (New York: Pantheon, 1978; originally published, 1968), 57; Iris Chang, *The Rape of Nanking: The Forgotten Holocaust of World War II* (New York: Basic Books, 1999); estimates of the number of Chinese killed in Nanking and its vicinity range up to 340,000. See Daqing Yang, "Convergence or Divergence? Historical Writings on the Rape of Nanking," *American Historical Review* 104: 3 (June 1999), 850.

6. Meirion Harries and Susie Harries, *Soldiers of the Sun: The Rise and Fall of the Imperial Japanese Army* (New York: Random House, 1991), 223.

7. Evans F. Carlson, *Twin Stars Over China* (New York: Dodd, Mead, 1940), 168.

8. Yergin, *Prize*, 307.

9. Akira Iriye, *Power and Culture: The Japanese-American War, 1941–1945* (Cambridge: Harvard University Press, 1981), 12; Ronald H. Spector, *Eagle Against the Sun: The American War with Japan* (New York: Vintage, 1985; originally published, 1984), 62.

10. James W. Morley, ed., *Deterrent Diplomacy: Japan, Germany, and the USSR, 1935–1940* (New York: Columbia University Press, 1976), 298–99; Herbert P. Bix, *Hirohito and The Making of Modern Japan* (New York: HarperCollins, 2000), 374.

11. Jonathan Marshall, *To Have and Have Not: Southeast Asian Raw Materials and the Origins of the Pacific War* (Berkeley: University of California Press, 1950) x.

12. Ibid., 13.

13. Senate Naval Affairs Committee, hearings, *Nomination of William Franklin Knox* (Washington: U.S. Government Printing Office, 1940), 9.

14. "Japan furnishes" and Gallup Poll of June 1939 in Yergin, *Prize*, 310. *The Good Earth* was also made into a popular Hollywood movie.

15. Asada Sadao, "The Japanese Navy and the United States," in *Pearl Harbor As History*, Dorothy Borg and Shumpei Okamoto, eds. (New York: Columbia University Press, 1973), 251. For Yamamoto, see Hiroyuki Agawa, *The Reluctant Admiral: Yamamoto and the Imperial Navy* (Tokyo: Kodansha, 1979).

16. Quoted in Yergin, *Prize*, 317.

17. Quoted in Iriye, *Power and Culture*, 27.

18. Quoted in Marshall, *Have and Have Not*, 124.

19. Yergin, *Prize*, 318.

20. Iriye, *Power and Culture*, 28.

21. Quoted in Yergin, *Prize*, 320.

22. Quoted in Ienaga, *Pacific War*, 133.

23. Quoted in Spector, *Eagle Against the Sun*, 76.

24. Quoted in Marshall, *Have and Have Not*, 135.

25. Bix, *Hirohito*, 408–18.

26. Bix, *Hirohito*, 410.

27. Quoted in Yergin, *Prize*, 322.

28. Michael A. Barnhart, *Japan Prepares for Total War: The Search for Economic Security, 1919–1941* (Ithaca: Cornell University Press, 1987), 263.

29. Quoted in Bix, *Hirohito*, 416.

30. Agawa, *Reluctant Admiral*, 79–84, 138–40. For the best description and analysis of the Pearl Harbor plan, see Gordon W. Prange with David M. Goldstein and Katherine V. Dillon, *At Dawn We Slept: The Untold Story of Pearl Harbor* (New York: Penguin, 1991; originally published, 1981).

31. Quoted in Bix, *Hirohito*, 428.

32. Ireye, *Power and Culture*, 31.

33. Bix, *Hirohito*, 428–29.

34. Quoted in Ienega, *Pacific War*, 135.

35. Quoted in ibid., 140.

36. Quoted in Bix, *Hirohito*, 435.

37. Hull and Nomura quotations are from Prange, *At Dawn*, 554.

38. David Kahn, "Why Weren't We Warned?" *World War II*, Pearl Harbor Commemorative Issue (2001), 97.

39. Captain Mitsuo Fuchida, "I Led the Air Attack on Pearl Harbor," *U.S. Naval Institute Proceedings* (September 1952), 939–52.

40. Interview with James F. Anderson by John T. Matson, U.S. Naval Institute, 1981.

41. Interview with Stephen Bower Young by DLM; Young, *Trapped at Pearl Harbor: Escape from Battleship Oklahoma* (Croton-on-Hudson, N.Y.: North River, and Annapolis, Md.: Naval Institute Press, 1991), passim.

42. Quoted in Yergin, *Prize*, 327.

43. Samuel Eliot Morison, *Two-Ocean War: A Short History of the United States Navy in the Second World War* (Boston: Little, Brown, 1963), 59.

44. Quoted in Ienaga, *Pacific War*, 141.

45. Quoted in Bix, *Hirohito*, 437.

46. Robert Sherwood, *Roosevelt and Hopkins: An Intimate History* (New York: Harper, 1950), 428.

47. Quoted in John Keegan, *The Second World War* (New York: Viking, 1989), 240.

48. Gerhard L. Weinberg, *A World at Arms: A Global History of World War II* (Cambridge: Cambridge University Press, 1994), 250–55, 262.

49. Robert Guillain, *I Saw Tokyo Burning: An Eyewitness Narrative from Pearl Harbor to Hiroshima* (Garden City, N.Y.: Doubleday, 1981), 1–3.

50. James Jones, *WW II* (New York: Ballantine, 1975), 25.

51. Quoted in Hans G. Von Lehmann, "Japanese Landing Operations in World War II," in Merrill L. Bartlett, ed., *Assault from the Sea: Essays on the History of Amphibious Warfare* (Annapolis, Md.: Naval Institute Press, 1983), 195.

52. Edwin Ramsey, oral history, *American Experience*, WGBH, Boston.

53. Lester I. Tenney, *My Hitch in Hell: The Bataan Death March* (Washington and London: Brassey's, 1995), 20–21.

54. William Manchester, *American Caesar: Douglas MacArthur, 1880–1964* (New York: Dell, 1978), 230, 233.

55. Quoted in ibid., 233.

56. Quoted in ibid., 269; see also 274.

57. Carlo D'Este, *Eisenhower: A Soldier's Life* (New York: Henry Holt, 2002), 294–96. Eisenhower also blamed MacArthur's air chief, Major General Louis H. Brereton.

58. MacArthur and Romulo quotations in Manchester, *American Caesar*, 311–12.

59. Quoted in D. Clayton James, *The Years of MacArthur, 1942–1945*, vol. 1 (Boston: Houghton Mifflin, 1975), 128.

60. Tenney, *Hitch*, 32–33.

61. Ibid., 34.

62. Ienaga, *Pacific War*, 49.

63. Quoted in Elizabeth M. Norman, *We Band of Angels: The Untold Story of American Nurses Trapped on Bataan by the Japanese* (New York: Random House, 1999), 13.

64. Tenney, *Hitch*, 42.

65. Interview with Hattie Brantley, Lou Reda Productions.

66. Ienaga, *Pacific War*, 53.

67. Frank Gibney, ed., *Senso: The Japanese Remember the Pacific War* (New York: M. E. Sharpe, 1995), 53–54; on Japan's armed forces, see Hayashi Saburo, *KOGUN: The Japanese Army in the Pacific War* (Quantico, Va.: Marine Corps Association, 1989).

68. Interview with Kermit Lay, Lou Reda Productions; Gavan Daws, *Prisoners of the Japanese: POWs of World War II in the Pacific* (New York: William Morrow, 1994), 75.

69. Lester Tenney's account is pieced together from three sources: his interview with DLM, his interview with Lou Reda Productions, and his book *My Hitch in Hell*.

70. Quoted in Arthur Zich, *The Rising Sun* (New York: Time-Life Books, 1977), 100.

71. Lay interview.

72. Tenney interview, Lou Reda Productions.

73. Ibid.

74. Lay interview.

75. Jeter A. Isely and Philip A. Crowl, *The U.S. Marines and Amphibious War: Its Theory, and Its Practice in the Pacific* (Princeton, N.J.: Princeton University Press, 1951), 76.

76. Morison, *Two-Ocean War*, 88.

77. Ibid.; Yergin, *Prize*, 351–54.

78. Weinberg, *World at Arms*, 324–26.

79. Quoted in Nathan Miller, *War at Sea: A Naval History of World War II* (New York: Oxford University Press, 1995), 235–36.

80. Ted W. Lawson, *Thirty Seconds Over Tokyo* (New York: Random House, 1943), 64–66.

81. Walter J. Boyne, *Clash of Titans: World War II at Sea* (New York: Simon & Schuster, 1995), 167.

82. Quoted in John Keegan, *Intelligence in War: Knowledge of the Enemy from Napoleon to Al-Qaeda* (New York: Alfred A. Knopf, 2003), 196.

83. Mitsuo Fuchida and Masatake Okumiya, *Midway: The Battle That Doomed Japan: The Japanese Navy's Story* (Annapolis, Md.: Naval Institute Press, 1955).

84. Dan Van der Vat, *The Pacific Campaign: The U.S.-Japanese Naval War, 1941–1945* (New York: Simon & Schuster, 1991 ed.), 180.

85. For an excellent analysis of the role of intelligence in the battle, see Keegan, *Intelligence in War*, Chapter 6.

86. Gilbert Cant, *America's Navy in World War II* (New York: John Day, 1943), 233–34.

87. Quoted in Walter Lord, *Incredible Victory* (New York: Harper & Row, 1967), 86.

88. Morison, *Two-Ocean War*, 156.

89. Victor Davis Hanson, *Carnage and Culture: Landmark Battles in the Rise of Western Power* (New York: Doubleday, 2001), 345.

90. Quoted in Richard Overy, *Why the Allies Won* (New York: W. W. Norton, 1996), 42.

91. Fuchida and Okumiya, *Midway*, 177.

92. Keegan, *Second World War*, 275, 278.

93. Clarence E. Dickinson and Boyden Sparks, "The Target Was Utterly Satisfying," in S. E. Smith, *The United States Navy in World War II* (New York: William Morrow, 1966), 279–80.

94. Fuchida and Okumiya, *Midway*, 177.

95. Quoted in Van der Vat, *Pacific Campaign*, 190.

96. Fletcher Pratt, *The Navy's War* (New York: Harper & Bros., 1944), 128–31

97. Quoted in Van der Vat, *Pacific Campaign*, 193.

98. Quoted in Lord, *Incredible Victory*, 251.

99. Quoted in Boyne, *Clash of Titans*, 193.

100. Fuchida and Okumiya, *Midway*, 11.

101. Quoted in Morison, *Two-Ocean War*, 162.

102. Quoted in Overy, *Why the Allies Won*, 43.

103. Jones, *WW II*, 39.

104. Jack Belden, *Retreat with Stilwell* (New York: Alfred A. Knopf, 1943), 305–58.

CHAPTER 2: THE HARD WAY BACK

1. Jones, *WW II*, 48.

2. William J. Murphy, "The Right Way. The Wrong Way. The Navy Way," unpublished ms, EC; Isely and Crowl, *Amphibious War*, 103.

3. Quoted in John A. Lorelli, *To Foreign Shores: U.S. Amphibious Operations in World War II* (Annapolis, Md.: Naval Institute Press, 1995), 50.

4. Quoted in Spector, *Eagle Against the Sun*, 195.

5. Thayer Soule, *Shooting the Pacific War: Marine Corps Combat Photography in WWII* (Lexington: University of Kentucky Press, 2000), 4.

6. William Manchester, *Goodbye, Darkness: A Memoir of the Pacific War* (Boston: Little, Brown, 1987), 209.

7. *Newsweek* (October 5, 1942), 20.

8. Quoted in Thomas Buell, *Master of Seapower: A Biography of Fleet Admiral Ernest J. King* (Boston: Little, Brown, 1980), 221.

9. E. B. Potter, *Bull Halsey* (Annapolis, Md.: Naval Institute Press), 157.

10. Quoted in Richard Tregaskis, *Guadalcanal Diary* (New York: Random House, 1943), 221.

11. Isely and Crowl, *Amphibious War*, 135.

12. Quoted in ibid.

13. Quoted in Miller, *War at Sea*, 286.

14. Ira Wolfert, *Battle for the Solomons* (Boston: Houghton Mifflin, 1943), 341.

15. Quoted in Richard B. Frank, *Guadalcanal: The Definitive Account of the Landmark Battle* (New York: Random House, 1990), 441.

16. Tregaskis, *Guadalcanal Diary*, 56.

17. Robert L. Schwartz, "The Big Bastard," in *The Best from "Yank, the Army Weekly"* (New York: E. P. Dutton, 1945), 43–47.

18. Quoted in Morison, *Two-Ocean War*, 208.

19. Interview with Paul Moore, Jr., Columbia University Oral History Collection.

20. Quoted in Desmond Flower and James Reeves, eds., *The War: 1939–1945, A Documentary History* (New York: Da Capo Press, 1997), 715.

21. Moore interview.

22. Major General Carl W. Hoffman, U.S. Marine Corps (ret.), oral history transcript, Marine Corps Oral History Collection, Marine Corps Historical Center, Washington, D.C.

23. Quoted in S. E. Smith, ed., *The United States Marine Corps in World War II* (New York: Random House, 1969), 266–67.

24. John Hersey, *Into the Valley: A Skirmish of the Marines* (New York: Alfred A. Knopf, 1943), 56.

25. Quoted in Kenneth S. Davis, *Experience of War* (Garden City, N.Y.: Doubleday, 1965), 308.

26. Quoted in Hersey, *Into the Valley*, 56.

27. James Jones, *The Thin Red Line* (New York: Charles Scribner's Sons, 1962), 156–57.

28. Quoted in Eric M. Bergerud, *Touched with Fire: The Land War in the South Pacific* (New York: Viking, 1996), 411–12.

29. Quoted in ibid., 412.

30. Quoted in James Merrill, *A Sailor's Admiral: A Biography of William E. Halsey* (New York: Crowell, 1976), 73.

31. Jones, *WW II*, 28.

32. James A. Michener, "After the War: Victories at Home," *Newsweek* (January 11, 1993), 26.

33. Quoted in Hersey, *Into the Valley*, 11; Isely and Crowl, *Amphibious War*, 144–45.

34. Quoted in Tregaskis, *Guadalcanal Diary*, 401.

35. John Hersey, "The Battle of the River," *Life* (November 23, 1942), 116.

36. Jones, *WW II*, 54.

37. Ira Wolfert, "Heroes Don't Win Wars," in Louis Snyder, ed., *Masterpieces of War Reporting* (New York: J. Messner, 1962), 191–95.; "desperate terrain" in Smith, ed., *Marine Corps*, 332.

38. Samuel E. Stavisky, *Marine Combat Correspondent: World War II in the Pacific* (New York: Ballantine, 1999), 80–81.

39. Quoted in Manchester, *Goodbye, Darkness*, 231.

40. Jones, *WW II*, 122–24.

41. George H. Johnston, *The Toughest Fighting in the World* (New York: Duell, Sloan & Pearce, 1943), 167–68.

42. Robert L. Eichelberger, *Our Jungle Road to Tokyo* (Nashville: Battery Classics, 1989), 21–23.

43. Ibid., 33–34.

44. Dave Richardson, "No Front Line in New Guinea," in Debs Myers, Jonathan Kilbourn, and Richard Harrity, eds., *Yank, the GI Story of the War* (New York: Duell, Sloan, and Pearce, 1947), 43.

45. Patrick J. Robinson, *The Fight for New Guinea* (New York: Random House, 1943), 165.

46. Eichelberger, *Our Jungle Road,* 48–49.

47. Diaries collected by Eichelberger's staff, in ibid., 53–55.

48. Quoted in ibid., 51.

49. Jay Luvass, ed., *Dear Miss Em: General Eichelberger's War in the Pacific, 1942–1945* (Westport, Conn: Greenwood Press, 1972), 64–65.

50. Quoted in Geoffrey Perret, *Old Soldiers Never Die: The Life of Douglas MacArthur* (New York: Random House, 1996), 329.

51. For the war in North Africa see Rick Atkinson, *An Army at Dawn: The War in North Africa, 1942–1943* (New York: Henry Holt, 2004).

52. For the Battle of the Atlantic, see Michael Gannon, *Operation Drumbeat: The Dramatic True Story of Germany's First U-Boat Attacks Along the American Coast in World War II* (New York: Harper & Row, 1990); Clay Blair, *Hitler's U-Boat War,* vol. 1, *The Hunters, 1939–42* (New York: Random House, 1996); and the definitive account by Samuel Eliot Morison, *The Battle of the Atlantic: September 1939–May 1943* (Boston: Little, Brown, 1957).

53. Karl Doenitz and R. H. Stevens with David Woodward, *Memoirs: Ten Years and Twenty Days* (Cleveland: World, 1959), 341.

54. Jones, *WW II,* 85.

55. Ernie Pyle, *Here Is Your War* (New York: Pocket, 1945), 555–57.

56. Dwight D. Eisenhower, *Crusade in Europe* (New York: Doubleday, 1948), 157. For a brilliant account of how the Allies recovered from the low point of 1942 and turned the tide of the war, see Overy, *Why the Allies Won.*

CHAPTER 3: AMPHIBIOUS ADVANCE

1. Robert Sherrod, *Tarawa: The Story of a Battle* (New York: Bantam, 1983; originally published, 1944), 30–31.

2. Quoted in Miller, *War at Sea,* 375.

3. Quoted in Manchester, *American Caesar,* 380.

4. Bix, *Hirohito,* 444.

5. Samuel Eliot Morison, The *History of U.S. Naval Operations During the Second World War,* vol. 4, *Coral Sea, Midway and Submarine Actions, May 1942–August 1943* (Boston: Little, Brown, 1953), 409.

6. Quoted in Manchester, *American Caesar,* 389.

7. Quoted in ibid., 391–92.

8. D. Clayton James, "Introduction: Rethinking the Pacific War," in Gunter Bischof and

Robert L. Dupont, eds., *The Pacific War Revisited* (Baton Rouge: Louisiana State University Press, 1997), 3.

9. Quoted in Manchester, *American Caesar*, 388.

10. Isely and Crowl, *Amphibious War*, 9.

11. Ibid, 10.

12. Quoted in ibid, 11.

13. A. A. Vandegrift, as told to Robert B. Aspray, *Once a Marine: The Memoirs of General A. A. Vandegrift* (New York: W. W. Norton, 1964), 235–36.

14. Isley and Crowl, *Amphibious War*, 3–13.

15. Spector, *Eagle Against the Sun*, 25.

16. Quoted in Joseph H. Alexander, *Storm Landings: Epic Amphibious Battles in the Central Pacific* (Annapolis, Md.: Naval Institute Press, 1997), 9.

17. Quoted in Isely and Crowl, *Amphibious War*, 4. Pete Ellis died of mysterious causes while visiting the Japanese islands of Palau in 1923. For Marine Corps amphibious theory see also Russell F. Weigley, *The American Way of War: A History of United States Military Strategy and Policy* (New York: Macmillan, 1973), Chapter 12; and Allan R. Millett, *Semper Fidelis: The History of the United States Marine Corps* (New York: Macmillan, 1980), Chapter 12. In December 1943 the United States had 1,878,152 military service personnel deployed against Japan and 1,810,367 deployed against Germany. This allocation of manpower was about to change dramatically in favor of Europe with the planning and preparation for the Normandy invasion in early 1944 (Weigley, *American Way of War*, 271).

18. Alexander, *Storm Landings*, 6.

19. Paul W. Kearney and Blake Clark, " 'Pete' Mitscher, Boss of Task Force 58," *The American Legion Magazine* (July 1945). For the great carrier fleets, see James H. Belote and William M. Belote, *Titans of the Seas: The Development and Operations of Japanese and American Carrier Task Forces During World War II* (New York: Harper & Row, 1975).

20. U.S. Marine Corps Correspondents, *Betio Beachhead* (New York: G. P. Putnam's Sons, 1945), passim.

21. Quoted in Charles T. Gregg, *Tarawa* (New York: Stein & Day, 1984), 162.

22. Quoted in Hanson W. Baldwin, "The Bloody Epic That Was Tarawa," *New York Times Magazine* (November 14, 1958), 19.

23. Interview with Robert Sherrod, Lou Reda Productions.

24. Quoted in Patrick L. McKiernan, "Tarawa: The Tide That Failed," in Merrill L. Bartlett, *Assault from Sea: Essays on the History of Amphibious Warfare* (Annapolis, MD: Naval Institute Press, 1983), 214.

25. Interview with Michael Ryan, Lou Reda Productions.

26. Baldwin, "The Bloody Epic," 68.

27. Karl Albrecht, "Tarawa Remembered," *Follow Me* (November–December, 1993), 28–31.

28. Quoted in Baldwin, "The Bloody Epic," 69.

29. Sherrod, *Tarawa*, xiii, 64.

30. Interview with Harry Jackson, Lou Reda Productions.

31. Quoted in Manchester, *Goodbye, Darkness*, 267.

32. Sherrod, *Tarawa*, 66.

33. Interview with Norman Hatch by DLM; interview with Norman Hatch, Marine Corps Oral History Collection, Marine Corps Historical Center, Washington, D.C.

34. Lieutenant Bonnie Little to wife, quoted in Joseph Alexander, *Utmost Savagery: The Three Days of Tarawa* (New York: Ivy, 1977), 106.

35. Sherrod interview.

36. Quoted in Manchester, *Goodbye, Darkness*, 267.

37. Hatch interview with DLM.

38. Hatch interview, Marine Corps Oral History Collection; Hatch interview with DLM.

39. Interview with Edward Heimberger (Eddie Albert), Lou Reda Productions.

40. Quoted in Alexander, *Utmost Savagery*, 192.

41. Hatch interview with DLM; interview with Norman Hatch, Lou Reda Productions; Hatch interview, Marine Corps Oral History Collection.

42. Sherrod, *Tarawa*, 90–92.

43. Quoted in Alexander, *Utmost Savagery*, 187.

44. Sherrod, *Tarawa*, 96.

45. Ibid., 96–97, 110.

46. Interview with Colonel William Jones, Lou Reda Productions; Joseph H. Alexander, *Across the Reef: The Marine Assault of Tarawa* (Washington, D.C.: Marine Corps Historical Center, 1993), 42.

47. Quoted in Sherrod, *Tarawa*, 113.

48. Manchester, *Goodbye, Darkness*, 282.

49. William Jones interview.

50. Quoted in Alexander, *Across the Reef*, 46.

51. Quoted in Sherrod, *Tarawa*, 100; Sherrod interview.

52. Carl Hoffman, Marine Corps Oral History Collection.

53. Sherrod, *Tarawa*, 113–14.

54. Heimberger (Albert) interview.

55. Quoted in Baldwin, "The Bloody Epic," 72.

56. Sherrod, *Tarawa*, 100–101.

57. Ibid., 132.

58. Quoted in ibid., 129.

59. Sherrod interview.

60. William Jones interview.

61. Quoted in Sherrod, *Tarawa*, 139.

62. Sherrod, *Tarawa*, 140; Sherrod interview.

63. *Life* (October 11, 1943); Davis quoted in Frederick S. Voss, *Reporting the War: The Journalistic Coverage of World War II* (Washington, D.C.: Smithsonian Institution Press, 1994), 34.

64. George S. Horne, "Tarawa's Captor Reviews Victory," *New York Times* (November 30, 1943).

65. Sherrod interview.

66. "Mid-Pacific Stronghold," *New York Times* (December 27, 1943).

67. Lt. Gen. Holland M. Smith, "Tarawa Observation and Analysis," in Smith, *Marine Corps*, 558–61.

68. Vandegrift, *Once a Marine*, 230.

CHAPTER 4: SAIPAN

1. Robert Capa, *Slightly Out of Focus* (New York: Modern Library, 1999), 111. On the invasion of Sicily, see Carlo D'Este, *Bitter Victory: The Battle for Sicily, July–August 1943* (London: Collins, 1988). For the Italian campaign, see Albert N. Garland and Howard McGaw Smyth, *United States Army in World War II: The Mediterranean Theater of Operations: Sicily and the Surrender of Italy* (Washington, D.C.: Center of Military History, U.S. Army, 1965).

2. Capa, *Slightly Out of Focus*, 111.

3. Theodore L. Gatchel, *At the Water's Edge: Defending Against the Modern Amphibious Assault* (Annapolis, Md.: Naval Institute Press, 1996), 132–33.

4. Bergerud, *Touched with Fire*, 61.

5. Quoted in ibid., 70.

6. Quoted in Patrick K. O'Donnell, *Into the Rising Sun* (New York: Free Press, 2002), 87–88.

7. Bergerud, *Touched with Fire*, 271.

8. Yuki Tanaka, *Hidden Horrors: Japanese War Crimes in World War II* (Boulder, CO: Westview Press, 1998), 114.

9. Quoted in O'Donnell, *Rising Sun*, 127.

10. Oral testimony of David C. Krechel, EC.

11. Quoted in Samuel Eliot Morison, *History of United States Naval Operations in World War II*, vol. 8, *New Guinea and the Marianas, March 1944 to August 1944* (Boston: Little, Brown, 1964), 5.

12. Quoted in Richard B. Frank, *Downfall: The End of the Imperial Japanese Empire* (New York: Random House, 1999), 48.

13. Robert Sherrod, *On to Westward: War in the Central Pacific* (New York: Duell, Sloan & Pearce, 1945), 14.

14. Quoted in Alexander, *Storm Landings*, 70.

15. Manchester, *Goodbye, Darkness*, 309.

16. Quoted in John C. Chapin, *Breaching the Marianas: The Battle for Saipan* (Washington, D.C.: Marine Corps Historical Center, 1994), 17, 36.

17. General Edwin Simmons, oral testimony, Lou Reda Productions; interview with Simmons by DLM.

18. Quoted in Alexander, *Storm Landings*, 62.

19. Sherrod, *On to Westward,* 50.

20. Quoted in Haruko Taya Cook, "The Myth of the Saipan Suicides," *Military History Quarterly* 7 (Spring 1995), 13.

21. Interview with John C. Chapin, Lou Reda Productions; Chapin, *Breaching the Marianas,* 2.

22. Sherrod, *On to Westward,* 55.

23. Henry Crowe, Marine Corps Oral History Collection, Marine Corps Historical Center, Washington, D.C.

24. Hatch interview by DLM.

25. Sherrod, *On to Westward,* 58.

26. Quoted in Bernard Naulty, *The Right to Fight: African-American Marines in World War II* (Washington, D.C.: Marine Corps Historical Center, 1995), 1.

27. Quoted in Henry Shaw and Ralph W. Donnelly, *Blacks in the Marine Corps* (Washington, D.C.: History and Museums Division, U.S. Marine Corps, 1975), 34.

28. Quoted in Naulty, *Right to Fight,* 20–21.

29. Quoted in Shaw and Donnelly, *Blacks in the Marine Corps,* 35.

30. Quoted in Morison, *New Guinea and the Marianas,* 200.

31. Quoted in ibid., 213.

32. Quoted in Boyne, *Clash of Titans,* 298.

33. Spruance and Nimitz quoted in Spector, *Eagle Against the Sun,* 305.

34. Interview, Lou Reda Productions.

35. Morison, *New Guinea and the Marianas,* 278.

36. Morison, *Two-Ocean War,* 343.

37. Quoted in Morison, *New Guinea and the Marianas,* 291.

38. Quoted in Boyne, *Clash of Titans,* 302.

39. Quoted in Morison, *New Guinea and the Marianas,* 302.

40. Ibid., 302–4.

41. Weinberg, *World at Arms,* 653.

42. Quoted in Chapin, *Breaching the Marianas,* 17–18.

43. Quoted in ibid., 29.

44. Quoted in ibid.

45. Chapin interview.

46. Quoted in Chapin, *Breaching the Marianas,* 19.

47. Birdie B. Daigle diary, EC; most U.S. Navy nurses in the Pacific served in hospitals far from the battlefront, but some, like Lieutenant Daigle, were assigned to field hospitals near the firing line.

48. Quoted in Walter A. McDougall, *Let the Sea Make a Noise: A History of the North Pacific from Magellan to MacArthur* (New York: Harper Perennial, 2004; originally published, 1993), 647.

49. Quoted in Sherrod, *On to Westward,* 89. For this controversy, see Harry A. Gailey, *Howlin' Mad Versus the Army: Conflict in Command, Saipan 1944* (Novato, Calif.: Presidio Press, 1986).

50. Quoted in Carl Hoffman, *Saipan: The Beginning of the End* (Washington, D.C.: Historical Division, U.S. Marine Corps, 1950), 223.

51. Sherrod, *On to Westward*, 23–24, 140.

52. Quoted in Cook, "Myth of the Saipan Suicides," 15.

53. Arnold Krammer, "Japanese Prisoners of War in America," *Pacific Historical Review* 52 (1983), 71–72, 82–83.

54. Philip A. Crowl, *The Campaign in the Marianas* (Washington, D.C.: Office of the Chief of Military History, 1959), 265–67.

55. Sherrod, *On to Westward*, 119–23.

56. David Nichols, ed., *Ernie's War: The Best of Ernie Pyle's World War II Dispatches* (New York: Simon & Schuster, 1987), 367.

57. Sherrod, *On to Westward*, 119–23.

58. Robert Sherrod, "Saipan," *Life* (August 28, 1944), 75.

59. Robert Sherrod, "The Nature of the Enemy," *Time* (August 28, 1944), 27; Sherrod, *On to Westward*, 144–47; interview with John McCullough by DLM.

60. Smith, ed., *Marine Corps*, 607.

61. Quoted in Carl Hoffman, *Saipan*, 260.

62. Quoted in Frank, *Downfall*, 30.

63. Quoted in Cook, "Myth of the Saipan Suicides," 17.

64. Cook, "Myth of the Saipan Suicides," 17.

65. Bix, *Hirohito*, 480.

66. Quoted in John W. Dower, *War Without Mercy: Race and Power in the Pacific War* (New York: Pantheon, 1986), 247.

67. Quoted in Andrew A. Rooney, *The Fortunes of War: Four Great Battles of World War II* (Boston: Little, Brown, 1962), 37.

68. Quoted in Chapin, *Breaching the Marianas*, 36.

69. Quoted in H. N. Oliphant, "How the Jap Soldier Thought," in *"Yank," the GI Story of the War*, 148–54.

70. Interview with Justice M. Chambers, Marine Corps Oral History Collection, Marine Corps Historical Center, Washington, D.C.

71. Manchester, *American Caesar*, 405.

72. Quoted in Spector, *Eagle Against the Sun*, 294.

73. Quoted in Manchester, *American Caesar*, 432.

74. Weinberg, *World at Arms*, 657.

75. Quoted in Manchester, *American Caesar*, 425.

76. The most prominent proponent of this thesis is D. Clayton James in *The Years of MacArthur*, vol. 2 (Boston: Houghton Mifflin, 1970–1975), 533–35. For a suggestive essay on how MacArthur's political clout may have influenced Roosevelt's decision to liberate the Philippines, see Michael Schaller, "General Douglas MacArthur and the Politics of the Pacific War," in Bischof and Dupont, eds., *Pacific War Revisited*, 17–40.

77. Quoted in Manchester, *American Caesar*, 427.

78. Robert Ross Smith, "Luzon Versus Formosa," in Kent Roberts Greenfield, ed., *Command Decisions* (Washington, D.C.: Office of Chief of Military History, 1960), 463–65.

79. Quoted in James H. Hallas, *The Devil's Anvil: The Assault on Peleliu* (Westport, Conn.: Praeger, 1994), 281.

80. Quoted in ibid., 280.

81. Sherrod, *On to Westward*, 148.

CHAPTER 5: A MARINE AT PELELIU

1. E. B. Sledge in Studs Terkel, *"The Good War": An Oral History of World War II* (New York: New Press, 1984), 65–66.

2. James D. Seidler, testimony, EC.

3. Unless otherwise indicated, all quotations from Eugene Sledge are from the following sources: E. B. Sledge, *With the Old Breed at Peleliu and Okinawa* (New York: Oxford University Press, 1990; originally published, 1981, Presidio Press); Sledge, oral testimony, Lou Reda Productions; Sledge interview with DLM. See also "The Old Breed and the Costs of War," in John V. Denson, ed., *The Costs of War: America's Pyrrhic Victories* (New Brunswick, N.J.: Transaction, 1997); Eugene B. Sledge, "Peleliu 1944: Why Did We Go There?," *U.S. Naval Institute Proceedings* 120 (September 1994); Eugene B. Sledge, with Colonel Joseph H. Alexander, "Sledgehammer's War and Peace: Reflections on Combat, North China Duty, and Homecoming," 1999, ms. I am grateful to the late Dr. Sledge for allowing me to quote from this book before it was published as *China Marine: An Infantryman's Life after World War II* (New York: Oxford University Press, 2003).

4. Quoted in George P. Hunt, *Coral Comes High* (New York: Harper & Bros., 1946), 13.

5. Officer and sergeant quoted in ibid., 40, 43.

6. Quoted in Hallas, *Devil's Anvil*, 41.

7. Quoted in ibid., 36.

8. Tom Lea, *Peleliu Landing* (El Paso, Tex.: Carl Hertzog, 1945), 4.

9. Russell Davis, *Marine at War* (New York: Scholastic, 1961), 95.

10. Tom Lea, "Peleliu: Tom Lea Paints Island Invasion," *Life* (June 11, 1945), 61.

11. Lea, *Peleliu Landing*, 1–8; Lea, "Peleliu," 61–66.

12. Lea, *Peleliu Landing*, 6–7.

13. Ibid., 7; Lea, "Peleliu," 61.

14. Jones, *WW II*, 118.

15. Lea, *Peleliu Landing*, 12–13.

16. Ibid., 12–15.

17. Hunt, *Coral Comes High*, 98.

18. Lea, *Peleliu Landing*, 17–18.

19. Ibid., 20–21.

20. Lea, "Peleliu," 66.

21. Interview with Benis Frank by DLM.

22. Interview with General Paul Henderson, Lou Reda Productions. For Puller, see Lieutenant Colonel Jon T. Hoffman, *Chesty: Lieutenant General Lewis B. Puller, USMC* (New York: Random House, 2001); for two fine accounts of the battle, see Harry A. Gailey, *Peleliu, 1944* (Annapolis, Md.: Nautical and Aviation Publishing Company of America, 1983), and Bill Sloan, *Brotherhood of Heroes: The Marines at Peleliu 1944—The Bloodiest Battle of the Pacific War* (New York: Simon & Schuster, 2005).

23. Interview with General Ray Davis, Lou Reda Productions.

24. Hunt, *Coral Comes High*, 112.

25. The description of this encounter is based on Sledge's later conversations with Harris.

26. Quoted in Hallas, *Devil's Anvil*, 176.

27. Hunt, *Coral Comes High*, 144.

28. Ibid., 112.

29. Frank interview.

30. Lea, *Peleliu Landing*, 34.

31. Lea, "Peleliu," 65.

CHAPTER 6: THE RETURN

1. Quoted in Manchester, *American Caesar*, 388–89. The campaign to recover the Philippines is covered exhaustively in Louis Morton, *The United States Army in World War II: The War in the Pacific: The Fall of the Philippines* (Washington, D.C.: Office of the Chief of Military History, Department of the Army, 1953).

2. Quoted in Bix, *Hirohito*, 481.

3. Quoted in Flower and Reeves, *The War*, 750.

4. Morison, *Two-Ocean War*, 449. For the most rousing action account of this titanic battle, focusing on the battle off Samar, see James D. Hornfischer, *The Last Stand of the Tin Can Sailors* (New York: Bantam, 2004).

5. Interview with Admiral Thomas C. Kinkaid, Columbia University Oral History Project.

6. Quoted in Samuel Eliot Morison, *Leyte* (Boston: Little, Brown, 1958), 288.

7. Morison, *Two-Ocean War*, 463.

8. Kinkaid interview.

9. Quoted in Manchester, *American Caesar*, 459.

10. Bix, *Hirohito*, 481.

11. Linwood B. Crider, personal testimony, EC; interview with Linwood Crider by DLM.

12. Eichelberger, *Our Jungle Road*, 182; 11th Airborne historian quoted in ibid.

13. Quoted in Manchester, *American Caesar*, 475.

14. "The Battle Begins for Luzon," *Life* (January 22, 1945), 19.

15. Quoted in Guillain, *I Saw Tokyo Burning*, 189.

16. Quoted in Rafael Steinberg, *Return to the Philippines* (New York: Time-Life Books, 1979), 114. For the Cabanatuan raid, see Forrest B. Johnson, *Hour of Redemption: The Ranger Raid on Cabanatuan* (New York: Manor Books, 1979); and Hampton Sides, *Ghost*

Soldiers: The Forgotten Epic Story of World War II's Most Dramatic Mission (New York: Doubleday, 2001).

17. Carl Mydans, "My God! It's Carl Mydans," *Life* (February 19, 1945), 20.

18. *New York Times,* "Week in Review" (February 11, 1945).

19. Nurses quoted in Norman, *We Band of Angels,* 203–4.

20. Mydans, "My God!" 98.

21. Quoted in Norman, *We Band of Angels,* 204.

22. Mydans, "My God!" 98–101.

23. Eichelberger, *Our Jungle Road,* 194–95.

24. James, *Years of MacArthur,* vol. 1, 626–35.

25. H. N. Oliphant, "How the Jap Soldier Thought," 22.

26. Fred Nixon, written testimony, EC.

27. Tenney interview with Lou Reda Productions.

28. Manchester, *American Caesar,* 413.

29. Carlos Romulo, *I See the Philippines Rise* (Garden City, N.Y.: Doubleday, 1946), 229.

30. Eichelberger, *Our Jungle Road,* 198–89.

31. Lieutenant Colonel Luis M. Burris, edited by Carol Heckman-Owen, "Blazing Trails with 'D' Battery in the War Against Japan," ms at EC.

32. Quoted in Norman, *We Band of Angels,* 213.

33. Burris, "Blazing Trails."

34. "MacArthur Is Home," *Life* (April 9, 1945), 31.

35. Manchester, *American Caesar,* 500.

36. Eichelberger, *Our Jungle Road,* 166.

37. Both quotations on the trials from Manchester, *American Caesar,* 569, 571.

38. Quoted in Stephen E. Ambrose, *American Heritage New History of World War II,* original text by C. L. Sulzberger (New York: Viking, 1997), 530.

CHAPTER 7: THE B-29S

1. Guillain, *I Saw Tokyo Burning,* 191.

2. I. J. Galantin, *Take Her Deep!: A Submarine Against Japan in World War II* (Chapel Hill, N.C.: Algonquin Books, 1987), 208–9.

3. Quoted in William Bradford Huie, "The Navy's Seabees," *Life* (October 9, 1944), 52; interview with Lou Reda by DLM. Reda served in the Seabees in the Pacific in World War II.

4. St. Clair McKelway, "A Reporter with the B-29s, IV—The People," *The New Yorker* (June 30, 1945), 35, 37–38, 40–43.

5. Charles W. Sweeney, *War's End: An Eyewitness Account of America's Last Atomic Mission* (New York: Avon, 1997), 43–44; Jacob Vander Meulen, *Building the B-29* (Washington, D.C.: Smithsonian Institute Press, 1995).

6. Interview with Harry George, Lou Reda Productions. Unless otherwise indicated, all quotations by B-29 crew members are from interviews conducted by Mark Natola, some of them for Lou Reda Productions, and by DLM.

7. McKelway, "B-29s, IV," 40–41.

8. Interview with General James V. Edmundson, Lou Reda Productions.

9. Robert Morgan with Ron Powers, *The Man Who Flew the Memphis Belle: Memoirs of a World War II Bomber Pilot* (New York: Dutton, 2001), 298.

10. General Curtis E. LeMay with MacKinlay Kantor, *Mission with LeMay* (Garden City, N.Y.: Doubleday, 1965), 332.

11. Ibid., 322.

12. St. Clair McKelway, "A Reporter with the B-29s, I—Possum, Rosy, and the Thousand Kids," *The New Yorker* (June 9, 1945), 28. The primary sources on the bombing of Japan are at the National Archives, which houses the main records of the Twentieth Air Force and the files of the United States Strategic Bombing Survey; the Curtis LeMay and Henry "Hap" Arnold papers are in the Library of Congress's Manuscript Room; the United States Air Force Historical Research Agency at Maxwell Air Force Base, Alabama, has extensive citations of unit histories and is the world's finest archive for the statistical accounts of the Army Air Forces in World War II. I used all of the above sources for this book and for a book I am writing about the U.S. Eighth Air Force in World War II.

13. Quoted in Kenneth P. Werrell, *Blankets of Fire: U.S. Bombers Over Japan During World War II* (Washington, D.C.: Smithsonian Institution Press, 1996), 133.

14. Morgan, *Memphis Belle*, 292.

15. John Ciardi, *Saipan: The War Diary of John Ciardi* (Fayetteville: University of Arkansas Press, 1988), 35. Other excellent memoirs are Earl Snyder, *General Leemy's Circus* (New York: Exposition Press, 1955); Chester Marshall, *Sky Giants Over Saipan* (Winona, Mo.: Apollo, 1984); Kevin Herber, *Maximum Effort* (Manhattan, Ks.: Sunflower, 1983); and Van Parker, *Dear Folks* (Memphis, Tenn.; Global, 1989).

16. Morgan, *Memphis Belle*, 288.

17. John Ciardi in Terkel, *"The Good War,"* 201.

18. Ciardi, *Saipan*, 40.

19. Ciardi in Terkel, *"The Good War,"* 200.

20. Ciardi, *Saipan*, 44, 58, 83, 90–94, 99–101.

21. Ibid., 93, 99–100.

22. Morgan, *Memphis Belle*, 303.

23. LeMay, *Mission*, 345.

24. Ciardi in Terkel, *"The Good War,"* 200.

25. Ibid., 276.

26. Kurt Vonnegut, Jr., *Slaughterhouse-Five or The Children's Crusade* (New York: Dell, 1969), 128–31, 153–54.

27. Ciardi, *Saipan*, xi, 97, 103.

28. Knox Burger, "Tokyo Fire Raid," in *"Yank," the GI Story of the War*, 274–76.

29. Quoted in Keith Wheeler, *Bombers Over Japan* (Alexandria, Va.: Time-Life Books, 1982), 168.

30. Interview with Robert Morgan by DLM, July 26, 2003; Morgan, *Memphis Belle*, 311.

31. St. Clair McKelway, "A Reporter with the B-29s, III—The Cigar, the Three Wings, and the Low-Level Attacks," *The New Yorker* (June 23, 1945), 36.

32. Morgan interview.

33. LeMay, *Mission*, 352.

34. McKelway, "B-29s, III," 36–38.

35. Michael S. Sherry, *The Rise of American Air Power: Creation of Armageddon* (New Haven: Yale University Press, 1987), 406, 278–79. For other sources on the fire raids, see Werrell, *Blankets of Fire*, Ronald Schaeffer, *Wings of Judgment* (New York: Oxford University Press, 1987); Conrad Crane, *Bombs, Cities, and Civilians* (Lawrence: University Press of Kansas, 1993); Haywood Hansell, *Strategic Air War Against Japan* (Maxwell AFB, Ala.: Air University, 1980); E. Bartlett Kopp, *Flames Over Tokyo* (New York: Donald I. Fine, 1991); and the seven-volume official history by Wesley Frank Craven and James Lea Cate, *The Army Air Forces in World War II* (Chicago: University of Chicago Press, 1948–58).

36. Gordon Daniels, "The Great Tokyo Air Raid, 9–10 March 1945," in W. G. Beasley, ed., *Modern Japan: Aspects of History, Literature and Society* (Berkeley: University of California Press, 1975), 123. See also Hoito Edoin (Edwin P. Hoyt), *The Night Tokyo Burned* (New York: St. Martin's Press, 1987).

37. Burger, "Tokyo Fire Raid," 276–77; interview with Knox Burger by DLM.

38. LeMay, *Mission*, 384.

39. Quoted in Richard Rhodes, *Dark Sun: The Making of the Hydrogen Bomb* (New York: Simon & Schuster, 1995), 21–22.

40. LeMay, *Mission*, 353.

41. United States Strategic Bombing Survey, "Statistical Appendix to Over-all Report (European War)," Record Group 243, National Archives, Washington, D.C., 1947, 10–31; Werrell, *Blankets of Fire,* 167–68. Werrell's book is the most reliable secondary account of the damage caused by the fire raids.

42. LeMay, *Mission*, 354–55, 368.

43. Quoted in Keith Wheeler, *Bombers Over Japan*, 98.

44. Craven and Cate, *The Army Air Forces in World II*, vol. 5, 756.

45. Sherry, *American Air Power*, 280.

46. Quoted in Bix, *Hirohito*, 491.

47. Bix, *Hirohito*, 491.

48. Williamson Murray and Allan R. Millett, *A War to Be Won: Fighting the Second World War* (Cambridge: Harvard University Press, 2000), 508. This is the best single-volume military history of the war.

49. Werrell, *Blankets of Fire*, 226–27, 237–38; Donald L. Miller, *The Story of World War II* (New York: Simon & Schuster, 2001), 481–82; 544 naval aircraft were lost in bombing and strafing operations against the home islands, almost 20 percent of Navy losses during the entire war.

50. Morgan interview.

51. Ciardi in Terkel, *"The Good War,"* 199–200.

52. Russell Brines, *Until They Eat Stones* (New York: J. B. Lippincott, 1944), 9, 11.

53. McKelway, "B-29s, IV," 42–45.

54. McKelway, "B-29s, III," 39.

55. Interview with Marty Schaffer by DLM.

56. Ibid.

57. Manchester, *Goodbye, Darkness,* 338. For the devastating impact of the blockade on Japan's economy, see United States Strategic Bombing Survey, Report No. 42, *The Japanese Wartime Standard of Living and Utilization of Manpower* (Washington, D.C.: Manpower, Food and Civilian Supplies Division, 1947); Mark P. Parillo, *The Japanese Merchant Marine in World War II* (Annapolis, Md.: Naval Institute Press, 1993); and Jerome B. Cohen, *Japan's Economy in War and Reconstruction* (Minneapolis: University of Minnesota Press, 1949).

58. Around 82 percent of these planes landed for fuel, and in some cases repairs as well. The remaining 18 percent that landed on the island required repairs in order to make it back to their bases on the Marianas. Twentieth Air Force Files, "A Brief Summary of B-29 Strategic Air Operations: 5 June 1944–14 August 1945," Air Force Historical Research Agency, Maxwell Air Force Base, Ala., n.d.

CHAPTER 8: UNCOMMON VALOR

1. William Sanders Clark, unpublished account of personal experiences, 1945, EC. All subsequent quotations by Clark are from this source.

2. Raymond Spruance, interview, July 9, 1965, Raymond A. Spruance Papers, Naval Historical Center, Washington, D.C.; see also Thomas B. Buell, *The Quiet Warrior: A Biography of Admiral Raymond A. Spruance* (Annapolis, Md: Naval Institute Press, 1987), 324–25.

3. Between November 1944 and early January 1945 the Japanese launched seven raids on the Marianas from Iwo Jima, destroying eleven Superforts and damaging forty-three others. The attacks stopped in mid-January when LeMay increased the number of bombing missions against Iwo Jima. See Craven and Cate, *The Army Air Forces in World War II,* vol. 5, 581–83.

4. Historian Robert Burrell argues that it was pressure from General Hap Arnold for airstrips for his fighter escorts that first persuaded Nimitz to back the assault on Iwo Jima, which Burrell sees as an unnecessary operation, not worth the high cost that the Marines paid. Nimitz and Spruance then convinced a reluctant King, who described the island as a "sink hole in the hands of whoever held it," to endorse the plan. See Burrell, "Breaking the Cycle of Iwo Jima Mythology: A Strategic Study of Operation Detachment," *The Journal of Military History,* 68: 4 (October 2004): 1143–86.

5. Jones, *WW II,* 235–36.

6. Typed copy at EC of article on the Battle of Iwo Jima by Brigadier General Wendell Duplantis (originally published in *Battle Creek Enquirer and News,* February 21, 1965), 1.

7. Sherrod, *On to Westward*, 153–56; Sherrod, "The First Three Days," *Life* (March 5, 1945), 41.

8. Quoted in Brig. Gen. Edwin M. Simmons, "The Island Campagn," in Jacob Neufeld, William T. Youngblood and Mary Lee Jefferson, eds., *Pearl to V-J Day: World War II in the Pacific* (Washington, D.C.: Air Force History and Museums Program, 2000), 34.

9. Sherrod, *On to Westward*, 154, 159.

10. John Lardner, "A Reporter at Large: D Day, Iwo Jima," *The New Yorker* (March 17, 1945), 48.

11. Interview with Andy Anderson, Lou Reda Productions.

12. Lardner, "D Day," 50.

13. Quoted in Keith Wheeler, *The Road to Tokyo* (New York: Time-Life Books, 1979), 60.

14. Quoted in Lynn Kessler, ed., with Edmond B. Bart, *Never in Doubt: Remembering Iwo Jima* (Annapolis, Md.: Naval Institute Press, 1999), 168–69.

15. Joe Rosenthal with W. C. Heinz, "The Picture That Will Live Forever," *Collier's* (February 18, 1955), 62; interview with Frank Crossland Caldwell, Lou Reda Productions.

16. Lardner, "D Day," 50–61.

17. Sherrod, *On to Westward*, 178; Sherrod, "The First Three Days," 44.

18. Quoted in Kessler, *Never in Doubt*, 12.

19. Quoted in ibid., 206–8.

20. Sherrod, "The First Three Days," 44.

21. Quoted in Kessler, *Never in Doubt*, 55.

22. Interview with General Fred E. Hayner, Lou Reda Productions.

23. Sherrod, "The First Three Days," 44.

24. Sherrod, *On to Westward*, 190.

25. Quoted in Keith Wheeler, *Road to Tokyo*, 41.

26. Quoted in Richard Wheeler, *Iwo* (New York: Lippincott & Crowell, 1980), 10.

27. Ibid., 33.

28. Quoted in Duplantis, 3.

29. Bill Reed, "Battle for Iwo," in *"Yank," the GI Story of the War*, 219–21.

30. Interview with Charles W. Lindberg, Lou Reda Productions; all subsequent quotations by Lindberg are from this source.

31. Quoted in Richard Wheeler, *Iwo*, 159.

32. Quoted in ibid., 161.

33. Rosenthal, "The Picture That Will Live Forever," 62–63; Hal Buell, *Moments: The Pulitzer Prize-Winning Photographs* (New York: Black Dog & Leventhal, 1999), 22; Richard Wheeler, *Iwo*, 157–64; Hatch interview with DLM.

34. Quoted in James Bradley with Ron Powers, *Flags of Our Fathers* (New York: Bantam, 2000), 220. For another fine account of the battle, see Bill D. Ross, *Iwo Jima—Legacy of Valor* (New York: Vintage, 1986); for the battle from the perspective of a medical officer,

see James S. Vedder, *Combat Surgeon: Up Front with the 27th Marines* (Novato, Calif.: Presidio Press, 1984).

35. Jeremy Paxman and Robert Harris, *A Higher Form of Killing: The Secret Story of Gas and Germ Warfare* (New York: Hill & Wang, 1983), 138; John Ellis van Courtland Moon, "Chemical Warfare: A Forgotten Lesson," *Bulletin of the Atomic Scientists* 45, no. 6 (July–August 1989), 40–43; Brooks E. Kleber and Dale Birdsell, *The Chemical Warfare Service: Chemicals in Combat, United States Army in World War II* (Washington, D.C.: Government Printing Office, 1966), 648–52.

36. Nichols, *Ernie's War*, 368, 374–77.

37. Hal Buell, *Moments*, 23: interview with Hal Buell, Lou Reda Productions.

38. Sherrod, *On to Westward*, 202.

39. C. P. Zurlinden, Jr., and others, "Iwo: The Red-Hot Rock," *Collier's* (April 4, 1945), 16–17.

40. Quoted in Broderick H. Johnson, ed., *Navajos and World War II* (Tsaile, Navajo Nation Ariz.: Navajo Community Press, 1977), 54–56.

41. John P. Langellier, *American Indians in the U.S. Armed Forces 1866–1945* (Mechanicsburg, Pa.: Stackpole, 2000), 8.

42. Quoted in Kessler, *Never in Doubt*, 166.

43. Quoted in Bruce Watson, "Jaysho, Moasi," *Smithsonian Magazine* 24, no. 5 (August 1993), 36; see also Ron McCoy, "Navajo Code-Talkers of World War II," *American West* 18 (1981), 67–73; and Alison R. Bernstein, *American Indians and World War II* (Norman: University of Oklahoma Press, 1991).

44. Quoted in Johnson, *Navajos and World War II*, 59–61.

45. Interview with Norma Crotty, Lou Reda Productions.

46. Richard Wheeler, *Iwo*, 201; George Green testimony, EC.

47. Keith Wheeler, *Road to Tokyo*, 55.

48. Quoted in Derrick Wright, *The Battle for Iwo Jima* (Somerset, U.K.: Sutton Publishing, 1999), 154.

49. Quoted in Richard Wheeler, *Iwo*, 223.

50. Hayner interview.

51. Richard Wheeler, *Iwo*, 231.

52. Quoted in ibid., 234.

53. See, for example, Burrell, "Breaking the Cycle," 1186.

54. Quoted in Kessler, *Never in Doubt*, 112–13.

55. Cooke, quoted in Smith, *Marine Corps*, 827.

CHAPTER 9: OKINAWA

1. Sledge, *Old Breed*, 171–73, 178.

2. For figures on the Normandy landings, see D'Este, *Eisenhower*, 534; Stephen E. Ambrose, *D-Day, June 6, 1944: The Climactic Battle of World War II* (New York: Simon & Schuster, 1994), 576; Andrew Gordon, "The Greatest Military Armada Ever Launched," and Williamson Murray, "A Visitor to Hell," both in Jane Penrose, ed., *The D-Day*

Companion: Leading Historians Explore History's Greatest Amphibious Assault (Oxford, U.K.: Osprey Publishing, 2004), 141–43, 161; Murray and Millett, *War to Be Won*, 420; and Adrian Lewis, *Omaha Beach: A Flawed Victory* (Chapel Hill: University of North Carolina Press, 2001), passim.

Statistics on the number of Marines taking part in the Okinawa operation are at the Marine Corps Historical Center, Washington, D.C. Navy records are at the Naval Historical Center, Washington, D.C. Army records are at the U.S. Army Military History Institute, Carlisle Barracks, Carlisle, Pennsylvania.

When Douglas MacArthur landed at Luzon on January 9, 1945, he had an assault force of approximately 175,000 troops, only slightly fewer than sailed into the waters around Okinawa.

3. Sledge, *Old Breed*, 179.
4. Interview with Mort Zimmerman by DLM; Morison, *Two-Ocean War*, 529; for the *Franklin*, see Roy W. Bruce, "Done Blowed the Ship to Hell," *Naval History* (March–April 1995), 41–47.
5. Sherrod, *On to Westward*, 265, 293–94
6. Sledge, *Old Breed*, 179; Manchester, *Goodbye, Darkness*, 399–400.
7. Sledge, *Old Breed*, 179; "Okinawa," *Life* (May 28, 1945), 90.
8. John Lardner, "A Reporter on Okinawa: II—The Tomb Life," *The New Yorker* (May 26, 1945).
9. Army Major General John R. Hodge commanded the XXIV Corps, which had three infantry Divisions—the 7th, 77th, and 96th, with the 27th in floating reserve and the 81st in area reserve. Marine Major General Roy S. Geiger commanded the III Amphibious Corps, comprised of the 1st and 6th Marine Divisions, with the 2nd Marine Division in floating reserve.
10. Isely and Crowl, *Amphibious War*, 15.
11. Quoted in Sherrod, *On to Westward*, 268–69.
12. Quoted in George Feifer, *Tennozan: The Battle of Okinawa and the Atomic Bomb* (New York: Ticknor & Fields, 1992), 136. This book and three others are excellent histories of the battle: Roy E. Appleman, James M. Burns, Russell A. Guegeler, and John Stevens, *Okinawa: The Last Battle* (Washington, D.C.: Historical Division, Department of the Army, 1948); William M. Belote and James H. Belote, *Typhoon of Steel: The Battle for Okinawa* (New York: Harper & Row, 1970); and Benis M. Frank and Henry I. Shaw, Jr., *Victory and Occupation* (Washington, D.C.: U.S. Marine Corps, 1968). Colonel Hiromichi Yahara and Frank Gibney gave an eyewitness account of the battle from the Japanese perspective in *The Battle for Okinawa* (New York: John Wiley, 1995).
13. Sherrod, *On to Westward*, 270.
14. John Lardner, "A Reporter on Okinawa: I—Suicides and Bushwhackers," *The New Yorker* (May 19, 1945), 34.
15. Sledge interview, Lou Reda Productions; Sledge interview with DLM.
16. Nichols, *Ernie's War*, 408–9.

17. Quoted in Gerald Astor, *Operation Iceberg: The Invasion and Conquest of Okinawa in World War II* (New York: Dell, 1995), 158.

18. Lardner, "Suicides," 34.

19. Quoted in E. B. Potter, *Nimitz* (Annapolis, Md.: Naval Institute Press, 1976), 372.

20. Manchester, *Goodbye, Darkness,* 409.

21. Raymond Sawyer, oral testimony, EC.

22. Evan Wylie, "Death of Ernie Pyle," in *"Yank," the GI Story of the War,* 230.

23. Sherrod, *On to Westward,* 296–97.

24. Manchester, *Goodbye, Darkness,* 406–7; interview with Lieutenant General Victor Krulak, Lou Reda Productions.

25. Guillain, *I Saw Tokyo Burning,* 204.

26. Victor Davis Hanson, *Ripples of Battle: How Wars of the Past Still Determine How We Fight, How We Live, and How We Think* (New York: Doubleday, 2003), 61.

27. Morison, *Two-Ocean War,* 550.

28. Quoted in Flower and Reeves, *The War,* 743.

29. Quoted in Feifer, *Tennozan,* 206.

30. Quoted in Astor, *Operation Iceberg,* 174.

31. Robert Leckie, *Okinawa: The Last Battle of World War II* (New York: Penguin, 1996 edition), 92–95. For an account of the *Yamato's* final voyage, see Russell Spurr, *A Glorious Way to Die* (New York: New Market Press, 1981).

32. Spector, *Eagle Against the Sun,* 538.

33. Quoted in Feifer, *Tennozan,* 224.

34. Vice Admiral M. L. Deyo, "Kamikaze," ms, U.S. Naval Historical Center, Washington, D.C.

35. Quoted in Morison, *Two-Ocean War,* 545.

36. Evan Wylie, "Kamikaze: Jap Suicide," in *"Yank," the GI Story of the War,* 269–70.

37. Morison, *Two-Ocean War,* 548–49.

38. Phelps Adams, "Attack on Carrier Bunker Hill," *New York Sun* (June 28, 1945).

39. Both quotations in Miller, *War at Sea,* 526.

40. Sherrod, *On to Westward,* 294; Mitscher quoted in Miller, *War at Sea.*

41. CINCPAC Headquarters Reports, 3rd Fleet Reports, and 5th Fleet Reports, U.S. Navy's Classified Records Branch, Washington Navy Yard, Washington D.C.; Japanese Monograph No. 83, *Okinawa Area Naval Operations, January–June 1945. Naval Air Operations,* Library of Congress, Washington, D.C.; Belote and Belote, *Typhoon,* 342–43. Belote and Belote put the total number of Japanese planes lost in the Okinawa campaign at 1,600.

    During the entire war, the Japanese lost 3,913 airmen on kamikaze missions that caused the death of at least 3,300 U.S. sailors and navy airmen. See Frank, *Downfall,* 181–82.

42. Zimmerman interview.

43. Hanson Baldwin, *Battles Lost and Won: Great Campaigns of World War II* (New York: Harper & Row, 1966), 377.

44. Quoted in Ambrose, *American Heritage New History of World War II*, 572.

45. Major General Wilburt S. Brown, oral history interview, Marine Corps Historical Center, Washington, D.C.

46. Manchester, *Goodbye, Darkness*, 411–12.

47. Sawyer, EC.

48. Ibid.

49. Sledge, "Sledgehammer's War and Peace," 21.

50. W. Eugene Smith, "24 Hours with Infantryman Terry Moore," *Life* (June 18, 1945), 20–25.

51. Sledge, "Sledgehammer's War and Peace," passim; Sledge interview, Lou Reda Productions; Sledge, *Old Breed*, 252–53, 269; Sledge interview with DLM.

52. Manchester, *Goodbye, Darkness*, 420, 429–30.

53. Sledge interview, Lou Reda Productions.

54. Manchester, *Goodbye, Darkness*, 451–53.

55. Quoted in ibid., 435.

56. Sledge, *Old Breed*, 223.

57. Feifer, *Tennozan*, 276.

58. Evan Regal and others quoted in Feifer, *Tennozan*, 415–19; Manchester, *Goodbye, Darkness*, 441–43.

59. Miyagi Kikuko, in Haruko Taya Cook and Theodore F. Cook, *Japan at War: An Oral History* (New York: New Press, 1992), 357.

60. Ibid., 360–62.

61. Sledge interview, Lou Reda Productions.

62. Sledge, *Old Breed*, 306–8; Sledge interview, Lou Reda Productions.

63. Approximately 100,000 American fighting men were killed in action or missing in action in the Pacific war. The 1st Marine Division had the highest number of days in contact with the enemy in the Pacific theater, approximately 225, and the highest losses of any American division—Marine or Army—in the theater. It suffered 19,284 casualties, which included 5,435 killed in action, a little over one quarter of the entire number of Marines killed in action in World War II (19,733).

64. Bruce I. Gudmundsson "Okinawa" in Robert Cowley, ed., *No End Save Victory: Perspectives on World War II* (New York: G. P. Putnam's Sons, 2001), 638.

65. Belote and Belote, *Typhoon*, 173–74, 263–66.

66. Meirion Harries and Susie Harries, *Soldiers of the Sun*, 428.

67. W. H. Lawrence, "Japan, Like Okinawa, Will Cost High Price," *New York Times* (June 24, 1945), 1.

68. Sledge, *Old Breed*, 312. For a succinct account of the military lessons of the Battle of Okinawa, see Jon T. Hoffman, "The Legacy and Lessons of Okinawa," *Marine Corps Gazette* 79 (April 1995), 64–71.

1. Marvin A. Kastenbaum, "A Teenage Warrior," ms, EC. For the Japanese annihilation campaigns in China, see Bix, *Hirohito*, 365–68.

2. Quotations in Richard Rhodes, "The Toughest Flying in the World," *World War II Chronicles* (New York: American Heritage, 1995), 40–47; interview with Ruven Greenberg, EC.

3. Charles J. Rolo, "Wingate's Circus," *Atlantic Monthly* (October 1943), 91–94.

4. Quoted in Mary Penick Motley, ed. *The Invisible Soldier: The Experience of the Black Soldier, World War II* (Detroit: Wayne State University Press, 1975.)

5. Gregory F. Michno, *Death on the Hellships: Prisoners at Sea in the Pacific War* (Annapolis, Md.: Naval Institute Press, 2001), 282–83. For different—and lower—figures, see Gavan Daws, *Prisoners of the Japanese*, 297.

6. Forrest Knox, in Donald Knox, *Death March: The Survivors of Bataan* (New York: Harcourt Brace Jovanovich, 1981), 338–40; William R. Evans, *Kora!* (Rogue River, Ore.: Atwood, 1986), 107, 112.

7. Interview with Melvin Rosen by DLM; Davis quoted in Knox, *Death March*, 350; John M. Wright, Jr., *Captured on Corregidor: Diary of an American P.O.W.* (Jefferson, N.C.: McFarland, 1988), 92; Daws, *Prisoners of the Japanese*, 294.

8. Interview with Maynard Booth, Lou Reda Productions; Rosen interviews by DLM and Lou Reda Productions; interview with William G. Adair, Lou Reda Productions; all Marion Lawton quotations in Knox, *Death March*, 356.

9. Rosen interview, Lou Reda Productions. For a powerful account of the journey of the last hell ship, see E. Bartlett Kerr, *Surrender and Survival: The Experience of American POWs in the Pacific, 1941–1945* (New York: William Morrow, 1985), Chapter 12. For graphic eyewitness accounts, see, in addition to the books previously mentioned, Manny Lawton, *Some Survived* (Chapel Hill, N.C.: Algonquin, 1984) and Sidney Smith, *Give Us This Day* (New York: W. W. Norton, 1957).

10. Quoted in Knox, *Death March*, 364–65.

11. Tenney interviews with DLM and Lou Reda Productions; Tenney, *Hitch*, 122–37.

12. Hewlett quoted in Knox, *Death March*, 368; these figures are from the Center for Internee Rights, and include merchant marines. In *Surrender and Survival*, 339, Kerr states that 25,600 American military personnel were captured by the Japanese and that 10,650 were killed or died in captivity, a mortality rate of 41.6 percent. Kerr does not include merchant marines; to put the German figures in perspective, 60 percent of the Russian military personnel captured by the Nazis did not survive the war.

13. Interview with Frank "Foo" Fujita by DLM; Fujita interview, Lou Reda Productions.

14. Tenney interview by DLM; Daws, *Prisoners of the Japanese*, 308.

15. Tenney, *Hitch*, 164; Tenney interview, Lou Reda Productions.

16. For the story of the Chichi Jima fliers, see James Bradley, *Flyboys: A True Story of Courage* (Boston: Little, Brown, 2003).

17. Daws, *Prisoners of the Japanese*, 322. For the terrifying ordeal of one captured American flier, see Fiske Hanley II, *Accused American War Criminal* (Austin, Tex.: Eakin Press, 1997); for Japanese atrocities against airmen POWs, see also Marc Landis, *The Fallen: A True Story of American POWS and Japanese Wartime Atrocities* (New York: John Wiley & Sons, 2004).

18. Interview with Ray Halloran by DLM; interviews with Ray Halloran and Robert Goldsworthy by Mark Natola.

19. LeMay, *Mission*, 376.

20. Terkel, *"The Good War,"* 201.

21. LeMay, *Mission*, 375.

22. Ibid., 375, 381.

23. Truman diary, June 17, 1945, in Robert H. Ferrell, ed., *Off the Record: The Private Papers of Harry S. Truman* (New York: Harper & Row, 1980), 47.

24. Quoted in Frank, *Downfall*, 143.

25. Ibid., 139–43; for the invasion plans, see ibid., Chapter 8.

26. Interview with McCloy, in David McCullough, *Truman* (New York: Simon & Schuster, 1992), 401.

27. Quoted in Daws, *Prisoners of the Japanese*, 325.

28. Sledge, "Sledgehammer's War and Peace," 1; Sledge interview by DLM.

29. Kastenbaum ms, EC.

30. D. M. Giangreco and Kathryn Moore, "Half a Million Purple Hearts," *American Heritage* (December 2000), 81–83. See also D. M. Giangreco, "Casualty Projections for the Invasion of Japan, 1945–46: Planning and Policy Implications," *Journal of Military History* 61, no. 3 (July 1997), 535; and D. M. Giangreco, "The Truth About Kamikazes," *Naval History* (May–June 1997), 25–30.

31. Herbert Bix, "Japan's Delayed Surrender: A Reinterpretation," *Diplomatic History* 19 (Spring 1995), 210; *Army Battle Casualties and Non-Battle Deaths in World War II, Final Report, 7 December 1941–31 December 1946* (Washington, D.C.: Statistical and Accounting Branch, Office of the Adjutant General), 10. For ULTRA intercepts, see Edward J. Drea, *In the Service of the Emperor: Essays on the Imperial Japanese Army* (Lincoln: University of Nebraska Press, 1998); and Drea, *MacArthur's ULTRA: Codebreaking and the War Against Japan, 1942–1945* (Lawrence: University Press of Kansas, 1992).

32. Frank, *Downfall*, 194, 202.

33. Quoted in ibid., 196.

34. Bix, "Japan's Delayed Surrender," 214.

35. Spector, *Eagle Against the Sun*, 543.

36. Guillian, *I Saw Tokyo Burning*, 209.

37. Interview with Paul Tibbets by DLM, January 26, 2002.

38. Interview with Frederick L. Ashworth by DLM.

39. Paul W. Tibbets, *The Flight of the Enola Gay* (Reynoldsburg, Ohio: Buckeye Aviation, 1969), 183.

40. Sweeney, *War's End*, 137–38. Sweeney retired from the service as a major general.

41. Tibbets interview.

42. Ibid.; Tibbets, *Enola Gay*, 192. It was LeMay's idea to have the bomb dropped by a single, unescorted plane. See Leslie R. Groves, *Now It Can Be Told: The Story of the Manhattan Project* (New York: Harper & Row, 1962), 284.

43. Interview with Raymond Biel by Mark Natola.

44. Quoted in Groves, *Now It Can Be Told*, 308.

45. Quotations in General Groves, Memorandum to the Secretary of War, 18 July 45, quoted in ibid., 433–40. For a perceptive analysis of the story of the bomb, see Martin Sherwin, *A World Destroyed: Hiroshima and the Origins of the Arms Race* (New York: Vintage, 1987).

46. Robert H. Ferrell, ed., *Dear Bess: The Letters from Harry to Bess Truman, 1910–1959* (New York: W. W. Norton, 1983), 519. For an excellent account of the decision to use the bomb, see Samuel Walker, *Prompt and Utter Destruction: Truman and the Use of Atomic Bombs Against Japan* (Chapel Hill: University of North Carolina Press, 1997).

47. Quoted in David M. Kennedy, *Freedom from Fear: The American People in Depression and War, 1929–1945* (New York: Oxford University Press, 1999), 845.

48. Quoted in Barton J. Bernstein, "The Perils and Politics of Surrender: Ending the War with Japan and Avoiding the Third Atomic Bomb," *Pacific Historical Review* 46 (February 1977), 5.

49. Bix, "Japan's Delayed Surrender," 222–23. For a suggestive essay on this issue, see Ian Buruma, "The War over the Bomb," *New York Review of Books* (September 21, 1995), 26–34.

50. Barton J. Bernstein, "Understanding the Atomic Bomb and the Japanese Surrender: Missed Opportunities, Little-Known Near Disasters, and Modern Memory," *Diplomatic History* 19 (Spring 1995), 240.

51. Quoted in McCullough, *Truman*, 437.

52. Groves, *Now It Can Be Told*, 265.

53. "The Atomic Age," *Life* (August 20, 1945), 32.

54. Terkel, *"The Good War,"* 506–13.

55. Groves, *Now It Can Be Told*, 306. Groves initially expected a second plutonium bomb "to be ready about August 24," with "additional ones arriving in increasing numbers from there on" (309). For the sinking of the *Indianapolis*, see Doug Stanton, *In Harm's Way: The Sinking of the USS* Indianapolis *and the Extraordinary Story of Its Survivors* (New York: Henry Holt, 2001).

56. Quoted in McCullough, *Truman*, 448.

57. Groves, *Now It Can Be Told*, 309.

58. Sweeney, *War's End*, 163–64.

59. Tibbets, *Enola Gay*, 186.

60. Colonel Paul Tibbets, Jr., as told to Wesley Price, "How to Drop an Atom Bomb," *Saturday Evening Post* (June 8, 1946), 136; Tibbets, *Enola Gay*, 226–27; and Tibbets interview.

61. All quotations in Tibbets, *Enola Gay,* 228 and Tibbets interview.

62. Quoted in McCullough, *Truman,* 454.

63. Tibbets, "How to Drop an Atom Bomb," 136; Tibbets interview.

64. Tibbets, *Enola Gay,* 237.

65. Quoted in Feifer, *Tennozan,* 567.

66. Sweeney, *War's End,* 176.

67. Morrison in Terkel, *"The Good War,"* 513.

68. Quoted in Flower and Reeves, *The War,* 1032.

69. Hajimi Kito in Terkel, *"The Good War,"* 539.

70. Michihiko Hachiya, *Hiroshima Diary: The Journal of a Japanese Physician, August 6–September 30, 1945* (Chapel Hill: University of North Carolina Press, 1955), 1–9.

71. Quoted in Robert Jay Lifton, *Death in Life: Survivors of Hiroshima* (New York: Random House, 1967), 79.

72. Hachiya, *Hiroshima Diary,* 97.

73. LeMay, *Mission,* 387.

74. Trolley in Terkel, *"The Good War,"* 544.

75. LeMay, *Mission,* 382.

76. Quoted in McCullough, *Truman,* 455.

77. Ferrell, *Off the Record,* 52.

78. Interview with Ray Gallagher by DLM; interview with Ray Gallagher by Mark Natola.

79. Quoted in Gordon Thomas and Max Morgan Witts, *Enola Gay* (New York: Stein & Day, 1977); Tibbets interview.

CHAPTER 11: VICTORY

1. Ashworth interview. Unless otherwise indicated all quoted passages are from interviews by DLM and Mark Natola with the men on *Bockscar.* Ashworth was especially helpful in re-creating the flight of *Bockscar.* General Sweeney was interviewed by my associate Mark Natola but would not release the interview for publication. Subsequently, I made several unsuccessful attempts to get in touch with him. The interview he did with Natola stays close to the substance of his autobiography, *War's End,* which I have used in this chapter to give his account of the mission. General Sweeney died in 2004.

2. Sweeney, *War's End,* 4.

3. Ibid., 198.

4. William L. Laurence, "A Giant Pillar of Purple Fire," *New York Times* (September 9, 1945).

5. Sweeney, *War's End,* 200.

6. Morrison in Terkel, *"The Good War,"* 513.

7. Sweeney, *War's End,* 203.

8. Tibbets interview; Paul Tibbets, *Return of the Enola Gay* (Columbus, Oh.: Mid Coast Marketing, 1998), 248 (revised edition of Tibbets's earlier book).

9. Sweeney, *War's End*, 209; Purnell quoted in Groves, *Now It Can Be Told*, 344.

10. Laurence, "A Giant Pillar of Purple Fire."

11. Sweeney (*War's End*, 212) claims that Hopkins's message was garbled in transmission and came out as "Sweeney aborted."

12. Tibbets interview.

13. Sweeney, *War's End*, 211.

14. Ibid., 213–15.

15. Ibid., 217.

16. Laurence, "A Giant Pillar of Purple Fire."

17. Ibid.

18. Sweeney, *War's End*, 223–26.

19. Tibbets, *Return of the Enola Gay*, 250; Tibbets interview.

20. Quoted in McCullough, *Truman*, 459.

21. Ferrell, *Off the Record*, 61. The standard volume on the end of the war in the Pacific is Robert J. C. Butow, *Japan's Decision to Surrender* (Stanford, Calif.: Stanford University Press, 1954).

22. Groves, *Now It Can Be Told*, 352–53.

23. *New York Times*, August 15, 1945.

24. The figure of 405,399 deaths is the number of service personnel who died during their service in the war. The approximate figure of the number of persons who died in combat is 291,557. *Army Battle Casualties and Nonbattle Deaths in World War II: Final Report 7 December–31 November 1946*, Department of the Army; for recent data on the human cost of the war, see Murray and Millett, *A War to Be Won*, Chapter 20; and Weinberg, *A World at Arms*, 894–920. In warfare all figures on casualties are approximate.

25. Paul Fussell, "Thank God for the Atomic Bomb," reprinted in Kai Bird and Lawrence Lischultz, eds., *Hiroshima's Shadow* (Stony Creek, Conn.: Pamphleteer's Press, 1998), 217–18.

26. Sledge, *Old Breed*, 312–15.

27. Interview with Fiske Hanley by DLM; interview with Fiske Hanley, Lou Reda Productions; Frank Fujita, oral testimony, Lou Reda Productions; Frank Fujita, *Foo: A Japanese-American Prisoner of the Rising Sun* (Denton: University of North Texas Press, 1993), 1–5, 312–16; Halloran interview by DLM.

28. Goldsworthy interview.

29. Quoted in Charles Smith, *Securing the Surrender: Marines and the Occupation of Japan* (Washington, D.C.: Marine Corps Historical Center, 1997), 10.

30. Tenney, *Hitch*, 172.

31. Douglas MacArthur, *Reminiscences* (New York: McGraw-Hill, 1964), 271–77.

32. Quoted in Morison, *Two-Ocean War*, 576.

33. Dale Kramer, "Fall of Japan," in *"Yank," the GI Story of the War*, 291.

34. MacArthur, *Reminiscences*, 275–77.

EPILOGUE: REMEMBERING

1. Sweeney, *War's End*, 247.

2. Tibbets, *Enola Gay*, 240–43.

3. Sweeney, *War's End*, 257.

4. Tibbets, *Enola Gay*, 243; Tibbets interview.

5. Bob Greene, *Duty: A Father, His Son, and the Man Who Won the War* (New York: William Morrow, 2000), 19–20.

6. Tibbets, *Enola Gay*, 8.

7. The Committee for the Compilation of Materials on Damage Caused by the Atomic Bombs in Hiroshima and Nagasaki, Eisei Ishikawa, trans., and David L. Swain, *Hiroshima and Nagasaki: The Physical, Medical, and Social Effects of the Atomic Bombings* (New York: Basic Books, 1981), 6.

8. Takashi Nagai, *The Bells of Nagasaki* (Tokyo: Kodansha International, 1984), 6, 114–18.

9. Jones, *WW II*, 255–56.

10. Halloran interview; Chester Marshall with Ray "Hap" Halloran, *Hap's War: The Incredible Survival Story of a P.O.W. Slated for Execution* (Collierville, Tenn.: Global Press, 1998).